Microsoft®
Excel
Developer's
Kit

Version 5 *for*
Microsoft Windows™
and the Apple® Macintosh®

Microsoft
P R E S S

PUBLISHED BY
Microsoft Press
A Division of Microsoft Corporation
One Microsoft Way
Redmond, Washington 98052-6399

Library of Congress Cataloging-in-Publication Data
Microsoft Excel developer's kit : version 5 for Microsoft Windows and
    the Apple Macintosh / Microsoft Corporation.
        p.   cm.
    Includes index.
    ISBN 1-55615-632-4
    1. Computer software--Development.   2. Microsoft Excel for
Windows.   3. Macintosh (Computer)--Programming.   I. Microsoft
Corporation.
QA76.76.D47M52   1994
005.26--dc20   94-6319
                                                                                CIP

Printed and bound in the United States of America.

 2 3 4 5 6 7 8 9 MLML 9 8 7 6 5 4

Distributed to the book trade in Canada by Macmillan of Canada, a division of Canada Publishing Corporation.

A CIP catalogue record for this book is available from the British Library.

Microsoft Press books are available through booksellers and distributors worldwide. For further information about international editions, contact your local Microsoft Corporation office. Or contact Microsoft Press International directly at fax (206) 936-7329.

Contents

Introduction

The Microsoft® Excel Developer's Kit provides information for software developers who want to develop applications that interact with Microsoft Excel. The Microsoft Excel Developer's Kit is a programming and technical reference. It is not a guide to Microsoft Excel macro language or Visual Basic™ programming, and it assumes an understanding of Microsoft Excel's capabilities as exposed to the user.

This book contains everything you need to know to use the Microsoft Excel Developer's Kit. It assumes that you already know C and that you are familiar with Microsoft Excel and Visual Basic, Applications Edition or the Microsoft Excel 4.0 macro language. Visual Basic is described in the *Microsoft Excel Visual Basic User's Guide* and the *Microsoft Excel Visual Basic Language Reference.* The Microsoft Excel macro language is described completely in the *Microsoft Excel User's Guide* and the online Microsoft Excel Macro Functions Help.

If you plan to develop applications for Microsoft Windows™, you should know the basics of Microsoft Windows programming and how to write DLLs. Similarly, if you plan to develop applications for the Apple® Macintosh®, you should know about programming in the Apple Macintosh environment before you start.

Note Developing a Microsoft Windows DLL is nearly identical to developing an Apple Macintosh code resource. In this book, the term "DLL" is often used to refer to either.

Two disks accompany this book: one disk for use with Microsoft Windows and one for use with the Apple Macintosh. For information on the contents of these disks, see "Sample Files," later in this chapter.

Because Microsoft Excel includes two macro languages and other extension mechanisms, it is not always easy to determine which parts of Microsoft Excel are best suited for your application. The following sections outline the available components, typical scenarios for use, and disadvantages of each.

C API and Reference

Chapter 1 describes the Microsoft Excel Application Programming Interface (C API). Chapter 2 is a function reference for the API.

You can use the C API to create new custom worksheet functions (functions that can be entered into a cell on a worksheet), to create new macro functions optimized for use from Microsoft Excel 4.0 macro sheets, and to create add-ins written in C but using Microsoft Excel commands and functions to perform actions and calculate values.

Although you can write worksheet functions in both Visual Basic and the Microsoft Excel macro language, if the function requires high-speed or data-intensive calculations, it may be more appropriate to write the function in C. The Microsoft Excel C API is the best way to integrate external custom worksheet functions with Microsoft Excel.

Applications that require high-speed data transfer from an external source into Microsoft Excel can use the C API. A typical use of this capability is a macro function that retrieves data from an external database and puts the data on a worksheet. Other examples include a function that retrieves data from an external source, such as a stock ticker, or a calculation-intensive statistical analysis function (the Microsoft Excel Analysis Toolpack that ships with Excel 5.0 is in fact written using the C API).

Disadvantages of the C API include the following:

- Because the C API is optimized for use from the Microsoft Excel macro language and the worksheet, it is not a very good mechanism for writing external functions to be used by Visual Basic (although Visual Basic and the C API can be combined into hybrid solutions).

- The C API is not object-oriented (because it is based on the Microsoft Excel 4.0 macro language). You cannot use the C API to access Visual Basic objects, properties, and methods.

- Because the C API can be used only from a DLL loaded in the Microsoft Excel process, an external application cannot use the C API to control Excel.

- The C API cannot be used unless Microsoft Excel has explicitly called the DLL function in response to a menu, toolbar, cell calculation, or event.

Calling DLLs from VBA

Chapter 6 provides examples of DLL functions written in C that can be called from Visual Basic in Microsoft Excel. Text and examples show how Visual Basic data types (such as arrays, objects, and variants) are passed to DLL functions from Microsoft Excel.

Because Visual Basic is more powerful than the Microsoft Excel macro language, you can often write almost all of your custom functions and procedures in Visual Basic. Even with the added power of Visual Basic, however, it may be faster to perform some tasks from a C-language DLL. You may also need to write an external DLL function in C because you need to call a system-level function with a parameter-passing style or memory-management constraint not supported by Visual Basic.

Examples of tasks that must be performed in C include calls to Microsoft Mail API (MAPI) functions that use arrays of structures contained within an enclosing structure or functions that require dynamic memory allocation. Visual Basic's built-in data types and memory-management systems cannot support these complex tasks; therefore a Visual Basic macro that needs to call these functions must call an intermediate C-language function that builds the structures or manages memory to match the function's calling conventions.

It is also appropriate to write DLL functions that are called from Visual Basic if you need to perform speed-intensive calculations (which is one of the same reasons you'd use the C API). If you need to use Microsoft Excel objects as a part of the calculation, you can use the techniques in Chapter 6 to pass objects and other complex parameters to a DLL function and then use the techniques in Chapter 7 to manipulate the Microsoft Excel objects.

You cannot use the information in Chapter 6 to write a custom function that will be used only from a worksheet. The calling conventions described in this chapter apply to DLL functions called from Visual Basic, not functions called from a worksheet or macro sheet. Use Chapters 1 and 2 if you are writing a custom function that will be called from a worksheet.

Using IDispatch

Chapter 7 describes techniques that allow your C or C++ application or DLL to use OLE Automation to control Microsoft Excel with the OLE 2 IDispatch interface. This is essentially what Visual Basic Professional and other applications do when they access Microsoft Excel objects, properties, and methods using OLE Automation.

You should use this chapter if you're using Microsoft Excel as a component of a larger application—using the charting or PivotTable™ components of Microsoft Excel to display your application's data, for example. Controlling Microsoft Excel with OLE Automation lets you create the data in Microsoft Excel and use Visual Basic methods and properties to control the presentation of the data.

The OLE Automation techniques in Chapter 7 can also be used to examine and manipulate Microsoft Excel objects from C-language DLL functions called from Visual Basic. A likely scenario is a database access function that returns result data to a worksheet range. The DLL function would accept the destination Range object as a parameter and use IDispatch to place the data in the range.

The disadvantage of using OLE Automation is that the IDispatch interface is complex. If your application is small, the efforts to use IDispatch may not be justified. IDispatch is also not as closely tied to Microsoft Excel as the C API, but its programming model matches the Microsoft Excel object model, and it works across processes (unlike the C API).

File Format

Chapter 3 describes the binary interchange file format (BIFF) for workbooks (Microsoft Excel 5 workbooks include worksheets, macro sheets, and Visual Basic modules); Chapter 4 describes the BIFF for charts (charts are also included in workbooks, but their BIFF records are specific to charts); and Chapter 5 describes the workspace BIFF.

Appendixes

Appendix A, "Dynamic Data Exchange and XlTable Format," documents the dynamic data exchange (DDE) formats supported by Microsoft Excel and provides detailed information about the high-performance XlTable DDE format. Appendix B, "The EXCEL5.INI File," details the functionality of the EXCEL5.INI file (or the Excel Settings (5) file on the Apple Macintosh) and describes how settings in the file work with Microsoft Excel. Appendix C, "Displaying Custom Help," provides information about creating custom help files for your application, and Appendix D, "File Converter API," shows how to use the Microsoft Excel file converter API to allow conversion from external file formats.

Sample Files

Files for Windows

The Windows sample code disk contains the following directories.

- The INCLUDE directory contains the header file XLCALL.H, which must be included in all C source files that call Microsoft Excel functions. The subdirectories in this directory contain the XLCALL.H file translated into several languages.

- The LIB directory contains the library file XLCALL.LIB. If you need to call Microsoft Excel functions, this library file is linked to your code. XLCALL.LIB is a Windows import library; it doesn't contain any actual code. You can use IMPORT statements in your linker definition (.DEF) file instead of linking to this library.

- The SAMPLE directory contains several subdirectories with sample source code, which is intended as a learning resource and includes extensive comments.

- The BIFF directory contains the BIFF file-dumping programs, DUMPBIFF.EXE and BIFFVIEW.EXE, and other BIFF sample code.

- The HELP directory contains sample files for Appendix C, "Displaying Custom Help."

Files for the Apple Macintosh

The Macintosh sample code disk contains a compressed archive of the following directories.

- The Include folder contains the header file xlcall.h, which must be included in all C source files that call Microsoft Excel functions. The folders within the Include folder contain the xlcall.h file translated into several languages.

- The Sample Code folder contains several folders with sample source code, which is intended as a learning resource and includes extensive comments. The folders within the Sample Code folder are Circum, Examples, Framework, and SwitchSn.

The Microsoft Support Network

The Microsoft Support Network offers you a wide range of choices and access to high-quality, responsive technical support. Microsoft recognizes that support needs vary from user to user; the Microsoft Support Network allows you to choose the type of support that best meets your needs, with options ranging from electronic bulletin boards to annual support programs.

Services vary outside the United States and Canada. In other locations, contact a local Microsoft subsidiary for information. The Microsoft Support Network is subject to Microsoft's then-current prices, terms, and conditions, and is subject to change without notice.

Product Support Within the United States and Canada

In the United States and Canada, the following support services are available through the Microsoft Support Network:

Electronic Services

These services are available 24 hours a day, 7 days a week, including holidays.

Microsoft FastTips for Applications (800) 936-4100 on a touch-tone telephone. Receive automated answers to common questions, and access a library of technical notes, all delivered by recording or fax. You can use the following keys on your touch-tone telephone after you reach FastTips:

To	Press
Advance to the next message	*
Repeat the current message	7
Return to the beginning of FastTips	#

CompuServe Interact with other users and Microsoft support engineers, or access the Microsoft Knowledge Base to get product information. At any ! prompt, type **go microsoft** to access Microsoft forums, or type **go mskb** to access the Microsoft Knowledge Base. For an introductory CompuServe® membership kit, call (800) 848-8199, operator 519.

Microsoft Download Service Access, via modem, the Driver Library and the most current technical notes (1200, 2400, or 9600 baud; no parity; 8 data bits; 1 stop bit). In the United States, call (206) 936-6735. In Canada, call (905) 507-3022.

Internet Access the Driver Library and the Microsoft Knowledge Base. The Microsoft Internet FTP archive host, ftp.microsoft.com, supports anonymous login. When logging in as anonymous, you should type your complete electronic-mail name as your password.

Standard Support

Microsoft support engineers provide 90 days of no-charge support for the Microsoft Excel Developer's Kit. In the United States, support engineers are available via a toll call between 6:00 A.M. and 6:00 P.M. Pacific time, Monday through Friday, excluding holidays. Call (206) 635-7048.

In Canada, support engineers are available via a toll call between 8:00 A.M. and 8:00 P.M. Eastern time, Monday through Friday, excluding holidays. Call (905) 568-3503.

When you call, you should be at your computer and have the appropriate product documentation at hand. Be prepared to give the following information:

- The version number of Microsoft Excel that you are using
- The type of hardware that you are using
- The exact wording of any messages that appeared on your screen
- A description of what happened and what you were doing when the problem occurred
- A description of how you tried to solve the problem

Priority Support

The Microsoft Support Network offers priority telephone access to Microsoft support engineers 24 hours a day, 7 days a week, except holidays.

- In the United States, call (900) 555-2100; $2 (U.S.) per minute, $25 (U.S.) maximum. Charges appear on your telephone bill. Not available in Canada.
- In the United States, call (800) 936-5700; $25 (U.S.) per incident, billed to your VISA card, MasterCard, or American Express card. In Canada, call (800) 668-7975; $30 per incident, billed to your VISA card, MasterCard, or American Express card.

Text Telephone

Microsoft text telephone (TT/TDD) services are available for the deaf or hard-of-hearing. In the United States, using a TT/TDD modem, dial (206) 635-4948 between 6:00 A.M. and 6:00 P.M. Pacific time, Monday through Friday, excluding holidays. In Canada, using a TT/TDD modem, dial (905) 568-9641 between 8:00 A.M. and 8:00 P.M. Eastern time, Monday through Friday, excluding holidays.

Other Support Options

The Microsoft Support Network offers annual support plans. For information, in the United States, contact the Microsoft Support Network Sales and Information group at (800) 936-3500 between 6:00 A.M. and 6:00 P.M. Pacific time, Monday through Friday, excluding holidays. In Canada, call (800) 668-7975 between 8:00 A.M. and 8:00 P.M. Eastern time, Monday through Friday, excluding holidays.

Product Support Worldwide

Microsoft provides product support services throughout the world. For the Microsoft Excel Developer's Kit, support information is available on the CompuServe forums described in the preceding section. For more information about Microsoft product support, contact the Microsoft subsidiary office that serves your country. Microsoft subsidiary offices and the countries they serve are listed in the *Microsoft Excel User's Guide* for Microsoft Excel version 5.0.

Note Microsoft's support services are subject to Microsoft prices, terms, and conditions in place at the time the service is used.

Microsoft Solution Provider Program

Microsoft Solution Providers are independent organizations that provide consulting, integration, development, training, technical support or other services for Microsoft products. Microsoft Solution Providers implement business solutions for companies of all sizes and industries by taking advantage of today's micro-computer technology for graphical and client-server applications. Microsoft equips Solution Providers with information, business development assistance and tools that help create additional value with Microsoft-based software technology.

To locate a Microsoft Solution Provider in your area, or for more information on the Microsoft Solution Provider program in the U.S., call Microsoft at (800) 426-9400. In Canada, call (800) 563-9048. Outside the U.S. and Canada, contact your local Microsoft Office.

Microsoft Developer Network

The Microsoft Developer Network is the definitive source of systems-related SDKs, DDKs, operating systems, and programming information on developing applications for the Microsoft Windows and Windows NT™ operating systems. Offered as an annual membership program, the Developer Network streamlines your access to Microsoft development information and technology through the Development Library, the Development Platform, and the *Developer Network News.*

The Development Library provides the information you need at your fingertips. This unique Windows-based CD-ROM reference packs thousands of pages of information on programming for Windows in one place, and the Library's full-text search engine makes it all readily available. Updated quarterly, the Development Library is the comprehensive source of programming information on all Microsoft development products and system software.

The Development Platform brings you CD-ROMs containing the latest in Microsoft's operating systems and all systems-related SDKs and DDKs—both domestic and international versions. You get the latest releases at least once each quarter, including generally available pre-release software, so you can always be confident you're working with current software. The bimonthly *Developer Network News* publishes up-to-the-minute information about Microsoft's systems strategy, development products, and services.

To join the Developer Network, in the U.S. and Canada call (800) 759-5474. In Europe, call +31 10 258 8864. In Japan, call 03-5461-2617. Everywhere else, call (402) 691-0173.

C H A P T E R   1

The Microsoft Excel Applications Programming Interface

This chapter describes the Applications Programming Interface (API) for Microsoft Excel version 5.0. You can use the API to develop programs that call Microsoft Excel. Chapter 2, "Applications Programming Interface Function Reference," is a companion chapter to this one: it describes in detail the functions that are useful when working with the API.

The first part of this chapter discusses writing DLL functions and calling them from a Microsoft Excel macro sheet or worksheet. For information about using DLL functions with Visual Basic, see Chapter 6, "Using DLLs from Visual Basic." The second part of this chapter, "Calling Microsoft Excel from C," discusses the API calls that allow a C-language application to call into Microsoft Excel.

Microsoft Excel exposes its objects as OLE Automation objects. OLE 2 allows another application, called an *OLE Automation Controller,* to access the exposed objects and use their properties and methods with the IDispatch interface. For more information about using the Microsoft Excel IDispatch interface, see Chapter 7, "Using the OLE 2 IDispatch Interface."

Depending on your application, you may wish to use the C API, a DLL called from Visual Basic, the OLE 2 IDispatch interface, or some hybrid combination. The introduction to this book discusses when each of these solutions is most appropriate and gives guidelines for selecting an approach best suited to your application.

Microsoft Excel 5.0 has two macro languages: the Microsoft Excel 4.0 macro language and Visual Basic. Throughout this chapter, we use the term "macro language" to mean the Microsoft Excel 4.0 macro language.

Why Use the C Applications Programming Interface?

The Microsoft Excel 4.0 macro language is a fast, powerful, and portable tool for enhancing Microsoft Excel. You can create user-defined functions, write scripts that control Microsoft Excel, create new commands, and even create entire applications using Microsoft Excel as a platform. However, the macro language is not always powerful enough. You may already have large libraries of code written in another language. You may need the speed and security of compiled high-level languages. Or perhaps you need to interface with external libraries or databases.

The API can provide all these capabilities for you to use with a compiler for a high-level language. With the tools in this package you can:

- Create functions and commands in a high-level language such as C or Pascal.
- Dynamically link and call functions between the macro language and a high-level language.

If you know C and the Microsoft Excel macro language, you'll be able to write add-ins in C. In most cases, translating existing macro sheets into C is a straightforward task. You will not have to learn a large API in order to use C to develop add-ins. As a benefit, your add-ins will run faster, and they will be able to access functionality available only from C. For example, if you already have large libraries written in C (or any language that can be called from C), you will be able to use them with Microsoft Excel.

Getting Started

There are four possible ways of calling your C code from Microsoft Excel:

- From a Visual Basic module. You write a custom function in C and use the Declare statement to reference the function in the Visual Basic module. For more information about using DLLs with Visual Basic, see Chapter 6, "Using DLLs from Visual Basic."
- From a worksheet. You write a user-defined function in C, which Microsoft Excel users can enter on worksheets and evaluate. Your code is called whenever Microsoft Excel needs to calculate that function.
- From a macro sheet. You write a custom procedure in C, which can be called from a Microsoft Excel macro.
- From a menu, button, ON function, shortcut key, or toolbar. You write a custom procedure in C, which can be attached to a menu item, to a tool on the toolbar, to an event with an ON function, to a shortcut key, or to a button or other object on a worksheet drawing layer.

There is a difference between user-defined functions, which simply compute values based on their parameters and return the values, and user-defined commands, which actually perform actions. You can write functions or commands in C or in the Microsoft Excel built-in macro language. The following section describes calling DLLs from Microsoft Excel. For information on calling Microsoft Excel from your add-ins, see "Calling Microsoft Excel from C" on page 8.

Note Writing DLLs is slightly more complex than writing normal Windows code, which in turn is more complex than writing normal C programs. Make sure you understand both before you begin.

Creating DLL Files in C

The Microsoft Windows DLL examples in this chapter were prepared and tested with 16-bit Microsoft Windows version 3.1 using Microsoft Visual C++, version 1.5. If you use another compiler, you may also need the Microsoft Windows SDK.

Creating a Microsoft Windows DLL with Visual C++ is very simple. When you create a new project for your DLL, select "Windows dynamic link library (DLL)" from the list of project types. For more information, select the Visual Workbench command from the Help menu and search for the "DLLs: Building" topic in the Help.

When you create a simple DLL with Visual C++, you do not need to write a LibMain or WEP function. However, if your DLL must perform some action when it is initialized or unloaded, you will need LibMain and/or WEP (the example DLL in Chapter 2 uses a LibMain function to initialize string byte counts when the DLL is first loaded).

A Simple Example

The CIRCUM.MAK project in the SAMPLE\CIRCUM directory builds a simple Microsoft Windows DLL. The DLL contains a single exported function, called CalcCircum, which takes the radius of a circle as its argument and returns the circle's circumference.

```
double FAR * FAR PASCAL __export CalcCircum (double FAR *pdRadius)
{
    *pdRadius *= 6.283185308;

    return pdRadius;
}
```

Functions that will be called from Microsoft Excel in 16-bit Microsoft Windows version 3.1 should be declared as FAR PASCAL __export, as shown in the example. DLL functions in Microsoft Windows NT should be declared with the __stdcall calling convention.

For more information about using this DLL, see "Calling the Function from Within Microsoft Excel" on page 5. For information about calling a DLL from Visual Basic, see Chapter 6, "Using DLLs from Visual Basic."

Creating Code Resource Files in C

The Apple Macintosh code-resource examples in this chapter were prepared and tested with Symantec THINK C™.

To create a code resource that can be used with Microsoft Excel, you must set some compiler and project options before you build the code resource.

To set the compiler options, choose Options from the Edit menu. Select "Compiler Options" from the list box, set the "8-byte doubles" check box, and clear the "'\p' is unsigned char[]" check box. Microsoft Excel uses eight-byte IEEE floating-point values for all numbers.

To set the project options, choose Set Project Type from the Build menu. Select the dialog-box settings as shown in the following illustration.

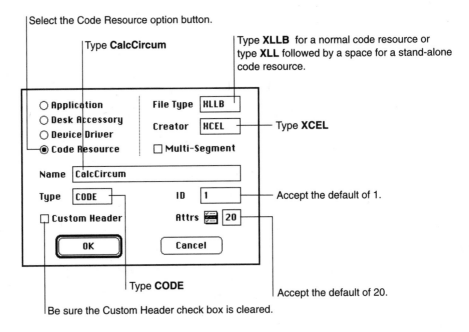

Select the Code Resource option button.

Type **CalcCircum**

Type **XLLB** for a normal code resource or type **XLL** followed by a space for a stand-alone code resource.

Type **XCEL**

Accept the default of 1.

Type **CODE**

Accept the default of 20.

Be sure the Custom Header check box is cleared.

For more information about writing code resources, see the *THINK C User's Guide*.

Note The default libraries (ANSI and ANSI-small) provided by THINK C assume that globals are offset to A5, not A4. To offset globals to A4, use the ANSI-A4 library to compile code resources. For more information, see the *THINK C User's Guide.*

To use this code resource, you must put the actual file with the code resource into the Microsoft Excel folder. Using a system software version 7.0 alias will not work.

A Simple Example

The Circum Project in the Sample Code:Circum folder builds a simple Apple Macintosh code resource. The code resource contains a single exported function, called CalcCircum, which takes the radius of a circle as its argument and returns the circle's circumference.

```
double pascal CalcCircum (double *pdRadius)
{
    *pdRadius *= 6.283185308;

    return pdRadius;
}
```

Code-resource functions that will be called from Microsoft Excel should be declared with the pascal calling convention, as shown in the example.

Calling the Function from Within Microsoft Excel

Once you have created a code resource or DLL, you should be able to call the DLL or code resource from within Microsoft Excel. The procedure is the same for Windows or the Macintosh.

Note The examples in this chapter discuss calling a DLL function from a worksheet or macro sheet. For information about calling DLL functions from Visual Basic, see Chapter 6, "Using DLLs from Visual Basic."

Functions for Linking DLLs or Code Resources

Microsoft Excel uses three key functions to link to DLLs or code resources. These functions are the same whether you are using Microsoft Excel for Windows or for the Macintosh. The first function, REGISTER, establishes a dynamic link to a function that resides in a DLL or code resource. The CALL function then calls that DLL or code resource function. Finally, the UNREGISTER function breaks the link, allowing the operating system to remove the DLL from memory. For example, see the following macro.

	A	B
1	fCircum	=REGISTER("CIRCUM","CalcCircum","EE")
2		=CALL(fCircum,100)
3		=UNREGISTER(fCircum)
4		=RETURN()

Cell B1 has the defined name fCircum.

Registering the Function

Cell B1 registers the function CalcCircum, which is exported by a DLL called CIRCUM.DLL. (On the Macintosh, cell B1 registers the code resource called CalcCircum, which resides in a file called Circum.) If the function is found, REGISTER returns a number called a *register ID*. That number can then be used as the first argument to the CALL and UNREGISTER functions.

The third argument to the REGISTER function informs Microsoft Excel what data types the CalcCircum function expects and what data type it will return. The first letter is a code describing the return type: in this case, E, meaning a pointer to a floating-point number. The next letter or letters describe all the arguments. The CalcCircum function takes a pointer to a floating-point number as its single argument, so the second letter of the code is E. Microsoft Excel supports several data types, such as integers, floating-point numbers, strings, arrays, and Booleans.

There is even a special code for the Microsoft Excel internal data type, the XLOPER; for more information, see "The XLOPER Data Type" on page 9. All of the data types are described under "REGISTER" on page 76, and in the online Microsoft Excel Macro Function Reference.

After the registration, cell B2 calls the function, with an argument of 100. The result becomes the value of B2. Finally, B3 unregisters the function, allowing the DLL or code resource to be removed from memory.

Running the Function

Now try running the CalcCircum function. Make sure the name fCircum is defined to refer to B1. To do this, select A1:B1; then choose the Create... command from the Name submenu on the Insert Menu, and choose the OK button. To run the macro, choose the Macro command from the Tools menu, type **fCircum**, and choose the Run button. The DLL should load and run the function. A quick way to see all the return values in the macro sheet is to press CTRL+` (accent grave). Microsoft Excel then switches into Display Values mode, and you see something like the following illustration.

	A	B
1	fCircum	-540868608
2		628.3185308
3		TRUE
4		TRUE

The value in B1 is the result of registering the function; in other words, it is the register ID. This value may vary from session to session. The value in B2 is the result of evaluating the CalcCircum function. The values in B3 and B4 indicate that both of the commands in these cells were evaluated successfully. You can press CTRL+` again to switch back to Display Formulas mode.

Registering a Function Automatically

For registering functions you need to use only once, there is a shortcut. You can use an alternate form of the CALL function, which automatically registers and then calls a function. The following illustration shows this form.

	B
6	=CALL("CIRCUM","CalcCircum","EE",100)
7	=RETURN()

This shortcut is helpful because it can be entered directly on a worksheet, as well as on a macro sheet. This is one way you can allow worksheets to use functions that are defined in a DLL.

Defining a Name for the Function

Although the preceding methods are effective, you ideally would like to be able to provide "native" functions, which look to the user like ordinary Microsoft Excel functions. To do this, you can use the full form of the REGISTER function on a worksheet. The following illustration shows this form.

	B
9	=REGISTER("CIRCUM","CalcCircum","EE","CalcCircum","radius",1,"Math & Trig")
10	=CalcCircum(100)
11	=RETURN()

In this example, in addition to registering the function, REGISTER defines a new name so that you can refer to the function directly. To do this, you need to specify the Microsoft Excel internal name, the names of the arguments, and the category to which this function belongs. Now, when the user chooses the Function... command from the Insert menu, the new function appears in the list under Math & Trig, as shown in the following illustration.

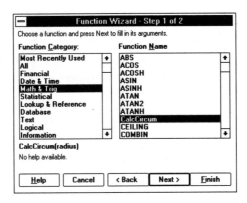

For more information about using the different forms of REGISTER, see page 76. For more information about using the different forms of CALL, see page 61.

Calling Microsoft Excel from C

Earlier in this chapter, you learned how to call DLLs and code resources from Microsoft Excel. However, in the CIRCUM example, you didn't actually drive Microsoft Excel; you just calculated a function and returned the result. In Microsoft Excel 5.0, it is possible to call internal Microsoft Excel functions directly from the code in your DLL.

Note The examples in this chapter discuss using the C API to call internal Microsoft Excel functions. For information about using the OLE 2 IDispatch interface to access Microsoft Excel Visual Basic objects, methods, and properties, see Chapter 7, "Using the OLE 2 IDispatch Interface."

Driving Microsoft Excel from C is straightforward because there is only one function, Excel4, to learn. The following is the function prototype:

```
int _cdecl Excel4(int iFunction, LPXLOPER pxRes, int iCount, ...)
```

The Excel4 function takes three or more arguments:

- The first argument is an integer that identifies which internal Microsoft Excel function you want to call.

- The second argument is a pointer to a buffer where the result is to be stored.

- The third argument is an integer that specifies how many arguments you want to pass to the function.

The third argument is followed by the actual arguments to the Microsoft Excel function. All the arguments to Microsoft Excel functions and their return values must always be specified as far pointers to XLOPER data structures, which are discussed in the following section. The return value indicates success or an error code. The keyword _cdecl indicates that the function uses the C calling convention as opposed to the Pascal calling convention.

To use this function, you need to know the following:

- What an XLOPER is and how to construct and examine one.

- How to specify which function or command equivalent you want Microsoft Excel to perform.

The next two sections discuss these two issues. Then you will be ready to start programming Microsoft Excel in C.

The XLOPER Data Type

Microsoft Excel is *polymorphic*. Cells can hold many different types of values: strings, numbers, arrays, error values, or logical values. Internally, this is accomplished by using a special, 10-byte data type called an XLOPER. Every XLOPER has 2 bytes that indicate the type of data and 8 bytes that indicate the actual data. The 8 bytes are used differently, depending on the data type—sometimes they contain a pointer to data that is stored elsewhere.

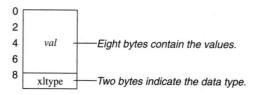

There are 12 different types of XLOPERs. You specify a type by entering a *type constant* in the *xltype* field of the XLOPER. The type constants are defined for you in XLCALL.H and are listed in the following table.

Type constant	xltype	Type of value
xltypeNum	0x0001	Numeric (IEEE floating-point)
xltypeStr	0x0002	String (byte-counted)
xltypeBool	0x0004	Logical (TRUE or FALSE)
xltypeRef	0x0008	General reference (external and/or disjoint)
xltypeErr	0x0010	Error
xltypeFlow	0x0020	Flow control in a macro
xltypeMulti	0x0040	Array
xltypeMissing	0x0080	Missing argument in a function call
xltypeNil	0x0100	None (for example, an empty cell)
xltypeSRef	0x0400	Single rectangular reference to current sheet
xltypeInt	0x0800	Integer (rarely used; use xltypeNum)
xltypeBigData	0x0802	Persistent data storage

Windows   The file XLCALL.H contains the definition of the XLOPER structure. In Windows, the definition appears as follows:

```
typedef struct xloper
{
    union
    {
        double num;                  /* xltypeNum */
        LPSTR str;                   /* xltypeStr */
        WORD bool;                   /* xltypeBool */
        WORD err;                    /* xltypeErr */
        short int w;                 /* xltypeInt */
        struct
        {
            WORD count;              /* always = 1 */
            XLREF ref;
        } sref;                      /* xltypeSRef */
        struct
        {
            XLMREF far *lpmref;
            DWORD idSheet;
        } mref;                      /* xltypeRef */
        struct
        {
```

```
            struct xloper far *lparray;
            WORD rows;
            WORD columns;
        } array;                        /* xltypeMulti */
        struct
        {
            union
            {
                short int level;        /* xlflowRestart */
                short int tbctrl;       /* xlflowPause */
                DWORD idSheet;          /* xlflowGoto */
            } valflow;
            WORD rw;                    /* xlflowGoto */
            BYTE col;                   /* xlflowGoto */
            BYTE xlflow;
        } flow;                         /* xltypeFlow */
        struct
        {
            union
            {
                BYTE far *lpbData;       /* data passed in */
                HANDLE hdata;            /* data returned */
            } h;
            long cbData;
        } bigdata;                      /* xltypeBigData */
    } val;
    WORD xltype;
} XLOPER, FAR *LPXLOPER;

typedef struct xlref
{
    WORD rwFirst;
    WORD rwLast;
    BYTE colFirst;
    BYTE colLast;
} XLREF, FAR *LPXLREF;

typedef struct xlmref
{
    WORD count;
    XLREF reftbl[1];        /* actually reftbl[count] */
} XLMREF, FAR *LPXLMREF;
```

Macintosh The definition of the XLOPER structure is slightly different on the
Macintosh. The names are the same, but "far" is omitted because all pointers are 4
bytes. In addition, types are defined differently; for example, "short unsigned"
instead of "WORD." This will not prevent you from porting C source files directly
between the Macintosh and Windows.

Types of XLOPERs

Following are diagrams of the various types of XLOPERs.

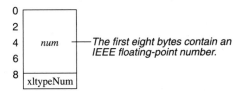

xltypeNum: Declared as double in C

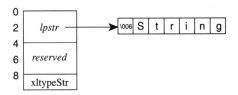

xltypeStr: Points to a byte-counted ("Pascal") string

Caution When you get string XLOPERs from Microsoft Excel, they are not always null-terminated! Do not attempt to pass them directly to C string-handling functions, such as `strcpy()`, that expect null-terminated strings.

Note Be sure to use an `unsigned char` or `(BYTE)` for the byte count. This is important because it is possible to create negative string lengths otherwise. For example:

```
LPSTR s;
WORD w;

w = s[0];         /* Bad */
w = (BYTE) s[0]; /* Good */
```

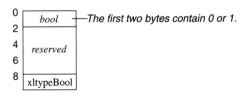

xltypeBool: The logical (Boolean) type

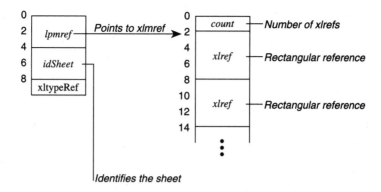

Identifies the sheet

xltypeRef: A general, external, or disjoint reference.
You can use the xlSheetId function to get
the sheet ID number.

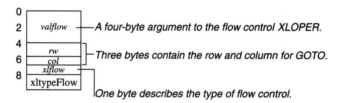

Error Code	Defined Constant	Value
#NULL!	xlerrNull	0
#DIV/0!	xlerrDiv0	7
#VALUE!	xlerrValue	15
#REF!	xlerrRef	23
#NAME?	xlerrName	29
#NUM!	xlerrNum	36
#N/A	xlerrNA	42

The first two bytes contain one of
the Microsoft Excel error codes.

xltypeErr: The error type

xltypeFlow: The type used for flow control functions on
macro sheets

For more information, see "Advanced Flow Control in Macro Sheets" on page 48.

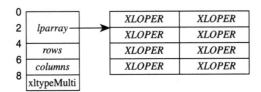

xltypeMulti: Contains a pointer to a two-dimensional (row major) array of XLOPERs, and the number of rows and columns in that array

xltypeMissing: A missing argument in a function call. This type can be used only as an argument to a function.

xltypeNil: An empty cell on a sheet

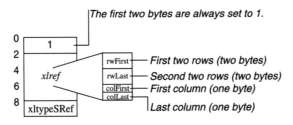

xltypeSref: A single rectangular reference to the current sheet

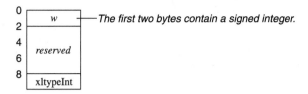

The first two bytes contain a signed integer.

xltypeInt: Integers are rarely used in Microsoft Excel; you will generally use xltypeNum.

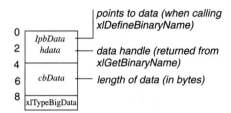

points to data (when calling xlDefineBinaryName)

data handle (returned from xlGetBinaryName)

length of data (in bytes)

xltypeBigData: Used with defined binary names for persistent data storage.

Examples of XLOPERs in C

Following are some examples showing how to construct various types of XLOPERs in C. As a convention, XLOPER variable names start with a lowercase "x."

To construct an integer XLOPER with value 27

```
XLOPER xInt;

xInt.xltype = xltypeInt;
xInt.val.w = 27;
```

To construct a numeric (floating-point) XLOPER with the value 3.141592654

```
XLOPER xPi;

xPi.xltype = xltypeNum;
xPi.val.num = 3.141592654;
```

To construct an XLOPER containing the string "Excel String"

```
XLOPER xStr;

xStr.xltype = xltypeStr;
xStr.val.str = (LPSTR)"\014Excel String";
/* Notice the octal byte count in front of the string. */
```

Macintosh On the Macintosh only, you can use THINK C to create byte-counted string constants by putting \p in front of the string, so that you don't have to do the counting yourself. The following code is one way to create the string "Excel String."

```
XLOPER xStr;

xStr.xltype = xltypeStr;
xStr.val.str = "\pExcel String";
```

To construct an XLOPER containing the logical value TRUE

```
XLOPER xBool;

xBool.xltype = xltypeBool;
xBool.val.bool = 1;
```

To construct an XLOPER containing a zero divide (#DIV/0!) error

```
XLOPER xZeroDivide;

xZeroDivide.xltype = xltypeErr;
xZeroDivide.val.err = xlerrDiv0;
```

To construct an XLOPER containing the array {1,2}

```
XLOPER rgx[2];
XLOPER xArray;

rgx[0].xltype = rgx[1].xltype = xltypeInt;
rgx[0].val.w = 1;
rgx[1].val.w = 2;
xArray.xltype = xltypeMulti;
xArray.val.array.lparray = (LPXLOPER) &(rgx[0]);
xArray.val.array.rows = 1;
xArray.val.array.columns = 2;
```

To construct a bigdata XLOPER

```
XLOPER xData;

xData.xltype = xltypeBigData;
xData.val.bigdata.h.lpbData = lpbData;        // pointer to the data
xData.val.bigdata.cbData = cbData;            // data length in bytes
```

For more information about using bigdata XLOPERs, see "Persistent Storage," later in this chapter.

Using Reference XLOPERs

References are not only one of the most common features in the macro language —
they are also the most confusing! In the Microsoft Excel macro language, you have
to remember when to use a local reference and when to use an external reference.
You also have to remember when to use R1C1 notation and when to use A1
notation. Sometimes references are specified as strings; sometimes they are not. To
help keep all this straight, the C API is designed to simplify specifying references.
This section describes the different types of references and how to construct
XLOPERs that specify them.

The first thing you must do is decide which sheet you want to refer to. There are
three possibilities: the current sheet, the active sheet, or an external sheet.

Current Sheet

The current sheet is the sheet that is currently being calculated. This may be a
macro sheet (in the case of a running macro) or a worksheet (in the case of a user-
defined function). The current sheet is not necessarily the one that appears in front
on the screen, as shown in the following example.

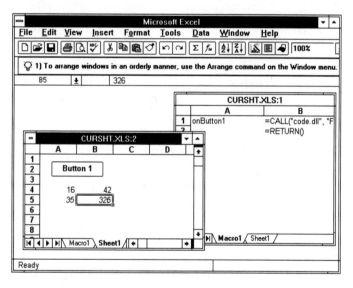

The user is working on Sheet1 and clicks Button 1. This executes a macro on
Macro1. While that macro is running, it calls your DLL. Macro1 is now the current
sheet because it is the one being calculated.

To create a reference to the current sheet, you create an xltypeSRef XLOPER, as shown in the following example.

```
XLOPER xRef;

xRef.xltype = xltypeSRef;
xRef.val.sref.count = 1;
xRef.val.sref.ref.rwFirst  = 0;
xRef.val.sref.ref.rwLast   = 2;
xRef.val.sref.ref.colFirst = 0;
xRef.val.sref.ref.colLast  = 2;
```

This creates a reference to the cells A1:C3 in the upper-left corner of the current sheet. Notice how rows and columns are always zero-based inside Microsoft Excel.

Tips for Creating References

- To create a reference to a single cell, set rwFirst = rwLast and colFirst = colLast.

- To create a reference to an entire column, set rwFirst = 0 and rwLast = 0x3FFF.

- To create a reference to an entire row, set colFirst = 0 and colLast = 0xFF.

- To create a reference to the entire sheet, set rwFirst = colFirst = 0, rwLast = 0x3FFF, and colLast = 0xFF.

- To create a nonadjacent reference on the current sheet, you must create an external reference. The xltypeSRef type does not support nonadjacent references. See the following section, "External Sheet."

Active Sheet

The active sheet is the sheet that the user sees in front on the screen. For example, in the preceding illustration the active sheet would be Sheet1. To create a reference to the active sheet, you need to find out the sheet ID of the active sheet and then construct an external reference to that sheet ID. See the following section, "External Sheet."

External Sheet

Technically, an external sheet is any sheet except the current sheet. This means the active sheet is an external sheet unless the current sheet and the active sheet are the same. For example, when you are executing a user-defined function during recalculation on a worksheet, the active sheet might be the same as the current sheet. External references are the most common type of reference used in C functions. That is because you need an external reference to refer to the active (front) sheet, which is probably the sheet used to call the DLL. To construct an external reference, you need to find the sheet ID of the sheet you want and build the external reference XLOPER.

To find the sheet ID of the sheet you want, use the xlSheetId function. For more information about how to call the xlSheetId function, see "xlSheetId" on page 126. The xlSheetId function has two forms. If it is called with no arguments, it returns the sheet ID of the active sheet, that is, the sheet that the user sees in front. If it is called with one argument, of type xltypeStr, it returns the sheet ID of the named sheet. The xlSheetId type returns its result by putting the sheet ID in the val.mref.idSheet field of the result XLOPER. For example:

```
XLOPER xRef;

if (xlretSuccess!=Excel4(xlSheetId,&xRef,0)) {
    error("No active sheet!");
}


/*
**   Now xRef.val.mref.idSheet contains the
**   sheet ID of the active sheet.
*/
```

If this succeeds, the sheet ID for xRef is filled in. Or, you might want an external reference to a named sheet. The following example shows how to obtain the sheet ID of SHEET1 in BOOK1.XLS.

```
XLOPER xRef, xFileName;

xFileName.xltype = xltypeStr;
xFileName.val.str = "\021[BOOK1.XLS]SHEET1";

if (xlretSuccess !=
        Excel4(xlSheetId, &xRef, 1, (LPXLOPER)&xFileName)) {
    error ("SHEET1 not found");
}
```

The next step is to build the external reference XLOPER. This is an XLOPER of type xltypeRef, which is the most general reference type. The following code constructs a rectangular reference to the active sheet:

```
XLOPER xRef;
XLMREF xlmref;

if (xlretSuccess!=Excel4(xlSheetId,&xRef,0)) {
    error();
}
else {
```

```
    xRef.xltype = xltypeRef;
    xRef.val.mref.lpmref = (LPXLMREF) &xlmref;
    xlmref.count = 1;
    xlmref.reftbl[0].rwFirst = 0;
    xlmref.reftbl[0].rwLast  = 3;
    xlmref.reftbl[0].colFirst= 0;
    xlmref.reftbl[0].colLast = 3;
}
```

This code generates a reference to 16 cells in the upper-left corner of the active (front) sheet. This would be called !A1:D4 in the macro language. If you want to specify a nonadjacent reference, you can use a different value for count. You will also have to allocate more memory for xlmref. Then, you can fill in reftbl[*n*] for the (*n*+1)th rectangular region. The reftbl[*n*] reference is easily expanded using the XLMREF and XLREF constructs defined in XLCALL.H. Dynamically allocate space for the XLMREF and specify sizeof(XLMREF) + sizeof(XLREF) * (*n*−1) where *n* is the number of nonadjacent references you want to build.

Note As a shortcut, you can use an idSheet number of 0 in your XLOPER to get the current sheet. Microsoft Excel automatically fills in the correct idSheet number. When you get external references from Microsoft Excel, you always get an actual idSheet number, not 0, even if they refer to the current sheet.

Using XLOPERs to Communicate with C Functions

You can use XLOPERs when your function is called by C. This is the most flexible way to communicate with Microsoft Excel. To do this, use the R data type in the third argument to the REGISTER function. For example:

```
=REGISTER("myDLL","myFunc","RR","MyFunc","Value")
```

This would register a function declared as:

```
LPXLOPER myFunc(LPXLOPER px);
```

You can also use data type P in the third argument. The distinction between data types P and R is significant only when the argument being passed is specified as a reference. Type R passes the reference as xltypeRef. Data type P passes the value represented by the reference.

Specifying Microsoft Excel Functions

The Excel4 function is used to call any of the Microsoft Excel functions or command equivalents. These function or command equivalents are the same as those defined in the *Microsoft Excel Function Reference* and the online Microsoft Excel Macro Function Reference.

Of course, many functions in the Microsoft Excel Macro Language do not make sense in DLLs. For example, you would never want to call the GOTO function or the ARGUMENT function from a DLL because its behavior wouldn't make sense outside of a macro sheet.

To understand how to specify a function, you need to know something about how Microsoft Excel works internally. Microsoft Excel contains two tables: the *function* table and the *command-equivalent* table. These tables are simply arrays of pointers to internal Microsoft Excel functions.

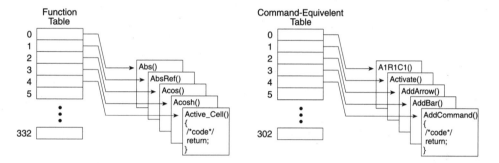

The command-equivalent table is very much like the function table, with entries that point to Microsoft Excel command equivalents. When you use Excel4, you will need to know the index of the Microsoft Excel function or command equivalent. These are defined for you in XLCALL.H:

```
#define xlfCount 0
#define xlfIsna 2
#define xlfIserror 3
#define xlfSum 4
#define xlfAverage 5
#define xlfMin 6
#define xlfMax 7
#define xlfRow 8
#define xlfColumn 9
#define xlfNa 10
        .
        .
        .
```

```
#define xlcBeep (0 | xlCommand)
#define xlcOpen (1 | xlCommand)
#define xlcOpenLinks (2 | xlCommand)
#define xlcCloseAll (3 | xlCommand)
#define xlcSave (4 | xlCommand)
#define xlcSaveAs (5 | xlCommand)
#define xlcFileDelete (6 | xlCommand)
#define xlcPageSetup (7 | xlCommand)
#define xlcPrint (8 | xlCommand)
#define xlcPrinterSetup (9 | xlCommand)
        .
        .
        .
```

The name of each function or command equivalent is based on the name in the *Microsoft Excel Function Reference* or the online Microsoft Excel Macro Function Reference. Functions are prefixed with "xlf," while command equivalents are prefixed with "xlc." You will also notice that all the command equivalents have their xlCommand bit set, so Microsoft Excel knows whether to use the command-equivalent table or the function table. You can also easily determine whether you have a function or a command equivalent. It is important to distinguish between the two: a function returns a value, and a command equivalent executes some action.

Calling the Dialog Box Forms of Functions

In the macro language, most command equivalents that have dialog boxes can be called either with the dialog box or without it. In the *dialog box form* of the function, the name is followed by a question mark. For example, SAVE.AS will not prompt the user with a dialog box, but SAVE.AS? will. To use the dialog box form in C, simply set the xlPrompt bit (defined in XLCALL.H). For example, this code deletes the file BOOK1.XLS:

```
XLOPER xResult, xBook1;

xBook1.xltype = xltypeStr;
xBook1.val.str = "\011BOOK1.XLS";

Excel4(xlcFileDelete, &xResult, 1, (LPXLOPER)&xBook1);
```

The following code displays the Delete dialog box, offering all the *.BAK files as candidates for deletion:

```
XLOPER xResult, xFilter;

xFilter.xltype = xltypeStr;
xFilter.val.str = "\005*.BAK";

Excel4(xlcFileDelete | xlPrompt, &xResult, 1, (LPXLOPER) &xFilter);
```

Using International Versions of Microsoft Excel

So far, you have read about running DLLs on only the U.S. version of Microsoft Excel. However, you may want to create an international DLL. This is a DLL that will work with any international version of Microsoft Excel.

The first argument to the Excel4 function, specifying which function to execute, is universal. Every version of Microsoft Excel uses the same function codes, although the name the user may see for the codes is different in international versions. For example, the SUM function is called SOMME in French Microsoft Excel, but it still uses function code 4. A problem arises only when you need to refer to this function by name; for example, if you want to place a SUM formula in a cell, and you are calling the FORMULA function. In the U.S. version, you could call FORMULA("=SUM(1,2)"), but this would not be understood in the French version.

To get around this problem, you can set the international bit (xlIntl). This tells Microsoft Excel to treat the following command as if it were executed in U.S. Microsoft Excel. As a result, setting the xlIntl bit and calling FORMULA("=SUM(1,2)") has the same effect on any version of Microsoft Excel. The French Microsoft Excel user simply sees =SOMME(1,2) entered on the sheet.

Excel4

Now that you know all about XLOPERs and specifying functions, you can take a closer look at the Excel4 function:

```
int _cdecl Excel4(int iFunction, LPXLOPER pxRes, int iCount, ...)
```

First, notice that this function is _cdecl. This means that it uses the C calling convention (as opposed to the Pascal calling convention). This is helpful because the C calling convention allows for a function with a variable number of arguments. In Microsoft Windows NT, the Excel4 function uses the __stdcall calling convention, which also allows for a variable number of arguments. For more information about calling conventions, see your compiler documentation.

The function takes at least three arguments. The following three arguments must always be present.

- The iFunction argument is the function code. You should always use one of the defined constants from XLCALL.H.

- The pxRes argument is a pointer to an XLOPER that you have allocated for the result of the function. This is where Microsoft Excel will put the result of your function call. If you use 0, Microsoft Excel discards the return value. However, it is a very good idea to check the result from Excel4.

- The iCount argument is the number of arguments you are going to pass, from 0 to 30. Microsoft Excel never allows more than 30 arguments in a function call.

Following the iCount argument are the arguments to the Microsoft Excel function itself. These must all be LPXLOPERs, that is, far pointers to XLOPERs that you have allocated. As a rule, all arguments to all Microsoft Excel functions and command-equivalents are always specified as (far) pointers to XLOPERs. In order to represent a missing (omitted) argument, create an XLOPER of type xltypeMissing, and pass a pointer to that, or use a NULL pointer.

Windows With Microsoft Windows, it is a good idea to always cast these arguments to LPXLOPER. That way, you can be sure the compiler will not accidentally pass a near pointer, causing general chaos. For example, always write:

```
Excel4(xlfGetCell, &xResult, 1, (LPXLOPER) &MyInt);
```

Instead of:

```
Excel4(xlfGetCell, &xResult, 1, &MyInt); /* BAD!!! */
```

When you include XLCALL.H, the Excel4 function prototype automatically casts the second argument (the return value) to an LPXLOPER. All the other arguments, starting with the fourth, need to have casts.

More About Using the Excel4 Function

You should always check the return value from Excel4. If it is not xlretSuccess, something has prevented the call from succeeding. For example, one of the XLOPERs may not be valid; Microsoft Excel may be low on memory; or you may have used an invalid number of arguments. For a list of the possible return values, see "Excel4" on page 70. If Excel4 does not return xlretSuccess, the XLOPER returned will contain a #VALUE! error.

Note The Excel function in the framework library automatically checks the return value to aid in debugging.

Be careful to distinguish between a Microsoft Excel function failing and the Excel4 function failing. When a Microsoft Excel function fails, Excel4 succeeds but pxRes contains one of the Microsoft Excel error codes. When Excel4 fails, it actually returns one of the xlret... failure codes. There is a fine distinction between a failure in Microsoft Excel and a failure in the callback mechanism.

You can call Excel4 only when control has been passed to your code by Microsoft Excel. You are not able to call back into Microsoft Excel at any time you want. In other words, you cannot set up a timer with a callback address, return control to Microsoft Excel, and then in your callback function start calling Excel4. Neither can you create a DLL that interacts with Microsoft Excel but is loaded and called by another application. To communicate with Microsoft Excel from another application you should use OLE Automation or DDE. For more information about OLE Automation, see Chapter 7, "Using the OLE2 IDispatch Interface." For more information about DDE, see Appendix A, "Dynamic Data Exchange and XlTable Format."

Important Unless Microsoft Excel has called you, Microsoft Excel will not be ready to handle callbacks.

Note Even though the Excel4 and Excel4v functions are named for Microsoft Excel version 4.0, they work with both Microsoft Excel version 4.0 and 5.0. The current Excel4 and Excel4v functions will continue to work even with future versions of Microsoft Excel, although future versions may implement additional callback functions. This ensures that any add-ins you develop now will still work with future versions of Microsoft Excel.

There is an additional function, Excel4v, which works like Excel4, but it takes an array of LPXLOPERs passed by reference instead of on the stack:

```
int FAR PASCAL Excel4v(int iFunction, LPXLOPER pxRes,
    int iCount, LPXLOPER FAR rgx[]);
```

This function allows you to wrap up Excel4 in another function. For example:

```
int FAR MyExcel4(int iFunction, LPXLOPER pxRes, int iCount, ...)
{
    int result = Excel4v(iFunction, pxRes, iCount,
        (LPXLOPER FAR *) (&iCount+1));
    assert(result == xlretSuccess);
    return result;
}
```

Macintosh You can call Excel4 or Excel4v directly in Windows, just by linking with XLCALL.LIB. However, if you want to call Excel4 or Excel4v on the Apple Macintosh, you have to load the code resource where these functions reside and get a pointer to them. These two functions are stored as code resources in the Microsoft Excel executable file itself. The following is an example of how you would load them:

```
#include <SetUpA4.h>
#include "xlcall.h"

Handle hExcel4, hExcel4v;
short wStateSav, wStateSav2;
short (*Excel4)(short,LPXLOPER,short,...);
short pascal (*Excel4v)(short,LPXLOPER,short,LPXLOPER *);

signed long int pascal main (i)
    signed long int i;
{
    RememberA0();
    SetUpA4();

    hExcel4 = GetNamedResource('CODE',"\pExcel4");
    wStateSav = HGetState(hExcel4);
    HLock(hExcel4);
    Excel4 = (ProcPtr) *hExcel4;

    hExcel4v = GetNamedResource('CODE',"\pExcel4v");
    wStateSav2 = HGetState(hExcel4v);
    HLock(hExcel4v);
    Excel4v = (ProcPtr) *hExcel4v;

    /* Your code here */

    HSetState(hExcel4, wStateSav);
    HSetState(hExcel4v, wStateSav2);
    RestoreA4();

    return /* whatever you want to return here - must be local */;
}
```

Memory Management

The biggest disadvantage of writing code in a high-level language, instead of the Microsoft Excel macro language, is the problem of dealing with memory management. This section discusses several critical issues in memory management. You should understand this section fully before attempting to write Microsoft Excel DLLs.

Memory Used for XLOPERs

Where is the memory used for XLOPERs allocated and freed? First, consider the simple case in which Microsoft Excel calls a function in a DLL that returns a value. Microsoft Excel allocates and frees the arguments it passes, so you don't have to worry about them.

The only potential problem is the return value. If your function returns a simple value, there is no problem using the normal C return value. However, sometimes your function needs to return an XLOPER. That XLOPER may be contained in 10 bytes as usual, but it might also have pointers to large blocks of data that are stored elsewhere. The simplest way to return such data is to allocate some static memory and return a pointer to the memory. Following are examples for Windows and the Macintosh of a simple DLL that returns a string XLOPER.

Windows Example

```
LPXLOPER FAR ReturnString(void)
{
    static XLOPER x;

    x.xltype = xltypeStr;
    x.val.str = "\004Test";

    return (LPXLOPER) &x;
}
```

Macintosh Example

```
pascal LPXLOPER main (void)
{
    static XLOPER x;
    LPXLOPER px;

    RememberA0();
    SetUpA4();

    x.xltype = xltypeStr;
    x.val.str = "\pTest";

    px = &x;
    RestoreA4();

    return px;
}
```

Next, consider the case in which the DLL calls a Microsoft Excel function using Excel4. Again, the caller (the DLL) allocates the arguments. The caller must allocate 10 bytes for the return value XLOPER as well, and a pointer to this XLOPER is passed as the second argument to Excel4 so that Microsoft Excel knows where to place the return value.

This works for simple XLOPERs without any pointers. But what happens when Excel4 must return a string? The XLOPER contains a pointer to memory that has been allocated by Microsoft Excel from its own memory management system. You need to let Microsoft Excel know when you are finished with that data so that Microsoft Excel can free its memory. This is done using the xlFree function, which takes one or more XLOPERs and tells Microsoft Excel that it can free any associated memory.

For example, if the XLOPER is a string, calling xlFree on it frees the string, not the XLOPER itself. Similarly, if the XLOPER is an array of strings, xlFree frees everything except the top-level XLOPER. To summarize, whenever Excel4 returns an XLOPER containing a pointer, you must call xlFree on that XLOPER.

A safe rule is to call xlFree on every return value you get back from Excel4. If you pass xlFree an XLOPER that does not contain a pointer, nothing happens. If xlFree is accidentally called twice on the same XLOPER, Microsoft Excel ignores the second call.

Do not modify XLOPERs that you get back from Microsoft Excel. If you do, the Microsoft Excel memory manager will not be able to free them properly and may crash.

Example of xlFree

The following example uses the xlFree function to return a string.

```
/*
** Use Microsoft Excel to get input from the user,
** then copy it into our own memory space.
*/

XLOPER xQuery, xResponse, x2;
static unsigned char rgchResult[64] = "";
unsigned char i;

xQuery.xltype = xltypeStr;
xQuery.val.str = "\022What is your name?";

x2.xltype = xltypeNum;
x2.val.num = 2;

Excel4(xlfInput, &xResponse, 2, (LPXLOPER) &xQuery, (LPXLOPER) &x2);

if (xResponse.xltype == xltypeStr) {
```

```
/*
** Now Microsoft Excel has allocated memory for the
** string in its own memory space. Copy the string out
** to our own memory, while converting to a C
** (null-terminated) string.
*/

for (i=1;
        (i <= (unsigned char)xResponse.val.str[0]) && (i < 64);
        i++) {
    rgchResult[i - 1] = xResponse.val.str[i];
}

rgchResult[i - 1] = '\0';

}


/*
** Let Microsoft Excel free the string from its memory.
*/

Excel4(xlFree, 0, 1, (LPXLOPER) &xResponse);
```

Returning XLOPERs That Still Need to Be Freed by Microsoft Excel

As explained in the previous section, it is important to call the xlFree function on any XLOPERs that return values from callback functions because Microsoft Excel may have allocated some memory for these values and needs to free this memory. For example, suppose we need a DLL function that returns the name of the current sheet. That DLL function calls GET.DOCUMENT(1) to get the name of the sheet. For example:

```
/*
** BAD!
*/
LPXLOPER FAR PASCAL __export GetSheetName(void)
{
    static XLOPER x1, xSheetName;

    x1.xltype = xltypeInt;
    x1.val.w  = 1;

    Excel4(xlfGetDocument, &xSheetName, 1, (LPXLOPER)&x1);

    return (LPXLOPER)&xSheetName;
}
```

What's wrong with this code? It calls GET.DOCUMENT(1), which returns a string. This string is then allocated by Microsoft Excel. However, the code never calls xlFree on the return value, so Microsoft Excel loses the memory associated with the string. You can waste quite a bit of memory this way, and it can never be retrieved.

You could try calling the xlFree function on xSheetName before returning it. Unfortunately, the contents of an XLOPER are undefined after xlFree, so that probably wouldn't work. You could allocate your own, static XLOPER, with your own, static buffer to keep the string. This would require copying out the data yourself, and would waste static (global) memory.

Microsoft Excel supports a special bit called xlbitXLFree (0x1000). You can turn on this bit in the xltype field of any XLOPER returned from Microsoft Excel. If your function returns an XLOPER in which the xlbitXLFree bit is 1, Microsoft Excel copies out the data it needs from the XLOPER and frees it for you. For example, you could rewrite the preceding function as:

```
/*
** GOOD!
*/
LPXLOPER FAR PASCAL __export GetSheetName()
{
    static XLOPER x1, xSheetName;

    x1.xltype = xltypeInt;
    x1.val.w  = 1;

    Excel4(xlfGetDocument, &xSheetName, 1, (LPXLOPER)&x1);

    xSheetName.xltype |= xlbitXLFree;

    return (LPXLOPER)&xSheetName;
}
```

Microsoft Excel frees xSheetName for you after the function has returned.

Returning XLOPERs That Still Need to Be Freed by the DLL

Another common problem occurs when you want to write a function that returns a very large XLOPER (for example, a large array full of strings) as the return value. As described in "Memory Used for XLOPERS" on page 27, you can simply allocate the space for the return value as your own global memory by declaring it static. This works for small return values. But for very large arrays, this can consume quite a bit of memory.

To address this problem, Microsoft Excel allows you to set the xlbitDLLFree bit (0x4000) in the xltype field of the XLOPERs that you return from your functions. To use it, you allocate any extra memory that you need for your XLOPER using your own memory allocation routines. You then set the xlbitDLLFree bit in the xltype field to true (1). Finally, you return a pointer to the XLOPER to Microsoft Excel using the normal return statement. Microsoft Excel automatically copies out the data in the XLOPER; then, it calls back the DLL to give you a chance to free the memory that was allocated. It does this by calling the xlAutoFree function, which your DLL must provide. Microsoft Excel passes one argument, which is the XLOPER that is ready to be freed. See the following examples.

Windows Example

```
LPXLOPER FAR PASCAL __export GetString(void)
{
    static XLOPER x;

    x.xltype = xltypeStr;
    x.val.str = GlobalLock(GlobalAlloc(GMEM_MOVEABLE, 8));

    lstrcpy(x.val.str, "\006Sample");

    x.xltype |= xlbitDLLFree;

    return (LPXLOPER)&x;
}


void FAR PASCAL __export xlAutoFree(LPXLOPER px)
{
    /*
    ** We'll take advantage of the fact that in
    ** protected mode Windows, handles are the
    ** the same as selectors.
    */

    GlobalUnlock(HIWORD(px->val.str));
    GlobalFree(HIWORD(px->val.str));

    return;
}
```

Macintosh Example

```
/*
** The following code goes in the
** GetString code resource
*/

LPXLOPER pascal main (void)
{
    static XLOPER x;
    LPXLOPER px;
    Handle h;

    RememberA0();
    SetUpA4();

    h = NewHandle(8);
    HLock(h);

    x.xltype = xltypeStr;
    x.val.str = (char *)*h;

    strcpy(x.val.str, "\pSample");

    x.xltype |= xlbitDLLFree;
    px = &x;

    RestoreA4();
    return px;
}


/*
** The following code goes in the
** xlAutoFree code resource
*/

int pascal main(LPXLOPER px)
{
    Handle h;

    RememberA0();
    SetUpA4();
```

```
        h = RecoverHandle(px->val.str);
        HUnlock(h);
        DisposHandle(h);

        RestoreA4();

        return 1;
}
```

When the GetString function is called from Microsoft Excel, it allocates memory
from the system. Then GetString turns on the xlbitDLLFree bit in x.xltype and
returns x. When Microsoft Excel sees that this bit is on, it copies out the data it
needs and then calls xlAutoFree to free the data. (In this code sample, xlAutoFree is
not very robust. In a real application with more than one DLL function, you may
want to write a version of xlAutoFree that actually checks the type of the
LPXLOPER being passed and uses that information to decide how to free it.) With
Windows, make sure that you export xlAutoFree in your .DEF file.

Setting Names in DLLs

You can use DLLs even though no macro sheet is present. However, you may want
to define some names to help you keep data between calls to your DLL. For
example, you may want to call xlfSetName from a DLL even though there is no
macro sheet where you can define the name.

For this purpose, Microsoft Excel has a special, hidden name space that is
accessible to DLLs. This allows you to store temporary names in Microsoft Excel.
However, it is important to remember that this name space is shared by all DLLs
within the same instance of Microsoft Excel. Therefore, if you want to ensure that
your names do not conflict with names defined by another DLL, be sure to begin all
your names with a unique prefix, preferably the name of your DLL. For example, if
your DLL is called MYDLL.DLL, create names such as MYDLL_hWnd.

Following are ways you might use the hidden name space:

- When you create Microsoft Excel 4.0 user-defined dialog boxes with list boxes,
  you need to use a name to store the list of items in the list box. For an example
  of this, see the function fDialog in GENERIC.C. (For Windows, this is in the
  FRAMEWRK subdirectory of the sample source code. For the Macintosh, it is
  in the file fDialog.c in the Framework folder). Note that this applies to
  Microsoft Excel 4.0 dialog boxes created with the DIALOG.BOX macro
  function, not Microsoft Excel 5.0 dialog sheets.

- You can keep instance-specific static data when running with Windows. For
  more information, see "Multiple Instances of Microsoft Excel" on page 35.

- On the Macintosh, every function resides in its own code resource and has a separate static data space. You can use the Microsoft Excel hidden name space to pass data between different functions (code resources) in the same file.

The hidden name space is not accessible when the DLL is calculating a function on a worksheet. If the DLL function was called as part of a normal recalculation on a worksheet, names refer to the current sheet unless the DLL was registered as a macro type DLL (the data type string contained "#"). However, if the DLL was called from a macro sheet or if the DLL function was invoked through a menu, keyboard shortcut, toolbar, or otherwise, names will refer to the hidden name space.

Persistent Storage

The xlDefineBinaryName and xlGetBinaryName functions provide a mechanism for storing data and referencing it by name. Data with a defined binary name is stored with the workbook when you save the workbook. When the workbook is reloaded, the data is again available to any application which knows the data name.

Your application defines a name by passing the name (a string XLOPER) and a pointer to the data (in a bigdata XLOPER) to the xlDefineBinaryName function. Once the name is defined, you can use the xlGetBinaryName function to return a handle for the data whenever you need it.

For more information about the xlDefineBinaryName and xlGetBinaryName functions, see Chapter 2, "Applications Programming Interface Function Reference."

Using the Stack

Windows Only In Microsoft Windows, DLLs must share the same stack space as Microsoft Excel. When a DLL is first called, there is usually about 15K of space left on the stack. When that DLL calls the Excel4 function, Microsoft Excel consumes even more space on the stack. Microsoft Excel tests the amount of available stack space before it runs the function or command specified by the Excel4 function. If the stack would be overrun, Microsoft Excel will not run the command or function, and the Excel4 function call fails. This means that it is very important to use as little stack space as possible. Don't put large data structures on the stack. Declare local variables as static if at all possible. Avoid calling functions recursively.

In 16-bit Microsoft Windows, the Excel4 function stack check requires 8.5K available stack space when the function is called from a DLL called from a macro sheet or in response to an event or button press, and 4K available stack space when the function is called from a DLL called from a calculating worksheet.

Note   Microsoft Excel 4.0 did not perform this stack checking. Microsoft Excel 5.0 tests for adequate stack space for the most stack-intensive function or command every time you call the Excel4 function. If there is not enough stack space available for the most stack-intensive function or command, your function call will fail, even if it could run with the available stack space. This "worst case" stack check may cause some Excel4 function calls which worked in Microsoft Excel version 4.0 to fail in Microsoft Excel version 5.0.

To help you in debugging, a function called xlStack is provided, which returns the number of bytes left on the stack. If you suspect that you are overrunning the stack, call this function frequently to see how much stack space is left.

Finally, if you desperately need more stack space than the 15K that you normally get, you can use the Windows functions SwitchStackTo and SwitchStackBack. For more information about these functions, see the documentation for the Microsoft Windows Software Development Kit.

Important   You must always use the original stack when calling the Excel4 function.

Multiple Instances of Microsoft Excel

Windows Only   You must consider the possibility that your DLL will be called by more than one running instance of Microsoft Excel. If this happens, remember that your DLL has only one global data segment. For example, consider this code:

```
int i=0;

int FAR PASCAL __export test(void)
{
    return ++i;
}
```

This returns successive integers as long as there is only one copy of Microsoft Excel using this DLL. But if there are multiple instances of Microsoft Excel running at the same time and intermittently calling this DLL, there will still be only one copy of the variable i between all the instances. This means that your DLL cannot save state as easily as a normal C program can. What can you do about this, if you need a DLL to maintain a state that is distinct for each instance of Microsoft Excel?

The usual solution is to use a block of memory called an *instance block*. For example, you have a program Zoo with two functions: see_bears and see_fish. You can create an initialization function init_zoo, which allocates an instance block of memory (using LocalAlloc or GlobalAlloc) that contains all of the state that is instance-specific. The function init_zoo returns a pointer (or handle) to this memory. Then see_bears and see_fish take this handle as the first argument. Finally, exit_zoo frees the global memory. The code might look like this:

```
typedef struct tagInstanceBlock
{
    int a;
    int b;
} INSTANCEBLOCK;

HANDLE FAR PASCAL __export init_zoo()
{
    return GlobalAlloc(GMEM_MOVEABLE, sizeof(INSTANCEBLOCK));
}

void FAR PASCAL __export see_bears(HANDLE hInstBlock)
{
    INSTANCEBLOCK FAR *pib;

    pib = GlobalLock(hInstBlock);

    // Now use pib->a and pib->b as instance-specific
    // variables

    GlobalUnlock(hInstBlock);
}

void FAR PASCAL __export exit_zoo(HANDLE hInstBlock)
{
    GlobalFree(hInstBlock);
}
```

There are other ways around this problem. For example, you can store all instance-specific information on sheets, using Microsoft Excel to maintain your state. You can also store the instance handle in a name on the sheet or in the hidden name space. Or you can simply prevent multiple instances of Microsoft Excel from using your DLL. You can call the xlGetInst function to find out the instance handle of the instance that is calling you, so that you can distinguish between different instances.

Global Data in Code Resources

Macintosh Only   Normally, Macintosh applications refer to their globals (and statics) as offsets of the A5 register. Formerly, code resources couldn't allocate any global memory at all. However, if you are using THINK C, you can declare global variables in code resources. These global variables are put in the same segment as the main function. Unfortunately, these global variables are referred to by offsetting A4, not A5. This means that you have to set up the A4 register before you can use any global variables. THINK C includes a header file SetUpA4.h, which makes this easier.

The first thing you do is include the header file <SetUpA4.h>. Then, when your main function enters, call RememberA0 and then SetUpA4 before any other executable instruction. Avoid initializing local variables because the initialization code may also affect the value of register A0. Just before exiting, call RestoreA4. The structure of your code resource will look like this:

```
#include <SetUpA4.h>
#include "xlcall.h"

LPXLOPER pascal main (LPXLOPER xArg)
{
    static XLOPER x;
    LPXLOPER px;

    RememberA0();
    SetUpA4();

    /*
    ** Your code here ...
    */

    /*
    ** To return an XLOPER, you must return
    ** a non-static pointer to a static XLOPER,
    ** which is why we play this little trick
    ** with px and x.
    */

    px = &x;
    RestoreA4();

    return px;
}
```

You cannot access any globals after calling RestoreA4, because the A4 register from which you are trying to access them has been overwritten! So make sure that your return value is a local variable, not a global or static one. This is a frequent cause of programming errors in code resources.

For more information about special considerations for code resources, see your compiler manual.

High Bandwidth Communications

The Microsoft Excel DLL interface has been optimized to maximize performance for the two most common operations: getting values out of cells and putting values into cells. This has been done with two special functions, xlCoerce and xlSet. These are only available from DLLs.

xlCoerce

The xlCoerce function can be used for two different purposes: getting values from cells and converting XLOPERs from one type to another. Although these tasks seem unrelated, they are implemented in the same way.

To understand xlCoerce, consider how Microsoft Excel itself uses this function. Microsoft Excel is polymorphic, allowing a user to pass any type of value to a function; but a function may not understand the data type being passed to it. For example, the SIN function requires a number. The user may enter =SIN("25") in a cell, passing a string argument. Although the user has provided a string, Microsoft Excel knows that the function requires a number, so it uses xlCoerce to coerce the string into a number. The xlCoerce function takes two arguments: an XLOPER to coerce and the target type.

Coercing a String to a Number

The following example shows how to create a string "25" and coerce it to a number:

```
XLOPER xStr, xNum, xDestType;

/* Create the string "25" */
xStr.xltype = xltypeStr;
xStr.val.str = "\002" "25";

/* Create the second parameter (xltypeNum) */
xDestType.xltype = xltypeInt;    /* xDestType is an integer */
xDestType.val.w = xltypeNum; /* Destination is a number */

Excel4(xlCoerce, &xNum, 2, (LPXLOPER) &xStr, (LPXLOPER) &xDestType);
```

You can specify more than one target type. Some functions behave differently based on whether an argument is a string or a number. This is called function overloading.

For example, the DELETE.MENU function can take a string or a number as its second argument. To cover this possibility, xlCoerce allows you to specify multiple target types.

Coercing an Unknown to a String or a Number

The following example converts the unknown XLOPER x into a string or a number:

```
XLOPER xDestType, xStrOrNum;

xDestType.xltype = xltypeInt;   /* xDestType is an integer */
xDestType.val.w = xltypeStr | xltypeNum; /* String or number */
Excel4(xlCoerce, &xStrOrNum, 2, (LPXLOPER) &x, (LPXLOPER) &xDestType);
```

Using xlCoerce with References

The xlCoerce function works even when the source XLOPER is a reference. Therefore, if you coerce a reference to Sheet1!A1 to a string, xlCoerce looks up the current value of A1 and converts it to a string. In fact, you can coerce a reference to any nonreference type, which has the effect of looking up the value of that cell. This is the fastest way to get the value from a cell. Because this operation is so common, it is the default behavior of xlCoerce. If the second argument (destination type) is omitted, it is assumed that you want to coerce a reference to any nonreference type or, in other words, look up the value of a cell.

Getting a Value from a Cell

The following example shows code for the function LookupCell, which finds the value of any single cell on the active (front) sheet by constructing an external reference and then coercing it.

```
/*
** LookupCell
** Looks up the value of a cell on the active sheet
**
** Arguments:
**
**   LPXLOPER pxResult    Room for an XLOPER to store result
**   int iRow             0-based row
**   int iColumn          0-based column
**
** Returns:
**
**   pxResult
**
** Important! You must remember to call xlFree on pxResult when
** you are done!
*/
```

```
LPXLOPER LookupCell(LPXLOPER pxResult, int iRow, int iColumn)
{
    XLOPER xRef;
    XLMREF xlmref;

    /* Get Sheet ID of active sheet */
    Excel4(xlSheetId, &xRef, 0);
    xRef.xltype = xltypeRef;
    xRef.val.mref.lpmref = (LPXLMREF)&xlmref;

    xlmref.count = 1;
    xlmref.reftbl[0].rwFirst=xlmref.reftbl[0].rwLast=iRow;
    xlmref.reftbl[0].colFirst=xlmref.reftbl[0].colLast=iColumn;

    /*
    ** Since there is only one argument to xlCoerce, Microsoft Excel
    ** will coerce to ANY nonreference type
    */

    Excel4(xlCoerce, pxResult, 1, (LPXLOPER)&xRef);

    return pxResult;
}
```

Similarly, you can coerce a rectangular reference. This allows you to look up a rectangular range of cells, all at once, and returns an xltypeMulti (Microsoft Excel array).

xlSet

When you buy an airline ticket, you generally have to choose between a full-fare ticket with no restrictions and a much cheaper ticket with restrictions. The cheaper ticket might be nonrefundable or require a Saturday night stay.

Similarly, in Microsoft Excel there are two ways to enter information into cells. The usual way, available in the macro language, is to use the FORMULA function, called xlcFormula from C. This is the expensive, unrestricted way. It takes a long time, but you can put almost anything anywhere and, if you don't like the result, you can undo it by calling xlcUndo.

However, there is a much faster function called xlSet. It is only available from the C API, and comes with two restrictions:

- You can enter only constants, not formulas, into cells. This allows Microsoft Excel to skip recomputing the internal formula dependency tree.
- You cannot undo with the xlSet function. This saves time, since Microsoft Excel does not have to record the information required to undo the action.

In spite of these restrictions, xlSet is very useful. In most database access scenarios, you need to write a large table of constant values into a rectangular range of cells. This can all be done with one call to Microsoft Excel.

Note Because xlSet is a command-equivalent function, it does not work in user-defined functions.

The following code creates a large array and places it into the active sheet, in one step:

```
int i,j;
static XLOPER rgx[10][10], xArray, xRef;
XLMREF xlmref;

if (xlretSuccess != Excel4(xlSheetId, &xRef, 0))
    return;

xRef.xltype = xltypeRef;
xRef.val.mref.lpmref = (LPXLMREF) &xlmref;
xlmref.count = 1;
xlmref.reftbl[0].rwFirst  = 0;
xlmref.reftbl[0].rwLast   = 9;
xlmref.reftbl[0].colFirst = 0;
xlmref.reftbl[0].colLast  = 9;

for (i=0; i<10; i++)
{
    for (j=0; j<10; j++)
    {
        rgx[i][j].xltype = xltypeNum;
        rgx[i][j].val.num = i * 10 + j;
    }
}

xArray.xltype = xltypeMulti;
xArray.val.array.lparray = (LPXLOPER) &rgx;
xArray.val.array.rows = xArray.val.array.columns = 10;

Excel4(xlSet, 0, 2, (LPXLOPER) &xRef, (LPXLOPER) &xArray);
```

By using xlCoerce and xlSet, you can speed up data transfer dramatically.

Creating Stand-alone DLLs (XLLs)

Up to this point, only DLLs that are registered and called from macro sheets have been discussed. However, Microsoft Excel 5.0 also supports stand-alone DLLs. These are DLLs (or code resources) that the user opens by choosing Open from the File menu and selecting a DLL file or by using the Microsoft Excel 5.0 Add-In Manager. (The user can also put DLL files in the Microsoft Excel startup directory, in which case they are opened at run time.) By convention, stand-alone DLLs are called XLLs. They should be given a filename with the extension .XLL for Windows or a file type of 'XLL ' on the Macintosh.

Note The easiest way to create a stand-alone XLL is to start with the sample generic code provided in the FRAMEWRK subdirectory or folder.

When using an XLL, the user never sees a macro sheet or Add-In sheet. Therefore, an XLL must be able to do everything an XLA (Add-In) can do. In particular, XLLs need a way to provide functions that run automatically at open time, close time, and so on.

When developing an XLL, you need to:

- Define the interface to Microsoft Excel. An XLL should export a few functions that are called by Microsoft Excel and the Microsoft Excel Add-In Manager.

- Define the user interface to the XLL. Does the XLL use pull-down menus? Toolbars? Shortcut keys? Or does it only provide additional functions for use on worksheets?

The Interface to Microsoft Excel

To write an XLL, you should provide three functions (described in this section) that are called by Microsoft Excel and three functions that are called by the Add-In Manager. For information about the functions called by the Add-In Manager, see "Supporting the Add-In Manager" on page 45.

The functions in the following table are called by Microsoft Excel.

This function	Is called when
xlAutoOpen()	The XLL is opened.
xlAutoClose()	The XLL is closed.
xlAutoRegister()	Microsoft Excel needs to register a function but doesn't know the argument and return value types.

For more information on these three functions, see "xlAutoOpen," "xlAutoClose," and "xlAutoRegister" on pages 106, 103, and 107, respectively.

Opening an XLL

You can open an XLL in the same ways you open any Microsoft Excel file. You can use the Open command on the File menu, the Microsoft Excel startup directory, the command line, or the OPEN= entries in EXCEL4.INI. You can open an XLL in the macro language by calling the REGISTER function with only one argument (the name of the XLL). Here is what happens:

1. Microsoft Excel tries to register a function in your XLL called xlAutoOpen, which should be declared as type "A" (returns a Boolean, no parameters). For more information, see "xlAutoOpen" on page 106.

2. If that succeeds, Microsoft Excel runs the xlAutoOpen function. This function should:

   - Call xlfRegister to register all the functions that the XLL makes available.

   - Add any menus or menu items that the XLL makes available.

   - Do any other necessary initialization.

   - Return 1.

   There is no guarantee that xlAutoOpen will be called before a function in your XLL is run. For example, the user can simply register and call one of the functions without opening the XLL, bypassing xlAutoOpen.

3. Microsoft Excel unregisters the xlAutoOpen function, since it is no longer needed.

Important   Calling xlAutoOpen is the only way the Open command loads an XLL. This function is required in every DLL with the extension XLL.

Unregistering the Entire XLL

A user can call the function UNREGISTER and specify the name of your XLL. For example, if UNREGISTER("GENERIC.XLL") is called from a Microsoft Excel macro or another DLL, this instructs Microsoft Excel to remove that DLL from memory. Here is what happens:

1. Microsoft Excel tries to register a function called xlAutoClose, which should be declared as type A.

2. If xlAutoClose is found, Microsoft Excel runs the xlAutoClose function. This function should:

   - Do any necessary global cleanup.

   - Remove any menus or menu items that were added in xlAutoOpen.

   - Delete any names that were created in xlAutoOpen. Remember that calling xlfRegister with a fourth argument causes a name to be created. You can delete names by calling xlfSetName with the second argument omitted. This is important; otherwise, the names will still appear in the Paste Function dialog box.

3. When xlAutoClose returns, Microsoft Excel unregisters all functions registered in that DLL, no matter who registered them or how often they were registered in that instance of Microsoft Excel.

Note While you are developing XLLs, you may find it convenient to call the UNREGISTER function, with the name of your XLL as its argument, from a macro in Microsoft Excel. This ensures that the XLL is completely unloaded. Thus you can compile a new version of the XLL in another process without conflicts.

Quitting Microsoft Excel

When the user quits Microsoft Excel, all loaded XLLs are unregistered as described in the previous section. The xlAutoClose function is called for every XLL that has one.

Be aware that it is still possible that your XLL will be removed from memory without xlAutoClose being called. For example, the user could unregister every function individually, and xlAutoClose will never be called.

Note There is no menu item that allows a user to close an XLL.

Registering Functions Without a Type String

You may want to allow end users to register functions in your XLL without specifying the *type_text* argument (for more information on the *type_text* argument, see "REGISTER" on page 76). This makes it easier for users to load individual XLL functions. To do this, you need to provide the xlAutoRegister function. Here is what happens:

1. A macro sheet calls REGISTER, specifying the name of the XLL and the name of the function but omitting the *type_text* argument.

2. Microsoft Excel tries to register a function in the XLL called xlAutoRegister, which should be of type PP (which takes a value LPXLOPER and returns a value LPXLOPER). If this fails, the REGISTER function returns #VALUE!

3. If this succeeds, Microsoft Excel calls xlAutoRegister, passing the name of the function (as xltypeStr) as the argument. xlAutoRegister should:

   - Determine whether the function name is recognized. If it is not, your xlAutoRegister function should return #VALUE! as an xltypeErr.

   - If the function is recognized, xlAutoRegister should call xlfRegister as usual, specifying at least the first three arguments (including *type_text*).

   - Return the same value as returned by xlfRegister (an xltypeNum if a success or an xltypeErr if a failure).

Note If xlAutoRegister calls xlfRegister without providing the *type_text* argument, an infinite loop results.

Supporting the Add-In Manager

There are some additional steps you can take to work with the Microsoft Excel Add-In Manager.

This function	Is called when the Add-In Manager
xlAutoAdd()	Adds an XLL.
xlAutoRemove()	Removes an XLL.
xlAddInManagerInfo()	Needs additional information from the XLL.

Adding New XLLs with the Add-In Manager

The following steps describe how to use the Add-In Manager to add new XLLs.

1. The user runs the Add-Ins... command from the Tools Menu and selects the check box next to the name of the Add-In or chooses the Browse button if the Add-In is in a different directory.

    a. If the user chooses the Browse button, the Add-In Manager displays the Browse dialog box, allowing the user to select XLA files or XLL files. On the Macintosh, all files of type 'XLA ', 'XLA3', 'XLA4', and 'XLL ' are listed.

    b. The user chooses a file. If it is an XLL file, the Add-In Manager attempts to register and run the xlAutoAdd function in the XLL. This function takes no arguments. Your XLL can optionally display a message telling the user that the XLL is now available and how to get it.

2. The Add-In Manager calls REGISTER() on the XLL, which causes the XLL's xlAutoOpen function to run.

3. The Add-In Manager attempts to register and run a function called xlAutoAdd in the XLL. This function takes no arguments. It can do anything you want it to do before your Add-In is added by the Add-In Manager.

4. The Add-In Manager also adds an OPEN= line to the EXCEL.INI file. This causes Microsoft Excel to automatically open your XLL whenever Microsoft Excel runs.

5. The Add-In Manager tries to register and call the xlAddInManagerInfo function in your XLL to find out more information about the XLL. For more information, see the following section, "Supporting the Add-In Manager's Long Names."

Removing XLLs with the Add-In Manager

1. The user runs the Add-Ins... command from the Tools menu and deselects the check box for the XLL.

2. The Add-In Manager attempts to register and run a function called xlAutoRemove in the XLL. This function takes no arguments. It can do anything you want it to do before your Add-In is removed with the Add-In Manager.

3. The Add-In Manager calls UNREGISTER on the XLL, which causes the XLL's xlAutoClose function to run and unregisters all the functions in the XLL, removing it from memory.

4. The Add-In Manager also removes the OPEN= line from the EXCEL.INI file.

Supporting the Add-In Manager's Long Names

The Add-In Manager can optionally display a longer, more descriptive name for your XLL, in addition to the filename. When running with MS-DOS®, this is preferable to seeing only the eight-character filename. To support this, the Add-In Manager attempts to register and call a function in your XLL named xlAddInManagerInfo. This function is of type "PP", which takes a value LPXLOPER and returns a value LPXLOPER. When the Add-In Manager needs a long filename, it calls this function with 1 as the argument. Your xlAddInManagerInfo function should check this argument. If it is 1, the function should return an xltypeStr containing the long name of the XLL Add-In. If the argument is not 1, the function should return a #VALUE! error.

REGISTER.ID

REGISTER.ID is a Microsoft Excel macro function that facilitates connecting XLLs to menus, tools, event handlers, and other items that require you to provide the address of a subroutine. The REGISTER.ID function is a direct replacement for any function that requires a macro reference. An example would be a menu that needs to call the function MyFunc in an XLL named MYXLL.XLL.

In the second column of the menu definition table you would place REGISTER.ID("MYXLL.XLL","MyFunc"). When the menu executes the REGISTER.ID, if the XLL has already been registered, it calls the function. If the XLL has not been registered, Microsoft Excel registers it by calling xlAutoRegister and then calls the function.

The Generic Template for XLLs

The sample code in the FRAMEWRK directory (or Framework folder on the Macintosh disk) contains a template you can use for writing your own Microsoft Excel XLLs. This code demonstrates many of the features of the Microsoft Excel C API. To see the generic Add-In code, open GENERIC.C on the Windows disk. On the Macintosh disk, open the C source files in the Framework folder.

When you open the compiled generic Add-In (GENERIC.XLL on the Windows disk or Generic on the Macintosh disk) in Microsoft Excel, it creates a new Generic menu with the four commands listed in the following table.

Command	Action
Dialog	Displays a Microsoft Excel dialog box
Dance	Moves the selection around until you press ESC
Native Dialog	Displays a Windows or Macintosh dialog box that was created using the Windows API or the Macintosh User Interface Toolbox
Exit	Closes GENERIC.XLL or Generic and removes the menu

The generic Add-In also provides two functions, Func1 and FuncSum, which can be used whenever the generic Add-In is open. These functions appear in the Generic Add-In category in the Paste Function dialog box. Also, these functions can be registered without loading all of the generic Add-In. To do this, use the following formulas.

Windows
=REGISTER("GENERIC.XLL","FUNC1")
=REGISTER("GENERIC.XLL","FUNCSUM")

Macintosh
=REGISTER("GENERIC","FUNC1")
=REGISTER("GENERIC","FUNCSUM")

Advanced Flow Control in Macro Sheets

Ordinarily, when Microsoft Excel runs a macro, it does so by evaluating successive cells, one at a time, from top to bottom. However, simple top-to-bottom execution does not allow for any of the flow-control constructs that are essential in a high-level language. Microsoft Excel solves this problem by using the flow-control XLOPER, named xltypeFlow. If a function on the sheet returns a flow-control XLOPER, then, instead of going on to the next cell, Microsoft Excel executes the flow-control command contained in that XLOPER.

	A
1	=ECHO(FALSE)
2	=BEEP()
3	=ALERT("Hi there!")
4	=GOTO(A3)

Microsoft Excel evaluates these cells in sequence.

This call returns a Goto XLOPER, so control jumps to A3.

This is how Microsoft Excel controls all flow on macro sheets. It means that functions such as GOTO and RETURN can be implemented as first-class functions. Therefore you can write your own versions of GOTO and HALT. This capability also explains how statements such as this work:

=IF(Boolean,GOTO(A3),GOTO(A4))

This capability allows you to write and understand flow-control functions. For example, suppose you want a function that checks the sign of a number and then performs one action if the sign is negative, another action if it is zero, and yet another action if it is positive. The macro could look like the following illustration.

	A	B
11		
12	Run2(b)	=SWITCH.SIGN(0,B14,B16,B18)
13		=ALERT("Shouldn't be reached")
14		=ALERT("Negative")
15		=RETURN()
16		=ALERT("Zero")
17		=RETURN()
18		=ALERT("Positive")
19		=RETURN()

You can use flow-control XLOPERs to write this function, as shown in the following code example.

Windows Example

```
#include <windows.h>
#include <xlcall.h>

LPXLOPER FAR PASCAL __export SwitchSign(double d, LPXLOPER pxNeg,
    LPXLOPER pxZero, LPXLOPER pxPos)
{
    // pxNeg, pxZero, and pxPos must be local references.

    static XLOPER xGoto, xError, xSheet;
    LPXLOPER pxChosen;

    if (d < 0)
        pxChosen = pxNeg;
    else if (d == 0)
        pxChosen = pxZero;
    else
        pxChosen = pxPos;

    if (pxChosen->xltype != xltypeSRef) {
```

```
            xError.xltype = xltypeErr;
            xError.val.err = xlerrValue;
            return &xError;
    }

    // Figure out the Sheet ID of the current sheet, which we need
    // to make xGoto

    Excel4(xlSheetId, &xSheet, 0);

    xGoto.xltype = xltypeFlow;
    xGoto.val.flow.xlflow = xlflowGoto;
    xGoto.val.flow.valflow.idSheet = xSheet.val.mref.idSheet;
    xGoto.val.flow.rw = pxChosen->val.sref.ref.rwFirst;
    xGoto.val.flow.col = pxChosen->val.sref.ref.colFirst;

    return &xGoto;
}
```

Macintosh Example

```
#include <SetUpA4.h>
#include "xlcall.h"
#include "Framework.h"

LPXLOPER pascal main(double *d, LPXLOPER pxNeg,
    LPXLOPER pxZero, LPXLOPER pxPos)
{
    static XLOPER xGoto;
    XLOPER xError, xSheet;
    LPXLOPER pxChosen;

    RememberA0();
    SetUpA4();
    InitFramework();

    if (*d < 0)
        pxChosen = pxNeg;
    else if (*d == 0)
        pxChosen = pxZero;
    else
        pxChosen = pxPos;

    if (pxChosen->xltype != xltypeSRef) {
```

```
        xError.xltype = xltypeErr;
        xError.val.err = xlerrValue;
        pxChosen = &xError;

        QuitFramework();
        RestoreA4();

        return pxChosen;
    }
    Excel(xlSheetId, &xSheet, 0);

    xGoto.xltype = xltypeFlow;
    xGoto.val.flow.xlflow = xlflowGoto;
    xGoto.val.flow.valflow.idSheet = xSheet.val.mref.idSheet;
    xGoto.val.flow.rw = pxChosen->val.sref.ref.rwFirst;
    xGoto.val.flow.col = pxChosen->val.sref.ref.colFirst;

    pxChosen = &xGoto;

    QuitFramework();
    RestoreA4();

    return pxChosen;
}
```

This sample code is in the SWITCHSN directory or SwitchSn folder.

Note You can return flow control XLOPERs from your C functions, and you can pass them to Excel4. The only thing you can't do with flow-control XLOPERs is pass them into C functions from Microsoft Excel. In other words, you cannot pass the return value from the GOTO function to one of your own functions. This means you can't write IF in C.

Tips and Special Considerations

This section contains tips for developing DLLs and code resources for Microsoft Excel.

Looking Up Names

In the macro language, you can find out what names refer to simply by invoking them. The only way to do this from a DLL is to call the function xlfEvaluate, which is the equivalent of the macro language function EVALUATE. In the macro language, EVALUATE is not very useful because things are evaluated automatically anyway. However, from C, xlfEvaluate is quite useful.

The xlfEvaluate function takes any string containing a valid Microsoft Excel expression (anything that could be typed into a worksheet cell) and evaluates it using the standard Microsoft Excel evaluator. For example:

```
XLOPER x1, x2;

/* Evaluate the string "15+17" */
x1.xltype = xltypeStr;
x1.val.str = "\005" "15+17";

Excel4(xlfEvaluate, &x2, 1, (LPXLOPER) &x1);

/* x2 now contains 32 */
```

Although you can theoretically evaluate any expression, remember that the string you pass has to be parsed, which is a slow process. So if speed is important, avoid using xlfEvaluate.

Note Calling xlfEvaluate is equivalent to pressing F9 in the formula bar. It cannot evaluate external references to sheets that are not open.

The xlfEvaluate function is most commonly used to look up the values assigned to names in a sheet. For example:

```
XLOPER x1, x2;

/* Look up the defined name "profits" on the active sheet */
x1.xltype = xltypeStr;
x1.val.str = "\010!profits";

Excel4(xlfEvaluate, &x2, 1, (LPXLOPER) &x1);
Excel4(xlFree, 0, 1, (LPXLOPER) &x2);

/* x2 now contains whatever "profits" was defined as */
```

Note that xlfEvaluate cannot evaluate command equivalents, because they cannot be entered into cells on worksheets.

Calling Macro Language Functions from DLLs

The "Calling the Function from Within Microsoft Excel" section, on page 5, discussed using REGISTER and CALL to call DLL functions from the macro language. You can also call macro language functions from DLLs.

You can use xlUDF to call *user-defined functions,* that is, functions defined in a macro sheet or Add-In. For the first argument to xlUDF, use a reference to the function you want to execute. Then pass all the arguments to the function you are calling. For example, if you had a user-defined function named FUNC, you could call FUNC(5) as follows:

```
XLOPER xFuncStr, xFuncRef, x5, xResult;

xFuncStr.xltype = xltypeStr;
xFuncStr.val.str = "\004FUNC";

x5.xltype = xltypeNum;
x5.val.num = 5;

/*
** Lookup the name FUNC using EVALUATE
*/

Excel4(xlfEvaluate, &xFuncRef, 1, (LPXLOPER) &xFuncStr);
Excel4(xlUDF, &xResult, 2, (LPXLOPER) &xFuncRef, (LPXLOPER) &x5);

/*
** After using xResult, don't forget to free it:
*/

Excel4(xlFree, &xResult, 2, (LPXLOPER) &xResult, (LPXLOPER) &xFuncRef);
```

Performing Lengthy Operations

Both Windows and the Macintosh use *cooperative multitasking.* This means that every application must explicitly give up the processor so that other applications can run. Normally, Microsoft Excel gives up the processor frequently, allowing background tasks to run smoothly.

If you expect your DLL function to take a long time, you will need to:

- Give up the processor as frequently as possible.
- Determine whether the user has canceled the function by pressing ESC. If the user has canceled, you may want to terminate the lengthy operation.

There is a single function called xlAbort that handles both of these tasks at once. First it yields, giving other applications in the system a chance to run. Then it checks whether the user has canceled by pressing ESC. If so, xlAbort returns TRUE; if not, it returns FALSE.

When the user cancels the function by pressing ESC, the DLL should clean up and return as quickly as possible. However, you might want to prompt the user to confirm the cancellation, offering the option of continuing. If the user wants to continue, the pending cancellation can be cleared by calling xlAbort with one argument, an xltypeBool with the value FALSE.

For an example of the xlAbort function, see the fDance function in GENERIC.C in the FRAMEWRK directory on the Windows disk, or see the fDance.c file in the Framework folder on the Macintosh disk.

Dealing with Uncalculated Cells

During the recalculation of a worksheet, Microsoft Excel uses sophisticated heuristics to determine which cells are scheduled to be recalculated and in which order. This means that if you enter a function on a worksheet that calls a DLL and that function tries to look up the value of another cell, you cannot be sure whether the value has been recalculated yet. You need to be concerned about this only if all of the following conditions apply:

- You are writing a DLL function that will be entered on a worksheet.
- That function looks at the value of other cells on the worksheet.
- The DLL is not a macro type (the data type string does not contain "#").

If your DLL functions are not meant to be entered on worksheets, or if they do not try to find out the values of cells elsewhere on the worksheet (for example, using xlCoerce), you do not need to worry about the possibility of uncalculated cells.

Here is an example scenario: A DLL function called GetB5 returns the value of cell B5. The function would look like this:

```
LPXLOPER FAR PASCAL __export GetB5(void)
{
    static XLOPER xResult, xReference, xNum;

    xReference.xltype = xltypeSRef;
    xReference.val.sref.count = 1;
    xReference.val.sref.ref.rwFirst =
        xReference.val.sref.ref.rwLast   = 4;
    xReference.val.sref.ref.colFirst =
        xReference.val.sref.ref.colLast = 1;

    xNum.xltype = xltypeInt;
    xNum.val.w = xltypeNum;

    Excel4(xlCoerce, &xResult, 2, (LPXLOPER)&xReference,
        (LPXLOPER)&xNum);

    return &xResult;
}
```

This could be registered with a *type_text* argument of "R!". The exclamation point means that the function is volatile and needs to be recalculated whenever the sheet changes. To work around this, set recalculation to manual. Next, enter the following formulas on a worksheet.

Formulas

	B
1	15
2	=B1+1
3	=B2+1
4	=B3+1
5	=B4+1
6	

Values

	B
1	15
2	16
3	17
4	18
5	19
6	

Microsoft Excel schedules the cells to be calculated in descending order. That is, first B1 will be calculated, then B2, then B3, and so on. What happens when we insert the GetB5 call on line B6?

Formulas

	B
1	15
2	=B1+1
3	=B2+1
4	=B3+1
5	=B4+1
6	=GetB5()

Values

	B
1	15
2	16
3	17
4	18
5	19
6	19

Initially, the value is correct. But Microsoft Excel has no way of knowing that the function GetB5 depends on the value of Cell B5. So if you change B1 . . .

Formulas

	B
1	25
2	=B1+1
3	=B2+1
4	=B3+1
5	=B4+1
6	=GetB5()

Values

	B
1	25
2	16
3	17
4	18
5	19
6	19

. . . and then recalculate by pressing F9, Microsoft Excel schedules B6 to be calculated first. Now when GetB5 tries to look at the value of B5, it finds that the cell has not been calculated yet. The xlCoerce function call returns xlretUncalced. However, Microsoft Excel remembers that it moved to that uncalculated cell and schedules B5 to be recalculated again later. The GetB5 function returns a wrong value, Microsoft Excel recalculates B2 through B5, and finally, calls GetB5 once again. So the final values are correct:

Formulas

	B
1	25
2	=B1+1
3	=B2+1
4	=B3+1
5	=B4+1
6	=GetB5()

Values

	B
1	25
2	26
3	27
4	28
5	29
6	29

Finally, Microsoft Excel now knows that B6 is dependent on B5, and rightly schedules it to be calculated last in the future. GetB5 will not see xlretUncalced again.

Experienced macro language users will recognize that this is not the behavior of the Microsoft Excel macro language. If GetB5 had been written in the macro language, the first recalculation would simply have given the wrong value. Microsoft Excel would still reschedule B6, so the next recalculation would be correct. If, for some reason, you require this macro language behavior, you can specify # in the *type_text* argument to the REGISTER function.

Getting the Instance and Windows Handles

Windows Only   To program in the Windows environment, it is sometimes helpful to find out the Microsoft Excel instance handle (hInst) or top-level window handle (hWnd). Two special functions, xlGetInst and xlGetHwnd, have been provided for this purpose.

For example, you might need the instance handle so you can call the Windows function MakeProcInstance(). The window handle is useful for creating child windows and custom Windows dialog boxes.

Considerations for the Function Wizard

The Function Wizard allows the user to construct an expression's arguments interactively. As a part of this process, the Function Wizard evaluates functions with the user's proposed arguments and displays the result. For simple functions that quickly calculate a value this process does not cause a problem. Unfortunately, functions that access external data as a part of calculations, or functions that require a significant amount of time in order to calculate don't work well, because the time required to calculate or retrieve external data is annoying long.

The Function Wizard cannot automatically determine which functions should not be calculated during expression construction. It is therefore up to each XLL function to refuse to calculate if not appropriate. Functions can determine if they are being called from the Function Wizard by trying to run a command. The Function Wizard evaluates all expressions in "function mode," which causes commands to fail.

For example, the following example calls the ACTIVATE command with no parameters (this command was chosen because it does nothing if no parameters are specified). If the ACTIVATE command succeeds (the Excel4 function returns xlretSuccess) and the XLL function was called from a running macro, ACTIVATE returns TRUE and the XLL function calculates normally. If ACTIVATE returns FALSE, the XLL function was called because the Function Wizard is constructing an expression, so the XLL function does not calculate. If the ACTIVATE command fails, the XLL function was called from a worksheet. In this case, there is no way to determine if the function was called by the Function Wizard, and the function fails.

```
LPXLOPER FAR PASCAL __export LongCalculation(WORD arg1, WORD arg2)
{
    XLOPER xInWizard;
    static XLOPER xReturn;

    if (xlretSuccess == Excel4(xlcActivate, &xInWizard, 0)) {
        if (xRet.val.bool == FALSE) {
            // ACTIVATE returns FALSE if the command fails.
            // This occurs when the Function Wizard
            // is in use. Return without doing lengthy
            // calculations.
            xReturn.xltype = xltypeBool;
            xReturn.val.bool = FALSE;
            return &xReturn;
        }
    }
    else {
        // Function is being called from a worksheet. Macro-only
        // functions should fail if this is the case.
        xReturn.xltype = xltypeErr;
        xReturn.val.err = xlerrValue;
        return &xReturn;
    }

    // function is not being called from a worksheet or the Function
    // Wizard. Calculate normally.

    //  ... calculate and set up return value ...
    return &xReturn;
}
```

C H A P T E R   2

Applications Programming Interface Function Reference

Introduction

This chapter lists alphabetically the Microsoft Excel functions most useful for creating and working with DLLs designed to be called from Microsoft Excel 4.0 macro sheets (for information about using DLLs with Visual Basic, see Chapter 6, "Using DLLs from Visual Basic"). You can call almost any function from a DLL, with the exception of some macro control functions. These macro control functions are listed in the following section. For information about functions not included in this chapter, see the online Microsoft Excel Macro Function Reference.

This chapter contains Microsoft Windows and Apple Macintosh (THINK C) code examples. Source code for the examples is in the SAMPLE directory on the Windows disk and in the Sample Code folder on the Macintosh disk. In the text, every example includes the path and filename of the corresponding disk file. If there is a description of the example, it usually appears under the Windows Example heading and it is not repeated for the Macintosh example.

Functions Included in This Chapter

The functions listed in this chapter include the following:

- The Excel4 and Excel4v callback functions.
- Functions you are likely to use to interact with Microsoft Excel DLLs from a macro sheet: CALL, REGISTER, REGISTER.ID, and UNREGISTER.
- Functions that are especially useful in DLLs: CALLER and EVALUATE.

- Microsoft Excel special service functions, which can only be called from DLLs:

xlAbort	xlFree	xlSheetId
xlCoerce	xlGetBinaryName	xlSheetNm
xlDisableXLMsgs	xlGetHwnd	xlStack
xlEnableXLMsgs	xlGetInst	xlUDF
xlDefineBinaryName	xlSet	

- Functions you should provide in your XLL to qualify as a stand-alone DLL (XLL):

xlAddInManagerInfo	xlAutoClose	xlAutoRegister
xlAutoAdd	xlAutoOpen	xlAutoRemove

- Functions in the Framework library, which provide a good starting point for writing Microsoft Excel DLLs and XLLs.

Some Microsoft Excel functions have arguments that make them easier to use in DLLs. These include ADD.COMMAND, ADD.MENU, ADD.TOOL, ADD.TOOLBAR, and DIALOG.BOX, which accept an array as well as a reference as an argument. For information about these functions, see the online Microsoft Excel Macro Function Reference.

The following are the macro control functions that cannot be called from DLLs:

BREAK	ENDIF	IF	RETURN
ELSE	FOR	NEXT	WHILE
ELSEIF	FOR.CELL		

Functions in the Framework Library

The Framework library was created to help make writing XLLs easier. It includes simple functions for managing XLOPER memory, creating temporary XLOPERs, robustly calling the Excel4 function, and printing debugging strings on an attached terminal.

The functions included in this library help simplify a piece of code that looks like this . . .

```
XLOPER xMissing, xBool;
xMissing.xltype = xltypeMissing;
xBool.xltype = xltypeBool;
xBool.val.bool = 0;
Excel4(xlcDisplay, 0, 2, (LPXLOPER) &xMissing, (LPXLOPER) &xBool);
```

. . . to look like this:

```
Excel(xlcDisplay, 0, 2, TempMissing(), TempBool(0));
```

The following functions are included in the Framework library:

debugPrintf	TempActiveRef	TempNum
Excel	TempActiveCell	TempStr
FreeAllTempMemory	TempActiveRow	TempBool
InitFramework	TempActiveColumn	TempInt
QuitFramework	TempMissing	TempErr

Using these functions shortens the amount of time required to write a DLL or XLL. Starting development from the sample application GENERIC also shortens development time. Use GENERIC.C as a template to help set up the framework of an XLL and then replace the existing code with your own.

The Framework library is especially useful on the Apple Macintosh, where the Excel4 and Excel4v functions are stored as code resources in the Microsoft Excel executable file and you must load the code resource and obtain a pointer to these functions before you can call them. The Framework library does this work automatically, so you can call the Excel and Excel4 functions directly.

The temporary XLOPER functions create XLOPER values using memory from a local heap managed by the Framework library. The XLOPER values remain valid until you call the FreeAllTempMemory function or the Excel function (the Excel function frees all temporary memory before it returns).

To use the Framework library functions, you must include the FRAMEWRK.H file in your C code and add the FRAMEWRK.C or FRAMEWRK.LIB files to your code project.

CALL (Form 1)

Called from a macro sheet or worksheet. This function calls a registered function in a DLL or a code resource. The function must already have been registered using REGISTER or REGISTER.ID.

Returns the return value from the function that was called.

Syntax

```
CALL(register_id,argument1, ...)
```

register_id (xltypeNum) The register ID of the function. You can get this using REGISTER.

argument1, ... Zero or more arguments to the function that is being called. These arguments are optional.

Remark

If the function was originally registered, and a function name was specified in the *function_text* argument, this function can alternately be called as follows:

```
=function_text(argument1, ...)
```

Example

The following example registers the CalcCircum function in CIRCUM.DLL then calls the function using the defined name for cell B1.

	A	B
1	fCircum	=REGISTER("CIRCUM","CalcCircum","EE")
2		=CALL(fCircum,100)
3		=UNREGISTER(fCircum)
4		=RETURN()

Cell B1 has the defined name fCircum.

Related Functions

CALL (Form 2), REGISTER, REGISTER.ID, UNREGISTER

CALL (Form 2)

Called from a macro sheet or worksheet. If the function is not yet registered, it is registered when called, and then the specified procedure in the DLL or code resource is called. If the function is already registered, it is called without reregistering.

Returns the return value from the function that was called.

Syntax

```
CALL(module_text,procedure,type_text,argument1, ...)
```

module_text (xltypeStr)

Windows The name of the DLL containing the function.

Macintosh The name of the file containing the code resource.

procedure (xltypeStr or xltypeNum)

Windows If a string, the name of the function to call. If a number, the ordinal export number of the code function to call. For clarity and robustness, always use the string form.

Macintosh If a string, the name of the code resource to call. If a number, the resource number of the resource to call. For clarity and robustness, always use the string form.

type_text (xltypeStr) An optional string specifying the types of all the arguments to the function, and the type of the return value of the function. You can omit this argument for a stand-alone DLL (XLL) that provides the xlAutoRegister function. For more information about data types, see the "Remarks" section under "REGISTER (Form 1)" on page 77.

argument1, ... Zero or more arguments to the function. These arguments are optional.

Remark
This form of call is equivalent to using Call (Form 1), as follows:

=CALL(REGISTER.ID(*module_text*, *procedure*, *type_text*), *argument1*, ...)

Example
The following example registers and calls the CalcCircum function in CIRCUM.DLL.

	B
6	=CALL("CIRCUM","CalcCircum","EE",100)
7	=RETURN()

Related Functions
CALL (Form 1), REGISTER, REGISTER.ID, UNREGISTER

CALLER

Called from a macro sheet or DLL.

Returns information about the cell, range of cells, command on a menu, tool on a toolbar, or object that called the macro that is currently running.

Code called from	Returns
DLL	The Register ID.
A single cell	A cell reference.
Menu	A four-element array, containing the bar ID, the menu position, the submenu position, and the command position. On 16-bit Microsoft Windows, the submenu is included only in Microsoft Excel versions 5.0c and later.

Code called from	Returns
Toolbar	A two-element array. The first element is the toolbar number for built-in toolbars or a toolbar name for custom toolbars. The second item is the position on the toolbar.
Graphic object	The object identifier (object name).
ON.ENTER	A reference to the cell being entered.
ON.DOUBLECLICK	The cell that was double-clicked (not necessarily the active cell).
Auto_Open, AutoClose, Auto_Activate or Auto_Deactivate macro	Name of the calling sheet.
Other methods not listed	#REF! error.

The return value is one of the following XLOPER data types: xltypeRef, xltypeSRef, xltypeNum, xltypeStr, xltypeErr, or xltypeMulti. For more information about XLOPERs, see "The XLOPER Data Type" on page 9.

Syntax

From a macro sheet:

```
CALLER()
```

From a DLL:

```
Excel4(xlfCaller, (LPXLOPER) pxRes,0);
```

Windows Example

\SAMPLE\EXAMPLE\EXAMPLE.C

```
short int FAR PASCAL __export CallerExample(void)
{
    XLOPER xRes;

    Excel4(xlfCaller, (LPXLOPER)&xRes, 0);
    Excel4(xlcSelect, 0, 1, (LPXLOPER)&xRes);
    Excel4(xlFree, 0, 1, (LPXLOPER)&xRes);
    return 1;
}
```

Macintosh Example

:Sample Code:Examples:CallerExample.c

```
short int pascal main(void)
{
```

```
    XLOPER xRes;

    RememberA0();
    SetUpA4();
    InitFramework();

    Excel4(xlfCaller, (LPXLOPER)&xRes, 0);
    Excel4(xlcSelect, 0, 1, (LPXLOPER)&xRes);
    Excel4(xlFree, 0, 1, (LPXLOPER)&xRes);

    QuitFramework();
    RestoreA4();

    return 1;
}
```

Remark

This function is the only exception to the rule that worksheet functions can be called only from DLLs that were called from worksheets.

debugPrintf

Framework library function, called from a DLL. This function writes a debugging string to an attached terminal. The terminal should be set up for 9600 baud, 8 data bits, no parity, and 1 stop bit.

This function does not return a value.

Syntax

```
void far cdecl debugPrintf(LPSTR lpFormat, arguments);
```

lpFormat (LPSTR) The format string, which is identical to what you would use with the `sprintf` function.

arguments Zero or more arguments to match the format string.

Windows Example

This function prints a string to show that control was passed to the routine.

\SAMPLE\EXAMPLE\EXAMPLE.C

```
short int far pascal debugPrintfExample(void)
{
    debugPrintf("Made it!\r");
    return 1;
}
```

Macintosh Example

:Sample Code:Examples:debugPrintfExample.c

```
short int pascal main(void)
{
    RememberA0();
    SetUpA4();
    InitFramework();

    debugPrintf("Made it!\r");

    QuitFramework();
    RestoreA4();

    return 1;
}
```

EVALUATE

Called from a macro sheet or DLL. This function uses the Microsoft Excel parser and function evaluator to evaluate any expression that could be entered in a worksheet cell.

Returns the result of evaluating the string.

Syntax

From a macro sheet:

```
EVALUATE(formula_text)
```

formula_text (xltypeStr) The string to evaluate, optionally beginning with an equal sign (=).

From a DLL:

```
Excel4(xlfEvaluate, LPXLOPER pxRes, 1, LPXLOPER pxFormulaText)
```

Remarks

Limitations

The string can contain only functions, not command equivalents. It is equivalent to pressing F9 from the formula bar.

Primary Use

The primary use of the EVALUATE function is to allow DLLs to find out the value assigned to a defined name on a sheet.

External References

EVALUATE cannot be used to evaluate references to an external sheet that is not open.

Macro Example

The following example takes a text value, a5, and jumps to the location it represents by using the EVALUATE function.

	A
1	a5
2	=EVALUATE(A1&"()")
3	=RETURN()
4	
5	=ALERT("Made it!")
6	=RETURN()

Windows Example

This example uses xlfEvaluate to coerce the text "!B38" to the contents of cell B38.

\SAMPLE\EXAMPLE\EXAMPLE.C

```
short int FAR PASCAL __export EvaluateExample(void)
{
    XLOPER xFormulaText, xRes, xRes2, xInt;

    xFormulaText.xltype = xltypeStr;
    xFormulaText.val.str = "\004!B38";
    Excel4(xlfEvaluate, (LPXLOPER)&xRes, 1,
        (LPXLOPER)&xFormulaText);

    xInt.xltype = xltypeInt;
    xInt.val.w = 2;
    Excel4(xlcAlert, (LPXLOPER)&xRes2, 2,
        (LPXLOPER)&xRes, (LPXLOPER)&xInt);
    Excel4(xlFree, 0, 1, (LPXLOPER)&xRes);
    Excel4(xlFree, 0, 1, (LPXLOPER)&xRes2);

    return 1;
}
```

Macintosh Example

:Sample Code:Examples:EvaluateExample.c

```
short int pascal main(void)
{
    XLOPER xFormulaText, xRes, xRes2, xInt;

    RememberA0();
    SetUpA4();
    InitFramework();

    xFormulaText.xltype = xltypeStr;
    xFormulaText.val.str = "\004!B38";
    Excel4(xlfEvaluate, (LPXLOPER)&xRes, 1,
        (LPXLOPER)&xFormulaText);

    xInt.xltype = xltypeInt;
    xInt.val.w = 2;
    Excel4(xlcAlert, (LPXLOPER)&xRes2, 2,
        (LPXLOPER)&xRes, (LPXLOPER)&xInt);
    Excel4(xlFree, 0, 1, (LPXLOPER)&xRes);
    Excel4(xlFree, 0, 1, (LPXLOPER)&xRes2);

    QuitFramework();
    RestoreA4();

    return 1;
}
```

Excel

Framework library function, called from a DLL. This is a wrapper for the Excel4 function. It checks to see that none of the arguments are zero, which would indicate that a temporary XLOPER failed. If an error occurs, it prints a debug message. When finished, it frees all temporary memory.

Returns one of the following (int).

Value	Return code	Description
0	xlretSuccess	The function was called successfully. This does not mean that the function did not return a Microsoft Excel error value; to find that out, you have to look at the resulting XLOPER.

Value	Return code	Description
1	xlretAbort	An abort occurred (internal abort). You might get this if a macro closes its own macro sheet by calling CLOSE, or if Microsoft Excel is out of memory. In this case you must exit immediately. The DLL can call only xlFree before it exits. The user will be able to save any work interactively using the Save command on the File menu.
2	xlretInvXlfn	An invalid function number was supplied. If you are using constants from XLCALL.H, this shouldn't happen.
4	xlretInvCount	An invalid number of arguments was entered. Remember that no Microsoft Excel function can take more than 30 arguments, and some require a fixed number of arguments.
8	xlretInvXloper	An invalid XLOPER structure or an argument of the wrong type was used.
16	xlretStackOvfl	(Windows only) A stack overflow occurred. Use xlStack to monitor the amount of room left on the stack. Don't allocate large local (automatic) arrays on the stack if possible; make them static. (Note that a stack overflow may occur without being detected.)
32	xlretFailed	A command-equivalent function failed. This is equivalent to a macro command displaying the macro error alert dialog box.
64	xlretUncalced	An attempt was made to dereference a cell that has not been calculated yet, because it was scheduled to be recalculated after the current cell. In this case the DLL needs to exit immediately. It can call only xlFree before it exits. For more information, see "Dealing with Uncalculated Cells" on page 54.

Syntax

```
Excel(int iFunction, LPXLOPER pxRes, int iCount, LPXLOPER
argument1, ...)
```

iFunction (int) A number indicating the command, function, or special function you want to call. For a list of valid *iFunction* values and related information, see the "Remarks" section under "Excel4" on page 72.

pxRes (LPXLOPER) A pointer to an allocated XLOPER (10 bytes) that will hold the result of the evaluated function.

iCount (int) The number of arguments that will be passed to the function.

argument1, ... (LPXLOPER) The optional arguments to the function. All arguments must be pointers to XLOPERs. For Windows, remember to cast these arguments to far pointers.

Windows Example

This example passes a bad argument to the Excel function, which sends a message to the debugging terminal.

\SAMPLE\EXAMPLE\EXAMPLE.C

```
short int far pascal ExcelExample(void)
{
    Excel(xlcDisplay, 0, 1, 0);
    return 1;
}
```

Macintosh Example

:Sample Code:Examples:ExcelExample.c

```
short int pascal main(void)
{
    RememberA0();
    SetUpA4();
    InitFramework();

    Excel(xlfOffset, 0, 1, 0);

    QuitFramework();
    RestoreA4();

    return 1;
}
```

Related Function

Excel4

Excel4

Called from a DLL. This function calls an internal Microsoft Excel macro function or special command from a DLL or code resource.

Returns one of the following (int).

Value	Return code	Description
0	xlretSuccess	The function was called successfully. This does not mean that the function did not return a Microsoft Excel error value; to find that out, you have to look at the resulting XLOPER.
1	xlretAbort	An abort occurred (internal abort). You might get this if a macro closes its own macro sheet by calling CLOSE, or if Microsoft Excel is out of memory. In this case you must exit immediately. The DLL can call only xlFree before it exits. The user will be able to save any work interactively using the Save command on the File menu.
2	xlretInvXlfn	An invalid function number was supplied. If you are using constants from XLCALL.H, this shouldn't happen.
4	xlretInvCount	An invalid number of arguments was entered. Remember that no Microsoft Excel function can take more than 30 arguments, and some require a fixed number of arguments.
8	xlretInvXloper	An invalid XLOPER structure or an argument of the wrong type was used.
16	xlretStackOvfl	(Windows only) A stack overflow occurred. Use xlStack to monitor the amount of room left on the stack. Don't allocate large local (automatic) arrays on the stack if possible; make them static. (Note that a stack overflow may occur without being detected.)
32	xlretFailed	A command-equivalent function failed. This is equivalent to a macro command displaying the macro error alert dialog box.
64	xlretUncalced	An attempt was made to dereference a cell that has not been calculated yet, because it was scheduled to be recalculated after the current cell. In this case the DLL needs to exit immediately. It can call only xlFree before it exits. For more information, see "Dealing with Uncalculated Cells" on page 54.

Syntax

```
Excel4(int iFunction, LPXLOPER pxRes, int iCount, LPXLOPER
argument1, ...)
```

iFunction (int) A number indicating the command, function, or special function you want to call. For a list of valid *iFunction* values, see the following "Remarks" section.

pxRes (LPXLOPER) A pointer to an allocated XLOPER (10 bytes) that will hold the result of the evaluated function.

iCount (int) The number of arguments that will be passed to the function.

argument1, ... (LPXLOPER) The optional arguments to the function. All arguments must be pointers to XLOPERs. For Windows, remember to cast these arguments to far pointers.

Remarks

Valid *iFunction* values

Valid *iFunction* values are any of the xlf... or xlc... constants defined in XLCALL.H or any of the following special functions:

xlAbort	xlEnableXLMsgs	xlGetInst	xlSheetNm
xlCoerce	xlFree	xlSet	xlStack
xlDefineBinaryName	xlGetBinaryName	xlSheetId	xlUDF
xlDisableXLMsgs	xlGetHwnd		

Different Types of Functions

Excel4 distinguishes between three classes of functions. The functions are classified according to the three states in which Microsoft Excel may be running the DLL. Class 1 applies when the DLL is called from a worksheet as a result of recalculation. Class 2 applies when the DLL is called from within a function macro or from a worksheet where it was registered with a number sign (#) in the type text. Class 3 applies when a macro is called from an object, macro, menu, toolbar, shortcut key, or the Tools/Macro/Run command. The following table shows what functions are valid in each class.

Class 1	Class 2	Class 3
Any worksheet function	Any worksheet function	Any function, including xlSet and command-equivalent functions
Any xl... function except xlSet	Any xl... function except xlSet	
xlfCaller	Macro sheet functions that return a value but perform no action	

Displaying the Dialog Box for a Command-Equivalent Function

If a command-equivalent function has an associated dialog box, you can set the xlPrompt bit in *iFunction*. This means that Microsoft Excel will display the appropriate dialog box before carrying out the command.

Writing International DLLs

If you set the xlIntl bit in *iFunction*, the function or command will be carried out as if it were being called from an International Macro Sheet. This means that the command will behave as it would on the U.S. version of Microsoft Excel, even if it is running on an international (localized) version.

xlretUncalced or xlretAbort

After receiving one of these return values, your DLL needs to clean up and exit immediately. Callbacks into Microsoft Excel, except xlFree, are disabled after receiving one of these return values.

Windows Example

This example uses the Excel4 function to select the cell from which it was called.

\SAMPLE\EXAMPLE\EXAMPLE.C

```
short int FAR PASCAL __export Excel4Example(void)
{
    XLOPER xRes;

    Excel4(xlfCaller, (LPXLOPER)&xRes, 0);
    Excel4(xlcSelect, 0, 1, (LPXLOPER)&xRes);
    Excel4(xlFree, 0, 1, (LPXLOPER)&xRes);

    return 1;
}
```

Macintosh Example

:Sample Code:Examples:Excel4Example.c

```
short int pascal main(void)
{
    XLOPER xRes;

    RememberA0();
    SetUpA4();
    InitFramework();

    Excel4(xlfCaller, (LPXLOPER)&xRes, 0);
    Excel4(xlcSelect, 0, 1, (LPXLOPER)&xRes);
    Excel4(xlFree, 0, 1, (LPXLOPER)&xRes);

    QuitFramework();
    RestoreA4();

    return 1;
}
```

Related Functions

Excel4v, Excel

Excel4v

Called from a DLL. This function calls an internal Microsoft Excel function from a DLL or code resource. This form accepts its arguments as an array.

Returns the same value as Excel4.

Syntax

Windows

```
int pascal Excel4v(int iFunction, LPXLOPER pxRes, int iCount,
LPXLOPER FAR rgx[])
```

Macintosh

```
int pascal Excel4v(int iFunction, LPXLOPER pxRes, int iCount,
LPXLOPER rgx[])
```

iFunction (int) A number indicating the command, function, or special function you want to call. For more information, see the "Remarks" section under "Excel4" on page 72.

pxRes (LPXLOPER) A pointer to an allocated XLOPER (10 bytes) that will hold the result of the evaluated function.

iCount (int) The number of arguments that will be passed to the function.

rgx (LPXLOPER []) An array containing the arguments to the function. All arguments in the array must be pointers to XLOPERs. In Windows, remember to cast these arguments to a far pointer.

Remark

This function is provided so you can write a wrapper function that calls Excel4. Otherwise, it behaves exactly like Excel4.

Examples

For a Windows example of this function, see the code for the Excel function in FRAMEWRK.C in the FRAMEWRK directory. For a Macintosh example, see the file Framework.c in the Framework folder.

Related Functions

Excel4, Excel

InitFramework

Framework library function, called from a DLL. This function initializes the Framework library. On the Macintosh, this function must be called before any calls are made to the Framework library.

This function does not return a value.

Syntax

```
InitFramework(void);
```

This function has no arguments.

Windows Example

This example uses the InitFramework function to free all temporary memory.

\SAMPLE\EXAMPLE\EXAMPLE.C

```
short int FAR PASCAL __export InitFrameworkExample(void)
{
    InitFramework();
    return 1;
}
```

Macintosh Example

:Sample Code:Examples:InitFrameworkExample.c

```
short int pascal main(void)
(
    RememberA0();
    SetUpA4();
    InitFramework();

    QuitFramework();
    RestoreA4();

    return 1;
}
```

QuitFramework

Macintosh Only   Framework library function, called from a DLL. This function shuts down the Framework library. This function must be called before the function returns.

This function does not return a value.

Syntax

```
QuitFramework(void);
```

This function has no arguments.

Macintosh Example

This example uses the InitFramework function to free all temporary memory. It then calls the QuitFramework function to shut down the Framework library.

:Sample Code:Examples:QuitFrameworkExample.c

```
short int pascal main(void)
{
    RememberA0();
    SetUpA4();
    InitFramework();

    QuitFramework();
    RestoreA4();

    return 1;
}
```

REGISTER (Form 1)

Called from a Microsoft Excel 4.0 macro sheet or DLL. This function makes a function or command in a DLL or code resource available to Microsoft Excel, and returns the register ID identifying the function for use by CALL and UNREGISTER.

Returns the register ID of the function (xltypeNum), which can be used in subsequent CALL and UNREGISTER calls.

Syntax

From a macro sheet:

```
REGISTER(module_text,procedure,type_text,function_text,
argument_text,macro_type,category,shortcut_text)
```

From a DLL:

```
Excel4(xlfRegister, LPXLOPER pxRes, 8,
    LPXLOPER pxModuleText,   LPXLOPER pxProcedure,
    LPXLOPER pxTypeText,     LPXLOPER pxFunctionText,
    LPXLOPER pxArgumentText,LPXLOPER pxMacroType,
    LPXLOPER pxCategory,     LPXLOPER pxShortcutText);
```

module_text (xltypeStr)

Windows The name of the DLL containing the function.

Macintosh The name of the file containing the code resource.

procedure (xltypeStr or xltypeNum)

Windows If a string, the name of the function to call. If a number, the ordinal export number of the function to call. For clarity and robustness, always use the string form.

Macintosh If a string, the name of the code resource to call. If a number, the resource number of the resource to call. For clarity and robustness, always use the string form.

type_text (xltypeStr) An optional string specifying the types of all the arguments to the function and the type of the return value of the function. For more information, see the following "Remarks" section. This argument can be omitted for a stand-alone DLL (XLL) that includes an xlAutoRegister function.

function_text (xltypeStr) The name of the function as it will appear in the Function Wizard. This argument is optional; if omitted, the function will not be available in the Function Wizard, and it can be called only using the CALL function.

argument_text (xltypeStr) An optional text string describing the arguments to the function. The user sees this in the Function Wizard. If omitted, it will be constructed based on the *type_text*.

macro_type (xltypeNum) An optional argument indicating the type of function. Use 0 for none, 1 for a function (default), or 2 for a command. This argument can be used to define hidden functions (use *macro_type* = 0) or to define functions available only from macro sheets (use *macro_type* = 2).

category (xltypeStr or xltypeNum) An optional argument allowing you to specify which category the new function or command should belong to. The Function Wizard divides functions by type (category). You can specify a category name or a sequential number, where the number is the position in which the category appears in the Function Wizard. For more information, see "Category Names" on page 83. If omitted, the User Defined category is assumed.

shortcut_text (xltypeStr) A one-character, case-sensitive string specifying the control key that will be assigned to this command. For example, "A" will assign this command to CONTROL+SHIFT+A. This argument is optional and is used for commands only.

Remarks

Data Types

In the CALL, REGISTER, and REGISTER.ID functions, the *type_text* argument specifies the data type of the return value and the data types of all arguments to the DLL function or code resource. The first character of *type_text* specifies the data type of the return value. The remaining characters indicate the data types of all the arguments. For example, a DLL function that returns a floating-point number and takes an integer and a floating-point number as arguments would require "BIB" for the *type_text* argument.

The following table contains a complete list of the data type codes that Microsoft Excel recognizes, a description of each data type, how the argument or return value is passed, and a typical declaration for the data type in the C programming language.

Code	Description	Pass by	C declaration
A	Logical (FALSE = 0, TRUE = 1)	Value	`short int`
B	IEEE 8-byte floating-point number	Value (Windows)	`double` (Windows)
		Reference (Macintosh)	`double *` (Macintosh)
C	Null-terminated string (maximum string length = 255 characters)	Reference	`char *`
D	Byte-counted string (first byte contains length of string, maximum string length = 255 characters)	Reference	`unsigned char *`
E	IEEE 8-byte floating-point number	Reference	`double *`
F	Null-terminated string (maximum string length = 255 characters)	Reference (modify in place)	`char *`
G	Byte-counted string (first byte contains length of string, maximum string length = 255 characters)	Reference (modify in place)	`unsigned char *`
H	Unsigned 2-byte integer	Value	`unsigned short int`
I	Signed 2-byte integer	Value	`short int`
J	Signed 4-byte integer	Value	`long int`
K	Array	Reference	`FP *`
L	Logical (FALSE = 0, TRUE = 1)	Reference	`short int *`
M	Signed 2-byte integer	Reference	`short int *`
N	Signed 4-byte integer	Reference	`long int *`

Code	Description	Pass by	C declaration

O	Array	Reference	Three arguments are passed:
			`unsigned short int *`
			`unsigned short int *`
			`double []`

P	Microsoft Excel OPER data structure	Reference	`OPER *`
R	Microsoft Excel XLOPER data structure	Reference	`XLOPER *`

When working with the data types displayed in the preceding table, keep the following in mind:

- The C-language declarations are based on the assumption that your compiler defaults to 8-byte doubles, 2-byte short integers, and 4-byte long integers.

- In the Microsoft Windows programming environment, all pointers are far pointers. For example, you should declare the D data type code as `unsigned char far *` in Microsoft Windows.

- All functions in DLLs and code resources are called using the Pascal calling convention. Most C compilers allow you to use the Pascal calling convention by adding the `pascal` keyword to the function declaration, as shown in the following example:

```
pascal void main (rows,columns,a)
```

- If a function uses a pass-by-reference data type for its return value, you can pass a null pointer as the return value. Microsoft Excel will interpret the null pointer as the #NUM! error value.

Additional Data Type Information

This section contains detailed information about the E, F, G, K, O, P, and R data types, and other information about the *type_text* argument.

E Data Type

Microsoft Excel expects a DLL using the E data type to pass pointers to floating-point numbers on the stack. This can cause problems with some languages (for example, Borland® C++) that expect the number to be passed on the coprocessor emulator stack. The workaround is to pass a pointer to the number on the coprocessor stack. The following example shows how to return a double from Borland C++:

```
typedef double FAR * lpDbl;
extern "C" lpDbl FAR PASCAL _export AddDbl(double D1,
    double D2, WORD npDbl)
{
```

```
    lpDbl Result;
    Result = (lpDbl)MK_FP(_SS, npDbl);
    *Result = D1 + D2;
    return (Result);
}
```

F and G Data Types

With the F and G data types, a function can modify a string buffer that is allocated by Microsoft Excel. If the return value type code is F or G, then Microsoft Excel ignores the value returned by the function. Instead, Microsoft Excel searches the list of function arguments for the first corresponding data type (F or G) and then takes the current contents of the allocated string buffer as the return value. Microsoft Excel allocates 256 bytes for the argument, so the function may return a larger string than it received.

K Data Type

The K data type uses a pointer to a variable-size FP structure. You should define this structure in the DLL or code resource as follows:

```
typedef struct _FP
{
    unsigned short int rows;
    unsigned short int columns;
    double array[1];      /* Actually, array[rows][columns] */
} FP;
```

The declaration double array[1] allocates storage only for a single-element array. The number of elements in the actual array equals the number of rows multiplied by the number of columns.

O Data Type

The O data type can be used only as an argument, not as a return value. It passes three items: a pointer to the number of rows in an array, a pointer to the number of columns in an array, and a pointer to a two-dimensional array of floating-point numbers.

Instead of returning a value, a function can modify an array passed by the O data type. To do this, you could use ">O" as the *type_text* argument. For more information about modifying an array, see the section "Modifying in Place—Functions Declared as Void" on page 82.

The O data type was created for direct compatibility with FORTRAN DLLs, which pass arguments by reference.

P Data Type

The P data type is a pointer to an OPER structure. The OPER structure contains 8 bytes of data, followed by a 2-byte identifier that specifies the type of data. With the P data type, a DLL function or code resource can take and return any Microsoft Excel data type.

The OPER structure is defined as follows:

```
typedef struct _oper
{
    union
    {
        double num;
        unsigned char *str;
        unsigned short int bool;
        unsigned short int err;
        struct
        {
            struct _oper *lparray;
            unsigned short int rows;
            unsigned short int columns;
        } array;
    } val;
    unsigned short int type;
} OPER;
```

The *type* field contains one of the values listed in the following table.

Type	Description	Val field to use
1	Numeric	num
2	String (first byte contains length of string)	str
4	Boolean (logical)	bool
16	Error: the error values are: 0 #NULL! 7 #DIV/0! 15 #VALUE! 23 #REF! 29 #NAME? 36 #NUM! 42 #N/A	err
64	Array	array
128	Missing argument	
256	Empty cell	

The last two values can be used only as arguments, not return values. The missing argument value (128) is passed when the caller omits an argument. The empty cell value (256) is passed when the caller passes a reference to an empty cell.

R Data Type—Calling Microsoft Excel Functions from DLLs

The R data type is a pointer to an XLOPER structure, which is an enhanced version of the OPER structure. In Microsoft Excel version 5.0, you can use the R data type to write DLLs and code resources that call Microsoft Excel functions. With the XLOPER structure, a DLL function can pass sheet references and implement flow control, in addition to passing data. For more information about flow control, see the section "Advanced Flow Control in Macro Sheets" on page 48.

Volatile Functions and Recalculation

Microsoft Excel usually calculates a DLL function (or a code resource) only when it is entered into a cell, when one of its precedents changes, or when the cell is calculated during a macro. On a worksheet, you can make a DLL function or code resource volatile, which means that it recalculates every time the worksheet recalculates. To make a function volatile, add an exclamation point (!) as the last character in the *type_text* argument.

For example, in Microsoft Excel for Windows, the following worksheet formula recalculates every time the worksheet recalculates:

```
CALL("User","GetTickCount","J!")
```

Modifying in Place—Functions Declared as Void

You can use a single digit *n* for the return type code in *type_text,* where *n* is a number from 1 to 9. This tells Microsoft Excel to take the value of the variable in the location pointed to by the *n*th argument in *type_text* as the return value. This is also known as modifying in place. The *n*th argument must be a pass-by-reference data type (C, D, E, F, G, K, L, M, N, O, P, or R). The DLL function or code resource also must be declared with the `void` keyword in the C language (or the `procedure` keyword in the Pascal language).

For example, a DLL function that takes a null-terminated string and two pointers to integers as arguments can modify the string in place. Use "1FMM" as the *type_text* argument, and declare the function as void.

Previous versions of Microsoft Excel used the > character to modify the first argument in place—there was no way to modify any argument other than the first. The > character is equivalent to $n = 1$ in Microsoft Excel version 5.0.

Handling Uncalculated Cells

Appending a number sign (#) to the end of *type_text* changes the way the DLL handles uncalculated cells when called from a worksheet. If the number sign is present, dereferencing uncalculated cells returns the old values (this is the behavior found in the macro language). If the number sign is not present, evaluating an uncalculated cell will result in an xlretUncalced error, and the current function will be called again once the cell has been calculated. In addition, if the number sign is not present, the DLL may call only Class 1 functions. If the number sign is present, the DLL may call any Class 2 function. For more information about working with uncalculated cells, see the section "Dealing with Uncalculated Cells" on page 54.

Category Names

Here are some guidelines for determining which category you should put your XLL functions in (the *category* argument to REGISTER).

- If the function does something that could be done by the user as a part of your add-in's user interface, you should put the function in the Commands category.

- If the function returns information about the state of the add-in or any other useful information, you should put the function in the Information category.

- An add-in should never add functions or commands to the User Defined category. This category is for the exclusive use of end-users.

Example for a Macro

The following example registers the CalcCircum function in CIRCUM.DLL, then calls the function using the defined name for cell B1.

	A	B
1	fCircum	=REGISTER("CIRCUM","CalcCircum","EE")
2		=CALL(fCircum,100)
3		=UNREGISTER(fCircum)
4		=RETURN()

Cell B1 has the defined name fCircum.

Examples

For a Windows example of this function, see the code for the xlAutoOpen function in GENERIC.C in the FRAMEWRK directory. For a Macintosh example, see the file xlAutoOpen.c in the Framework folder.

Related Functions

CALL, REGISTER.ID, UNREGISTER

REGISTER (Form 2)

Called from a macro sheet or DLL. This function can only be used on an XLL containing an xlAutoOpen procedure. This function registers the xlAutoOpen function, calls it, and then unregisters it.

Returns the name of the DLL or code resource (xltypeStr).

Syntax

From a macro sheet:

```
REGISTER(module_text)
```

From a DLL:

```
Excel4(xlfRegister, LPXLOPER pxRes, 1, LPXLOPER pxModuleText);
```

module_text (xltypeStr)

Windows The name of the DLL containing the function.

Macintosh The name of the file containing the code resource.

Remark

This function is to an XLL what OPEN is to a worksheet. A Macro Record of a File Open operation on an XLL will show that REGISTER(*module_text*) is recorded. If OPEN is performed on an XLL, the open function registers xlAutoOpen but does not run it. If an action similar to Open is needed for an XLL, use this form of REGISTER instead.

REGISTER.ID

Called from a macro sheet or DLL. If a function is already registered, returns the existing register ID for that function without reregistering it. If a function is not yet registered, registers it and returns a register ID.

Returns the register ID of the function (xltypeNum), which can be used in subsequent CALL and UNREGISTER calls.

Syntax

From a macro sheet:

```
REGISTER.ID(module_text,procedure,type_text)
```

From a DLL:

```
Excel4(xlfRegisterId, LPXLOPER pxRes, 3, LPXLOPER pxModuleText,
LPXLOPER pxProcedure, LPXLOPER pxTypeText);
```

module_text (xltypeStr)

Windows The name of the DLL containing the function.

Macintosh The name of the file containing the code resource.

procedure (xltypeStr or xltypeNum)

Windows If a string, the name of the function to call. If a number, the ordinal export number of the function to call. For clarity and robustness, always use the string form.

Macintosh If a string, the name of the code resource to call. If a number, the resource number of the resource to call. For clarity and robustness, always use the string form.

type_text (xltypeStr) An optional string specifying the types of all the arguments to the function and the type of the return value of the function. For more information, see the following "Remark" section. This argument can be omitted for a stand-alone DLL (XLL) defining xlAutoRegister.

Remark

This function is useful when you don't want to worry about maintaining a register ID, but need one later for unregistering. It is also useful for assigning to menus, tools, and buttons when the function you want to assign is in a DLL.

Related Functions

CALL, REGISTER, UNREGISTER

TempActiveCell

Framework library function, called from a DLL. This function creates a temporary XLOPER containing a reference to a single cell on the active sheet.

Returns a reference XLOPER (xltypeRef) containing the reference of the cell passed in.

Syntax

```
TempActiveCell(WORD rw, BYTE col);
```

rw (WORD) The row of the cell. All arguments are zero-based.

col (BYTE) The column of the cell.

Windows Example

This example uses the TempActiveCell function to display the contents of cell B121 on the active sheet.

\SAMPLE\EXAMPLE\EXAMPLE.C

```
short int far pascal TempActiveCellExample(void)
{
    Excel4(xlcAlert, 0, 1, (LPXLOPER) TempActiveCell(120,1));
    return 1;
}
```

Macintosh Example

:Sample Code:Examples:TempActiveCellExample.c

```
short int pascal main(void)
(
    RememberA0();
    SetUpA4();
    InitFramework();

    Excel4(xlcAlert, 0, 1, (LPXLOPER)TempActiveCell(120,1));

    QuitFramework();
    RestoreA4();

    return 1;
}
```

TempActiveColumn

Framework library function, called from a DLL. This function creates a temporary XLOPER containing a reference to an entire column on the active sheet.

Returns a reference XLOPER (xltypeRef) containing a reference to the column passed in.

Syntax

```
TempActiveColumn(BYTE col);
```

col (BYTE) The column number of the cell. The argument is zero-based.

Windows Example

The following example uses TempActiveColumn to select an entire column.

\SAMPLE\EXAMPLE\EXAMPLE.C

```
short int FAR PASCAL __export TempActiveColumnExample(void)
{
    Excel4(xlcSelect, 0, 1, TempActiveColumn(1));
    return 1;
}
```

Macintosh Example

:Sample Code:Examples:TempActiveColumnExample.c

```
short int pascal main(void)
(
    RememberA0();
    SetUpA4();
    InitFramework();

    Excel4(xlcSelect, 0, 1, TempActiveColumn(1));

    QuitFramework();
    RestoreA4();

    return 1;
}
```

TempActiveRef

Framework library function, called from a DLL. This function creates a temporary XLOPER containing a rectangular reference to the active sheet.

Returns a reference XLOPER (xltypeRef) containing the reference passed in.

Syntax

```
TempActiveRef(WORD rwFirst, WORD rwLast, BYTE colFirst, BYTE colLast);
```

rwFirst (WORD) The starting row of the reference. All arguments are zero-based.

rwLast (WORD) The ending row of the reference.

colFirst (BYTE) The starting column number of the reference.

colLast (BYTE) The ending column number of the reference.

Windows Example

This example uses the TempActiveRef function to select cells A112:C117.

\SAMPLE\EXAMPLE\EXAMPLE.C

```
short int FAR PASCAL __export TempActiveRefExample(void)
{
    Excel4(xlcSelect, 0, 1, TempActiveRef(111, 116, 0, 2));
    return 1;
}
```

Macintosh Example

:Sample Code:Examples:TempActiveRefExample.c

```
short int pascal main(void)
(
    RememberA0();
    SetUpA4();
    InitFramework();

    Excel4(xlcSelect, 0, 1, TempActiveRef(111,116, 0, 2));

    QuitFramework();
    RestoreA4();

    return 1;
}
```

TempActiveRow

Framework library function, called from a DLL. This function creates a temporary XLOPER containing a reference to an entire row on the active sheet.

Returns a reference XLOPER (xltypeRef) containing a reference to the row passed in.

Syntax

```
TempActiveRow(WORD rw);
```

rw (WORD) The row of the cell. The argument is zero-based.

Windows Example

The following example uses the TempActiveRow function to select an entire row.

\SAMPLE\EXAMPLE\EXAMPLE.C

```
short int FAR PASCAL __export TempActiveRowExample(void)
{
    Excel4(xlcSelect, 0, 1, TempActiveRow(120));
    return 1;
}
```

Macintosh Example

:Sample Code:Examples:TempActiveRowExample.c

```
short int pascal main(void)
(
    RememberA0();
    SetUpA4();
    InitFramework();

    Excel4(xlcSelect, 0, 1, TempActiveRow(120));

    QuitFramework();
    RestoreA4();

    return 1;
}
```

TempBool

Framework library function, called from a DLL. This function creates a temporary logical (TRUE/FALSE) XLOPER.

Returns a Boolean XLOPER (xltypeBool) containing the logical value passed in.

Syntax

```
TempBool(int b);
```

b (int) Use 0 to return a FALSE XLOPER; use any other value to return a TRUE XLOPER.

Windows Example

The following example uses the TempBool function to clear the status bar. Temporary memory is freed when the Excel function is called.

\SAMPLE\EXAMPLE\EXAMPLE.C

```
short int FAR PASCAL __export TempBoolExample(void)
{
    Excel(xlcMessage, 0, 1, TempBool(0));
    return 1;
}
```

Macintosh Example

:Sample Code:Examples:TempBoolExample.c

```
short int pascal main(void)
(
    RememberA0();
    SetUpA4();
    InitFramework();

    Excel(xlcMessage, 0, 1, TempBool(0));

    QuitFramework();
    RestoreA4();

    return 1;
}
```

TempErr

Framework library function, called from a DLL. This function creates a temporary error XLOPER.

Returns an error XLOPER (xltypeErr) containing the error code passed in.

Syntax

```
TempErr(WORD err);
```

err (WORD) The error code to place in the integer OPER. The error codes, which are defined in XLCALL.H, are shown in the following table.

Error	Error value	Decimal equivalent
#NULL	xlerrNull	0
#DIV/0!	xlerrDiv0	7
#VALUE!	xlerrValue	15
#REF!	xlerrRef	23
#NAME?	xlerrName	29
#NUM!	xlerrNum	36
#N/A	xlerrNA	42

Windows Example

This example uses the TempErr function to return a #VALUE! error to Microsoft Excel.

\SAMPLE\EXAMPLE\EXAMPLE.C

```
LPXLOPER FAR PASCAL __export TempErrExample(void)
{
    return TempErr(xlerrValue);
}
```

Macintosh Example

:Sample Code:Examples:TempErrExample.c

```
LPXLOPER pascal main(void)
{
    XLOPER xErr;

    RememberA0();
    SetUpA4();
    InitFramework();

    xErr.xltype = xltypeErr;
    xErr.val.err = xlerrValue;

    QuitFramework();
    RestoreA4();

    return TempErr(xlerrValue);
}
```

TempInt

Framework library function, called from a DLL. This function creates a temporary integer XLOPER.

Returns an integer XLOPER (xltypeInt) containing the value passed in.

Syntax

```
TempInt(short int i);
```

i (short int) The integer to place in the integer OPER.

Windows Example

This example uses the TempInt function to pass an argument to xlfGetWorkspace.

\SAMPLE\EXAMPLE\EXAMPLE.C

```
short int FAR PASCAL __export TempIntExample(void)
{
    XLOPER xRes;

    Excel(xlfGetWorkspace, (LPXLOPER)&xRes, 1, (LPXLOPER)TempInt(44));
    Excel(xlFree, 0, 1, (LPXLOPER)&xRes);
    return 1;
}
```

Macintosh Example

:Sample Code:Examples:TempIntExample.c

```
short int pascal main(void)
{
    XLOPER xRes;

    RememberA0();
    SetUpA4();
    InitFramework();

    Excel(xlfGetWorkspace, (LPXLOPER)&xRes, 1, (LPXLOPER)TempInt(44));
    Excel(xlFree, 0, 1, (LPXLOPER)&xRes);

    QuitFramework();
    RestoreA4();

    return 1;
}
```

TempMissing

Framework library function, called from a DLL. This function creates a temporary XLOPER containing a "missing" argument. It is used to simulate a missing argument when calling Microsoft Excel.

Returns a missing XLOPER (xltypeMissing).

Syntax

```
TempMissing(void);
```

This function has no arguments.

Windows Example

This example uses the TempMissing function to provide a missing argument to xlcActivateNext, which causes Microsoft Excel to switch to the next sheet.

\SAMPLE\EXAMPLE\EXAMPLE.C

```
short int FAR PASCAL __export TempMissingExample(void)
{
    XLOPER xBool;

    xBool.xltype = xltypeBool;
    xBool.val.bool = 0;
    Excel(xlcWorkspace, 0, 4, (LPXLOPER)TempMissing(),
        (LPXLOPER)TempMissing(), (LPXLOPER)TempMissing(),
        (LPXLOPER)&xBool);
    return 1;
}
```

Macintosh Example

:Sample Code:Examples:TempMissingExample.c

```
short int pascal main(void)
{
    XLOPER xBool;

    RememberA0();
    SetUpA4();
    InitFramework();

    xBool.xltype = xltypeBool;
    xBool.val.bool = 0;
    Excel(xlcWorkspace, 0, 4, (LPXLOPER)TempMissing(),
        (LPXLOPER)TempMissing(), (LPXLOPER)TempMissing(),
        (LPXLOPER)&xBool);

    QuitFramework();
    RestoreA4();

    return 1;
}
```

TempNum

Framework library function, called from a DLL. This function creates a temporary numeric (IEEE floating-point) XLOPER. Returns a numeric XLOPER (xltypeNum) containing the value passed in.

Syntax

```
TempNum(double d);
```

d (double) The number to place in the numeric OPER.

Windows Example

This example uses the TempNum function to pass an argument to xlfGetWorkspace.

\SAMPLE\EXAMPLE\EXAMPLE.C

```
short int FAR PASCAL __export TempNumExample(void)
{
    XLOPER xRes;

    Excel(xlfGetWorkspace, (LPXLOPER)&xRes, 1, (LPXLOPER)TempNum(44));
    Excel(xlFree, 0, 1, (LPXLOPER)&xRes);
    return 1;
}
```

Macintosh Example

:Sample Code:Examples:TempNumExample.c

```
short int pascal main(void)
{
    XLOPER xRes;

    RememberA0();
    SetUpA4();
    InitFramework();

    Excel(xlfGetWorkspace, (LPXLOPER)&xRes, 1, (LPXLOPER)TempNum(44));
    Excel(xlFree, 0, 1, (LPXLOPER)&xRes);

    QuitFramework();
    RestoreA4();

    return 1;
}
```

TempStr

Framework library function, called from a DLL. This function creates a temporary string XLOPER. The first character of the string passed in will be overwritten by a byte count.

Returns a string XLOPER (xltypeStr) containing the string passed in.

Syntax

```
TempStr(LPSTR str);
```

str (LPSTR) A pointer to the string to place in the XLOPER.

Windows Example

This example uses the TempStr function to create a string for a message box.

\SAMPLE\EXAMPLE\EXAMPLE.C

```
short int FAR PASCAL __export TempStrExample(void)
{
    Excel4(xlcAlert, 0, 1, TempStr(" Made it!"));
    return 1;
}
```

Macintosh Example

:Sample Code:Examples:TempStrExample.c

```
short int pascal main(void)
(
    RememberA0();
    SetUpA4();
    InitFramework();

    Excel4(xlcAlert, 0, 1, TempStr(" Made it!"));

    QuitFramework();
    RestoreA4();

    return 1;
}
```

UNREGISTER (Form 1)

Called from a macro sheet or DLL. This function reduces by one the use count of a function in a DLL or code resource. Each time REGISTER is called, the use count is increased by one. Each time UNREGISTER is called, the use count is decreased by one. When the use count of all the functions in a DLL reaches zero, the DLL is unloaded from memory.

If successful, returns TRUE (xltypeBool).

Syntax

From a macro sheet:

```
UNREGISTER(register_id)
```

From a DLL:

```
Excel4(xlfUnregister, LPXLOPER pxRes, 1, LPXLOPER pxRegisterId);
```

register_id (xltypeNum) The registered ID of the function to unregister, which you get from calling REGISTER or REGISTER.ID.

Remark

If you specified the *function_text* argument to REGISTER, you need to explicitly delete the name by calling SET.NAME and omitting the second argument, so that the function will no longer appear in the Function Wizard.

Example from a Macro Sheet

The following example registers the CalcCircum function in CIRCUM.DLL, calls the function using the defined name for cell B1, and then unregisters the function.

	A	B
1	fCircum	=REGISTER("CIRCUM","CalcCircum","EE")
2		=CALL(fCircum,100)
3		=UNREGISTER(fCircum)
4		=RETURN()

Cell B1 has the defined name fCircum.

Examples

For a Windows example of this function, see the code for the fExit function in GENERIC.C in the FRAMEWRK directory. For a Macintosh example, see the file fExit.c in the Framework folder.

Related Functions

CALL, REGISTER, REGISTER.ID, UNREGISTER (Form 2)

UNREGISTER (Form 2)

Called from a macro sheet or DLL. This function forces a DLL or code resource to be unloaded completely. It unregisters all of the functions in a DLL (or all of the code resources in a file), even if they are currently in use by another macro, no matter what the use count. This function registers xlAutoClose, calls xlAutoClose, unregisters xlAutoClose, and then unregisters all other functions in the DLL.

If successful, returns TRUE (xltypeBool). If unsuccessful, returns FALSE.

Syntax

From a macro sheet:

```
UNREGISTER(module_text)
```

From a DLL:

```
Excel4(xlfUnregister, LPXLOPER pxRes, 1, LPXLOPER pxModuleText);
```

module_text (xltypeStr)

Windows The name of the DLL containing the functions.

Macintosh The name of the file containing the code resources.

Remarks

Proceed Carefully

Beware of this form of the function. Since Microsoft Excel keeps use counts for every DLL function and code resource, it is possible to register a function in two different places. However, if you use this form of UNREGISTER, you will be guaranteed to delete all the registrations that exist.

Deleting all registrations is useful when you are developing DLLs, so that you can be sure a DLL is completely unloaded from Microsoft Excel while you compile a new version.

Remember to Delete Names

If you specified the *function_text* argument to REGISTER, you need to explicitly delete the names by calling SET.NAME and omitting the second argument, so that the function will no longer appear in the Function Wizard.

Related Functions

CALL, REGISTER, REGISTER.ID, UNREGISTER (Form 1)

xlAbort

Called from a DLL. This function yields the processor to other tasks in the system and checks whether the user has pressed ESC to cancel a macro.

Returns TRUE (xltypeBool) if the user has pressed ESC.

Syntax

```
Excel4(xlAbort, LPXLOPER pxRes, 1, LPXLOPER pxRetain)
```

pxRetain (xltypeBool) If FALSE, this function will also clear any pending abort (if you want to continue despite the user abort). This argument is optional; if omitted, this function will check for a user abort without clearing it.

Remarks

Frequent Calls May Be Needed

Functions that will likely take a long time must call this function frequently to yield the processor to other tasks in the system.

Avoid Sensitive Language

Microsoft recommends against using the term "Abort" in your user interface. Use "Cancel," "Halt," or "Stop."

Windows Example

The following code repetitively moves the active cell on a sheet until one minute has elapsed or until you press ESC. It calls the function xlAbort occasionally. This yields the processor, allowing cooperative multitasking.

\SAMPLE\FRAMEWRK\GENERIC.C

```
int FAR PASCAL __export fDance(void)
{
    DWORD dtickStart;
    XLOPER xAbort, xConfirm;
    int boolSheet;
    int col=0;
    char rgch[32];

    // Check what kind of sheet is active. If it is
    // a worksheet or macro sheet, this function will
    // move the selection in a loop to show activity.
    // In any case, it will update the status bar
    // with a countdown.

    // Call xlSheetId; if that fails the current sheet
    // is not a macro sheet or worksheet. Next, get the
    // time at which to start. Then start a while loop
```

```
// that will run for one minute. During the while loop,
// check if the user has pressed ESC. If true, confirm
// the abort. If the abort is confirmed, clear the message
// bar and return; if the abort is not confirmed, clear
// the abort state and continue. After checking for an
// abort, move the active cell if on a worksheet or macro.
// Then update the status bar with the time remaining.

// This block uses TempActiveCell(), which creates a
// temporary XLOPER. The XLOPER contains a reference to
// a single cell on the active sheet.
// This function is part of the framework library.

boolSheet = (Excel4(xlSheetId, 0, 0) == xlretSuccess);

dtickStart = GetTickCount();

while (GetTickCount() < dtickStart + 60000L) {
    Excel(xlAbort, &xAbort, 0);
    if (xAbort.val.bool) {
        Excel(xlcAlert, &xConfirm, 2,
            TempStr(" Are you sure you want to cancel?"),
            TempNum(1));

        if (xConfirm.val.bool) {
            Excel(xlcMessage, 0, 1, TempBool(0));
            return 1;
        }
    else {
            Excel(xlAbort, 0, 1, TempBool(0));
        }
    }

    if (boolSheet)  {
        Excel(xlcSelect, 0, 1, TempActiveCell(0,(BYTE)col));
        col = (col + 1) & 3;
    }
    wsprintf(rgch," 0:%lu",
        (60000 + dtickStart - GetTickCount()) / 1000L);
    Excel(xlcMessage, 0, 2, TempBool(1), TempStr(rgch));
}
Excel(xlcMessage, 0, 1, TempBool(0));

return 1;
}
```

Macintosh Example
:Sample Code:Framework:fDance.c

```c
int pascal main(void)
{
    long dtickStart,dtickCurrent;
    XLOPER xAbort, xConfirm;
    int boolSheet;
    int col=0;
    char rgch[32];

    RememberA0();
    SetUpA4();

    InitFramework();

    boolSheet = (Excel4(xlSheetId, 0, 0) == xlretSuccess);

    GetDateTime(&dtickStart);
    GetDateTime(&dtickCurrent);

    while (dtickCurrent - dtickStart < 60) {
        Excel(xlAbort, &xAbort, 0);
        if (xAbort.val.bool) {
            Excel(xlcAlert, &xConfirm, 2,
                TempStr(" Are you sure you want to cancel"),
                TempNum(1));

            if (xConfirm.val.bool) {
                Excel(xlcMessage, 0, 1, TempBool(0));
                QuitFramework();
                RestoreA4();
                return 1;
            }
            else {
                Excel(xlAbort, 0, 1, TempBool(0));
            }
        }
        if (boolSheet) {
            Excel(xlcSelect, 0, 1, TempActiveCell(0,col));
            col = (col + 1) & 3;
        }

        GetDateTime(&dtickCurrent);
        sprintf(rgch, " 0:%lu", dtickStart + 60 - dtickCurrent);

        Excel(xlcMessage, 0, 2, TempBool(1), TempStr(rgch));
```

```
        }

        Excel(xlcMessage, 0, 1, TempBool(0));
        QuitFramework();
        RestoreA4();
    return 1;
    }
```

xlAddInManagerInfo

Provided by stand-alone DLLs that are intended to work with the Add-In Manager.
This function provides information about a stand-alone DLL (XLL) for the benefit
of the Add-In Manager.

If *pxAction* is 1, returns a string (xltypeStr) containing the long name of the DLL.

If *pxAction* is any other value, returns a #VALUE! error.

Syntax
Windows
```
LPXLOPER FAR PASCAL xlAddInManagerInfo(LPXLOPER pxAction);
```

Macintosh
```
pascal LPXLOPER xlAddInManagerInfo(LPXLOPER pxAction);
```

pxAction (xltypeInt or xltypeNum) The information that is needed.

Windows Example
\SAMPLE\FRAMEWRK\GENERIC.C

```
LPXLOPER FAR PASCAL __export xlAddInManagerInfo(LPXLOPER xAction)
{
    static XLOPER xInfo, xIntAction;

    /*
    ** This code coerces the passed-in value to an integer.
    ** This is how the code determines what is being requested.
    ** If it receives a 1, it returns a string representing
    ** the long name. If it receives anything else, it
    ** returns a #VALUE! error.
    */

    Excel(xlCoerce, &xIntAction, 2, xAction, TempInt(xltypeInt));

    if(xIntAction.val.w == 1)    {
        xInfo.xltype = xltypeStr;
        xInfo.val.str = "\026Example Standalone DLL";
    }
```

```
        else {
            xInfo.xltype = xltypeErr;
            xInfo.val.err = xlerrValue;
        }
        return (LPXLOPER)&xInfo;
}
```

Macintosh Example
:Sample Code:Framework:xlAddInManagerInfo.c

```
LPXLOPER pascal main(LPXLOPER xAction)
{
    static XLOPER xInfo, xIntAction;
    int i,j;

    RememberA0();
    SetUpA4();
    InitFramework();

    Excel(xlCoerce, &xIntAction, 2, xAction, TempInt(xltypeInt));

    if(xIntAction.val.w == 1)    {
        xInfo.xltype = xltypeStr;
        xInfo.val.str = "\026Example Standalone DLL";
    }
    else {
        xInfo.xltype = xltypeErr;
        xInfo.val.err = xlerrValue;
    }
    return (LPXLOPER)&xInfo;
}
```

xlAutoAdd

Provided by every stand-alone DLL. This function will be called by the Add-In Manager when a stand-alone DLL (XLL) is added by the user.

Should return 1 (int).

Syntax
Windows
```
int FAR PASCAL xlAutoAdd(void);
```

Macintosh
```
pascal int xlAutoAdd(void);
```

This function has no arguments.

Remark

Use this function if there is anything your XLL needs to do when it is added by the Add-In Manager.

Windows Example

\SAMPLE\FRAMEWRK\EXAMPLE.C

```
int FAR PASCAL __export xlAutoAdd(void)
{
    // Display a dialog box indicating that
    // the XLL was successfully added
    Excel(xlcAlert, 0, 2,
        TempStr(" Thank you for adding Example.XLL!"),
        TempInt(2));
    return 1;
}
```

Macintosh Example

:Sample Code:Framework:xlAutoAdd.c

```
int pascal main(void)
(
    RememberA0();
    SetUpA4();
    InitFramework();

    // Display a dialog box indicating that
    // the XLL was successfully added
    Excel(xlcAlert, 0, 2,
        TempStr(" Thank you for adding Example!"),
        TempInt(2));

    QuitFramework();
    RestoreA4();

    return 1;
}
```

Related Function

xlAutoRemove

xlAutoClose

Provided by every stand-alone DLL. This entry point is called by Microsoft Excel when the user quits. It is also called when a Microsoft Excel macro calls UNREGISTER, giving a string argument that is the name of this XLL. Finally, this entry point will be called when the Add-In Manager is used to remove this XLL.

Must return 1 (int).

Syntax
Windows
```
int FAR PASCAL xlAutoClose(void);
```

Macintosh
```
pascal int xlAutoClose(void);
```

This function has no arguments.

Remarks
This function should:

- Remove any menus or menu items that were added in xlAutoOpen.
- Perform any necessary global cleanup.
- Delete any names that were created, especially names of exported functions. Remember that registering functions may cause some names to be created, if the fourth argument to REGISTER is present.

This function does not have to unregister the functions that were registered in xlAutoOpen. Microsoft Excel automatically does this after xlAutoClose returns.

Windows Example
\SAMPLE\FRAMEWRK\GENERIC.C

```
int FAR PASCAL __export xlAutoClose(void)
{
    int i;

    /*
    ** This block first deletes all names added by xlAutoOpen or by
    ** xlAutoRegister.
    */

    for (i = 0; i < rgFuncsRows; i++)
        Excel(xlfSetName, 0, 1, TempStr(rgFuncs[i][2]));

    return 1;
}
```

Macintosh Example

:Sample Code:Framework:xlAutoClose.c

```
int pascal main(void)
{
    int i;
    XLOPER x;

    RememberA0();
    SetUpA4();
    InitFramework();

    for (i = 0; i < rgFuncsRows; i++)
        Excel(xlfSetName, 0, 1, TempStr(rgFuncs[i][2]));

    QuitFramework();
    RestoreA4();

    return 1;
}
```

Related Function

xlAutoOpen

xlAutoFree

Provided by some DLLs. This routine is called by Microsoft Excel when DLL-managed memory needs to be freed. Inside the xlAutoFree function, callbacks into Microsoft Excel are disabled, with one exception: xlFree can be called to free Microsoft Excel allocated memory. This function receives a pointer to the XLOPER to be freed as the only argument.

This function does not return a value.

Syntax

Windows

```
void FAR PASCAL xlAutoFree(LPXLOPER pxFree);
```

Macintosh

```
pascal void xlAutoFree(LPXLOPER pxFree);
```

pxFree (LPXLOPER) A pointer to the memory to be freed.

Remarks

If the xlAutoFree function you provide looks at the xltype field of *pxFree,* remember that the xlbitDLLFree bit will still be set.

Windows   In Windows, xlStack, xlEnableXLMsgs, and xlDisableXLMsgs can also be called.

Windows Example

\SAMPLE\EXAMPLE\EXAMPLE.C

```
void FAR PASCAL __export xlAutoFree(LPXLOPER pxFree)
{
    GlobalUnlock(hArray);
    GlobalFree(hArray);
    return;
}
```

Macintosh Example

:Sample Code:Examples:xlAutoFree.c

```
int pascal main(LPXLOPER px)
{
    Handle h;

    RememberA0();
    SetUpA4();

    h = RecoverHandle(px->val.str);
    HUnlock(h);
    DisposHandle(h);

    RestoreA4();

    return 1;
}
```

xlAutoOpen

Provided by every stand-alone DLL. The only thing Microsoft Excel does when the user opens an XLL file is call the XLL's xlAutoOpen function.

The xlAutoOpen function should:

- Register all the functions you want to make available while this XLL is open.
- Add any menus or menu items that this XLL supports.
- Perform any other initialization that you need.

Must return 1 (int).

Syntax

Windows

```
int FAR PASCAL xlAutoOpen(void);
```

Macintosh

```
pascal int xlAutoOpen(void);
```

This function has no arguments.

Remarks

This function is called by Microsoft Excel whenever the XLL is opened, either by choosing Open from the File menu, or because the XLL is in the Excel startup directory. This function is registered but not called if an XLL is opened with OPEN. It is also called when a macro calls REGISTER with the name of this DLL as the only argument.

Examples

For a Windows example of this function, see the code for the xlAutoOpen function in GENERIC.C in the FRAMEWRK directory. For a Macintosh example, see the file xlAutoOpen.c in the Framework folder.

Related Functions

xlAutoClose, xlAutoRegister

xlAutoRegister

Provided by some stand-alone DLLs (XLLs). This entry point is called by Microsoft Excel when a REGISTER or CALL statement tries to register a function without specifying the *type_text* argument. If that happens, Microsoft Excel calls xlAutoRegister, passing the name of the function that the user tried to register. xlAutoRegister should use the normal xlRegister function to register the function; but, this time, it must specify the *type_text* argument. This function is required only if the DLL wants to support registering its individual entry points automatically.

If the function name is unknown, this function returns a #VALUE! error (xltypeErr). Otherwise, it returns whatever REGISTER returned (xltypeNum).

Syntax

Windows

```
LPXLOPER FAR PASCAL xlAutoRegister(LPXLOPER pxName);
```

Macintosh

```
pascal LPXLOPER xlAutoRegister(LPXLOPER pxName);
```

pxName (xltypeStr) The name of the function that needs to be registered. Not case-sensitive.

Windows Example

\SAMPLE\FRAMEWRK\GENERIC.C

```
LPXLOPER FAR PASCAL __export xlAutoRegister(LPXLOPER pxName)
{
    static XLOPER xDLL, xRegId;
    int i;

    // This block first initializes xRegId to a
    // #VALUE! error.   This is done in case a function
    // is not found to register.    Next, the code loops
    // through the functions in rgFuncs[]     and uses
    // lpstricmp to determine if the current row in
    // rgFuncs[] represents the function that needs
    // to be registered.    When it finds the proper row,
    // the function is registered and the    register ID
    // is returned to Microsoft Excel. If no matching
    // function is found, an xRegId is returned
    // containing a #VALUE! error.

    xRegId.xltype = xltypeErr;
    xRegId.val.err = xlerrValue;

    for (i = 0; i < rgFuncsRows; i++) {
        if (!lpstricmp(rgFuncs[i][0], pxName->val.str))  {
            Excel(xlGetName, &xDLL, 0);

            Excel(xlfRegister, 0, 8,
                (LPXLOPER)&xDLL,
                (LPXLOPER)TempStr(rgFuncs[i][0]),
                (LPXLOPER)TempStr(rgFuncs[i][1]),
                (LPXLOPER)TempStr(rgFuncs[i][2]),
                (LPXLOPER)TempStr(rgFuncs[i][3]),
                (LPXLOPER)TempStr(rgFuncs[i][4]),
                (LPXLOPER)TempStr(rgFuncs[i][5]),
                (LPXLOPER)TempStr(rgFuncs[i][6]));

            /* Free the XLL filename */
            Excel(xlFree, 0, 1, (LPXLOPER)&xDLL);
```

```
            return (LPXLOPER)&xRegId;
        }
    }

    return (LPXLOPER)&xRegId;
}
```

Macintosh Example

:Sample Code:Framework:xlAutoRegister.c

```
LPXLOPER pascal main(LPXLOPER pxName)
{
    static XLOPER xDLL, xArgs[7], xRegId;
    int i, j;

    RememberA0();
    SetUpA4();
    InitFramework();

    xRegId.xltype = xltypeErr;
    xRegId.val.err = xlerrValue;

    for (i = 0; i < rgFuncsRows; i++)    {
        if (!lpstricmp(rgFuncs[i][0], pxName->val.str)) {
            Excel(xlGetName, &xDLL, 0);

            Excel(xlfRegister, 0, 8,
                    (LPXLOPER)&xDLL,
                    (LPXLOPER)TempStr(rgFuncs[i][0]),
                    (LPXLOPER)TempStr(rgFuncs[i][1]),
                    (LPXLOPER)TempStr(rgFuncs[i][2]),
                    (LPXLOPER)TempStr(rgFuncs[i][3]),
                    (LPXLOPER)TempStr(rgFuncs[i][4]),
                    (LPXLOPER)TempStr(rgFuncs[i][5]),
                    (LPXLOPER)TempStr(rgFuncs[i][6]));

            /** Free XLL name **/
            Excel(xlFree, 0, 1, (LPXLOPER)&xDLL);

            return (LPXLOPER)&xRegId;
        }
    }


    QuitFramework();
    RestoreA4();

    return (LPXLOPER)&xRegId;
}
```

Related Function

xlAutoOpen

xlAutoRemove

Provided by every stand-alone DLL (XLL). This function is called by the Add-In Manager when a stand-alone DLL is removed by the user.

Must return 1 (int).

Syntax

Windows

```
int FAR PASCAL xlAutoRemove(void);
```

Macintosh

```
pascal int xlAutoRemove(void);
```

This function has no arguments.

Remark

Use this function if your XLL needs to complete any task when it is removed by the Add-In Manager.

Windows Example

\SAMPLE\FRAMEWRK\GENERIC.C

```
int FAR PASCAL __export xlAutoRemove(void)
{
    /*
     * Display a dialog box indicating that
     * the XLL was successfully removed
     */
    Excel(xlcAlert, 0, 2,
        TempStr(" Thank you for removing Example.XLL!"),
        TempInt(2));
    return 1;
}
```

Macintosh Example

:Sample Code:Framework:xlAutoRemove.c

```
int pascal main(void)
(
    RememberA0();
    SetUpA4();
    InitFramework();

    // Display a dialog box indicating that
    // the XLL was successfully removed
    Excel(xlcAlert, 0, 2,
        TempStr(" Thank you for removing Example!"),
        TempInt(2));

    QuitFramework();
    RestoreA4();

    return 1;
}
```

Related Function

xlAutoAdd

xlCoerce

Called from a DLL. This function converts one type of XLOPER to another, or looks up cell values on a sheet.

Returns the coerced value.

Syntax

```
Excel4(xlCoerce, LPXLOPER pxRes, 2, LPXLOPER pxSource,
LPXLOPER pxDestType);
```

pxSource The source XLOPER that needs to be converted. May be a reference if you want to look up cell values.

pxDestType (xltypeInt) A bit mask of which types you are willing to accept. You should use the bitwise OR operator (|) to specify multiple possible types. If this argument is omitted, it is assumed that you want to convert a reference to any nonreference type (this is handy for looking up cell values). This argument is optional.

Windows Example

\SAMPLE\EXAMPLE\EXAMPLE.C

```c
short int FAR PASCAL __export xlCoerceExample(short int iVal)
{
    XLOPER xStr, xInt, xDestType;

    xInt.xltype = xltypeInt;
    xInt.val.w = iVal;

    xDestType.xltype = xltypeInt;
    xDestType.val.w = xltypeStr;

    Excel4(xlCoerce, &xStr, 2, (LPXLOPER)&xInt,
        (LPXLOPER)&xDestType);

    Excel4(xlcAlert, 0, 1, (LPXLOPER)&xStr);
    Excel4(xlFree, 0, 1, (LPXLOPER)&xStr);

    return 1;
}
```

Macintosh Example

:Sample Code:Examples:XlCoerceExample.c

```c
short int pascal main(short int iVal)
{
    XLOPER xStr, xInt, xDestType;
    RememberA0();
    SetUpA4();
    InitFramework();

    xInt.xltype = xltypeInt;
    xInt.val.w = iVal;

    xDestType.xltype = xltypeInt;
    xDestType.val.w = xltypeStr;

    Excel4(xlCoerce, &xStr, 2, (LPXLOPER)&xInt,
        (LPXLOPER)&xDestType);

    Excel4(xlcAlert, 0, 1, (LPXLOPER)&xStr);
    Excel4(xlFree, 0, 1, (LPXLOPER)&xStr);

    QuitFramework();
    RestoreA4();

    return 1;
}
```

Related Function

xlSet

xlDefineBinaryName

Called from a DLL. Used to allocate persistent storage for a bigdata XLOPER. Data with a defined binary name is saved with the workbook, and can be accessed by name at any time.

Syntax

```
Excel4(xlDefineBinaryName, 0, 2, LPXLOPER pxName, LPXLOPER pxData);
```

pxName String XLOPER specifying the name of the data.

pxData Bigdata XLOPER specifying the data. When you call this function, the **lpbData** member of the bigdata structure should point to the data whose name is to be defined, and the **cbData** member should contain the length of the data in bytes.

If the *pxData* argument is not specified, the named allocation specified by *pxName* is deleted.

Remarks

There is a bug in the 16-bit Windows version of Microsoft Excel version 5.0 that affects this function (the bug does not exist on Windows NT, the Apple Macintosh version, or maintenance releases of 16-bit Windows Microsoft Excel with version numbers greater than 5.0a). When Microsoft Excel saves and reloads a workbook containing named binary data, the named data is shifted right six bytes (the first six bytes are undefined, and the last six bytes are truncated). This *only* occurs when the workbook is reloaded, so it does not affect an application that uses named data for temporary storage while a workbook is open and deletes the name before the workbook is saved.

If your application uses named data for persistent storage when the workbook is saved, you can work around this bug by using the following steps:

1. Pad your data with six extra trailing bytes when you define the name. This prevents data loss when the workbook is reloaded. You can access the allocation with the xlGetBinaryName function without problems until the workbook is saved and reloaded.

2. When the workbook is reloaded, and you access the named data with the xlGetBinaryName function, shift the pointer you receive by six bytes (add six to the pointer).

3. Delete the existing name and redefine the name using the shifted pointer (remember to add six bytes of padding at the end of the allocation). If you do not redefine the name before you save the workbook, the named data will be shifted again (for a total of *12* bytes) the next time the workbook is loaded.

Windows Example

This example accepts a name, a pointer to data, and the length of the data. It uses the xlDefineBinaryName function to allocate memory for the data, and returns the result of the Excel4 function (success or failure).

```
int FAR PASCAL __export xlDefineBinaryNameExample(LPSTR lpszName,
    LPBYTE lpbData, long cbData)
{
    char stBuf[255];
    XLOPER xName, xData;

    lstrcpy(stBuf + 1, lpszName);
    stBuf[0] = lstrlen(lpszName);

    xName.xltype = xltypeStr;
    xName.val.str = stBuf;

    xData.xltype = xltypeBigData;
    xData.val.bigdata.h.lpbData = lpbData;
    xData.val.bigdata.cbData = cbData;

    return Excel4(xlDefineBinaryName, 0, 2, (LPXLOPER)&xName,
        (LPXLOPER)&xData);
}
```

Macintosh Example

```
int pascal xlDefineBinaryNameExample(char *lpszName,
    unsigned char *lpbData, long cbData)
{
    int iRet;
    char szBuf[255];
    XLOPER xName, xData;

    RememberA0();
    SetUpA4();
    InitFramework();

    strcpy(szBuf + 1, lpszName);
    szBuf[0] = strlen(lpszName);
```

```
xName.xltype = xltypeStr;
xName.val.str = szBuf;

xData.xltype = xltypeBigData;
xData.val.bigdata.h.lpbData = lpbData;
xData.val.bigdata.cbData = cbData;

iRet = Excel4(xlDefineBinaryName, 0, 2,
    (LPXLOPER)&xName, (LPXLOPER)&xData);

QuitFramework();
RestoreA4();
return iRet;
}
```

Related Function
xlGetBinaryName

xlDisableXLMsgs

Windows Only   Called from a DLL. This function restores the DLL's context. It should be called after you have called xlEnableXLMsgs, when the portions of code that may yield to Microsoft Excel have been executed.

This function does not return a value.

Syntax
```
Excel4(xlDisableXLMsgs, 0, 0);
```

This function has no arguments.

Remark
This function is very fast and adds little overhead to the DLL.

Examples
For a Windows example of this function, see the code for the fShowDialog function in GENERIC.C in the FRAMEWRK directory.

Related Function
xlEnableXLMsgs

xlEnableXLMsgs

Windows Only Called from a DLL. This function restores Microsoft Excel's context. It should be called before any operations that may yield control to Microsoft Excel. This puts Microsoft Excel into a state in which it is ready to receive messages and use the math coprocessor.

This function does not return a value.

Syntax

```
Excel4(xlEnableXLMsgs, 0, 0);
```

This function has no arguments.

Remark

This function is very fast and adds little overhead to the DLL.

Examples

For a Windows example of this function, see the code for the fShowDialog function in GENERIC.C in the FRAMEWRK directory.

Related Function

xlDisableXLMsgs

xlFree

Called from a DLL. Allows Microsoft Excel to free auxiliary memory associated with an XLOPER. xlFree frees the auxiliary memory and resets the pointer to NULL but does not destroy other parts of the XLOPER.

This function does not return a value.

Syntax

```
Excel4(xlFree, 0, n, LPXLOPER px, ...)
```

px, ... One or more XLOPERs to free.

Remark

You must free every XLOPER that you get as a return value from Excel4 or
Excel4v if that XLOPER uses auxiliary memory (if it contains pointers). It is
always safe to free XLOPERs even if they did not use auxiliary memory, as long as
you got them from Excel4.

Windows Example

This example calls GET.WORKSPACE(1) to return (as a string) the platform on
which Microsoft Excel is currently running. The code copies this returned string
into a buffer for later use. The standard `strcpy` function is not used to copy the
string to the buffer because `strcpy` expects a null-terminated string and the
returned value is a byte-counted string. The code places the buffer back into the
XLOPER for later use with the Excel function. Finally, the code displays the string
in an alert box.

\SAMPLE\EXAMPLE\EXAMPLE.C

```
short int FAR PASCAL __export xlFreeExample(void)
{
    XLOPER xRes, xInt;
    char buffer[10];
    int i, len;

    xInt.xltype = xltypeInt;
    xInt.val.w = 1;
    Excel(xlfGetWorkspace, (LPXLOPER)&xRes, 1, (LPXLOPER)&xInt);
    len = (BYTE)xRes.val.str[0];
    for(i = 0; i <= len; i++)
        buffer[i] = xRes.val.str[i];
    Excel(xlFree, 0, 1, (LPXLOPER)&xRes);
    xRes.val.str = buffer;

    Excel(xlcAlert, 0, 1, (LPXLOPER)&xRes);
    return 1;
}
```

Macintosh Example

:Sample Code:Examples:xlFreeExample.c

```
short int pascal main(void)
(
    XLOPER xRes, xInt;
    char buffer[10];
    int i, len;

    RememberA0();
    SetUpA4();
    InitFramework();

    xInt.xltype = xltypeInt;
    xInt.val.w = 1;
    Excel(xlfGetWorkspace, (LPXLOPER)&xRes, 1, (LPXLOPER)&xInt);
    len = (char)xRes.val.str[0];
    for(i = 0; i <= len; i++)
        buffer[i] = xRes.val.str[i];
    Excel(xlFree, 0, 1, (LPXLOPER)&xRes);
    xRes.val.str = buffer;

    Excel(xlcAlert, 0, 1, (LPXLOPER)&xRes);

    QuitFramework();
    RestoreA4();

    return 1;
}
```

xlGetBinaryName

Called from a DLL. Used to return a handle for data saved by the
xlDefineBinaryName function. Data with a defined binary name is saved with the
workbook, and can be accessed by name at any time.

Syntax

```
Excel4(xlGetBinaryName, LPXLOPER pxRes, 1, LPXLOPER pxName);
```

pxRes Bigdata XLOPER. When the function returns, the **hdata** member of the
XLOPER contains a handle for the named data.

pxName String XLOPER specifying the name of the data.

Microsoft Excel owns the memory handle returned in **hdata**. In Microsoft Windows, the handle is a global memory handle (allocated by the GlobalAlloc function). On the Apple Macintosh, the handle is a standard memory handle (returned by the NewHandle function). You can lock and dereference the handle, but you must not reallocate or free the handle. If you need to change the size of the named allocation, you must delete the existing name and create a new one.

Remarks

There is a bug in the 16-bit Windows version of Microsoft Excel version 5.0 that affects this function (the bug does not exist on Windows NT, the Apple Macintosh version, or maintenance releases of 16-bit Windows Microsoft Excel with version numbers greater than 5.0a). When Microsoft Excel saves and reloads a workbook containing named binary data, the named data is shifted right six bytes (the first six bytes are undefined, and the last six bytes are truncated). This *only* occurs when the workbook is reloaded, so it does not affect an application that uses named data for temporary storage while a workbook is open and deletes the name before the workbook is saved.

If your application uses named data for persistent storage when the workbook is saved, you can work around this bug by using the following steps:

1. Pad your data with six extra trailing bytes when you define the name. This prevents data loss when the workbook is reloaded. You can access the allocation with the xlGetBinaryName function without problems until the workbook is saved and reloaded.

2. When the workbook is reloaded, and you access the named data with the xlGetBinaryName function, shift the pointer you receive by six bytes (add six to the pointer).

3. Delete the existing name and redefine the name using the shifted pointer (remember to add six bytes of padding at the end of the allocation). If you do not redefine the name before you save the workbook, the named data will be shifted again (for a total of *12* bytes) the next time the workbook is loaded.

Windows Example

This example accepts a name and the address of a pointer. It uses the xlGetBinaryName function to retrieve a handle for the named data, and then locks the handle and returns the locked pointer at the passed-in address.

```
int FAR PASCAL __export xlGetBinaryNameExample(LPSTR lpszName,
    LPBYTE FAR *lpbData)
{
    int iRet;
    char stBuf[255];
    XLOPER xName, xData;

    lstrcpy(stBuf + 1, lpszName);
    stBuf[0] = lstrlen(lpszName);

    xName.xltype = xltypeStr;
    xName.val.str = stBuf;

    if ((iRet = Excel4(xlGetBinaryName, (LPXLOPER)&xData, 1,
            (LPXLOPER)&xName)) !=xlretSuccess)
        return iRet;
    *lpbData = GlobalLock(xData.val.bigdata.h.hdata);

    return iRet;
}
```

Macintosh Example

This example accepts a name and the address of a pointer. It uses the xlGetBinaryName function to retrieve a handle for the named data, and returns the handle at the passed-in address.

```
int pascal xlGetBinaryNameExample(char *lpszName, Handle *phData)
{
    int iRet;
    char szBuf[255];
    XLOPER xName, xData;

    RememberA0();
    SetUpA4();
    InitFramework();

    strcpy(szBuf + 1, lpszName);
    szBuf[0] = strlen(lpszName);

    xName.xltype = xltypeStr;
    xName.val.str = szBuf;
```

```
    if ((iRet = Excel4(xlGetBinaryName,
            (LPXLOPER)&xData, 1, (LPXLOPER)&xName)) != xlretSuccess)
        phData = NULL;
    else
        *phData = xData.val.bigdata.h.hdata;

    QuitFramework();
    RestoreA4();
    return iRet;
}
```

Related Function
xlDefineBinaryName

xlGetHwnd

Windows Only   Called from a DLL. This function returns the window handle of the top-level Microsoft Excel window.

Contains the window handle (xltypeInt) in the val.w field.

Syntax
```
Excel4(xlGetHwnd, LPXLOPER pxRes, 0);
```

This function has no arguments.

Remark
This function is useful for writing Windows API code.

Windows Example
For a Windows example of this function, see the code for the fShowDialog function in GENERIC.C in the FRAMEWRK directory.

Related Function
xlGetInst

xlGetInst

Windows Only   Called from a DLL. This function returns the instance handle of the instance of Microsoft Excel that is currently calling a DLL.

The instance handle (xltypeInt) will be in the val.w field.

Syntax

```
Excel4(xlGetInst, LPXLOPER pxRes, 0);
```

This function has no arguments.

Remark

This function can be used to distinguish between multiple running instances of Microsoft Excel that are calling the DLL.

Windows Example

The following example compares the instance of the last copy of Microsoft Excel that called it to the current copy of Microsoft Excel that called it. If they are the same, it returns 1; if not, it returns 0.

\SAMPLE\EXAMPLE\EXAMPLE.C

```
short int FAR PASCAL __export xlGetInstExample(void)
{
    XLOPER xRes;
    static HANDLE hOld = 0;
    int iRet;

    Excel4(xlGetInst, (LPXLOPER)&xRes, 0);

    if((unsigned int)xRes.val.w != hOld)
        iRet = 0;
    else
        iRet = 1;

    hOld = xRes.val.w;

    return iRet;
}
```

Related Function

xlGetHwnd

xlGetName

Called from a DLL. Use this function to find the full path and filename of the DLL in the form of a string.

Returns the path and filename (xltypeStr).

Syntax

```
Excel4(xlGetName, LPXLOPER pxRes, 0);
```

This function has no arguments.

Remark

Macintosh On the Macintosh, this function may return xltypeNil if the DLL encountered low memory conditions at the time it was registered.

Windows Example

\SAMPLE\EXAMPLE\EXAMPLE.C

```
short int FAR PASCAL __export xlGetNameExample(void)
{
    XLOPER xRes;

    Excel4(xlGetName, (LPXLOPER)&xRes, 0);
    Excel4(xlcAlert, 0, 1, (LPXLOPER)&xRes);
    Excel4(xlFree, 0, 1, (LPXLOPER)&xRes);
    return 1;
}
```

Macintosh Example

:Sample Code:Examples:xlGetNameExample.c

```
short int pascal main(void)
{
    XLOPER xRes;

    RememberA0();
    SetUpA4();
    InitFramework();

    Excel4(xlGetName, (LPXLOPER)&xRes, 0);

    Excel4(xlcAlert, 0, 1, (LPXLOPER)&xRes);

    Excel4(xlFree, 0, 1, (LPXLOPER)&xRes);

    QuitFramework();
    RestoreA4();

    return 1;
}
```

xlSet

Called from a DLL. This function puts constant values into cells or ranges very quickly.

If successful, returns TRUE (xltypeBool). If unsuccessful, returns FALSE.

Syntax

```
Excel4(xlSet, LPXLOPER pxRes, 2, LPXLOPER pxReference,
LPXLOPER pxValue);
```

pxReference (xltypeRef or xltypeSRef) A rectangular reference describing the target cell or cells. The reference must describe adjacent cells.

pxValue The value to put in the cell or cells. For more information, see the following "Remarks" section.

Remarks

pxValue Argument

pxValue can either be a value or an array. If it is a value, the entire destination range is filled with that value. If it is an array (xltypeMulti), the elements of the array are put into the corresponding locations in the rectangle.

If you use a horizontal array for the second argument, it is duplicated down to fill the entire rectangle. If you use a vertical array, it is duplicated right to fill the entire rectangle. If you use a rectangular array, and it is too small for the rectangular range you want to put it in, that range is padded with #N/As.

To clear an element of the destination rectangle, use an xltypeNil XLOPER in the source array. To clear the entire destination rectangle, omit the second argument.

Restrictions

xlSet cannot be undone. In addition, it destroys any undo information that may have been available before.

xlSet can put only constants, not formulas, into cells.

xlSet behaves as a Class 3 command-equivalent function; that is, it is available only inside a DLL when the DLL is called from an object, macro, menu, toolbar, shortcut key, or the Run button in the Macro dialog box (accessed from the Tools menu).

Windows Example

The following example fills B205:B206 with the value that was passed in from a macro.

\SAMPLE\EXAMPLE\EXAMPLE.C

```
short int FAR PASCAL __export xlSetExample(short int iVal)
{
    XLOPER xRef, xValue;

    xRef.xltype = xltypeSRef;
    xRef.val.sref.count = 1;
    xRef.val.sref.ref.rwFirst = 204;
    xRef.val.sref.ref.rwLast = 205;
    xRef.val.sref.ref.colFirst = 1;
    xRef.val.sref.ref.colLast = 1;
    xValue.xltype = xltypeInt;
    xValue.val.w = iVal;

    Excel4(xlSet, 0, 2, (LPXLOPER)&xRef, (LPXLOPER)&xValue);
    return 1;
}
```

Macintosh Example

:Sample Code:Examples:xlSetExample.c

```
short int pascal main(short int iVal)
{
    XLOPER xRef, xValue;

    RememberA0();
    SetUpA4();
    InitFramework();

    xRef.xltype = xltypeSRef;
    xRef.val.sref.count = 1;
    xRef.val.sref.ref.rwFirst = 204;
    xRef.val.sref.ref.rwLast = 205;
    xRef.val.sref.ref.colFirst = 1;
    xRef.val.sref.ref.colLast = 1;
    xValue.xltype = xltypeInt;
    xValue.val.w = iVal;
    debugPrintf("iVal : %d\r", iVal);
    Excel4(xlSet, 0, 2, (LPXLOPER)&xRef, (LPXLOPER)&xValue);
    Excel4(xlcAlert, 0, 1, (LPXLOPER)&xRef);
    Excel4(xlFree, 0, 0, (LPXLOPER)&xRef);

    QuitFramework();
    RestoreA4();

    return 1;
}
```

Related Function

xlCoerce

xlSheetId

Called from a DLL. This function finds the sheet ID of a named sheet in order to construct external references.

Returns the sheet ID in *pxRes->val.mref.idSheet.*

Syntax

```
Excel4(xlSheetId, LPXLOPER pxRes, 1, LPXLOPER pxSheetName);
```

pxSheetName (xltypeStr) The name of the book and sheet you want to find out about. This argument is optional; if omitted, xlSheetId returns the sheet ID of the active (front) sheet.

Remark

The sheet must be open to use this function. There is no way to construct a reference to an unopened sheet from DLLs. For more information about using xlSheetId to construct references, see "Using Reference XLOPERs," on page 17.

Windows Example

\SAMPLE\EXAMPLE\EXAMPLE.C

```
short int FAR PASCAL __export xlSheetIdExample(void)
{
    XLOPER xSheetName, xRes;

    xSheetName.xltype = xltypeStr;
    xSheetName.val.str = "\021[BOOK1.XLS]Sheet1"";
    Excel4(xlSheetId, (LPXLOPER)&xRes, 1, (LPXLOPER)&xSheetName);
    Excel4(xlcAlert, 0, 1, TempNum(xRes.val.mref.idSheet));
    Excel4(xlFree, 0, 1, (LPXLOPER)&xRes);
    return 1;
}
```

Macintosh Example

:Sample Code:Examples:xlSheetIdExample.c

```
short int pascal main(void)
(
    XLOPER xSheetName, xRes;

    RememberA0();
    SetUpA4();
    InitFramework();

    xSheetName.xltype = xltypeStr;
    xSheetName.val.str = "\021[BOOK1.XLS]Sheet1";
    Excel4(xlSheetId, (LPXLOPER)&xRes, 1, (LPXLOPER)&xSheetName);
    Excel4(xlcAlert, 0, 1, TempNum(xRes.val.mref.idSheet));
    Excel4(xlFree, 0, 1, (LPXLOPER)&xRes);

    QuitFramework();
    RestoreA4();

    return 1;
}
```

Related Functions

xlSheetNm

xlSheetNm

Called from a DLL.

Returns the name of the sheet (xltypeStr), given an external reference.

Syntax

```
Excel4(xlSheetNm, LPXLOPER pxRes, 1, LPXLOPER pxExtref);
```

pxExtref (xltypeRef) An external reference to the sheet whose name you want.

Remark

This function returns the name of the sheet in the form "[Book1]Sheet1".

Windows Example

The following example returns the name of the sheet from which the function was called.

\SAMPLE\EXAMPLE\EXAMPLE.C

```
short int FAR PASCAL __export xlSheetNmExample(void)
{
    XLOPER xRes, xSheetName;

    Excel4(xlfCaller, (LPXLOPER)&xRes, 0);
    Excel4(xlSheetNm, (LPXLOPER)&xSheetName, 1, (LPXLOPER)&xRes);
    Excel4(xlcAlert, 0, 1, (LPXLOPER)&xSheetName);
    Excel4(xlFree, 0, 1, (LPXLOPER)&xSheetName);
    return 1;
}
```

Macintosh Example

:Sample Code:Examples:xlSheetNmExample.c

```
short int pascal main(void)
{
    XLOPER xRes, xSheetName;

    RememberA0();
    SetUpA4();
    InitFramework();

    Excel4(xlfCaller, (LPXLOPER)&xRes, 0);
    Excel4(xlSheetNm, (LPXLOPER)&xSheetName, 1, (LPXLOPER)&xRes);
    Excel4(xlcAlert, 0, 1, (LPXLOPER)&xSheetName);
    Excel4(xlFree, 0, 1, (LPXLOPER)&xSheetName);

    QuitFramework();
    RestoreA4();

    return 1;
}
```

Related Function

xlSheetId

xlStack

Windows Only   Called from a DLL. This function checks the amount of space left on the stack.

Returns the number of bytes (xltypeInt) remaining on the stack.

Syntax

```
Excel4(xlStack, LPXLOPER pxRes, 0);
```

This function has no arguments.

Remarks

Microsoft Excel has a limited amount of space on the stack, and you should take care not to overrun this space. First, never put large data structures on the stack. Make as many local variables as possible static. Avoid calling functions recursively; that will quickly fill up the stack.

If you suspect that you are overrunning the stack, call this function frequently to see how much stack space is left.

If you desperately need more stack space than the 12K or so that you normally get, you can use the Windows functions SwitchStackTo and SwitchStackBack.

Windows Example

The following example displays an alert message containing the amount of stack space left.

\SAMPLE\EXAMPLE\EXAMPLE.C

```
short int FAR PASCAL __export xlStackExample(void)
{
    XLOPER xRes;

    Excel4(xlStack, (LPXLOPER)&xRes, 0);
    Excel4(xlcAlert, 0, 1, (LPXLOPER)&xRes);
    return 1;
}
```

xlUDF

Calls a user-defined function. This function allows you to call macro language functions from DLLs.

Returns the return value from the user-defined function.

Syntax

```
Excel4(xlUDF, LPXLOPER pxRes, int iCount, LPXLOPER pxRef,
LPXLOPER pxArg1, ...);
```

pxRef (xltypeRef or xltypeSRef) The reference of the function you want to call. If it is named, you can use xlfEvaluate to look up the name first.

pxArg1, ... Zero or more arguments to the user defined function.

Windows Example

The following example runs TestMacro on sheet Macro1 in BOOK1.XLS. Make
sure that the macro is on a sheet named Macro1.

\SAMPLE\EXAMPLE\EXAMPLE.C

```
short int FAR PASCAL __export xlUDFExample(void)
{
    XLOPER xMacroName, xMacroRef, xRes;

    xMacroName.xltype = xltypeStr;
    xMacroName.val.str = "\033[BOOK1.XLS]Macro1!TestMacro";
    Excel4(xlfEvaluate, (LPXLOPER)&xMacroRef, 1,
        (LPXLOPER)&xMacroName);
    Excel4(xlUDF, (LPXLOPER)&xRes, 1, (LPXLOPER)&xMacroRef);
    return 1;
}
```

Macintosh Example

:Sample Code:Examples:xlUDFExample.c

```
short int pascal main(void)
{
    XLOPER xMacroName, xMacroRef, xRes;

    RememberA0();
    SetUpA4();
    InitFramework();

    xMacroName.xltype = xltypeStr;
    xMacroName.val.str = "\033[BOOK1.XLS]Macro1!TestMacro";
    Excel4(xlfEvaluate, (LPXLOPER)&xMacroRef, 1,
        (LPXLOPER)&xMacroName);
    Excel4(xlUDF, (LPXLOPER)&xRes, 1, (LPXLOPER)&xMacroRef);

    QuitFramework();
    RestoreA4();

    return 1;
}
```

C H A P T E R   3

File Format

The binary interchange file format (BIFF) is the file format in which Microsoft Excel workbooks are saved on disk. Microsoft Excel version 5.0 uses compound files; this is the OLE 2 implementation of the Structured Storage Model standard. For more information on this technology, see the *OLE 2 Programmer's Reference, Volume One,* and *Inside OLE 2,* both published by Microsoft Press® and available from your local bookstore.

The Workbook Compound File

An OLE 2 compound file is essentially "a file system within a file." The compound file contains a hierarchical system of storages and streams. A storage is analogous to a directory, and a stream is analogous to a file in a directory. Each Microsoft Excel version 5.0 workbook is stored in a compound file, an example of which is shown in the following illustration. This file is a workbook that contains three sheets: a worksheet with a PivotTable, a Visual Basic module, and a chart.

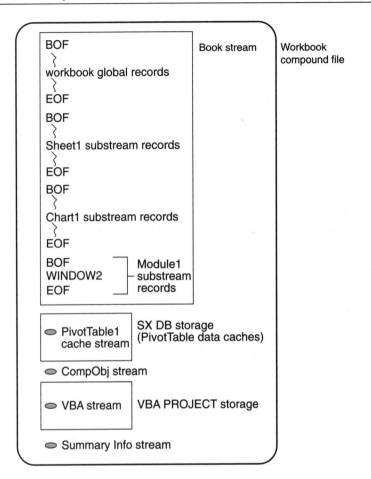

If a workbook contains embedded objects, then the file will also contain storages written by the applications that created the objects. The PivotTable data cache storage and VBA PROJECT storage are not documented. The CompObj stream contains OLE 2 component object data, and the Summary Info stream contains the standardized file summary information such as title, subject, author, and so on.

The Book stream begins with a BOF record, and then contains workbook global records up to the first EOF. The workbook global section contains one BOUNDSHEET record for each sheet in the workbook. You can use the dt field (document type), the lbPlyPos field (stream position of the BOF record for the sheet), and the cch/rgch fields (sheet name as a byte-counted string) to quickly read selected sheets in the workbook.

Each sheet in the workbook is stored after the workbook global section, beginning with BOF and ending with EOF. If you read the file in a continuous stream (instead of using the BOUNDSHEET records), you can test the dt field of each BOF record to determine the sheet type.

Other Microsoft Excel File Formats

Although chart records are written as part of the Book stream, they are documented in Chapter 4. Microsoft Excel creates several other files, some of which are documented in this book. The version 5.0 workspace file is documented in Chapter 5. The INI file (or preferences file) is documented in Appendix B. The toolbar file (.XLB extension in Microsoft Windows) is not documented.

This book contains BIFF documentation for Microsoft Excel version 5.0 only. For earlier versions of BIFF documentation, obtain a copy of the First Edition of this book. Both editions of this book are available on the Development Library (published by the Microsoft Developer Network). The Library is a CD-based reference source for Windows-based developers. For more information about this service, contact Microsoft Developer Network via Internet email (IP address devnetwk@microsoft.com), via Compuserve (address >INTERNET:devnetwk@microsoft.com), or call (800) 759-5474.

BIFF Record Information

Although different BIFF record types contain different information, every record has the same basic format. All BIFF records consist of the following three sections:

Record Number This 16-bit word identifies the record. The hexadecimal value of the record number is included in parentheses in the heading of the record description. For example, the EOF record's heading appears in this chapter as "EOF: End of File (0Ah)."

Record Data Length This 16-bit word equals the length of the following record data, in bytes. The record length depends on the type of data in the record. For example, the EOF record is always the same length, while a FORMULA record varies in length depending on the length of the formula itself.

Record Data This is the portion of the record containing the actual data that describes the formula, window, object, and so on.

The format for all BIFF records is described in the following table.

Offset	Length (bytes)	Contents
0	2	Record number
2	2	Record data length
4	Variable	Record data

A BIFF record has a length limit of 2084 bytes, including the record type and record length fields. Therefore, the record data field must be no longer than 2080 bytes. A large data object has a parent record and then one or more CONTINUE records to store the data. For example, embedded bitmapped graphic objects often use a parent IMDATA record and several CONTINUE records.

If a field (or a bit in a field) is marked "Reserved," then your application should treat the field or bit as a "don't-care" when you read or write the BIFF file. If a field (or a bit in a field) is marked "Reserved; must be zero," then you must write zeros to the field or bit when you write a BIFF file.

Byte Swapping

Microsoft Excel BIFF files are transportable across the MS-DOS/Windows (Intel® 80x86), and Apple Macintosh (Motorola® 680x0) operating systems, among others. To support transportability, Microsoft Excel writes BIFF files in the 80x86 format, where the low-order byte of the word appears first in the file, followed by the high-order byte. For example, the BOF record consists of six 16-bit words:

```
0809 0008 0500 0005 096C 07C9
```

and it appears in a BIFF file as:

```
09 08 08 00 00 05 05 00 6C 09 C9 07
```

Whenever Microsoft Excel for the Macintosh reads or writes a BIFF file, it calls a function that swaps the high- and low-order bytes of every 16-bit word in every record in the file. For 32-bit longs, the bytes in each 16-bit word are swapped first, and then the two 16-bit words are swapped. Be sure to include a byte-swap function in any custom BIFF utility you write for the Macintosh.

BIFF Versions

You can determine the BIFF version (and infer the Microsoft Excel version that wrote the file) by testing the high-order byte of the record number of the BOF record. For example, the first BOF record in a BIFF5 workbook file is:

09 08 08 00 00 05 05 00 6C 09 C9 07 (08h in high-order byte)

while the BOF record in a BIFF4 chart file is:

09 04 06 00 00 00 20 00 00 00 (04h in high-order byte)

In previous BIFF versions, some records (other than the BOF record) contained version information in the high-order byte of the record number. This proved to be redundant, so for BIFF5, only the high-order byte of the record number of the BOF record is significant.

Indexing in BIFF Records

In BIFF files, rows and columns are always stored zero-based, rather than with an offset of one as they appear in a sheet. For example, cell A1 is stored as row 0 (rw = 00h), column 0 (col = 00h); cell B3 is row 2 (rw = 02h), column 1 (col = 01h), and so on.

In most cases, you can use the variable-naming conventions in this chapter to determine if a variable is zero-based. Variable names that begin with the letter i are usally indexes, which are zero-based. For example, the variable ixfe occurs in every cell record; it is a zero-based index into the table of XF records. Variable names that begin with the letter c are usually counts, which are one-based. For example, many records contain a cch, which is a count of characters in the following string.

Undefined Cells in the Sheet

To reduce file size, cells that don't contain values or formulas and aren't referenced by formulas in any other cell are considered to be undefined cells. Such undefined cells don't appear in the BIFF file.

For example, if a worksheet has a value in cell A3, and the formula =A3+A4 in cell B10, then the only defined cells on the worksheet are A3, A4, and B10. No other cells need to exist.

Using this technique, entire rows can be undefined if they have no defined cells in them. In the preceding example, only rows 3, 4, and 10 are defined, so the file contains only three ROW records.

Cell Records

The term "cell records" refers to the BIFF record types that actually contain cell data. Cell records that appear in BIFF5 files are shown in the following table.

Record	Contents
ARRAY	An array-entered formula
BLANK	An empty cell
BOOLERR	A boolean or error value
FORMULA	A cell formula, stored as parse tokens
LABEL	A string constant
NUMBER	An IEEE floating-point number
MULBLANK	Multiple empty cells (new to BIFF5)
MULRK	Multiple RK numbers (new to BIFF5)
RK	An RK number
RSTRING	Cell with character formatting
SHRFMLA	A shared formula (new to BIFF5)
STRING	A string that represents the result of a formula

Microsoft Excel stores cell records in blocks that have at most 32 rows. Each row that contains cell records has a corresponding ROW record in the block, and each block contains a DBCELL record at the end of the block. For more information about row blocks and about optimizing your code when searching for cell records, see "Finding Cell Records in BIFF Files" on page 255.

BIFF Record Order

BIFF record order has changed as the file format has evolved. The simplest way to determine BIFF record order is to create a workbook in Microsoft Excel and then use the BiffView utility to examine the record order.

BIFF Utilities

There are two BIFF utilities in the BIFF directory on the Windows disk that accompanies this book. Use the BiffView utility (BIFFVIEW.EXE, a Windows program) to examine BIFF5 workbook files. Use DUMPBIFF.EXE (an MS-DOS program) to examine the BIFF5 workspace file.

BIFF Records: Alphabetical Order

Number	**Record**	**Page**
94	LHRECORD: .WK? File Conversion Information	181
98	LPR: Sheet Was Printed Using LINE.PRINT( )	182
C1	MMS: ADDMENU/DELMENU Record Group Count	182
BE	MULBLANK: Multiple Blank Cells	183
BD	MULRK: Multiple RK Cells	183
18	NAME: Defined Name	184
1C	NOTE: Note Associated with a Cell	186
03	NUMBER: Cell Value, Floating-Point Number	187
5D	OBJ: Describes a Graphic Object	187
63	OBJPROTECT: Objects Are Protected	215
D3	OBPROJ: Visual Basic Project	215
DE	OLESIZE: Size of OLE Object	216
92	PALETTE: Color Palette Definition	216
41	PANE: Number of Panes and Their Position	216
13	PASSWORD: Protection Password	217
4D	PLS: Environment-Specific Print Record	218
0E	PRECISION: Precision	218
2B	PRINTGRIDLINES: Print Gridlines Flag	218
2A	PRINTHEADERS: Print Row/Column Labels	219
12	PROTECT: Protection Flag	219
89	PUB: Publisher	219
B9	RECIPNAME: Recipient Name	220
0F	REFMODE: Reference Mode	220
27	RIGHTMARGIN: Right Margin Measurement	220
7E	RK: Cell Value, RK Number	221
08	ROW: Describes a Row	224
D6	RSTRING: Cell with Character Formatting	225
5F	SAVERECALC: Recalculate Before Save	226
AF	SCENARIO: Scenario Data	226
AE	SCENMAN: Scenario Output Data	227
DD	SCENPROTECT: Scenario Protection	228
A0	SCL: Window Zoom Magnification	228

BIFF Records: Record Number Order

Number	Record	Page
1D	SELECTION: Current Selection	228
1E	FORMAT: Number Format	173
21	ARRAY: Array-Entered Formula	146
22	1904: 1904 Date System	145
23	EXTERNNAME: Externally Referenced Name	165
25	DEFAULTROWHEIGHT: Default Row Height	161
26	LEFTMARGIN: Left Margin Measurement	180
27	RIGHTMARGIN: Right Margin Measurement	220
28	TOPMARGIN: Top Margin Measurement	245
29	BOTTOMMARGIN: Bottom Margin Measurement	153
2A	PRINTHEADERS: Print Row/Column Labels	219
2B	PRINTGRIDLINES: Print Gridlines Flag	218
2F	FILEPASS: File Is Password-Protected	170
31	FONT: Font Description	172
36	TABLE: Data Table	244
3C	CONTINUE: Continues Long Records	155
3D	WINDOW1: Window Information	246
3E	WINDOW2: Sheet Window Information	247
40	BACKUP: Save Backup Version of the File	150
41	PANE: Number of Panes and Their Position	216
42	CODEPAGE: Default Code Page	154
4D	PLS: Environment-Specific Print Record	218
50	DCON: Data Consolidation Information	159
51	DCONREF: Data Consolidation References	160
52	DCONNAME: Data Consolidation Named References	160
55	DEFCOLWIDTH: Default Width for Columns	161
59	XCT: CRN Record Count	250
5A	CRN: Nonresident Operands	157
5B	FILESHARING: File-Sharing Information	171
5C	WRITEACCESS: Write Access User Name	248
5D	OBJ: Describes a Graphic Object	187
5E	UNCALCED: Recalculation Status	245
5F	SAVERECALC: Recalculate Before Save	226
60	TEMPLATE: Workbook Is a Template	245

Number	Record	Page
AE	SCENMAN: Scenario Output Data	227
AF	SCENARIO: Scenario Data	226
B0	SXVIEW: View Definition	242
B1	SXVD: View Fields	240
B2	SXVI: View Item	241
B4	SXIVD: Row/Column Field IDs	237
B5	SXLI: Line Item Array	237
B6	SXPI: Page Item	239
B8	DOCROUTE: Routing Slip Information	163
B9	RECIPNAME: Recipient Name	220
BC	SHRFMLA: Shared Formula	230
BD	MULRK: Multiple RK Cells	183
BE	MULBLANK: Multiple Blank Cells	183
C1	MMS: ADDMENU/DELMENU Record Group Count	182
C2	ADDMENU: Menu Addition	145
C3	DELMENU: Menu Deletion	162
C5	SXDI: Data Item	235
CD	SXSTRING: String	239
D0	SXTBL: Multiple Consolidation Source Info	239
D1	SXTBRGIITM: Page Item Name Count	240
D2	SXTBPG: Page Item Indexes	240
D3	OBPROJ: Visual Basic Project	215
D5	SXIDSTM: Stream ID	236
D6	RSTRING: Cell with Character Formatting	225
D7	DBCELL: Stream Offsets	159
DA	BOOKBOOL: Workbook Option Flag	152
DC	SXEXT: External Source Information	236
DD	SCENPROTECT: Scenario Protection	228
DE	OLESIZE: Size of OLE Object	216
DF	UDDESC: Description String for Chart Autoformat	245
E0	XF: Extended Format	250
E1	INTERFACEHDR: Beginning of User Interface Records	179
E2	INTERFACEEND: End of User Interface Records	179
E3	SXVS: View Source	243

Record Descriptions

The first two fields in every BIFF record are record number and record length. Because these fields have the same offset and size in every BIFF record, they are not documented in the following descriptions. For more information about the record number and record length fields, see "BIFF Record Information" on page 133.

1904: 1904 Date System (22h)

The 1904 record stores the date system used by Microsoft Excel.

Record Data

Offset	Name	Size	Contents
4	f1904	2	= 1 if the 1904 date system is used

ADDIN: Workbook Is an Add-in Macro (87h)

This record has no record data field. If the ADDIN record is present in the BIFF file, it signifies that the macro is an add-in macro. The ADDIN record, if present, must immediately follow the first BOF record in the Book stream.

ADDMENU: Menu Addition (C2h)

The ADDMENU record stores a menu addition. When you add a menu object (a menu bar, a menu, a menu item, or a submenu item) to the user interface, Microsoft Excel writes a group of ADDMENU records for each object. The first record stores the menu bar, the second stores the menu, the third stores the menu item, and the fourth stores the submenu item (note how this identical to the menu hierarchy in the user interface). The number of records in the group depends on the level of the menu structure on which the addition occurs. For example, adding a menu to a menu bar causes two ADDMENU records to be written. Adding a submenu item to a menu item causes four records to be written.

If fInsert is true (equal to 01h), then the menu object is added at this level of the hierarchy. For example, if fInsert is true in the second ADDMENU record of the group, then Microsoft Excel adds a new menu to an existing menu bar. If fInsert is false (equal to 00h), then the record is a placeholder, and one of the following ADDMENU records in the group will define the menu addition.

For menu items and submenu items, the icetab field stores the index to the added command, if the item is attached to a built-in command. The icetabBefore field stores the index to the command before which the new command is added. If either of these indexes equals FFFFh, then the corresponding string from the rgch field is used instead of a built-in command.

The caitm field is equal to the number of following ADDMENU records that are to be inserted at this level of the menu hierarchy.

Record Data

Offset	Name	Size	Contents
4	icetabItem	2	Icetab of command
6	icetabBefore	2	Icetab of existing command before which the new command is inserted
8	caitm	1	Number of ADDMENU records at the next level of the menu hierarchy
9	fInsert	1	= 1, insert this menu object = 0, this is a placeholder record
10	rgch	var	stItem, stBefore, stMacro, stStatus, stHelp strings (see text)

The rgch field stores five concatenated strings, as described in the following table. Null strings will appear in the rgch field as a single byte (00h).

String	Contents
stItem	Text of menu object
stBefore	Text of item before which this item is added
stMacro	Macro name, encoded using a technique similar to the encoded filenames in the EXTERNSHEET record (for more information, see page 167)
stStatus	Status-bar text (for add-ins)
stHelp	Help filename and context ID (for add-ins)

ARRAY: Array-Entered Formula (21h)

An ARRAY record describes a formula that was array-entered into a range of cells. The range of cells in which the array is entered is defined by the rwFirst, rwLast, colFirst, and colLast fields.

The ARRAY record occurs directly after the FORMULA record for the upper-left corner cell of the array, that is, the cell defined by the rwFirst and colFirst fields.

The parsed expression is the array formula, stored in the Microsoft Excel internal format. For an explanation of the parsed format, see "Microsoft Excel Formulas" on page 259.

Record Data

Offset	Name	Size	Contents
4	rwFirst	2	First row of the array
6	rwLast	2	Last row of the array
8	colFirst	1	First column of the array
9	colLast	1	Last column of the array
10	grbit	2	Option flags
12	chn	4	(see text)
16	cce	2	Length of parsed expression
18	rgce	var	Parsed expression

The chn field should be ignored when reading the BIFF file. If you write a BIFF file, the chn field must be 00000000h.

The grbit field contains the following option flags.

Offset	Bits	Mask	Name	Contents
0	0	01h	fAlwaysCalc	Always calculate the formula
	1	02h	fCalcOnLoad	Calculate the formula when the file is opened
	7–2	FCh	(unused)	
1	7–0	FFh	(unused)	

AUTOFILTER: AutoFilter Data (9Eh)

This record stores data for an active AutoFilter.

Record Data

Offset	Name	Size	Contents
4	iEntry	2	Index of active AutoFilter
6	grbit	2	Option flags
8	doper1	10	DOPER structure for first filter condition (see text)
18	doper2	10	DOPER structure for second filter condition (see text)
28	rgch	var	String storage for vtString DOPER (see text)

The grbit field contains the following option flags.

Offset	Bits	Mask	Name	Contents
0	1-0	03h	wJoin	= 1 if custom filter conditions are ANDed = 0 if custom filter conditions are ORed
	2	04h	fSimple1	= 1 if the first condition is a simple equality (for optimization)
	3	08h	fSimple2	= 1 if the second condition is a simple equality (for optimization)
	7-4	F0h	(reserved)	
1	7-0	FFh	(reserved)	

The database oper structures (DOPERs) are 10-byte parsed definitions of the filter conditions that appear in the Custom AutoFilter dialog box. The DOPER structures are defined in the following sections.

DOPER Structure for RK Numbers (vt = 02h)

Offset	Name	Size	Contents
0	vt	1	Data type (see text)
1	grbitSgn	1	Comparison code (see text)
2	rk	4	RK number (see page 221)
6	(reserved)	4	

DOPER Structure for IEEE Floating-Point Numbers (vt = 04h)

Offset	Name	Size	Contents
0	vt	1	Data type (see text)
1	grbitSgn	1	Comparison code (see text)
2	num	8	IEEE floating-point number

DOPER Structure for Strings (vt = 06h)

Offset	Name	Size	Contents
0	vt	1	Data type (see text)
1	grbitSgn	1	Comparison code (see text)
2	(reserved)	4	
6	cch	1	Length of string (string is stored in rgch field that follows the DOPER structures)
7	(reserved)	3	

DOPER Structure for Boolean and Error Values (vt = 08h)

Offset	Name	Size	Contents
0	vt	1	Data type (see text)
1	grbitSgn	1	Comparison code (see text)
2	fError	1	Boolean/error flag
3	bBoolErr	1	Boolean value or error value
4	(reserved)	6	

The bBoolErr field contains the Boolean or error value, as determined by the fError field. If the fError field contains a 0, the bBoolErr field contains a Boolean value; if the fError field contains a 1, the bBoolErr field contains an error value.

Boolean values are 1 for true and 0 for false.

Error values are listed in the following table.

Error value	Value (hex)	Value (dec.)
#NULL!	00h	0
#DIV/0!	07h	7
#VALUE!	0Fh	15
#REF!	17h	23
#NAME?	1Dh	29
#NUM!	24h	36
#N/A	2Ah	42

The vt field contains the data type of the DOPER, as shown in the following table. For the DOPER types 00h, 0Ch, and 0Eh, the remaining 9 bytes of the DOPER are ignored.

vt	DOPER type
00h	Filter condition not used
02h	RK number
04h	IEEE number
06h	String
08h	Boolean or error value
0Ch	Match all blanks
0Eh	Match all non-blanks

The grbitSgn field corresponds to comparison operators as shown in the following table.

grbitSgn	Operator
01	<
02	=
03	<=
04	>
05	<>
06	>=

AUTOFILTERINFO: Drop-Down Arrow Count (9Dh)

This record stores the count of AutoFilter drop-down arrows. Each drop-down arrow has a corresponding OBJ record. If at least one AutoFilter is active (in other words, the range has been filtered at least once), there will be a corresponding FILTERMODE record in the file. There will also be one AUTOFILTER record for each active filter.

Record Data

Offset	Name	Size	Contents
4	cEntries	2	Number of AutoFilter drop-down arrows in the sheet

BACKUP: Save Backup Version of the File (40h)

The BACKUP record specifies whether or not Microsoft Excel should save backup versions of a file.

Record Data

Offset	Name	Size	Contents
4	fBackupFile	2	= 1 if Microsoft Excel should save a backup version of the file

BLANK: Cell Value, Blank Cell (01h)

A BLANK record describes an empty cell. The rw field contains the zero-based row number. The col field contains the zero-based column number.

Record Data

Offset	Name	Size	Contents
4	rw	2	Row
6	col	2	Column
8	ixfe	2	Index to XF record

BOF: Beginning of File (0809h)

The BOF record marks the beginning of the Book stream in the BIFF file. It also marks the beginning of record groups (or "substreams" of the Book stream) for sheets in the workbook. You can determine the BIFF version from the high-order byte of the record number field, as follows.

BOF Record Number Field

Offset	Name	Size	Contents
0	vers	1	ver: = 00 BIFF2 = 02 BIFF3 = 04 BIFF4 = 08 BIFF5
1	bof	1	09h

Record Data

Offset	Name	Size	Contents
4	vers	2	Version number (0500 for BIFF5)
6	dt	2	Substream type: 0005h = Workbook globals 0006h = Visual Basic module 0010h = Worksheet or dialog sheet 0020h = Chart 0040h = Microsoft Excel v4.0 macro sheet 0100h = Workspace file
8	rupBuild	2	Build identifier (internal use only)
10	rupYear	2	Build year (internal use only)

The dt field specifies whether the substream is a module, worksheet, chart, and so on.

The rupBuild and rupYear fields are reserved for internal Microsoft use. If you read a BIFF file, ignore the contents of these bytes. If you write a BIFF file, write 00 00 00 00 to these bytes.

BOOKBOOL: Workbook Option Flag (DAh)

This record saves a workbook option flag.

Record Data

Offset	Name	Size	Contents
4	fNoSaveSupp	2	=1 if the Save External Link Values option is off (Options dialog box, Calculation tab)

BOOLERR: Cell Value, Boolean or Error (05h)

A BOOLERR record describes a cell that contains a constant Boolean or error value. The rw field contains the zero-based row number. The col field contains the zero-based column number.

Record Data

Offset	Name	Size	Contents
4	rw	2	Row
6	col	2	Column
8	ixfe	2	Index to XF record
10	bBoolErr	1	Boolean value or error value
11	fError	1	Boolean/error flag

The bBoolErr field contains the Boolean or error value, as determined by the fError field. If the fError field contains a 0, the bBoolErr field contains a Boolean value; if the fError field contains a 1, the bBoolErr field contains an error value.

Boolean values are 1 for true and 0 for false.

Error values are listed in the following table.

Error value	Value (hex)	Value (dec.)
#NULL!	00h	0
#DIV/0!	07h	7
#VALUE!	0Fh	15
#REF!	17h	23
#NAME?	1Dh	29
#NUM!	24h	36
#N/A	2Ah	42

BOTTOMMARGIN: Bottom Margin Measurement (29h)

The BOTTOM MARGIN record specifies the bottom margin in inches when a sheet is printed. The num field is in 8-byte IEEE floating-point format.

Record Data

Offset	Name	Size	Contents
4	num	8	Bottom margin

BOUNDSHEET: Sheet Information (85h)

This record stores the sheet name, sheet type, and stream position.

Record Data

Offset	Name	Size	Contents
4	lbPlyPos	4	Stream position of the start of the BOF record for the sheet
8	grbit	2	Option flags
10	cch	1	Length of sheet name
11	rgch	var	Sheet name

The grbit field contains the following options.

Offset	Bits	Mask	Name	Contents
0	7-0	0Fh	dt	Sheet type: 00h = worksheet or dialog sheet 01h = Microsoft Excel v4.0 macro sheet 02h = chart 06h = Visual Basic module
1	1–0	03h	hsState	Hidden state: 00h = visible 01h = hidden 02h = very hidden (see text)
	7-2	FCh	(reserved)	

A Visual Basic procedure can set the **Visible** property of a sheet to create a very hidden sheet. A very hidden sheet can be made visible again by a Visual Basic procedure, but there is no way to make the sheet visible through the user interface of Microsoft Excel.

CALCCOUNT: Iteration Count (0Ch)

The CALCCOUNT record stores the Maximum Iterations option from the Options dialog box, Calculation tab.

Record Data

Offset	Name	Size	Contents
4	cIter	2	Iteration count

CALCMODE: Calculation Mode (0Dh)

The CALCMODE record stores options from the Options dialog box, Calculation tab.

Record Data

Offset	Name	Size	Contents
4	fAutoRecalc	2	Calculation mode: = 0 for manual = 1 for automatic = −1 for automatic, except tables

CODEPAGE: Default Code Page (42h)

The CODEPAGE record stores the default code page (character set) that was in use when the workbook was saved.

Record Data

Offset	Name	Size	Contents
4	cv	2	Code page the file is saved in: 01B5h (437 dec.) = IBM PC (Multiplan) 8000h (32768 dec.) = Apple Macintosh 04E4h (1252 dec.) = ANSI (Microsoft Windows)

COLINFO: Column Formatting Information (7Dh)

The COLINFO record describes the column formatting for a range of columns.

Record Data

Offset	Name	Size	Contents
4	colFirst	2	First formatted column (0-based)
6	colLast	2	Last formatted column (0-based)
8	coldx	2	Column width, in 1/256s of a character width
10	ixfe	2	Index to XF record that contains default format for column (for more information about the XF records, see page 250)
12	grbit	2	Options
14	(reserved)	1	Reserved; must be zero

The grbit field contains the following options.

Offset	Bits	Mask	Name	Contents
0	0	01h	fHidden	= 1 if the column range is hidden
	7–1	FEh	(unused)	
1	2–0	07h	iOutLevel	Outline level of column range
	3	08h	(reserved)	Reserved; must be zero
	4	10h	fCollapsed	= 1 if the column range is collapsed in outlining
	7–5	E0h	(reserved)	Reserved; must be zero

CONTINUE: Continues Long Records (3Ch)

Records that are longer than 2084 bytes (this includes the 4 bytes for record number and record length) must be split into several records. The first section appears in the base record; subsequent sections appear in CONTINUE records.

Record Data

Offset	Name	Size	Contents
4		var	Continuation of record data

COORDLIST: Polygon Object Vertex Coordinates (A9h)

This record stores the coordinates of the vertices in a polygon object.

Record Data

Offset	Name	Size	Contents
4	rgVTX	var	Array of vertex coordinates

The VTX structure is defined as follows:

```
typedef struct _vtx
    {
    unsigned short int x;
    unsigned short int y;
    }
        VTX;
```

The upper-left corner of a polygon's bounding rectangle is (x = 0h, y = 0h), and the lower-right corner is (x = 4000h, y = 4000h), as shown in the following illustration.

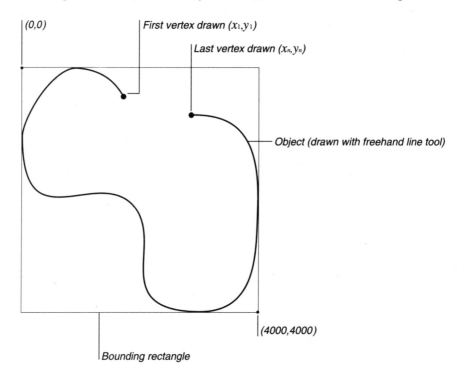

After the polygon is drawn, Microsoft Excel normalizes the coordinates in rgVTX to the bounding rectangle. The actual size of the polygon can be derived from the size of the bounding rectangle in the common object fields section of the OBJ record.

COUNTRY: Default Country and WIN.INI Country (8Ch)

This record contains localization information.

Record Data

Offset	Name	Size	Contents
4	iCountryDef	2	Default country index
6	iCountryWinIni	2	Country index from WIN.INI file

The default country index, iCountryDef, is determined by the localized version of Microsoft Excel that created the BIFF file. For example, all BIFF files created by the U.S. version of Microsoft Excel have iCountryDef = 1. If Microsoft Excel for Windows created the BIFF file, iCountryWinIni is equal to the index that corresponds to the country setting in the WIN.INI file. Country indexes are defined in the following table.

Index	Country	Index	Country
1	United States	49	Germany
2	Canada	52	Mexico
3	Latin America, except Brazil	55	Brazil
31	Netherlands	61	Australia
32	Belgium	64	New Zealand
33	France	81	Japan
34	Spain	82	South Korea
39	Italy	351	Portugal
41	Switzerland	354	Iceland
43	Austria	358	Finland
44	United Kingdom	785	Arabic
45	Denmark	886	Republic of China
46	Sweden	972	Israel
47	Norway		

CRN: Nonresident Operands (5Ah)

The CRN record describes nonresident operands in a formula. For example, if you have a worksheet that contains the formula =EXT.XLS!A1*A3, where EXT.XLS is not the active workbook, then the nonresident operand EXT.XLS!A1 generates a CRN record that describes the cell A1. If the nonresident operand contains more than one row, then there is one CRN record for each row. For example, if the formula =EXT.XLS!A1:A4*4 is array-entered on a worksheet, then there will be four CRN records.

If a worksheet contains two different formulas, and each formula has multiple nonresident operands, Microsoft Excel may create one CRN record or several CRN records, depending on how the nonresident cells are arranged. For example, suppose a worksheet contains two formulas (in different cells), =EXT.XLS!A1*2 and =EXT.XLS!B1*2. Because the nonresident operands are in a row, and are not separated by an empty cell, Microsoft Excel creates only one CRN record containing information for cells A1 and B1.

If, however, the formulas are =EXT.XLS!A1*2 and =EXT.XLS!C1*2, Microsoft Excel creates two CRN records because an empty cell (B1) separates the two operands, A1 and C1.

Record Data

Offset	Name	Size	Contents
4	colLast	1	Last column of nonresident operand
5	colFirst	1	First column of nonresident operand
6	rw	2	Row of nonresident operand
8	OPER	var	OPER structure; see following description

The OPER structure repeats for each cell in the nonresident operand. For example, the formula =SUM(EXT.XLS!A1:A3) produces one CRN record with three OPER structures.

OPER Structure if Cell Contains a Number

Offset	Name	Size	Contents
0	grbit	1	= 01h for cell that contains a number
1	num	8	IEEE floating-point number

OPER Structure if Cell Contains a String

Offset	Name	Size	Contents
0	grbit	1	= 02h for cell that contains a string
1	cch	1	Number of characters in string
2	rgch	var	String

OPER Structure if Cell Contains a Boolean Value

Offset	Name	Size	Contents
0	grbit	1	= 04h for cell that contains a Boolean value
1	f	2	= 1 if TRUE = 0 if FALSE
3	(unused)	6	

OPER Structure if Cell Contains an Error Value

Offset	Name	Size	Contents
0	grbit	1	= 10h for cell that contains an error value
1	err	2	Error value
3	(unused)	6	

DBCELL: Stream Offsets (D7h)

The DBCELL record stores stream offsets for the BIFF file. There is one DBCELL record for each block of ROW records and associated cell records. Each block can contain data for up to 32 rows. For more information about the DBCELL record, see "Finding Cell Records in BIFF Files" on page 255.

Record Data

Offset	Name	Size	Contents
4	dbRtrw	4	Offset from start of DBCELL record to start of first ROW record in the block; this is an offset to an earlier position in the stream
8	rgdb	var	Array of stream offsets (2-bytes each). For more information, see "Finding Cell Records in BIFF Files" on page 255.

DCON: Data Consolidation Information (50h)

The DCON record stores options from the Consolidate dialog box (Data menu).

Record Data

Offset	Name	Size	Contents
4	iiftab	2	Index to data consolidation function (see following table)
6	fLeftCat	2	= 1 if Left Column option is on
8	fTopCat	2	= 1 if Top Row option is on
10	fLinkConsol	2	= 1 if Create Links to Source Data option is on

The iiftab field, described in the following table, corresponds to the Function option in the Consolidate dialog box (Data menu).

Function	Iiftab
Average	0
Count Nums	1

Function	Iiftab
Count	2
Max	3
Min	4
Product	5
StdDev	6
StdDevp	7
Sum	8
Var	9
Varp	10

DCONNAME: Data Consolidation Named References (52h)

The DCONREF record contains the complete description of a named range of cells for the Consolidate command (Data menu). The stFile field contains an encoded workbook name; for information on this field, see "EXTERNSHEET" on page 167.

Record Data

Offset	Name	Size	Contents
4	cchName	1	Length of named range of source area
5	stName	var	Named range of source area for consolidation
var	cchFile	1	Length of workbook name
var	stFile	var	Workbook name

DCONREF: Data Consolidation References (51h)

The DCONNAME record contains the complete description of a range of cells for the Consolidate command (Data menu). The rgch field contains an encoded workbook name; for information on this field, see "EXTERNSHEET" on page 167.

Record Data

Offset	Name	Size	Contents
4	rwFirst	2	First row of source area for consolidation
6	rwLast	2	Last row of source area for consolidation
8	colFirst	1	First column of source area for consolidation
9	colLast	1	Last column of source area for consolidation

Offset	Name	Size	Contents
10	cch	1	Length of workbook name
11	rgch	1	Workbook name

DEFAULTROWHEIGHT: Default Row Height (25h)

The DEFAULTROWHEIGHT record specifies the height of all undefined rows in the sheet. The miyRw field contains the row height in units of 1/20 of a point. This record does not affect the row heights of any rows that are explicitly defined.

Record Data

Offset	Name	Size	Contents
4	grbit	2	Option flags (see following table)
6	miyRw	2	Default row height

The grbit field contains the following option flags.

Offset	Bits	Mask	Name	Contents
0	0	01h	fUnsynced	= 1 if all undefined rows have incompatible font height and row height
	1	02h	fDyZero	= 1 if all undefined rows have zero height
	2	04h	fExAsc	= 1 if all undefined rows have extra space above
	3	08h	fExDsc	= 1 if all undefined rows have extra space below
	7–4	F0h	(unused)	
1	7–0	FFh	(unused)	

DEFCOLWIDTH: Default Width for Columns (55h)

The DEFCOLWIDTH record specifies the width, measured in characters, for columns not explicitly sized in the COLWIDTH record.

Record Data

Offset	Name	Size	Contents
4	cchdefColWidth	2	Default width of the columns

DELMENU: Menu Deletion (C3h)

The DELMENU record stores a menu deletion and is very similar to the ADDMENU record. See the section "ADDMENU" on page 145 for more information about menu system modifications.

If fDelete is true (equal to 01h), then the menu object is deleted at this level of the hierarchy. For example, if fDelete is true in the second DELMENU record of the group, then Microsoft Excel deletes the specified menu from a menu bar. If fDelete is false (equal to 00h), then the record is a placeholder, and one of the following DELMENU records in the group will define the menu deletion.

For menu items and submenu items, the icetabItem field stores the index to the deleted command if the item is attached to a built-in command. If icetabItem equals FFFFh, then the stItem string from the rgch field is used instead.

Record Data

Offset	Name	Size	Contents
4	icetabItem	2	Icetab of command
6	cditm	1	Number of DELMENU records at the next level of the menu hierarchy
7	fDelete	1	= 1, delete this menu object = 0, this is a placeholder record
8	fMultiple	1	= 1 if this item has subitems
9	rgch	var	stItem (see text)

The first byte of the stItem string is the byte count, and the last byte is reserved.

DELTA: Iteration Increment (10h)

The DELTA record stores the Maximum Change value from the Options dialog box, Calculation tab. The number is in 8-byte IEEE floating-point format.

Record Data

Offset	Name	Size	Contents
4	numDelta	8	Maximum iteration change

DIMENSIONS: Cell Table Size (00h)

The DIMENSIONS record contains the minimum and maximum bounds of the sheet. It provides a concise indication of the sheet size.

Note that both the rwMac and colMac fields are one (1) greater than the actual last row and column. For example, a worksheet that exists between cells B3 and D6 would have the following dimensions in the dimensions record (note rows and columns are zero-based in BIFF files where row 1 and column A are both coded as 0):

rwMic   = 2 — indicates that 3 is the first row

colMic = 1 — indicates that B is the first column

rwMac   = 6 — indicates that 6 is the last row

colMac = 4 — indicates that D is the last column

Record Data

Offset	Name	Size	Contents
4	rwMic	2	First defined row on the sheet
6	rwMac	2	Last defined row on the sheet, plus 1
8	colMic	2	First defined column on the sheet
10	colMac	2	Last defined column on the sheet, plus 1
12	(reserved)	2	Reserved; must be zero

DOCROUTE: Routing Slip Information (B8h)

This record stores originator information for a routing slip and other information for document routing. The rgch field contains the concatenation of seven null-terminated strings: Subject, Message, Route ID, Custom Message Type, Book Title, Originator's Friendly Name, and Originator's System-specific Address. The lengths of the strings are contained in the seven fields, cchSubject through ulEIDSize.

Record Data

Offset	Name	Size	Contents
4	iStage	2	Routing stage
6	cRecip	2	Number of recipients
8	delOption	2	Delivery option: = 0, one at a time = 1, all at once
10	wFlags	2	Option flags
12	cchSubject	2	Length of Subject string
14	cchMessage	2	Length of Message string
16	cchRouteID	2	Length of Route ID string
18	cchCustType	2	Length of Custom Message Type string

Offset	Name	Size	Contents
20	cchBookTitle	2	Length of Book Title string
22	cchOrg	2	Length of Originator's Friendly Name string
24	ulEIDSize	4	Length of Originator's System-specific Address string
28	rgch	var	(see text)

The wFlags field contains the following option flags.

Offset	Bits	Mask	Name	Contents
0	0	01h	fRouted	= 1 if the document has been routed
	1	02h	fReturnOrig	= 1 if the document should be returned to originator
	2	04h	fTrackStatus	= 1 if status messaged should be sent
	3	08h	fCustomType	= 1 if status message is a custom message type
	6-4	70h	(reserved)	
	7	80h	fSaveRouteInfo	= 1 if the routing slip information should be saved
1	7-0	FFh	(reserved)	

EDG: Edition Globals (88h)

The EDG record contains information for the publisher/subscriber feature. This record can be created only by Microsoft Excel for the Macintosh. However, if any other platform version of Microsoft Excel encounters the EDG record in a BIFF file, it leaves the record in the file, unchanged, when the file is saved.

Record Data

Offset	Name	Size	Contents
4	lcsec	4	Count of section records that have ever been created in this document, plus 1 (includes published embedded charts)
8	crtpub	2	Count of PUB records in file (includes published embedded charts)
10	(reserved)	2	Reserved; must be zero

EOF: End of File (0Ah)

The EOF record marks the end of the workbook stream or the end of one of the substreams in the workbook stream. It has no record data field and is simply 0A000000h.

EXTERNCOUNT: Number of External References (16h)

The EXTERNCOUNT record specifies the number of externally referenced workbooks, DDE references, and OLE references contained in a Microsoft Excel workbook.

For example, a worksheet contains the following formulas in cells A1:A3:

=SALES.XLS!Profits

=Signal|System!Formats

=Signal|StockInfo!MSFT

This worksheet would have a value of 3 in the cxals field of the EXTERNCOUNT record, corresponding to the three external references SALES.XLS, Signal|System, and Signal|StockInfo.

Record Data

Offset	Name	Size	Contents
4	cxals	2	Number of external references

EXTERNNAME: Externally Referenced Name (23h)

The EXTERNNAME record stores an externally referenced name, DDE link, or OLE link. All EXTERNNAME records associated with a supporting workbook must directly follow the EXTERNSHEET record for the workbook. The order of EXTERNNAME records in a BIFF file should not be changed.

External Name

When the EXTERNNAME record stores an external name, fOle and fOleLink are both equal to zero (FALSE), and the record has the following form.

Offset	Name	Size	Contents
4	grbit	2	Option flags
6	(reserved)	4	Reserved; must be zero
10	cch	1	Length of external name

Offset	Name	Size	Contents
11	rgch	var	External name
var	cce	2	Length of name definition
var	rgce	var	Name definition, in parsed expression format; for more information see "Microsoft Excel Formulas" on page 259.

The grbit field contains the following option flags.

Bits	Mask	Name	Contents
0	0001h	fBuiltin	= 1 if name is a built-in name
1	0002h	fWantAdvise	N/A for External Names (must be zero)
2	0004h	fWantPict	N/A for External Names (must be zero)
3	0008h	fOle	N/A for External Names (must be zero)
4	0010h	fOleLink	N/A for External Names (must be zero)
15-5	FFE0h	(reserved)	Reserved; must be zero

DDE Link

When the EXTERNNAME record stores a DDE link, the record has the following form.

Offset	Name	Size	Contents
4	grbit	2	Option flags
6	(reserved)	4	Reserved; must be zero
10	cch	1	Length of external name
11	rgch	var	External name
var	rgoper	var	Array of OPERs that store the current value of the name; see Chapter 1 of this book for a description of the OPER structures

The grbit field contains the following option flags.

Bits	Mask	Name	Contents
0	0001h	fBuiltin	N/A for DDE links (must be zero)
1	0002h	fWantAdvise	= 0 for manual DDE links = 1 for automatic DDE links
2	0004h	fWantPict	= 1 if Microsoft Excel wants a cfPict clipboard format representation of the data; OBJ and IMDATA records store the image

Bits	Mask	Name	Contents
3	0008h	fOle	= 1 if this record stores the OLE StdDocumentName identifier (no rgoper follows rgch)
4	0010h	fOleLink	= 0 for DDE links
14-5	7FE0h	cf	The clipboard format for which the DDE Advise succeeded; this is used to reduce the time required for future Advise cycles
15	8000h	(reserved)	Reserved; must be zero

OLE Link

When the EXTERNNAME record stores an OLE link, fWantAdvise and fOleLink are equal to one (TRUE), and the record has the following form.

Offset	Name	Size	Contents
4	grbit	2	Option flags
6	lStgName	4	OLE 2 storage identifier
10	cch	1	Length of link name
11	rgch	var	Link name

The grbit field contains the following option flags.

Bits	Mask	Name	Contents
0	0001h	fBuiltin	N/A for OLE links (must be zero)
1	0002h	fWantAdvise	= 0 for manual OLE links = 1 for automatic OLE links
2	0004h	fWantPict	= 1 if Microsoft Excel wants a cfPict clipboard format representation of the data; OBJ and IMDATA records store the image
3	0008h	fOle	N/A for OLE links (must be zero)
4	0010h	fOleLink	= 1 for OLE links
15-5	FFE0h	(reserved)	Reserved; must be zero

EXTERNSHEET: External Reference (17h)

The EXTERNSHEET record specifies an externally referenced workbook. The cxals field of the EXTERNCOUNT record specifies the number of EXTERNSHEET records. You should not change the order of EXTERNSHEET records.

An externally referenced workbook is called a source workbook. The workbook that refers to it is called a dependent workbook.

Record Data

Offset	Name	Size	Contents
4	cch	1	Length of filename
5	rgch	var	Filename

The cch field contains the length of the source workbook filename. The rgch field contains the source workbook filename.

Filename Encoding

Whenever possible, filenames are encoded to make BIFF files transportable across file systems. Encoded filenames are identified by the first character of the rgch field. The first character of the rgch field may be any one of the following values.

Name	Value	Meaning
chEmpty	00	Reference to an empty workbook name (see text)
chEncode	01	Filename has been encoded (see following table)
chSelf	02	Self-referential external reference (see text)

chEmpty indicates that the filename is an external reference to an empty workbook name, as in the formula =Sheet1!$A$1.

chSelf indicates that the filename is an external reference where the dependent and source workbooks are the same. An example of this is a workbook SALES.XLS that contains the formula =SALES.XLS!$A$1.

A chDDE key (03h) can occur in the rgch field; it is not necessarily the first character in the field, as are chEmpty, chEncode, and chSelf. This key indicates that the external reference is a DDE or OLE link. In a DDE link, the chDDE key replaces the | (pipe) character that separates the DDE application and topic. In an OLE link, chDDE separates the classname and filename.

A chEncode at the beginning of rgch indicates that the filename of the source workbook has been encoded to a less system-dependent filename. The following special keys are recognized in the rgch field.

Name	Value	MS-DOS file system	Macintosh file system
chVolume	01	Represents an MS-DOS drive letter. It is followed by the drive letter. For example, the formula ='D:\SALES.XLS'!A1 generates the chVolume key when the dependent workbook is not on the D: drive. UNC filenames, such as \\server\share\myfile.xls generate an @ character after the chVolume key; this replaces the initial double backslash (\\).	Represents a single-character volume name. Because single-character volume names are uncommon on the Macintosh, the chLongVolume key is used to represent volume names that are longer than a single character.
chSameVolume	02	Indicates that the source workbook is on the same drive as the dependent workbook (the drive letter is omitted). For example, the formula ='\SALES.XLS'!A1 generates the chSameVolume key when the dependent workbook is not in the root directory.	Indicates that the source workbook is on the same volume as the dependent workbook (the volume name is omitted).
chDownDir	03	Indicates that the source workbook is in a subdirectory of the current directory. For example, the formula ='XL\SALES.XLS'!A1 generates the chDownDir key. The subdirectory name precedes the chDownDir key, and the filename follows it.	Indicates that the source workbook is in a folder in the current folder. For example, the formula =':XL:Sales1992'!A1 generates the chDownDir key. The folder name precedes the chDownDir key, and the filename follows it.

Name	Value	MS-DOS file system	Macintosh file system
chUpDir	04	Indicates that the source workbook is in the parent directory of the current directory. For example, the formula ='..\SALES.XLS'!A1 generates the chUpDir key.	Indicates that the source workbook is in the parent folder of the current folder. For example, the formula ='::Sales1992'!A1 generates the chUpDir key.
chLongVolume	05	(not used)	The chLongVolume key is followed by the length of the name (1 byte) and then by the volume name string.
chStartupDir	06	Indicates that the source workbook is in the startup directory (the XLSTART subdirectory of the directory that contains EXCEL.EXE).	Indicates that the source workbook is in the Excel Startup Folder (5), which is in the System Folder.
chAltStartupDir	07	Indicates that the source workbook is in the alternate startup directory.	Indicates that the source workbook is in the alternate startup folder.
chLibDir	08	Indicates that the source workbook is in the LIBRARY directory.	Indicates that the source workbook is in the Macro Library folder.

FILEPASS: File Is Password-Protected (2Fh)

If you type a protection password (File menu, Save As command, Options dialog box), the FILEPASS record appears in the BIFF file. The wProtPass field contains the encrypted password. All records after FILEPASS are encrypted; you cannot read these encrypted records.

Note that this record specifies a file protection password, as opposed to the PASSWORD record (type 13h), which specifies a sheet-level or workbook-level protection password.

Record Data

Offset	Name	Size	Contents
4	wProtPass	4	Encrypted password

FILESHARING: File-Sharing Information (5Bh)

This record stores file-sharing options selected in the Options dialog box, accessed with the Save As command (File menu). The write reservation password that you type in the dialog box is encrypted to an integer, wResPass. This record also contains the user name of the file's creator, stUNWriteRes.

Record Data

Offset	Name	Size	Contents
4	fReadOnlyRec	2	= 1 if the Read Only Recommended option is selected in the Options dialog box
6	wResPass	2	Encrypted password (if this field is zero, there is no write reservation password)
8	cch	1	Length of user name
9	stUNWriteRes	var	User name

FILTERMODE: Sheet Contains Filtered List (9Bh)

If the sheet contains a filtered list, the file will contain a FILTERMODE record. This record has no record data field.

FNGROUPCOUNT: Built-in Function Group Count (9Ch)

This record stores the number of built-in function groups (Financial, Math & Trig, Date & Time, and so on) in the current version of Microsoft Excel.

Record Data

Offset	Name	Size	Contents
4	cFnGroup	2	Number of built-in function groups

FNGROUPNAME: Function Group Name (9Ah)

This record stores the name of a custom function category.

Record Data

Offset	Name	Size	Contents
4	cch	1	Size of function category name
5	rgch	var	Function category name

FONT: Font Description (31h)

The workbook font table contains at least five FONT records. FONT records are numbered as follows: ifnt = 00h (the first FONT record in the table), ifnt = 01h, ifnt = 02h, ifnt = 03h, ifnt = 05h (minimum table), and then ifnt = 06h, ifnt = 07h, and so on. Notice that ifnt = 04h, never appears in a BIFF file. This is for backward-compatibility with previous versions of Microsoft Excel. If you read FONT records, remember to index the table correctly, skipping ifnt = 04h.

Record Data

Offset	Name	Size	Contents
4	dyHeight	2	Height of the font (in units of 1/20 of a point)
6	grbit	2	Font attributes (see following table)
8	icv	2	Index to color palette
10	bls	2	Bold style; a number from 100dec to 1000dec (64h to 3E8h) that indicates the character weight ("boldness"). Default values are 190h for normal text and 2BCh for bold text.
12	sss	2	Superscript/subscript: 00h = None 01h = Superscript 02h = Subscript
14	uls	1	Underline style: 00h = None 01h = Single 02h = Double 21h = Single Accounting 22h = Double Accounting
15	bFamily	1	Font family, as defined by the Windows API LOGFONT structure.
16	bCharSet	1	Character set, as defined by the Windows API LOGFONT structure.
17	(reserved)	1	Reserved; must be zero
18	cch	1	Length of font name
19	rgch	var	Font name

The grbit field contains the following font attributes.

Offset	Bits	Mask	Name	Contents
0	0	01h	(reserved)	Reserved; must be zero
	1	02h	fItalic	= 1 if font is italic
	2	04h	(reserved)	Reserved; must be zero

Offset	Bits	Mask	Name	Contents
0	3	08h	fStrikeout	= 1 if font is struck out
	4	10h	fOutline	= 1 if font is outline (Macintosh only)
	5	20h	fShadow	= 1 if font is shadow (Macintosh only)
	7-6	C0h	(reserved)	Reserved; must be zero
1	7–0	FFh	(unused)	

FOOTER: Print Footer on Each Page (15h)

The FOOTER record stores a print footer string for a sheet. This string appears at the bottom of every page when the sheet is printed.

Record Data

Offset	Name	Size	Contents
4	cch	1	Length of footer string (bytes)
5	rgch	var	Footer string

FORMAT: Number Format (1Eh)

The FORMAT record describes a number format in the workbook.

All the FORMAT records should appear together in a BIFF file. The order of FORMAT records in an existing BIFF file should not be changed. You can write custom number formats in a file, but they should be added at the end of the existing FORMAT records.

Record Data

Offset	Name	Size	Contents
4	ifmt	2	Format index code (for internal use only)
6	cch	1	Length of format string
7	rgch	var	Number format string

Microsoft Excel uses the ifmt field to identify built-in formats when it reads a file that was created by a different localized version.

FORMULA: Cell Formula (06h)

A FORMULA record describes a cell that contains a formula.

Record Data

Offset	Name	Size	Contents
4	rw	2	Row
6	col	2	Column
8	ixfe	2	Index to XF record
10	num	8	Current value of formula (see text)
18	grbit	2	Option flags
20	chn	4	(see text)
24	cce	2	Length of parsed expression
26	rgce	var	Parsed expression

The chn field should be ignored when reading the BIFF file. If you write a BIFF file, the chn field must be 00000000h.

The grbit field contains the following option flags.

Offset	Bits	Mask	Name	Contents
0	0	01h	fAlwaysCalc	Always calculate the formula
	1	02h	fCalcOnLoad	Calculate the formula when the file is opened
	2	04h	(reserved)	
	3	08h	fShrFmla	= 1 if formula is part of shared formula group
	7–4	F0h	(unused)	
1	7–0	FFh	(unused)	

For more information about shared formulas, see "SHRFMLA" on page 230.

The rw field contains the zero-based row number. The col field contains the zero-based column number.

If the formula evaluates to a number, the num field contains the current calculated value of the formula in 8-byte IEEE format. If the formula evaluates to a string, a Boolean, or an error value, the most-significant 2 bytes of the num field are FFFFh.

A Boolean value is stored in the num field as shown in the following table. For more information about Boolean values, see "BOOLERR" on page 152.

Offset	Name	Size	Contents
0	otBool	1	= 1 always
1	(reserved)	1	Reserved; must be zero
2	f	1	Boolean value

Offset	Name	Size	Contents
3	(reserved)	3	Reserved; must be zero
6	fExprO	2	= FFFFh

An error value is stored in the num field as shown in the following table. For more information about error values, see "BOOLERR" on page 152.

Offset	Name	Size	Contents
0	otErr	1	= 2 always
1	(reserved)	1	Reserved; must be zero
2	err	1	Error value
3	(reserved)	3	Reserved; must be zero
6	fExprO	2	= FFFFh

If the formula evaluates to a string, the num field has the structure shown in the following table.

Offset	Name	Size	Contents
0	otString	1	= 0 always
1	(reserved)	5	Reserved; must be zero
6	fExprO	2	= FFFFh

The string value is not stored in the num field; instead, it is stored in a STRING record that immediately follows the FORMULA record.

The cce field contains the length of the formula. The rgce field contains the formula in its parsed format. For more information, see "Microsoft Excel Formulas" on page 259.

GCW: Global Column Width Flags (ABh)

This record contains an array of 256 flag bits, where each bit represents a column of the sheet. If a bit is true, it means that the corresponding column has the Use Standard Width option on. If a bit is false, it means that the column has the Use Standard Width option off. If the Standard Width measurement has been changed (is no longer the default), then Microsoft Excel writes a STANDARDWIDTH record.

Record Data

Offset	Name	Size	Contents
4	cb	2	Number of bytes in global column width flags
6	grbitGCW	2	Global column width flags, columns A through P

Offset	Name	Size	Contents
8	grbitGCW	2	Global column width flags, columns Q through AF
...	...	...	...
4+cb	grbitGCW	2	Global column width flags, columns IG through IV

The grbitGCW field contains the following option flags.

Bits	Mask	Name	Contents
0 (LSB)	0001h	fGCWcol1	Flag for column 1 (for example, column A)
1	0002h	fGCWcol2	Flag for column 2 (for example, column B)
2	0004h	fGCWcol3	Flag for column 3 (for example, column C)
...	...	...	...
15	8000h	fGCWcol16	Flag for column 16 (for example, column P)

GRIDSET: State Change of Gridlines Option (82h)

This record indicates that the user changed the state of the Gridlines option in the Page Setup dialog box, Sheet tab.

Record Data

Offset	Name	Size	Contents
4	fGridSet	2	= 1 if user has ever changed the setting of the Gridlines option

GUTS: Size of Row and Column Gutters (80h)

This record contains the size of the row and column gutters, measured in screen units. The row and column gutters are the spaces that contain outline symbols. They are located above column headings and to the left of row headings.

Record Data

Offset	Name	Size	Contents
4	dxRwGut	2	Size of row gutter that appears to the left of the rows
6	dyColGut	2	Size of column gutter that appears above the columns
8	iLevelRwMac	2	Maximum outline level (for row gutter)
10	iLevelColMac	2	Maximum outline level (for column gutter)

HCENTER: Center Between Horizontal Margins (83h)

If the Horizontally option is selected in the Page Setup dialog box, Margins tab, then fHCenter = 1.

Record Data

Offset	Name	Size	Contents
4	fHCenter	2	= 1 if sheet is to be centered between horizontal margins when printed

HEADER: Print Header on Each Page (14h)

The HEADER record specifies a print header string for a sheet. This string appears at the top of every page when the sheet is printed.

Record Data

Offset	Name	Size	Contents
4	cch	1	Length of header string (bytes)
5	rgch	var	Header string

HIDEOBJ: Object Display Options (8Dh)

The HIDEOBJ record stores options selected in the Options dialog box, View tab.

Record Data

Offset	Name	Size	Contents
4	fHideObj	2	= 2 if Hide All option is on = 1 if Show Placeholders option is on = 0 if Show All option is on

HORIZONTALPAGEBREAKS: Explicit Row Page Breaks (1Bh)

The HORIZONTALPAGEBREAKS record contains a list of explicit row page breaks. The cbrk field contains the number of page breaks. The rgrw field is an array of 2-byte integers that specifies rows. Microsoft Excel sets a page break before each row contained in the list of rows in the rgrw field. The rows must be sorted in ascending order.

Record Data

Offset	Name	Size	Contents
4	cbrk	2	Number of page breaks
6	rgrw	var	Array of rows

IMDATA: Image Data (7Fh)

The IMDATA record contains the complete description of a bitmapped graphic object such as a drawing created by a graphics tool.

Record Data

Offset	Name	Size	Contents
4	cf	2	Image format: = 02h, Windows metafile or Macintosh PICT format = 09h, Windows bitmap format = 0Eh, Native format (see text)
6	env	2	Environment from which the file was written: = 1, Microsoft Windows = 2, Apple Macintosh
8	lcb	4	Length of the image data
12	data	var	Image data

For more information on the Microsoft Windows metafile file format, see the documentation for the Microsoft Windows Software Development Kit.

For more information on the Apple Macintosh PICT file format, see *The Programmer's Apple Mac Sourcebook* (published by Microsoft Press, ISBN 1-55615-168-3), section 2.087, "PICT File Format," or see *Inside Macintosh Volume V* (published by Addison-Wesley Publishing Company, Inc., ISBN 0-201-17719-6).

If the image is in Microsoft Windows bitmap format (cf = 09h) then the data field consists of a BITMAPCOREINFO data structure followed by the actual bitmap. The BITMAPCOREINFO data structure consists of a BITMAPCOREHEADER structure, followed by an array of RGBTRIPLE structures that define the color table. For more information on these structures, see the documentation for the Microsoft Windows Software Development Kit.

Native format (cf = 0Eh) stores an embedded object from another application. The image data is in the foreign application's format, and cannot be directly processed by Microsoft Excel.

INDEX: Index Record (0Bh)

Microsoft Excel writes an INDEX record immediately after the BOF record for each worksheet substream in a BIFF file. For more information about the INDEX record, see "Finding Cell Records in BIFF Files" on page 255.

Record Data

Offset	Name	Size	Contents
4	(reserved)	4	Reserved; must be zero
8	rwMic	2	First row that exists on the sheet
10	rwMac	2	Last row that exists on the sheet, plus 1
12	(reserved)	4	Reserved; must be zero
16	rgibRw	var	Array of file offsets to the DBCELL records for each block of ROW records. A block contains ROW records for up to 32 rows. For more information, see "Finding Cell Records in BIFF Files" on page 255.

The rwMic field contains the number of the first row in the sheet that contains a value or a formula that is referenced by a cell in some other row. Because rows (and columns) are always stored zero-based rather than one-based (as they appear on the screen), cell A1 is stored as row 0; cell A2 is row 1, and so on. The rwMac field contains the zero-based number of the last row in the sheet, plus 1.

INTERFACEEND: End of User Interface Records (E2h)

This records marks the end of the user interface section of the Book stream. It has no record data field.

INTERFACEHDR: Beginning of User Interface Records (E1h)

This records marks the beginning of the user interface section of the Book stream. It has no record data field.

ITERATION: Iteration Mode (11h)

The ITERATION record stores the Iteration option from the Options dialog box, Calculation tab.

Record Data

Offset	Name	Size	Contents
4	fIter	2	= 1 for iteration on

LABEL: Cell Value, String Constant (04h)

A LABEL record describes a cell that contains a string constant. The rw field contains the zero-based row number. The col field contains the zero-based column number. The string length is contained in the cch field and must be in the range of 0000h–00FFh (0–255). The string itself is contained in the rgch field.

Record Data

Offset	Name	Size	Contents
4	rw	2	Row
6	col	2	Column
8	ixfe	2	Index to XF record
10	cch	2	Length of the string
12	rgch	var	The string

LEFTMARGIN: Left Margin Measurement (26h)

The LEFTMARGIN record specifies the left margin in inches. The num field is in 8-byte IEEE floating-point format.

Record Data

Offset	Name	Size	Contents
4	num	8	Left margin

LHNGRAPH: Named Graph Information (95h)

Record Data

This record is similar to the .WKS NGRAPH record, except that the first 13 references are not written. Instead, there are 13 integers that indicate whether the references X, A–F, and Data Label A–F are defined.

LHRECORD: .WK? File Conversion Information (94h)

This record contains information that Microsoft Excel uses when it converts a .XLS file to a .WKS, .WK1, or .WK3 file, or vice versa.

Record Data

LHRECORD contains subrecords that resemble BIFF records. Each subrecord consists of the three fields described in the following table.

Offset (within subrecord)	Length (bytes)	Contents
0	2	Subrecord type (rtlh)
2	2	Length of subrecord data
4	var	Subrecord data

The following table describes the subrecords.

rtlh	Subrecord name	Contents
01h	(reserved)	Reserved for future use
02h	lhrtHpstGrHeader	Header string for /Graph Save Print help command
03h	lhrtHpstGrFooter	Footer string for /Graph Save Print help command
04h	lhrtNumGrLftMgn	Left margin for /Graph Save Print help command (IEEE number)
05h	lhrtNumGrRgtMgn	Right margin for /Graph Save Print help command (IEEE number)
06h	lhrtNumGrTopMgn	Top margin for /Graph Save Print help command (IEEE number)
07h	lhrtNumGrBotMgn	Bottom margin for /Graph Save Print help command (IEEE number)
08h	lhrtGrlh	Current /Graph View data. Structure similar to .WKS GRAPH record except that the first 13 references are not written. Instead, there are 13 integers that indicate whether the references X, A–F, and Data Label A–F are defined.
09h	lhrtcchGlColWidth	Current global column width (integer)
0Ah	(reserved)	Reserved for future use
0Bh	lhrttblType	Current table type: = 0, none (default) = 1, table1 = 2, table2
0Ch	(reserved)	Reserved for future use

LPR: Sheet Was Printed Using LINE.PRINT() (98h)

If this record appears in a file, it indicates that the sheet was printed using the LINE.PRINT() macro function. The LPR record stores options associated with this function.

Record Data

Offset	Name	Size	Contents
4	grbit	2	Option flags
6	cchMargLeft	2	Left margin, expressed as a count of characters
8	cchMargRight	2	Right margin, expressed as a count of characters
10	cliMargTop	2	Top margin, expressed as a count of lines
12	cliMargBot	2	Bottom margin, expressed as a count of lines
14	cliPg	2	Number of lines per page
16	cch	1	Length of printer setup string
17	rgch	var	Printer setup string

The grbit field contains the following option flags.

Offset	Bits	Mask	Name	Contents
0	0	01h	fWait	= 1, alert user after each sheet is printed
	1	02h	fFormatted	= 1, print headers and footers
	2	04h	fAutoLF	= 1, write only carriage return (CR) character (no line feed) at end of line
	7–3	F8h	(unused)	
1	7–0	FFh	(unused)	

MMS: ADDMENU/DELMENU Record Group Count (C1h)

This record stores the number of ADDMENU groups and DELMENU groups in the Book stream.

Record Data

Offset	Name	Size	Contents
4	caitm	1	Number of ADDMENU record groups
5	cditm	1	Number of DELMENU record groups

MULBLANK: Multiple Blank Cells (BEh)

The MULBLANK record stores up to the equivalent of 256 BLANK records; the MULBLANK record is a file size optimization. The number of ixfe fields can be determined from the ColLast field, and is equal to (colLast - colFirst + 1). The maximum length of the MULBLANK record is (256 x 2 + 10) = 522 bytes, because Microsoft Excel has at most 256 columns. Note that storing 256 blank cells in the MULBLANK record takes 522 bytes compared to 2560 bytes for 256 BLANK records.

Record Data

Offset	Name	Size	Contents
4	rw	2	Row number (0-based)
6	colFirst	2	Column number (0-based) of the first column of the multiple RK record
8	rgixfe	var	Array of indexes to XF records
10	colLast	2	Last column containing BLANKREC structure

MULRK: Multiple RK Cells (BDh)

The MULRK record stores up to the equivalent of 256 RK records; the MULRK record is a file size optimization. The number of 6-byte RKREC structures can be determined from the ColLast field, and is equal to (colLast - colFirst + 1). The maximum length of the MULRK record is (256 x 6 + 10) = 1546 bytes, because Microsoft Excel has at most 256 columns. Note that storing 256 RK numbers in the MULRK record takes 1546 bytes compared to 3584 bytes for 256 RK records.

Record Data

Offset	Name	Size	Contents
4	rw	2	Row number (0-based)
6	colFirst	2	Column number (0-based) of the first column of the multiple RK record
8	rgrkrec	var	Array of 6-byte RKREC structures
var	colLast	2	Last column containing RKREC structure

The RKREC structure is defined as follows:

```
typedef struct rkrec
        {
        SHORT ixfe;        /* index to XF record */
        long RK;     /* RK number */
        }
     RKREC;
```

NAME: Defined Name (18h)

The NAME record describes a defined name in the workbook.

Record Data

Offset	Name	Size	Contents
4	grbit	2	Option flags
6	chKey	1	Keyboard shortcut
7	cch	1	Length of the name text
8	cce	2	Length of the name definition
10	ixals	2	Index to sheet that contains this name, if the name is a local name (see text)
12	itab	2	This field is equal to ixals
14	cchCustMenu	1	Length of custom menu text
15	cchDescription	1	Length of description text
16	cchHelptopic	1	Length of help topic text
17	cchStatustext	1	Length of status bar text
18	rgch	var	Name text
var	rgce	var	Name definition (see text)
var	rgchCustMenu	var	Custom menu text
var	rgchDescr	var	Description text
var	rgchHelptopic	var	Help topic text
var	rgchStatustext	var	Status bar text

The grbit field contains the following option flags.

Bits	Mask	Name	Contents
0	0001h	fHidden	= 1 if name is hidden
1	0002h	fFunc	= 1 if name is a function
2	0004h	fOB	= 1 if name is a Visual Basic procedure

Bits	Mask	Name	Contents
3	0008h	fProc	= 1 if name is a function or command name on a macro sheet
4	0010h	fCalcExp	= 1 if name contains a complex function
5	0020h	fBuiltin	= 1 if name is a built-in name
11–6	0FC0h	fgrp	Function group index
12	1000h	fBig	= 1 if name refers to binary data (see text)
15–13	C000h	(reserved)	

If the fBig bit in the grbit field is equal to one, then the NAME record contains a name attached to binary data. These names can be created only by calling the xlDefineBinaryName function from the C API (see Chapters 1 and Chapter 2 of this book). The first byte is the length of the name, which is followed by the name string. Following the name string is the data to which the name refers. The data can be up to 2^{32} bytes long and may span multiple CONTINUE records.

The fCalcExp bit is set if the name definition contains a function that returns an array (for example, TREND, MINVERSE), contains a ROW or COLUMN function, or contains a user-defined function.

The chKey byte is significant only when the fProc bit is set in the grbit field. chKey is the keyboard shortcut for a command macro name. If the name is not a command macro name or has no keyboard shortcut, then chKey is meaningless.

The cch field contains the length of the name text and the rgch field contains the text itself. The cce field contains the length of the name definition and the rgce field contains the definition itself. The location of rgce within the record depends on the length of the name text (rgch) field.

The name definition (rgce) is stored in the Microsoft Excel parsed format. For more information, see "Microsoft Excel Formulas" on page 259.

The NAME record stores two types of names: global names and local names. A global name is defined for an entire workbook, and a local name is defined on a single sheet. For example, MyName is a global name, while Sheet1!MyName is a local name. The ixals field in the NAME record will be nonzero for local names and will index the list of EXTERNSHEET records for the sheets in the workbook. The following field, itab, is equal to ixals.

All NAME records should appear together in a BIFF file. The order of NAME records in an existing BIFF file should not be changed. You can add new names to a file, but they should be added at the end of the NAME list (block of NAME records). Microsoft Excel saves the names to the BIFF file in alphabetic order, but this is not a requirement; Microsoft Excel will sort the name list, if necessary, when it loads a BIFF file.

Built-in Names

Microsoft Excel contains several built-in names such as Criteria, Database, Auto_Open, and so on, for which the NAME records do not contain the actual name. Instead, cch always equals 1, and a single byte is used to identify the name as shown in the following table.

Built-in name	rgch
Consolidate_Area	00
Auto_Open	01
Auto_Close	02
Extract	03
Database	04
Criteria	05
Print_Area	06
Print_Titles	07
Recorder	08
Data_Form	09
Auto_Activate	0A
Auto_Deactivate	0B
Sheet_Title	0C

NOTE: Note Associated with a Cell (1Ch)

The NOTE record specifies a note associated with a cell.

Record Data

Offset	Name	Size	Contents
4	rw	2	Row of the note
6	col	2	Column of the note
8	cch	2	Length of the note (bytes)
10	rgch	var	The text of the note

The cell is given by the rw and col fields. The rw field contains the zero-based row number. The col field contains the zero-based column number.

The cch field contains the length of the note in bytes. The rgch field contains the text of the note in ASCII format.

Notes longer than 2048 characters (bytes) must be divided into several NOTE records, each record containing no more than 2048 characters. In this case, the first NOTE record contains the following fields.

Offset	Name	Size	Contents
4	rw	2	Row of the note
6	col	2	Column of the note
8	cch	2	Total length of the note
10	rgch	2048	The first 2048 characters of the note

Each successive NOTE record contains the following fields.

Offset	Name	Size	Contents
4	rw	2	= −1 always (FFFFh)
6	(reserved)	2	Reserved; must be zero
8	cch	2	Length of this section of the note
10	rgch	var	This section of the note

NUMBER: Cell Value, Floating-Point Number (03h)

A NUMBER record describes a cell containing a constant floating-point number. The rw field contains the zero-based row number. The col field contains the zero-based column number. The number is contained in the num field in 8-byte IEEE floating-point format.

Record Data

Offset	Name	Size	Contents
4	rw	2	Row
6	col	2	Column
8	ixfe	2	Index to XF record
10	num	8	Floating-point number value

OBJ: Describes a Graphic Object (5Dh)

BIFF files may contain several different variations of the OBJ record. They correspond to the graphic objects and dialog box controls available in Microsoft Excel: line object, rectangle object, check box object, and so on.

Record Data

The first 36 bytes of every OBJ record are fields that are common to all object types. The remaining fields are object-specific and are described in separate sections following the common object fields.

Common Object Fields

Offset	Name	Size	Contents
4	cObj	4	Count (1-based) of objects in file
8	OT	2	Object type: Group object: OT = 00h Line object: OT = 01h Rectangle object: OT = 02h Oval object: OT = 03h Arc object: OT = 04h Chart object: OT = 05h Text object: OT = 06h Button object: OT = 07h Picture object: OT = 08h Polygon object: OT = 09h Check box object: OT = 0Bh Option button object: OT = 0Ch Edit box object: OT = 0Dh Label object: OT = 0Eh Dialog frame object: OT = 0Fh Spinner object: OT = 10h Scroll bar object: OT = 11h List box object: OT = 12h Group box object: OT = 13h Drop-down object: OT = 14h
10	id	2	Object identification number
12	grbit	2	Option flags (see following table)
14	colL	2	Column containing the upper-left corner of the object's bounding rectangle
16	dxL	2	X (horizontal) position of the upper-left corner of the object's bounding rectangle, relative to the left side of the underlying cell, expressed in 1/1024th of the cell's width
18	rwT	2	Row containing the upper-left corner of the object's bounding rectangle
20	dyT	2	Y (vertical) position of the upper-left corner of the object's bounding rectangle, relative to the top of the underlying cell, expressed in 1/1024th of the cell's height

Offset	Name	Size	Contents
22	colR	2	Column containing the lower-right corner of the object's bounding rectangle
24	dxR	2	X (horizontal) position of the lower-right corner of the object's bounding rectangle, relative to the left side of the underlying cell, expressed in 1/1024th of the cell's width
26	rwB	2	Row containing the lower-right corner of the object's bounding rectangle
28	dyB	2	Y (vertical) position of the lower-right corner of the object's bounding rectangle, relative to the top of the underlying cell, expressed in 1/1024th of the cell's height
30	cbMacro	2	Length of the FMLA structure that stores the definition of the attached macro; see "FMLA Structure" on page 191. Some objects may store the length of the FMLA structure in a cbFmla that immediately preceded the FMLA; in these objects, cbMacro is ignored.
32	(reserved)	6	Reserved; must be zero

The grbit field at byte 12 contains the following flag bits.

Offset	Bits	Mask	Name	Contents
0	0	01h	fSel	= 1 if the object is selected
	1	02h	fAutoSize	= 1 if the object moves and sizes with cells
	2	04h	fMove	= 1 if the object moves with cells (Format Object dialog box, Properties tab)
	3	08h	(reserved)	Reserved; must be zero
	4	10h	fLocked	= 1 if the object is locked when the sheet is protected
	5	20h	(reserved)	Reserved; must be zero
	6	40h	(reserved)	Reserved; must be zero
	7	80h	fGrouped	= 1 if the object is part of a group of objects
1	0	01h	fHidden	= 1 if the object is hidden (can only be done from a macro)
	1	02h	fVisible	= 1 if the object is visible
	2	04h	fPrint	= 1 if the object is printable
	7-3	F8h	(reserved)	Reserved; must be zero

Line Object Fields

Offset	Name	Size	Contents
38	icv	1	Index to color palette for line color
39	lns	1	Line style: Solid: lns = 0 Dash: lns = 1 Dot: lns = 2 Dash-dot: lns = 3 Dash-dot-dot: lns = 4 Null (unused): lns = 5 Dark gray: lns = 6 Medium gray: lns = 7 Light gray: lns = 8
40	lnw	1	Line weight: Hairline: lnw = 0 Single: lnw = 1 Double: lnw = 2 Thick: lnw = 3
41	fAuto	1	Bit 0 = 1 if Automatic Border option is on (Format Object dialog box, Patterns tab). All other bits in fAuto are don't-care.
42	es	2	End style structure (see following table)
44	iqu	1	Quadrant index (direction of line): Starts upper left, ends lower right: iqu = 0 Starts upper right, ends lower left: iqu = 1 Starts lower right, ends upper left: iqu = 2 Starts lower left, ends upper right: iqu = 3
45	(reserved)	1	Reserved; must be zero
46	cchName	1	Length of name (null if no name)
47	stName	var	Name (null if no name; may contain a padding byte to force word-boundary alignment)
var	fmla	var	FMLA structure (see following section)

The end style structure (es) describes the arrowheads on the end point of the line. The structure contains four 4-bit fields as described in the following table.

Offset	Bits	Mask	Name	Contents
0	3–0	0Fh	sest	Arrowhead style: None: sest = 0 Open: sest = 1 Filled: sest = 2 Double-ended open: sest = 3 Double-ended filled: sest = 4
	7–4	F0h	sesw	Arrowhead width: Narrow: sesw = 0 Medium: sesw = 1 Wide: sesw = 2
1	3–0	0Fh	sesl	Arrowhead length: Short: sesl = 0 Medium: sesl = 1 Long: sesl = 2
	7–4	F0h	(unused)	

FMLA Structure

The FMLA structure stores a parsed expression for the macro that is attached to the object. For more information about parsed expressions, see "Microsoft Excel Formulas" on page 259. The FMLA structure is null if the object does not have a macro attached.

In some object types, the FMLA structure length is given by cbMacro in the common object fields. In other object types, the FMLA structure length is given by a cbFmla that immediately precedes the FMLA. In these object types, ignore cbMacro. There may be an optional padding byte at the end of the FMLA to force it to end on a word boundary. The FMLA structure has the following form.

Offset	Name	Size	Contents
0	cce	2	Length of parsed expression
2	(reserved)	4	
6	rgce	var	Parsed expression (may contain a padding byte to force word-boundary alignment)

Rectangle Object Fields

Offset	Name	Size	Contents
38	icvBack	1	Index to color palette for background color
39	icvFore	1	Index to color palette for foreground color
40	fls	1	Fill pattern

Offset	Name	Size	Contents
41	fAuto	1	Bit 0 = 1 if Automatic Fill option is on (Format Object dialog box, Patterns tab). All other bits in fAuto are don't-care.
42	icv	1	Index to color palette for line color
43	lns	1	Line style (see preceding section, "Line Object Fields")
44	lnw	1	Line weight (see preceding section, "Line Object Fields")
45	fAuto	1	Bit 0 = 1 if Automatic border option is on (Format Object dialog box, Patterns tab). All other bits in fAuto are don't-care.
46	frs	2	Frame style structure (see following table)
48	cchName	1	Length of name (null if no name)
49	stName	var	Name (null if no name; may contain a padding byte to force word-boundary alignment)
var	fmla	var	FMLA structure (see "FMLA Structure" on page 191)

The frame style structure (frs) contains 16 bits. Because dxyCorner overlaps the byte boundary, the structure is defined as a single 16-bit field instead of two 8-bit fields.

Offset	Bits	Mask	Name	Contents
0	0	0001h	frt	= 1 if rectangle has rounded corners (Format Object dialog box, Patterns tab)
	1	0002h	fShadow	= 1 if rectangle has a shadow border (Format Object dialog box, Patterns tab)
	9-2	03FCh	dxyCorner	Diameter of oval that describes rounded corners (if frt = 1)
	15–10	FC00h	(unused)	

Oval Object Fields

Offset	Name	Size	Contents
38	icvBack	1	Index to color palette for background color
39	icvFore	1	Index to color palette for foreground color
40	fls	1	Fill pattern
41	fAuto	1	Bit 0 = 1 if Automatic Fill option is on (Format Object dialog box, Patterns tab). All other bits in fAuto are don't-care.

Offset	Name	Size	Contents
42	icv	1	Index to color palette for line color
43	lns	1	Line style (see preceding section, "Line Object Fields")
44	lnw	1	Line weight (see preceding section, "Line Object Fields")
45	fAuto	1	Bit 0 = 1 if Automatic Border option is on (Format Object dialog box, Patterns tab). All other bits in fAuto are don't-care.
46	frs	2	Frame style structure (see following table)
48	cchName	1	Length of name (null if no name)
49	stName	var	Name (null if no name; may contain a padding byte to force word-boundary alignment)
var	fmla	var	FMLA structure (see "FMLA Structure" on page 191)

The frame style structure (frs) contains 16 bits. dxyCorner is not used for oval objects.

Offset	Bits	Mask	Name	Contents
0	0	0001h	frt	(not used for oval object)
	1	0002h	fShadow	= 1 if oval has a shadow border (Format Object dialog box, Patterns tab)
	2–9	03FCh	dxyCorner	(not used for oval object)
	10–15	FC00h	(unused)	

Arc Object Fields

Offset	Name	Size	Contents
38	icvBack	1	Index to color palette for background color
39	icvFore	1	Index to color palette for foreground color
40	fls	1	Fill pattern
41	fAuto	1	Bit 0 = 1 if Automatic Fill option is on (Format Object dialog box, Patterns tab). All other bits in fAuto are don't-care.
42	icv	1	Index to color palette for line color
43	lns	1	Line style (see preceding section, "Line Object Fields")
44	lnw	1	Line weight (see preceding section, "Line Object Fields")

Offset	Name	Size	Contents
45	fAuto	1	Bit 0 = 1 if Automatic Border option is on (Format Object dialog box, Patterns tab). All other bits in fAuto are don't-care.
46	iqu	1	Quadrant index (section of an oval that describes the arc): Upper-right quadrant of oval: iqu = 0 Upper-left quadrant of oval: iqu = 1 Lower-left quadrant of oval: iqu = 2 Lower-right quadrant of oval: iqu = 3
47	(reserved)	1	Reserved; must be zero
48	cchName	1	Length of name (null if no name)
49	stName	var	Name (null if no name; may contain a padding byte to force word-boundary alignment)
var	fmla	var	FMLA structure (see "FMLA Structure" on page 191)

Chart Object Fields

Offset	Name	Size	Contents
38	icvBack	1	Index to color palette for background color
39	icvFore	1	Index to color palette for foreground color
40	fls	1	Fill pattern
41	fAuto	1	Bit 0 = 1 if Automatic Fill option is on (Format Object dialog box, Patterns tab). All other bits in fAuto are don't-care.
42	icv	1	Index to color palette for line color
43	lns	1	Line style (see preceding section, "Line Object Fields")
44	lnw	1	Line weight (see preceding section, "Line Object Fields")
45	fAuto	1	Bit 0 = 1 if Automatic Border option is on (Format Object dialog box, Patterns tab). All other bits in fAuto are don't-care.
46	frs	2	Frame style structure (see preceding section, "Rectangle Object Fields")
48	grbit	2	Option flags (shown LSB to MSB): fLinked:1 = 1 if linked to chart sheet Reserved:15 Reserved; must be zero
50	(reserved)	16	Reserved; must be zero

Offset	Name	Size	Contents
66	cchName	1	Length of name (null if no name)
67	stName	var	Name (null if no name; may contain a padding byte to force word-boundary alignment)
var	fmla	var	FMLA structure (see "FMLA Structure" on page 191)

An embedded chart BIFF substream immediately follows the chart object record. This embedded chart file begins with a BOF record and ends with an EOF record. For more information on chart BIFF records, see Chapter 4, "File Format—Chart Records."

Text Object Fields

Offset	Name	Size	Contents
38	icvBack	1	Index to color palette for background color
39	icvFore	1	Index to color palette for foreground color
40	fls	1	Fill pattern
41	fAuto	1	Bit 0 = 1 if Automatic Fill option is on (Format Object dialog box, Patterns tab). All other bits in fAuto are don't-care.
42	icv	1	Index to color palette for line color
43	lns	1	Line style (see preceding section, "Line Object Fields")
44	lnw	1	Line weight (see preceding section, "Line Object Fields")
45	fAuto	1	Bit 0 = 1 if Automatic Border option is on (Format Object dialog box, Patterns tab). All other bits in fAuto are don't-care.
46	frs	2	Frame style structure (see preceding section, "Rectangle Object Fields")
48	cbText	2	Length of object text
50	(reserved)	2	Reserved; must be zero
52	cbRuns	2	Total length of all TXORUNS structures in record
54	ifntEmpty	2	If cbRuns = 0, then the text object is empty, and these 2 bytes contain the index to the FONT record for the object.
			If the object contains text, cbRuns > 0, and these 2 bytes are reserved.
56	(reserved)	2	Reserved; must be zero
58	grbit	2	Option flags (see following table)

Offset	Name	Size	Contents
60	rot	2	Orientation of text within object boundary (Format Object dialog box, Alignment tab): = 0 no rotation (text appears left to right) = 1 text appears top to bottom; letters are upright = 2 text is rotated 90 degrees counterclockwise = 3 text is rotated 90 degrees clockwise
62	(reserved)	12	Reserved; must be zero
74	cchName	1	Length of name (null if no name)
75	stName	var	Name (null if no name; may contain a padding byte to force word-boundary alignment)
var	fmla	var	FMLA structure (see "FMLA Structure" on page 191)
var	rgch	var	Object text; may contain a single padding byte at the end of the text for word-boundary alignment (cbText does not count this padding byte)
var	TXORUNS	8	TXORUNS structure; (see following description)
var	TXORUNS	8	TXORUNS structure; (see following description)

The grbit field at byte 58 contains the following option flags.

Offset	Bits	Mask	Name	Contents
0	0	01h	(reserved)	Reserved; must be zero
	3–1	0Eh	alcH	Horizontal text alignment: = 001 left-aligned = 010 centered = 011 right-aligned = 100 justified
	6–4	70h	alcV	Vertical text alignment: = 001 left-aligned = 010 centered = 011 right-aligned = 100 justified
	7	80h	fAutoTextSize	= 1 if Automatic Size option is on (Format Object dialog box, Alignment tab)
1	0	01h	(unused)	
	1	02h	fLockText	= 1 if the Lock Text option is on (Format Object dialog box, Protection tab)
	2	04h	fFuzzy	= 1 if object is selected (the broken border is displayed)
	7-3	F8h	(reserved)	Reserved; must be zero

The TXORUNS structure contains formatting information for the object text string. A TXORUNS structure occurs every time the text formatting changes. The TXORUNS structure is described in the following table.

Offset	Name	Size	Contents
0	ichFirst	2	Index to first character to which the formatting applies
2	ifnt	2	Index to FONT record
4	(reserved)	4	

There are always at least two TXORUNS structures in the text object record, even if the entire text string is normal font (ifnt = 0). The last TXORUNS structure, which ends the formatting information for the string, always has ichFirst = cbText, and ifnt = 0.

Button Object Fields

Offset	Name	Size	Contents
38	icvBack	1	Index to color palette for background color (fixed for buttons)
39	icvFore	1	Index to color palette for foreground color (fixed for buttons)
40	fls	1	Fill pattern (fixed for buttons)
41	grbit	1	Option flags (fixed for buttons)
42	icv	1	Index to color palette for line color (fixed for buttons)
43	lns	1	Line style (fixed for buttons)
44	lnw	1	Line weight (fixed for buttons)
45	fAuto	1	Bit 0 = 1 (fixed for buttons)
46	frs	2	Frame style structure (ignored for buttons)
48	cbText	2	Length of object text
50	(reserved)	2	Reserved; must be zero
52	cbRuns	2	Total length of all TXORUNS structures in record
54	ifntEmpty	2	If cbRuns = 0, then the button object is empty, and these 2 bytes contain the index to the FONT record for the object.
			If the object contains text, cbRuns > 0, and these 2 bytes are reserved.
56	(reserved)	2	Reserved; must be zero
58	grbit	2	Option flags (see following table):

Offset	Name	Size	Contents
60	rot	2	Orientation of text within object boundary (Format Object dialog box, Alignment tab): = 0, no rotation (text appears left to right) = 1, text appears top to bottom; letters are upright = 2, text is rotated 90 degrees counterclockwise = 3, text is rotated 90 degrees clockwise
62	(reserved)	6	Reserved; must be zero
68	grbit	2	Option flags (shown LSB to MSB): fDefault:1 = 1 if this is the default button fHelp:1 = 1 if this is the Help button fCancel:1 = 1 if this is the cancel button fDismiss:1 = 1 if this is the dismiss button Reserved:12 Reserved; must be zero
70	accel	2	Accelerator key character
72	accel2	2	Accelerator key character (Far East versions only)
74	cchName	1	Length of name (null if no name)
75	stName	var	Name (null if no name; may contain a padding byte to force word-boundary alignment)
var	fmla	var	FMLA structure (see "FMLA Structure" on page 191)
var	rgch	var	Object text; may contain a single padding byte at the end of the text for word-boundary alignment (cbText does not count this padding byte)
var	TXORUNS	8	TXORUNS structure; (see following description)
var	TXORUNS	8	TXORUNS structure; (see following description)

The grbit field at byte 58 contains the following option flags.

Offset	Bits	Mask	Name	Contents
0	0	01h	(reserved)	Reserved; must be zero
	3–1	0Eh	alcH	Horizontal text alignment: = 001 left-aligned = 010 centered = 011 right-aligned = 100 justified
	6–4	70h	alcV	Vertical text alignment: = 001 left-aligned = 010 centered = 011 right-aligned = 100 justified
	7	80h	fAutoTextSize	= 1 if Automatic Size option is on (Format Object dialog box, Alignment tab)

Offset	Bits	Mask	Name	Contents
1	0	01h	(unused)	
	1	02h	fLockText	= 1 if the Lock Text option is on (Format Object dialog box, Protection tab)
	2	04h	fFuzzy	= 1 if object is selected (the broken border is displayed)
	7-3	F8h	(reserved)	Reserved; must be zero

The TXORUNS structure contains formatting information for the object text string. A TXORUNS structure occurs every time the text formatting changes. The TXORUNS structure is described in the following table.

Offset	Name	Size	Contents
0	ichFirst	2	Index to first character to which the formatting applies
2	ifnt	2	Index to FONT record
4	(reserved)	4	

There are always at least two TXORUNS structures in the text object record, even if the entire text string is normal font (ifnt = 0). The last TXORUNS structure, which ends the formatting information for the string, always has ichFirst = cbText, and ifnt = 0.

Picture Object Fields

Offset	Name	Size	Contents
38	icvBack	1	Index to color palette for background color
39	icvFore	1	Index to color palette for foreground color
40	fls	1	Fill pattern
41	fAuto	1	Bit 0 = 1 if Automatic Fill option is on (Format Object dialog box, Patterns tab). All other bits in fAuto are don't-care.
42	icv	1	Index to color palette for line color
43	lns	1	Line style (see preceding section, "Line Object Fields")
44	lnw	1	Line weight (see preceding section, "Line Object Fields")
45	fAuto	1	Bit 0 = 1 if Automatic Border option is on (Format Object dialog box, Patterns tab). All other bits in fAuto are don't-care.
46	frs	2	Frame style structure (see preceding section, "Rectangle Object Fields")

Offset	Name	Size	Contents
48	cf	2	Image format: = 00h Text format = 01h Null format (no image data) = 02h Windows metafile or Macintosh PICT format = 09h Windows bitmap format
50	(reserved)	4	Reserved; must be zero
54	cbPictFmla	2	Length of picture FMLA structure (the FMLA that contains the link to the picture)
56	(reserved)	2	Reserved; must be zero
58	grbit	2	Option flags (see following table)
60	(reserved)	4	Reserved; must be zero
64	cchName	1	Length of name (null if no name)
65	stName	var	Name (null if no name; may contain a padding byte to force word-boundary alignment)
var	fmla	var	Attached macro FMLA structure (see "FMLA Structure" on page 191)
var	PictFmla	var	Picture FMLA structure (see "FMLA Structure" on page 191)
var	(reserved)	4	Reserved; must be zero

The grbit field at byte 58 contains the following option flags.

Offset	Bits	Mask	Name	Contents
0	0	01h	fAutoPict	= 0 if user manually sizes picture by dragging a handle
	1	02h	fDde	= 1 if reference in FMLA structure is a DDE reference
	2	04h	fIcon	= 1 if the picture is from a DDE link, and the only available representation of the picture is an icon
	7–3	F8h	(unused)	
1	7–0	FFh	(unused)	

Group Object Fields

A Group OBJ record precedes the OBJ records for the group members.

Offset	Name	Size	Contents
34	(reserved)	4	Reserved; must be zero
38	idNext	2	Object id number (id) of the object that follows the last object in this group. If there are no objects following the group, idNext = 0.
40	(reserved)	16	Reserved; must be zero

Polygon Object Fields

Offset	Name	Size	Contents
38	icvBack	1	Index to color palette for background color
39	icvFore	1	Index to color palette for foreground color
40	fls	1	Fill pattern
41	fAuto	1	Bit 0 = 1 if Automatic Fill option is on (Format Object dialog box, Patterns tab). All other bits in fAuto are don't-care.
42	icv	1	Index to color palette for line color
43	lns	1	Line style (see preceding section, "Line Object Fields")
44	lnw	1	Line weight (see preceding section, "Line Object Fields")
45	fAuto	1	Bit 0 = 1 if Automatic Border option is on (Format Object dialog box, Patterns tab). All other bits in fAuto are don't-care.
46	frs	2	Frame style structure (see preceding section, "Rectangle Object Fields")
48	wstate	2	If bit 0 = 1 the polygon is closed. All other bits are don't-care.
50	(reserved)	10	
60	iMacSav	2	Number of vertices in polygon (one-based)
62	(reserved)	8	
70	cchName	1	Length of name (null if no name)
71	stName	var	Name (null if no name; may contain a padding byte to force word-boundary alignment)
var	fmla	var	FMLA structure (see "FMLA Structure" on page 191)

For polygon objects, a COORDLIST record follows the OBJ record.

Check Box Object Fields

Offset	Name	Size	Contents
38	icvBack	1	Index to color palette for background color (fixed for check box objects)
39	icvFore	1	Index to color palette for foreground color (fixed for check box objects)
40	fls	1	Fill pattern (ignored for check box objects)
41	fAuto	1	(Ignored for check box objects)
42	icv	1	Index to color palette for line color (fixed for check box objects)
43	lns	1	Line style (ignored for check box objects)
44	lnw	1	Line weight (ignored for check box objects)
45	fAuto	1	(Ignored for check box objects)
46	frs	2	Frame style structure (ignored for check box objects)
48	(reserved)	10	Reserved; must be zero
58	grbit	2	Option flags (see following table)
60	(reserved)	20	Reserved; must be zero
80	cchName	1	Length of name (null if no name)
81	stName	var	Name (null if no name; may contain a padding byte to force word-boundary alignment)
var	cbFmla1	2	Length of FMLA structure for attached macro (never null)
var	fmla1	var	FMLA structure for attached macro (see "FMLA Structure" on page 191)
var	cbFmla2	2	Length of FMLA structure for cell link (never null)
var	fmla2	var	FMLA structure for cell link (see "FMLA Structure" on page 191)
var	cbText	2	Length of object text (never null)
var	rgch	var	Object text; may contain a single padding byte at the end of the text for word-boundary alignment (cbText does not count this padding byte)
var	fChecked	2	= 0 if check box is not checked = 1 if check box is checked = 2 if check box is gray (mixed)
var	accel	2	Accelerator key character
var	accel2	2	Accelerator key character (Far East versions only)

Offset	Name	Size	Contents
var	grbit	2	Option flags (shown LSB to MSB): fNo3d:1 = 1 if 3-d shading is off fBoxOnly:1 = 1 if only the box is drawn Reserved:14 Reserved; must be zero

The grbit field at byte 58 contains the following option flags.

Offset	Bits	Mask	Name	Contents
0	7-0	FFh	(reserved)	Reserved; must be zero
1	0	01h	(unused)	
	1	02h	fLockText	= 1 if the Lock Text option is on (Format Object dialog box, Protection tab)
	2	04h	fFuzzy	= 1 if object is selected (the broken border is displayed)
	7-3	F8h	(reserved)	Reserved; must be zero

Dialog Frame Object Fields

Offset	Name	Size	Contents
38	icvBack	1	Index to color palette for background color (fixed for dialog frame objects)
39	icvFore	1	Index to color palette for foreground color (fixed for dialog frame objects)
40	fls	1	Fill pattern (ignored for dialog frame objects)
41	grbit	1	Option flags (ignored for dialog frame objects)
42	icv	1	Index to color palette for line color (fixed for dialog frame objects)
43	lns	1	Line style (ignored for dialog frame objects)
44	lnw	1	Line weight (ignored for dialog frame objects)
45	fAuto	1	Bit 0 = 1 for dialog frame objects
46	frs	2	Frame style structure (ignored for dialog frame objects)
48	cbText	2	Length of object text
50	(reserved)	8	Reserved; must be zero
58	grbit	2	Option flags (see following table)
60	(reserved)	14	Reserved; must be zero
74	cchName	1	Length of name (null if no name)
75	stName	var	Name (null if no name; may contain a padding byte to force word-boundary alignment)
var	fmla	var	FMLA structure (see "FMLA Structure," p. 191)

Offset	Name	Size	Contents
var	rgch	var	Object text; may contain a single padding byte at the end of the text for word-boundary alignment (cbText does not count this padding byte)
var	TXORUNS	8	TXORUNS structure; (see following description)
var	TXORUNS	8	TXORUNS structure; (see following description)

The grbit field at byte 58 contains the following option flags.

Offset	Bits	Mask	Name	Contents
0	7-0	FFh	(reserved)	Reserved; must be zero
1	0	01h	(unused)	
	1	02h	fLockText	= 1 if the Lock Text option is on (Format Object dialog box, Protection tab)
	2	04h	fFuzzy	= 1 if object is selected (the broken border is displayed)
	7-3	F8h	(reserved)	Reserved; must be zero

The TXORUNS structure contains formatting information for the object text string, which is the dialog box caption. There are two TXORUNS structures in the dialog frame object record. The first has ichFirst = 00h and has ifnt pointing to the FONT record for the text. The second has ichFirst = cbText, and contains no other useful information. The TXORUNS structure is shown in the following table.

Offset	Name	Size	Contents
0	ichFirst	2	Index to first character to which the formatting applies
2	ifnt	2	Index to FONT record
4	(reserved)	4	

Drop-Down Object Fields

Offset	Name	Size	Contents
38	icvBack	1	Index to color palette for background color (fixed for drop-down objects)
39	icvFore	1	Index to color palette for foreground color (fixed for drop-down objects)
40	fls	1	Fill pattern (ignored for drop-down objects)
41	grbit	1	Option flags (ignored for drop-down objects)
42	icv	1	Index to color palette for line color (fixed for drop-down objects)
43	lns	1	Line style (ignored for drop-down objects)

Offset	Name	Size	Contents
44	lnw	1	Line weight (ignored for drop-down objects)
45	fAuto	1	Bit 0 = 1 for drop-down objects
46	frs	2	Frame style structure (ignored for drop-down objects)
48	(reserved)	4	Reserved; must be zero
52	iVal	2	Scroll bar position
54	iMin	2	Scroll bar minimum value
56	iMax	2	Scroll bar maximum value
58	dInc	2	Amount to scroll when arrow is clicked
60	dPage	2	Amount to scroll when scroll bar is clicked
62	fHoriz	2	= 1 if scroll bar is horizontal
64	dxScroll	2	Width of scroll bar
66	grbit	2	Option flags (shown LSB to MSB): (reserved):3 Reserved; must be zero fNo3d:1 = 1 if 3-d shading is off (reserved):12 Reserved; must be zero
68	(reserved)	18	Reserved; must be zero
86	ifnt	2	Index to FONT record for list box
88	(reserved)	14	Reserved; must be zero
102	xLeft	2	X (horizontal) position of the upper-left corner of the drop-down's bounding rectangle
104	yTop	2	Y (vertical) position of the upper-left corner of the drop-down's bounding rectangle
106	xRight	2	X (horizontal) position of the lower-right corner of the drop-down's bounding rectangle
108	yBot	2	Y (vertical) position of the lower-right corner of the drop-down's bounding rectangle
110	(reserved)	4	Reserved; must be zero
114	cchName	1	Length of name (null if no name)
115	stName	var	Name (null if no name; may contain a padding byte to force word-boundary alignment)
var	cbFmla1	2	Length of FMLA structure for attached macro (never null)
var	fmla1	var	FMLA structure for attached macro (see "FMLA Structure" on page 191)
var	cbFmla2	2	Length of FMLA structure for cell link (never null)
var	fmla2	var	FMLA structure for cell link (see "FMLA Structure" on page 191)

Offset	Name	Size	Contents
var	cbFmla3	2	Length of FMLA structure for input range (never null)
var	fmla3	var	FMLA structure for input range (see "FMLA Structure" on page 191)
var	cLines	2	Number of elements in list box (1-based)
var	iSel	2	Index of selected item (1-based)
var	grbit	2	Option flags (shown LSB to MSB): f(reserved):2 Reserved; must be zero fValidIds:1 = 1 if idEdit is valid fNo3d:1 = 1 if 3-d shading is off (reserved):12 Reserved; must be zero
var	(reserved)	2	Reserved; must be zero
var	grbit	2	Option flags (shown LSB to MSB): wStyle:2 Drop-down style: 0 = combo, 1 = combo edit, 2 = simple 3 = max (reserved):14 Reserved; must be zero
var	cLine	2	Maximum number of lines that drop-down contains before a scroll bar is added
var	dxMin	2	Minimum allowable width of the drop-down
var	(reserved)	2	Reserved; must be zero

Edit Box Object Fields

Offset	Name	Size	Contents
38	icvBack	1	Index to color palette for background color (fixed for edit box objects)
39	icvFore	1	Index to color palette for foreground color (fixed for edit box objects)
40	fls	1	Fill pattern (ignored for edit box objects)
41	grbit	1	Option flags (ignored for edit box objects)
42	icv	1	Index to color palette for line color (fixed for edit box objects)
43	lns	1	Line style (ignored for edit box objects)
44	lnw	1	Line weight (ignored for edit box objects)
45	fAuto	1	Bit 0 = 1 for edit box objects
46	frs	2	Frame style structure (ignored for edit box objects)
48	(reserved)	10	Reserved; must be zero

Offset	Name	Size	Contents
58	grbit	2	Option flags (see following table)
60	(reserved)	14	Reserved; must be zero
74	cchName	1	Length of name (null if no name)
75	stName	var	Name (null if no name; may contain a padding byte to force word-boundary alignment)
var	cbFmla	2	Length of FMLA structure for attached macro (never null)
var	fmla	var	FMLA structure for attached macro (see "FMLA Structure" on page 191)
var	cbText	2	Length of object text (never null)
var	rgch	var	Object text; may contain a single padding byte at the end of the text for word-boundary alignment (cbText does not count this padding byte)
var	ivtEdit	2	Edit validation: = 000, Text = 001, Integer = 010, Number = 011, Reference = 100, Formula
var	fMultiLine	2	= 1 if edit is multiline
var	fVScroll	2	= 1 if edit box has vertical scroll bar
var	idList	2	Object id of linked list box or linked drop-down, if edit box is part of a combination list-edit or combination drop-down edit. If idList = 0, then this is a simple edit box.

The grbit field at byte 58 contains the following option flags.

Offset	Bits	Mask	Name	Contents
0	7-0	FFh	(reserved)	Reserved; must be zero
1	0	01h	(unused)	
	1	02h	fLockText	= 1 if the Lock Text option is on (Format Object dialog box, Protection tab)
	2	04h	fFuzzy	= 1 if object is selected (the broken border is displayed)
	7-3	F8h	(reserved)	Reserved; must be zero

Group Box Object Fields

Offset	Name	Size	Contents
38	icvBack	1	Index to color palette for background color (fixed for group box objects)
39	icvFore	1	Index to color palette for foreground color (fixed for group box objects)
40	fls	1	Fill pattern (ignored for group box objects)
41	grbit	1	Option flags (ignored for group box objects)
42	icv	1	Index to color palette for line color (fixed for group box objects)
43	lns	1	Line style (ignored for group box objects)
44	lnw	1	Line weight (ignored for group box objects)
45	fAuto	1	Bit 0 = 1 for group box objects
46	frs	2	Frame style structure (ignored for group box objects)
48	(reserved)	10	Reserved; must be zero
58	grbit	2	Option flags (see following table)
60	(reserved)	26	Reserved; must be zero
86	cchName	1	Length of name (null if no name)
87	stName	var	Name (null if no name; may contain a padding byte to force word-boundary alignment)
var	cbFmla	2	Length of FMLA structure (never null)
var	fmla	var	FMLA structure (see "FMLA Structure," p. 191)
var	cbText	2	Length of object text (never null)
var	rgch	var	Object text; may contain a single padding byte at the end of the text for word-boundary alignment (cbText does not count this padding byte)
var	accel	2	Accelerator key character
var	accel2	2	Accelerator key character (Far East versions only)
var	grbit	2	Option flags (shown LSB to MSB): fNo3d:1 = 1 if 3-d shading is off (reserved):15 Reserved; must be zero

The grbit field at byte 58 contains the following option flags.

Offset	Bits	Mask	Name	Contents
0	7-0	FFh	(reserved)	Reserved; must be zero
1	0	01h	(unused)	
	1	02h	fLockText	= 1 if the Lock Text option is on (Format Object dialog box, Protection tab)

Offset	Bits	Mask	Name	Contents
	2	04h	fFuzzy	= 1 if object is selected (the broken border is displayed)
	7-3	F8h	(reserved)	Reserved; must be zero

Label Object Fields

Offset	Name	Size	Contents
38	icvBack	1	Index to color palette for background color (fixed for label objects)
39	icvFore	1	Index to color palette for foreground color (fixed for label objects)
40	fls	1	Fill pattern (ignored for label objects)
41	grbit	1	Option flags (ignored for label objects)
42	icv	1	Index to color palette for line color (fixed for label objects)
43	lns	1	Line style (ignored for label objects)
44	lnw	1	Line weight (ignored for label objects)
45	fAuto	1	Bit 0 = 1 for label objects
46	frs	2	Frame style structure (ignored for label objects)
48	cbText	2	Length of object text
50	(reserved)	8	Reserved; must be zero
58	grbit	2	Option flags (see following table)
60	(reserved)	14	Reserved; must be zero
74	cchName	1	Length of name (null if no name)
75	stName	var	Name (null if no name; may contain a padding byte to force word-boundary alignment)
var	fmla	var	FMLA structure (see "FMLA Structure" on page 191)
var	rgch	var	Object text; may contain a single padding byte at the end of the text for word-boundary alignment (cbText does not count this padding byte)
var	TXORUNS	8	TXORUNS structure; (see following description)
var	TXORUNS	8	TXORUNS structure; (see following description)

The grbit field at byte 58 contains the following option flags.

Offset	Bits	Mask	Name	Contents
0	7-0	FFh	(reserved)	Reserved; must be zero
1	0	01h	(unused)	

Offset	Bits	Mask	Name	Contents
	1	02h	fLockText	= 1 if the Lock Text option is on (Format Object dialog box, Protection tab)
	2	04h	fFuzzy	= 1 if object is selected (the broken border is displayed)
	7-3	F8h	(reserved)	Reserved; must be zero

The TXORUNS structure contains formatting information for the object text string, which is the label string. There are two TXORUNS structures in the label object record. The first has ichFirst = 00h and has ifnt pointing to the FONT record for the label. The second has ichFirst = cbText, and contains no other useful information. The TXORUNS structure is shown in the following table.

Offset	Name	Size	Contents
0	ichFirst	2	Index to first character to which the formatting applies
2	ifnt	2	Index to FONT record
4	(reserved)	4	

List Box Object Fields

Offset	Name	Size	Contents
38	icvBack	1	Index to color palette for background color (fixed for list box objects)
39	icvFore	1	Index to color palette for foreground color (fixed for list box objects)
40	fls	1	Fill pattern (ignored for list box objects)
41	grbit	1	Option flags (ignored for list box objects)
42	icv	1	Index to color palette for line color (fixed for list box objects)
43	lns	1	Line style (ignored for list box objects)
44	lnw	1	Line weight (ignored for list box objects)
45	fAuto	1	Bit 0 = 1 for list box objects
46	frs	2	Frame style structure (ignored for list box objects)
48	(reserved)	4	Reserved; must be zero
52	iVal	2	Scroll bar position
54	iMin	2	Scroll bar minimum value
56	iMax	2	Scroll bar maximum value
58	dInc	2	Amount to scroll when arrow is clicked
60	dPage	2	Amount to scroll when scroll bar is clicked
62	fHoriz	2	= 1 if scroll bar is horizontal

Offset	Name	Size	Contents
64	dxScroll	2	Width of scroll bar
66	grbit	2	Option flags (shown LSB to MSB): (reserved):3 Reserved; must be zero fNo3d:1 = 1 if 3-d shading is off (reserved):12 Reserved; must be zero
68	(reserved)	18	Reserved; must be zero
86	ifnt	2	Index to FONT record for list box
88	(reserved)	4	Reserved; must be zero
92	cchName	1	Length of name (null if no name)
93	stName	var	Name (null if no name; may contain a padding byte to force word-boundary alignment)
var	cbFmla1	2	Length of FMLA structure for attached macro (never null)
var	fmla1	var	FMLA structure for attached macro (see "FMLA Structure" on page 191)
var	cbFmla2	2	Length of FMLA structure for cell link (never null)
var	fmla2	var	FMLA structure for cell link (see "FMLA Structure" on page 191)
var	cbFmla3	2	Length of FMLA structure for input range (never null)
var	fmla3	var	FMLA structure for input range (see "FMLA Structure" on page 191)
var	cLines	2	Number of elements in list box (1-based)
var	iSel	2	Index of selected item (1-based)
var	grbit	2	Option flags (shown LSB to MSB): f(reserved):2 Reserved; must be zero fValidIds:1 = 1 if idEdit is valid fNo3d:1 = 1 if 3-d shading is off wListSelType:2 List box selection type: 0 = standard, 1 = multi-select, 2 = extended-select (reserved):10 Reserved; must be zero
var	idEdit	2	Object id of linked edit box, if list box is part of a combination list-edit. If idList = 0, then this is a simple list box.

Offset	Name	Size	Contents
var	rgbSel	var	Array of bytes, indicating which items are selected in a multi-select or extended-select list box. The number of elements in the array is equal to cLines. If an item is selected in the list box, then the corresponding element in the array = 1.

Option Button Object Fields

Offset	Name	Size	Contents
38	icvBack	1	Index to color palette for background color (fixed for option button objects)
39	icvFore	1	Index to color palette for foreground color (fixed for option button objects)
40	fls	1	Fill pattern (ignored for option button objects)
41	fAuto	1	(Ignored for option button objects)
42	icv	1	Index to color palette for line color (fixed for option button objects)
43	lns	1	Line style (ignored for option button objects)
44	lnw	1	Line weight (ignored for option button objects)
45	fAuto	1	(Ignored for option button objects)
46	frs	2	Frame style structure (ignored for option button objects)
48	(reserved)	10	Reserved; must be zero
58	grbit	2	Option flags (see following table)
60	(reserved)	32	Reserved; must be zero
92	cchName	1	Length of name (null if no name)
93	stName	var	Name (null if no name; may contain a padding byte to force word-boundary alignment)
var	cbFmla1	2	Length of FMLA structure for attached macro (never null)
var	fmla1	var	FMLA structure for attached macro (see "FMLA Structure" on page 191)
var	cbFmla2	2	Length of FMLA structure for cell link (never null)
var	fmla2	var	FMLA structure for cell link (see "FMLA Structure" on page 191)
var	cbText	2	Length of object text (never null)
var	rgch	var	Object text; may contain a single padding byte at the end of the text for word-boundary alignment (cbText does not count this padding byte)

Offset	Name	Size	Contents
var	fChecked	2	= 0 if option button is not checked = 1 if option button is checked
var	accel	2	Accelerator key character
var	accel2	2	Accelerator key character (Far East versions only)
var	grbit	2	Option flags (shown LSB to MSB): fNo3d:1 = 1 if 3-d shading is off fBoxOnly:1 = 1 if only the box is drawn Reserved:14 Reserved; must be zero
var	idRadNext	2	Object ID of the next option button in the group
var	fFirstBtn	2	= 1 if this option button is the first in the group

The grbit field at byte 58 contains the following option flags.

Offset	Bits	Mask	Name	Contents
0	7-0	FFh	(reserved)	Reserved; must be zero
1	0	01h	(unused)	
	1	02h	fLockText	= 1 if the Lock Text option is on (Format Object dialog box, Protection tab)
	2	04h	fFuzzy	= 1 if object is selected (the broken border is displayed)
	7-3	F8h	(reserved)	Reserved; must be zero

Scroll Bar Object Fields

Offset	Name	Size	Contents
38	icvBack	1	Index to color palette for background color (fixed for scroll bar objects)
39	icvFore	1	Index to color palette for foreground color (fixed for scroll bar objects)
40	fls	1	Fill pattern (ignored for scroll bar objects)
41	grbit	1	Option flags (ignored for scroll bar objects)
42	icv	1	Index to color palette for line color (fixed for scroll bar objects)
43	lns	1	Line style (ignored for scroll bar objects)
44	lnw	1	Line weight (ignored for scroll bar objects)
45	fAuto	1	Bit 0 = 1 for scroll bar objects
46	frs	2	Frame style structure (ignored for scroll bar objects)
48	(reserved)	4	Reserved; must be zero
52	iVal	2	Scroll bar position

Offset	Name	Size	Contents
54	iMin	2	Scroll bar minimum value
56	iMax	2	Scroll bar maximum value
58	dInc	2	Amount to scroll when arrow is clicked
60	dPage	2	Amount to scroll when scroll bar is clicked
62	fHoriz	2	= 1 if scroll bar is horizontal
64	dxScroll	2	Width of scroll bar
66	grbit	2	Option flags (shown LSB to MSB): (reserved):3 Reserved; must be zero fNo3d:1 = 1 if 3-d shading is off (reserved):12 Reserved; must be zero
68	cchName	1	Length of name (null if no name)
69	stName	var	Name (null if no name; may contain a padding byte to force word-boundary alignment)
var	cbFmla1	2	Length of FMLA structure for attached macro (never null)
var	fmla1	var	FMLA structure for attached macro (see "FMLA Structure" on page 191)
var	cbFmla2	2	Length of FMLA structure for cell link (never null)
var	fmla2	var	FMLA structure for cell link (see "FMLA Structure" on page 191)

Spinner Object Fields

Offset	Name	Size	Contents
38	icvBack	1	Index to color palette for background color (fixed for spinner objects)
39	icvFore	1	Index to color palette for foreground color (fixed for spinner objects)
40	fls	1	Fill pattern (ignored for spinner objects)
41	grbit	1	Option flags (ignored for spinner objects)
42	icv	1	Index to color palette for line color (fixed for spinner objects)
43	lns	1	Line style (ignored for spinner objects)
44	lnw	1	Line weight (ignored for spinner objects)
45	fAuto	1	Bit 0 = 1 for spinner objects
46	frs	2	Frame style structure (ignored for spinner objects)
48	(reserved)	4	Reserved; must be zero
52	iVal	2	Spinner position

Offset	Name	Size	Contents
54	iMin	2	Spinner minimum value
56	iMax	2	Spinner maximum value
58	dInc	2	Amount to scroll when spinner is clicked
60	(reserved)	2	Reserved; must be zero
62	fHoriz	2	= 1 if spinner is horizontal
64	dxScroll	2	Width of spinner
66	grbit	2	Option flags (shown LSB to MSB): (reserved):3 Reserved; must be zero fNo3d:1 = 1 if 3-d shading is off (reserved):12 Reserved; must be zero
68	cchName	1	Length of name (null if no name)
69	stName	var	Name (null if no name; may contain a padding byte to force word-boundary alignment)
var	cbFmla1	2	Length of FMLA structure for attached macro (never null)
var	fmla1	var	FMLA structure for attached macro (see "FMLA Structure" on page 191)
var	cbFmla2	2	Length of FMLA structure for cell link (never null)
var	fmla2	var	FMLA structure for cell link (see "FMLA Structure" on page 191)

OBJPROTECT: Objects Are Protected (63h)

The OBJPROTECT record stores an option from the Protection command.

Record Data

Offset	Name	Size	Contents
4	fLockObj	2	= 1 if objects are protected

OBPROJ: Visual Basic Project (D3h)

The contents of this record are reserved.

Record Data

Offset	Name	Size	Contents
4	(reserved)	var	

OLESIZE: Size of OLE Object (DEh)

This record stores the size of an embedded OLE object (when Microsoft Excel is a server).

Record Data

Offset	Name	Size	Contents
4	(reserved)	2	
6	rwFirst	2	First row
8	rwLast	2	Last row
10	colFirst	1	First column
11	colLast	1	Last column

PALETTE: Color Palette Definition (92h)

The PALETTE record describes the colors selected in the Options dialog box, Color tab. Each rgch field contains 4 bytes, rgbRed, rgbGreen, rgbBlue, and an unused byte. The 3 color bytes correspond to the Red, Green, and Blue values in the Color Picker dialog box, and the unused byte is don't-care. The Color Picker dialog box appears when you choose the Modify button in the Color tab. If the worksheet uses the default palette, the BIFF file does not contain the PALETTE record.

Record Data

Offset	Name	Size	Contents
4	ccv	2	Count of color values that follow
6	rgch	4	Color value of first color in palette
10	rgch	4	Color value of second color in palette
14	rgch	4	Color value of third color in palette
...	...	...	...
var	rgch	4	Color value of last (= ccv) color in palette

PANE: Number of Panes and Their Position (41h)

The PANE record describes the number and position of unfrozen panes in a window.

Record Data

Offset	Name	Size	Contents
4	x	2	Horizontal position of the split; zero if none
6	y	2	Vertical position of the split; zero if none
8	rwTop	2	Top row visible in the bottom pane
10	colLeft	2	Leftmost column visible in the right pane
12	pnnAct	2	Pane number of the active pane

The x and y fields contain the position of the vertical and horizontal splits, respectively, in units of 1/20 of a point. Either of these fields may be zero, indicating that the window is not split in the corresponding direction.

For a window with a horizontal split, the rwTop field is the topmost row visible in the bottom pane or panes. For a window with a vertical split, the colLeft field contains the leftmost column visible in the right pane or panes.

The pnnAct field indicates which pane is the active pane. The pnnAct field contains one of the following values:

    0 = bottom right
    1 = top right
    2 = bottom left
    3 = top left

If the window has frozen panes, as specified in the WINDOW2 record, then x and y have special meaning. If there is a vertical split, then x contains the number of columns visible in the top pane. If there is a horizontal split, then y contains the number of rows visible in the left pane. Both types of splits can be present in a window, as in unfrozen panes.

PASSWORD: Protection Password (13h)

The PASSWORD record contains the encrypted password for a protected sheet or workbook. Note that this record specifies a sheet-level or workbook-level protection password, as opposed to the FILEPASS record, which specifies a file password.

Record Data

Offset	Name	Size	Contents
4	wPassword	2	Encrypted password

PLS: Environment-Specific Print Record (4Dh)

The PLS record saves printer settings and printer driver information.

Record Data, Macintosh

Offset	Name	Size	Contents
4	wEnv	2	Operating environment: 0 = Microsoft Windows 1 = Apple Macintosh
6	rgb	var	TPrint structure (for more information on this structure, see *Inside Macintosh,* Volume II, page 149)

Record Data, Windows

Offset	Name	Size	Contents
4	wEnv	2	Operating environment: 0 = Microsoft Windows 1 = Apple Macintosh
6	rgb	var	DEVMODE structure (for more information on this structure, see the documentation for the Microsoft Windows Software Development Kit

PRECISION: Precision (0Eh)

The PRECISION record stores the Precision as Displayed option from the Options dialog box, Calculation tab.

Record Data

Offset	Name	Size	Contents
4	fFullPrec	2	= 0 if Precision As Displayed option is selected

PRINTGRIDLINES: Print Gridlines Flag (2Bh)

This record stores the Gridlines option from the Page Setup dialog box, Sheet tab.

Record Data

Offset	Name	Size	Contents
4	fPrintGrid	2	= 1 to print gridlines

PRINTHEADERS: Print Row/Column Labels (2Ah)

The PRINT HEADERS record stores the Row and Column Headings option from the Page Setup dialog box, Sheet tab.

Record Data

Offset	Name	Size	Contents
4	fPrintRwCol	2	= 1 to print row and column headers

PROTECT: Protection Flag (12h)

The PROTECT record stores the protection state for a sheet or workbook.

Record Data

Offset	Name	Size	Contents
4	fLock	2	= 1 if the sheet or workbook is protected

PUB: Publisher (89h)

The PUB record contains information for the publisher/subscriber feature. This record can be created only by Microsoft Excel for the Macintosh. However, if any other platform version of Microsoft Excel encounters the PUB record in a BIFF file, it leaves the record in the file, unchanged, when the file is saved.

Record Data

Offset	Name	Size	Contents
4	grbit	2	Option flags
6	ref	6	Reference structure describing the published area on the worksheet
12	sec	36	Section record associated with the published area
48	rgbAlias	var	Contents of the alias pointed to by the section record

The grbit field contains the following option flags.

Offset	Bits	Mask	Name	Contents
0	0	01h	fAprPrinted	= 1 if published appearance is shown when printed

Offset	Bits	Mask	Name	Contents
	1	02h	fSizPrinted	= 1 if published size is shown when printed
	7–2	FCh	(unused)	
1	7–0	FFh	(unused)	

RECIPNAME: Recipient Name (B9h)

This record stores recipient information for a routing slip. The rgch field contains the concatenation of two null-terminated strings: Recipient's Friendly Name, and Recipient's System-specific Address.

Record Data

Offset	Name	Size	Contents
4	cchRecip	2	Length of recipient's friendly name string
6	ulEIDSize	4	Length of recipient's system-specific address string
10	rgchRecip	var	(see text)

REFMODE: Reference Mode (0Fh)

The REFMODE record stores the Reference Style option from the Options dialog box, General tab.

Record Data

Offset	Name	Size	Contents
4	fRefA1	2	Reference mode: = 1 for A1 mode = 0 for R1C1 mode

RIGHTMARGIN: Right Margin Measurement (27h)

The RIGHT MARGIN record specifies the right margin in inches. The num field is in 8-byte IEEE floating-point format.

Record Data

Offset	Name	Size	Contents
4	num	8	Right margin

RK: Cell Value, RK Number (7Eh)

Microsoft Excel uses an internal number type, called an RK number, to save memory and disk space.

Record Data

Offset	Name	Size	Contents
4	rw	2	Row number
6	col	2	Column number
8	ixfe	2	Index to XF record that contains cell format
10	rk	4	RK number (see following description)

An RK number is either a 30-bit integer or the most-significant 30 bits of an IEEE number. The two LSBs of the 32-bit rk field are always reserved for RK type encoding; this is why the RK numbers are 30 bits, not the full 32. See the following diagram.

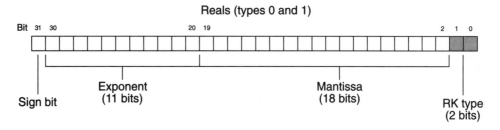

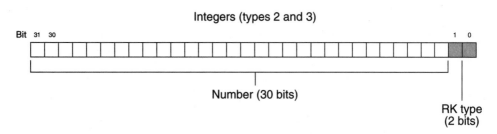

There are four different RK number types, as described in the following table.

RK type	Encode priority	Number (decimal)	RK number (hex)	Description of 30-bit encoding
0	1	1	3F F0 00 00	IEEE number

RK type	Encode priority	Number (decimal)	RK number (hex)	Description of 30-bit encoding
1	3	1.23	40 5E C0 01	IEEE number x 100
2	2	12345678	02 F1 85 3A	Integer
3	4	123456.78	02 F1 85 3B	Integer x 100

Microsoft Excel always attempts to store a number as an RK number instead of an IEEE number. There is also a specific priority of RK number encoding that the program uses. The following flowchart is a simplified version of the encoding algorithm. The algorithm always begins with an IEEE (full 64-bit) number.

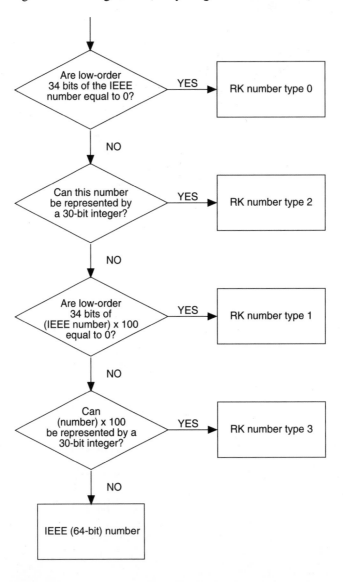

Microsoft*Press*®

Quality Computer Books

1-800-MSPRESS

You can use the following C code to demonstrate how to decode RK numbers:

Microsoft QuickC™

```c
double NumFromRk(long rk)
    {
    double num;
    if(rk & 0x02)
        {
        // int
        num = (double) (rk >> 2);
        }
    else
        {
        // hi words of IEEE num
        *((long *)&num+1) = rk & 0xfffffffc;
        *((long *)&num) = 0;
        }
    if(rk & 0x01)
        // divide by 100
        num /= 100;
    return num;
    }
main()
    {
    printf("%f\n", NumFromRk (0x02f1853b));
    }
```

THINK C

```c
short double NumFromRk(long int rk)
    {
    short double num;
    if(rk & 0x02)
        {
        /* int */
        num = (short double) (rk >> 2);
        }
    else
        {
        /* hi words of IEEE num */
        *((long int *)&num + 1) = 0;
        *((long int *)&num) = rk & 0xfffffffc;
        }
    if(rk & 0x01)
        /* divide by 100 */
        num /= 100;
    return num;
    }
main()
```

```
{
printf("%f\n", NumFromRk (0x02f1853b));
}
```

If you write a NUMBER record to a BIFF file, Microsoft Excel may convert the number to an RK number when it reads the file.

ROW: Describes a Row (08h)

A ROW record describes a single row in a Microsoft Excel sheet. ROW records and their associated cell records occur in blocks of up to 32 rows. Each block ends with a DBCELL record. For more information about row blocks and about optimizing your code when searching for cell records, see "Finding Cell Records in BIFF Files" on page 255.

Record Data

Offset	Name	Size	Contents
4	rw	2	Row number
6	colMic	2	First defined column in the row
8	colMac	2	Last defined column in the row, plus 1
10	miyRw	2	Row height
12	irwMac	2	Used by Microsoft Excel to optimize loading the file; if you are creating a BIFF file, set irwMac = 0
14	(reserved)	2	
16	grbit	2	Option flags
18	ixfe	2	If fGhostDirty = 1 (see grbit field), this is the index to the XF record for the row. Otherwise this field is undefined.
			Note: ixfe uses only the low-order 12 bits of the field (bits 11–0). Bit 12 is fExAsc, bit 13 is fExDsc, and bits 14 and 15 are reserved. fExAsc and fExDsc are set true if the row has extra space above or below, respectively.

The grbit field contains the following option flags.

Offset	Bits	Mask	Name	Contents
0	2–0	07h	iOutLevel	Index to outline level of row
	3	08h	(reserved)	
	4	10h	fCollapsed	= 1 if row is collapsed in outlining
	5	20h	fDyZero	= 1 if row height is set to zero

Offset	Bits	Mask	Name	Contents
0	6	40h	fUnsynced	= 1 if font height and row height are not compatible
	7	80h	fGhostDirty	= 1 if the row has been formatted, even if it contains all blank cells
1	7–0	FFh	(reserved)	

The rw field contains the zero-based row number. The colMic and colMac fields give the range of defined columns in the row.

The miyRw field contains the row height, in units of 1/20 of a point. The miyRw field may have the 8000h (2^{15}) bit set, indicating that the row is standard height. The low-order 15 bits must still contain the row height. If you hide the row, either by setting row height to zero, or by choosing the Hide command, miyRw still contains the original row height. This allows Microsoft Excel to restore the original row height when you choose the Unhide button.

Each row can have default cell attributes that control the format of all undefined cells in the row. By specifying default cell attributes for a particular row, you are effectively formatting all the undefined cells in the row without using memory for those cells. Default cell attributes do not affect the formats of cells that are explicitly defined.

For example, if you want all of row 3 to be left-aligned, then you could define all 256 cells in the row and specify that each individual cell be left-aligned. This would require storage for each of the 256 cells. An easy alternative would be to set the default cell for row 3 to be left-aligned and not define any individual cells in row 3.

RSTRING: Cell with Character Formatting (D6h)

When part of a string in a cell has character formatting, then an RSTRING record is written instead of the LABEL record.

Record Data

Offset	Name	Size	Contents
4	rw	2	Row
6	col	2	Column
8	ixfe	2	Index to XF record
10	cch	2	Length of string
12	rgch	var	String
var	cruns	1	Count of STRUN structures
var	rgstrun	var	Array of STRUN structures

The STRUN structure contains formatting information for the string. A STRUN structure occurs every time the text formatting changes. The STRUN structure is described in the following table.

Offset	Name	Size	Contents
0	ich	1	Index to first character to which the formatting applies
1	ifnt	1	Index to FONT record

SAVERECALC: Recalculate Before Save (5Fh)

If the Recalculate before Save option is selected in the Options dialog box, Calculation tab, then fSaveRecalc = 1.

Record Data

Offset	Name	Size	Contents
4	fSaveRecalc	2	= 1 to recalc before saving

SCENARIO: Scenario Data (AFh)

This records stores information for an individual scenario.

Record Data

Offset	Name	Size	Contents
4	cref	2	Number of changing cells
6	fLocked	1	= 1 if the scenario is locked for changes
7	fHidden	1	= 1 if the scenario is hidden
8	cchName	1	Length of name
9	cchComment	1	Length of comment
10	cchNameUser	1	Length of user name
11	rgch	var	Concatenation of scenario name string, user name string (preceded by duplicate of cchNameUser), and comment string (preceded by duplicate of cchComment)
var	rgRef	var	Array of cell references that contains changing cells (see text)
var	rgst	var	Array of byte-counted strings that contains changing cell values (see text)
var	rgIfmt	var	Array of ifmt for cell values (see text)

The changing cells for the scenario are stored in the three arrays at the end of the record. The rgRef array contains the cell addresses, as shown in the following table.

Offset	Name	Size	Contents
0	rw	2	Row number (zero-based)
2	col	2	Column number (zero-based)

The cell values are always stored as an array of byte-counted strings, as shown in the following table.

Offset	Name	Size	Contents
0	cch	1	Length of string
1	rgch	var	String

Finally, the cell number format indexes (ifmt) are stored as an array of 2-byte integers, following the array of cell value strings. These are only stored when the scenario contains cells with date/time number formats. If the cells contain any other number format, the rgIfmt will contain zeros.

SCENMAN: Scenario Output Data (AEh)

This records stores the general information for the set of scenarios on a worksheet.

Record Data

Offset	Name	Size	Contents
4	csct	2	Number of scenarios
6	isctCur	2	Index of current scenario
8	isctShown	2	Index of last displayed scenario
10	irefRslt	2	Number of reference areas in the following scenario result array
12	rgref	var	Scenario result array (see following table)

Each reference area in the scenario result array contains the following fields.

Offset	Name	Size	Contents
0	rwFirst	2	First row
2	rwLast	2	Last row
4	colFirst	1	First column
5	colLast	1	Last column

SCENPROTECT: Scenario Protection (DDh)

This record stores the scenario protection flag.

Record Data

Offset	Name	Size	Contents
4	fScenProtect	2	= 1 if scenarios are protected

SCL: Window Zoom Magnification (A0h)

This record stores the window zoom magnification.

Record Data

Offset	Name	Size	Contents
4	nscl	2	Numerator of reduced fraction
6	dscl	2	Denominator of reduced fraction

The magnification is stored as a reduced fraction. For example, if the magnification is 75%, nscl = 03h and dscl = 04h (3/4 = 0.75 = 75%). If the magnification is 11%, nscl = 0Bh (11 decimal) and dscl = 64h (100 decimal). If the BIFF file does not contain the SCL record, the magnification is 100%.

SELECTION: Current Selection (1Dh)

The SELECTION record stores the selection.

Record Data

Offset	Name	Size	Contents
4	pnn	1	Number of the pane described
5	rwAct	2	Row number of the active cell
7	colAct	2	Column number of the active cell
9	irefAct	2	Ref number of the active cell
11	cref	2	Number of refs in the selection
13	rgref	var	Array of refs

The pnn field indicates which pane is described. It contains one of the following values:

    0 = bottom right
    1 = top right
    2 = bottom left
    3 = top left

For a window that has no splits, the pnn field = 3.

The rwAct and colAct fields specify the active cell.

The irefAct field is a zero-based index into the array of ref structures (refs), specifying which ref contains the active cell. The rgref is an array because it is possible to create a multiple selection. In the case of a multiple selection, each selection is described by a ref, including the active cell (even if it is included in one of the other selections).

The selection (of cells) is described by the rgref array. The number of refs in the rgref field is equal to cref. Each ref in the array is 6 bytes long and contains the following fields.

Offset	Name	Size	Contents
0	rwFirst	2	First row in the reference
2	rwLast	2	Last row in the reference
4	colFirst	1	First column in the reference
5	colLast	1	Last column in the reference

If a selection is so large that it exceeds the maximum BIFF record size, it is broken down into multiple consecutive SELECTION records. Each record contains a portion of the larger selection. Only the cref and rgref fields vary in the multiple records; the pnn, rwAct, colAct, and irefAct fields are the same across all records in the group.

SETUP: Page Setup (A1h)

The SETUP record stores options and measurements from the Page Setup dialog box.

Record Data

Offset	Name	Size	Contents
4	iPaperSize	2	Paper size (see fNoPls in following table)
6	iScale	2	Scaling factor (see fNoPls in following table)
8	iPageStart	2	Starting page number

Offset	Name	Size	Contents
10	iFitWidth	2	Fit to width; number of pages
12	iFitHeight	2	Fit to height; number of pages
14	grbit	2	Option flags (see following table)
16	iRes	2	Print resolution (see fNoPls in following table)
18	iVRes	2	Vertical print resolution (see fNoPls in following table)
20	numHdr	8	Header margin (IEEE number)
28	numFtr	8	Footer margin (IEEE number)
36	iCopies	2	Number of copies (see fNoPls in following table)

The grbit field contains the following option flags.

Offset	Bits	Mask	Name	Contents
0	0	01h	fLeftToRight	Print over then down
	1	02h	fLandscape	= 0, Landscape mode = 1, Portrait mode (see fNoPls, below))
	2	04h	fNoPls	= 1, then the iPaperSize, iScale, iRes, iVRes, iCopies, and fLandscape data have not been obtained from the printer, so they are not valid
	3	08h	fNoColor	= 1, print black and white
	4	10h	fDraft	= 1, print draft quality
	5	20h	fNotes	= 1, print notes
	6	40h	fNoOrient	= 1, orientation not set
	7	80h	fUsePage	= 1, use custom starting page number instead of Auto
1	7–0	FFh	(unused)	

SHRFMLA: Shared Formula (BCh)

The SHRFMLA record is a file size optimization. It is used with the FORMULA record to compress the amount of storage required for the parsed expression (rgce). In earlier versions of Microsoft Excel, if you read an FORMULA record in which the rgce field contained a ptgExp parse token, then the FORMULA record contained an array formula. In Microsoft Excel version 5.0, this could indicate either an array formula or a shared formula.

If the record following the FORMULA is an ARRAY record, then the FORMULA record contains an array formula. If the record following the FORMULA is a SHRFMLA record, then the FORMULA record contains a shared formula. You can also test the fShrFmla bit in the FORMULA record's grbit field to determine this.

When reading a file, you must convert the FORMULA and SHRFMLA records to an equivalent FORMULA record if you plan to use the parsed expression. To do this, take all of the FORMULA record up to (but not including) the cce field and then append to that the SHRFMLA record from its cce field to the end. You must then convert some ptgs; this is explained later.

Following the SHRFMLA record will be one or more FORMULA records containing ptgExp tokens that have the same rwFirst and colFirst fields as those in the ptgExp in the first FORMULA. There is only one SHRFMLA record for each shared-formula record group.

To convert the ptgs, search the rgce field from the SHRFMLA record for any ptgRefN, ptgRefNV, ptgRefNA, or ptgAreaN ptgAreaNV, ptgAreaNA tokens. Add the corresponding FORMULA record's rw and col fields to the rwFirst and colFirst fields in the ptgs from the SHRFMLA. Finally, convert the ptgs as shown in the following table.

Convert this ptg	To this ptg
ptgRefN	ptgRef
ptgRefNV	ptgRefV
ptgRefNA	ptgRefA
ptgAreaN	ptgArea
ptgAreaNV	ptgAreaV
ptgAreaNA	ptgAreaA

For more information on ptgs and parsed expressions, see "Microsoft Excel Formulas" on page 259.

Remember that STRING records can appear after FORMULA records if the formula evaluates to a string.

If your code writes a BIFF file, always write standard FORMULA records; do not attempt to use the SHRFMLA optimization.

Record Data

Offset	Name	Size	Contents
4	rwFirst	2	First row
6	rwLast	2	Last row
8	colFirst	1	First column

Offset	Name	Size	Contents
9	colLast	1	Last column
10	(reserved)	2	
12	cce	2	Length of parsed expression
14	rgce	var	Parsed expression

SORT: Sorting Options (90h)

This record stores options from the Sort and Sort Options dialog boxes.

Record Data

Offset	Name	Size	Contents
4	grbit	2	Option flags
6	cchKey1	1	Length of string for sort key 1
7	cchKey2	1	Length of string for sort key 2
8	cchKey3	1	Length of string for sort key 3
9	rgchKey1	var	Sort key 1 string
var	rgchKey2	var	Sort key 2 string
var	rgchKey3	var	Sort key 3 string

The grbit field contains the following option flags.

Offset	Bits	Mask	Name	Contents
0	0	0001h	fCol	= 1 if Sort Left To Right option is on
	1	0002h	fKey1Dsc	= 1 if key 1 sorts in descending order
	2	0004h	fKey2Dsc	= 1 if key 2 sorts in descending order
	3	0008h	fKey3Dsc	= 1 if key 3 sorts in descending order
	4	0010h	fCaseSensitive	= 1 if sort is case-sensitive
	9-5	03E0h	iOrder	Index to table in First Key Sort Order option. The Normal sort order corresponds to iOrder = 0.
	10	0400h	fAltMethod	Used only in Far East versions of Microsoft Excel
	15-11	F800h	(reserved)	

SOUND: Sound Note (96h)

The SOUND record contains the complete description of a sound note.

Record Data

Offset	Name	Size	Contents
4	cf	2	Clipboard format; 4257h (16983 decimal) for sound notes
6	env	2	Environment from which the file was written: = 1, Microsoft Windows = 2, Apple Macintosh
8	lcb	4	Length of the sound data
12	data	var	Sound data

STANDARDWIDTH: Standard Column Width (99h)

The STANDARDWIDTH record records the measurement from the Standard Width dialog box.

Record Data

Offset	Name	Size	Contents
4	DxGCol	2	Standard column width, in 1/256s of a character width

STRING: String Value of a Formula (07h)

When a formula evaluates to a string, a STRING record occurs after the FORMULA record. If the formula is part of an array, then the STRING record occurs after the ARRAY record.

Record Data

Offset	Name	Size	Contents
4	cch	2	Length of the string
6	rgch	var	The string

STYLE: Style Information (93h)

Each style in a Microsoft Excel workbook, whether built-in or user-defined, requires a style record in the BIFF file. When Microsoft Excel saves the workbook, it writes the STYLE records in alphabetic order, the order that the styles appear in the drop-down list box.

Record Data-Built-In Styles

Offset	Name	Size	Contents
4	ixfe	2	Index to the style XF record.
			Note: ixfe uses only the low-order 12 bits of the field (bits 11–0). Bits 12, 13, and 14 are unused and bit 15 (fBuiltIn) is 1 for built-in styles.
6	istyBuiltIn	1	Built-in style number: = 00h Normal = 01h RowLevel_n = 02h ColLevel_n = 03h Comma = 04h Currency = 05h Percent = 06h Comma[0] = 07h Currency[0]
7	iLevel	1	Level of the outline style RowLevel_n or ColLevel_n (see text)

Record Data-User-Defined Styles

Offset	Name	Size	Contents
4	ixfe	2	Index to the style XF record.
			Note: ixfe uses only the low-order 12 bits of the field (bits 11–0). Bits 12, 13, and 14 are unused and bit 15 (fBuiltIn) is 0 for user-defined styles.
6	cch	1	Length of style name
7	rgch	1	Style name

The automatic outline styles, RowLevel_1 through RowLevel_7 and ColLevel_1 through ColLevel_7, are stored by setting istyBuiltIn to 01h or 02h, and then setting iLevel to the style level minus 1. If the style is not an automatic outline style, then ignore this field.

SUB: Subscriber (91h)

The SUB record contains information for the publisher/subscriber feature. This record can be created only by Microsoft Excel for the Macintosh. However, if any other platform version of Microsoft Excel encounters the SUB record in a BIFF file, it leaves the record in the file, unchanged, when the file is saved.

Record Data

Offset	Name	Size	Contents
4	ref	6	Reference structure describing the subscribed area on the worksheet
10	drwReal	2	Actual number of rows in the subscribed area
12	dcolReal	2	Actual number of columns in the subscribed area
14	grbit	2	Option flags
16	cbAlias	2	Size of rgbAlias
18	sec	36	Section record associated with the subscribed area
54	rgbAlias	var	Contents of the alias pointed to by the section record
xvar	stz	var	Null-terminated string containing the path of publisher. The first byte is a length byte, which does not count the terminating null byte.

The grbit field contains the following option flags.

Offset	Bits	Mask	Name	Contents
0	0	01h	(reserved)	
	1	02h	fObj	= 1 if subscribed in the object layer
	7–2	FCh	(reserved)	
1	7–0	FFh	(reserved)	

SXDI: Data Item (C5h)

This record contains information about the PivotTable data item.

Record Data

Offset	Name	Size	Contents
4	isxvdData	2	Field this data item is based on
6	iiftab	2	Index to aggregation function: = 00h, Sum = 01h, Count = 02h, Average = 03h, Max = 04h, Min = 05h, Product = 06h, Count Nums = 07h, StdDev = 08h, StdDevp = 09h, Var = 0Ah, Varp

Offset	Name	Size	Contents
8	df	2	Data display format: = 00h, Normal = 01h, Difference from = 02h, Percent of = 03h, Percent difference from = 04h, Running total in = 05h, Percent of row = 06h, Percent of column = 07h, Percent of total = 08h, Index
10	isxvd	2	Index to SXVD record used by data display format
12	isxvi	2	Index to SXVI record used by data display format
14	ifmt	2	Index to format table for this item
16	cchName	2	Length of name; if = FFFFh, then rgch is null and the name in the PivotTable cache storage is used
18	rgch	var	Name

SXEXT: External Source Information (DCh)

This record stores information about the SQL query string that retrieves external data for a PivotTable. The record is followed by SXSTRING records that contain the SQL strings and then by a SXSTRING record that contains the SQL server connection string.

Record Data

Offset	Name	Size	Contents
4	id	2	Connection ID of the SQL server
6	fError	2	= 1 if an error occurred during the last attempt to communicate with the server
8	cstSQL	2	Number of following SXSTRING records

SXIDSTM: Stream ID (D5h)

This record is a header record for a group of SXVS, SXEXT, and SXSTRING records that describe the PivotTable streams in the SX DB storage (the PivotTable cache storage). The idstm field identifies the stream.

Record Data

Offset	Name	Size	Contents
4	idstm	2	Stream ID

SXIVD: Row/Column Field IDs (B4h)

This record stores an array of field ID numbers (2-byte integers) for the row fields and column fields in a PivotTable. Two SXIVD records appear in the file: the first contains the array of row field IDs, and the second contains the array of column field IDs.

Record Data

Offset	Name	Size	Contents
4	rgisxvd	var	Array of 2-byte integers; contains either row field IDs or column field IDs

SXLI: Line Item Array (B5h)

The SXLI record stores an array of variable-length SXLI structures, which describe the row and column items in a PivotTable. There are two SXLI records for each PivotTable: the first stores row items, and the second stores column items.

Record Data

Offset	Name	Size	Contents
4	rgsxli	var	Array of SXLI structures

The SXLI structure has variable length but will always be at least 10 bytes long, with one element in the rgisxvi array (the index to the SXVI record for the item). The SXLI structure is shown in the following table.

Offset	Name	Size	Contents
0	cSic	2	Count of items that are identical to the previous element in rgsxvi; for 0 <= i < cSic rgisxvi[i] is the same as the previous line.
2	itmtype	2	Item type: = 00h, Data = 01h, Default = 02h, SUM = 03h, COUNTA = 04h, COUNT = 05h, AVERAGE = 06h, MAX = 07h, MIN = 08h, PRODUCT = 09h, STDEV = 0Ah, STDEVP = 0Bh, VAR = 0Ch, VARP = 0Dh, Grand total
4	isxviMac	2	Maximum index to the rgisxvi[i] array
6	grbit	2	Option flags; see following table
8	rgisxvi	2	Array of indexes to SXVI records; the number of elements in the array is (isxviMac + 1)

The grbit field contains the following flags.

Offset	Bits	Mask	Name	Contents
0	0	0001h	fMultiDataName	= 1, use the data field name for the subtotal (instead of using "Total")
	8-1	01F7h	iData	For a multi-data subtotal, iData is the index to the data field
	9	0200h	fSbt	= 1, this item is a subtotal
	10	0400h	fBlock	= 1, this item is a block total
	11	0800h	fGrand	= 1, this item is a grand total
	12	1000h	fMultiDataOnAxis	= 1, this axis contains multi-data
	15-13	E000h	(reserved)	Reserved; must be zero

SXPI: Page Item (B6h)

This record contains information for the PivotTable page item.

Record Data

Offset	Name	Size	Contents
4	isxvi	2	Index to SXVI record for the page item
6	isxvd	2	Index to SXVD record for the page item
8	idObj	2	Object ID for the page item drop-down arrow

SXSTRING: String (CDh)

This record contains a SQL query string, a SQL server connection string, or a page item name from a multiple-consolidation PivotTable.

Record Data

Offset	Name	Size	Contents
4	cch	2	Length of string
6	rgch	var	String

SXTBL: Multiple Consolidation Source Info (D0h)

This record stores information about multiple-consolidation PivotTable source data.

Record Data

Offset	Name	Size	Contents
4	cdref	2	Count (1-based) of DCONREF or DCONNAME records that follow the SXTBL record
6	csxtbpg	2	Count (1-based) of SXTBPG records that follow the DCONREF or DCONNAME records
8	grbitPages	2	(see following table)

The grbitPages field contains an encoded count of page fields as shown in the following table.

Offset	Bits	Mask	Name	Contents
0	14–0	7FFFh	cPages	Count (1-based) of page fields
	15	8000h	fAutoPage	= 1 if user selected the Create A Single Page Field For Me option in the PivotTable Wizard dialog box

SXTBPG: Page Item Indexes (D2h)

This record stores an array of page item indexes that represent the table references for a multiple-consolidation PivotTable.

Record Data

Offset	Name	Size	Contents
4	rgiitem	var	Array of two-byte indexes to page items (iitem)

SXTBRGIITM: Page Item Name Count (D1h)

This record stores the number of page item names in a multiple-consolidation PivotTable. The names are stored in SXSTRING records that follow the SXTBRGIITM.

Record Data

Offset	Name	Size	Contents
4	cItems	2	number of page item names (number of following SXTBRGIITM records)

SXVD: View Fields (B1h)

This record contains PivotTable view fields and other information.

Record Data

Offset	Name	Size	Contents
4	sxaxis	2	Axis: = 0, no axis = 1, row = 2, column = 4, page = 8, data
6	cSub	2	Number of subtotals attached
8	grbitSub	2	Item subtotal type (see following table)
10	cItm	2	Number of items
12	cchName	2	Length of name; if = FFFFh, then rgch is null and the name in the cache is used
14	rgch	var	Name

The subtotal type (grbitSub) bits are defined as shown in the following table.

Name	Contents
bitFNone	0000h
bitFDefault	0001h
bitFSum	0002h
bitFCounta	0004h
bitFAverage	0008h
bitFMax	0010h
bitFMin	0020h
bitFProduct	0040h
bitFCount	0080h
bitFStdev	0100h
bitFStdevp	0200h
bitFVar	0400h
bitFVarp	0800h

SXVI: View Item (B2h)

This record contains information about a PivotTable item.

Record Data

Offset	Name	Size	Contents
4	itmtype	2	Item type: = FEh, Page = FFh, Null = 00h, Data = 01h, Default = 02h, SUM = 03h, COUNTA = 04h, COUNT = 05h, AVERAGE = 06h, MAX = 07h, MIN = 08h, PRODUCT = 09h, STDEV = 0Ah, STDEVP = 0Bh, VAR = 0Ch, VARP = 0Dh, Grand total
6	grbit	2	Option flags

Offset	Name	Size	Contents
8	iCache	2	Index to PivotTable cache
10	cchName	2	Length of name; if = FFFFh, then rgch is null and the name in the cache is used
12	rgch	var	Name

The grbit field contains the following option flags.

Offset	Bits	Mask	Name	Contents
0	0	01h	fHidden	= 1 if item is hidden
	1	02h	fHideDetail	= 1 if detail is hidden
	7-2	FCh	(reserved)	Reserved, must be zero
1	7-0	FFh	(reserved)	Reserved, must be zero

SXVIEW: View Definition (B0h)

This record contains top-level PivotTable information.

Record Data

Offset	Name	Size	Contents
4	rwFirst	2	First row of PivotTable
6	rwLast	2	Last row of PivotTable
8	colFirst	2	First column of PivotTable
10	colLast	2	Last column of PivotTable
12	rwFirstHead	2	First row containing PivotTable headings
14	rwFirstData	2	First row containing PivotTable data
16	colFirstData	2	First column containing PivotTable data
18	iCache	2	Index to cache
20	(reserved)	2	Reserved; must be zero
22	sxaxis4Data	2	Default axis for data field
24	ipos4Data	2	Default position for data field
26	cDim	2	Number of fields
28	cDimRw	2	Number of row fields
30	cDimCol	2	Number of column fields
32	cDimPg	2	Number of page fields
34	cDimData	2	Number of data fields
36	cRw	2	Number of data rows
38	cCol	2	Number of data columns

Offset	Name	Size	Contents
40	grbit	2	Option flags
42	itblAutoFmt	2	Index to PivotTable autoformat
44	cchName	2	Length of PivotTable name
46	cchData	2	Length of data field name
48	rgch	var	PivotTable name, followed by name of data field

The grbit field contains the following option flags.

Offset	Bits	Mask	Name	Contents
0	0	0001h	fRwGrand	= 1 if PivotTable contains grand totals for rows
	1	0002h	fColGrand	= 1 if PivotTable contains grand totals for columns
	2	0004h	(reserved)	Reserved; must be zero
	3	0008h	fAutoFormat	= 1 if PivotTable has an autoformat applied
	4	0010h	fWH	= 1 if width/height autoformat is applied
	5	0020h	fFont	= 1 if font autoformat is applied
	6	0040h	fAlign	= 1 if alignment autoformat is applied
	7	0080h	fBorder	= 1 if border autoformat is applied
	8	0100h	fPattern	= 1 if pattern autoformat is applied
	9	0200h	fNumber	= 1 if number autoformat is applied
	15-10	FC00h	(reserved)	Reserved; must be zero

SXVS: View Source (E3h)

This record contains an integer that defines the data source for a PivotTable.

Record Data

Offset	Name	Size	Contents
4	vs	2	Data source: = 01h, Microsoft Excel list or database = 02h, External data source (Microsoft Query) = 04h, Multiple consolidation ranges = 08h, Another PivotTable = 10h, A Scenario Manager summary report

TABLE: Data Table (36h)

A TABLE record describes a data table created with the Table command (Data menu).

Record Data

Offset	Name	Size	Contents
4	rwFirst	2	First row of the table
6	rwLast	2	Last row of the table
8	colFirst	1	First column of the table
9	colLast	1	Last column of the table
10	grbit	2	Option flags
12	rwInpRw	2	Row of the row input cell
14	colInpRw	2	Column of the row input cell
16	rwInpCol	2	Row of the column input cell
18	colInpCol	2	Column of the column input cell

The grbit field contains the following option flags.

Offset	Bits	Mask	Name	Contents
0	0	01h	fAlwaysCalc	Always calculate the formula
	1	02h	fCalcOnLoad	Calculate the formula when the file is opened
	2	04h	fRw	= 1 input cell is a row input cell = 0 input cell is a column input cell
	3	08h	fTbl2	= 1 if two-input data table = 0 if one-input data table
	7–4	F0h	(unused)	
1	7–0	FFh	(unused)	

The area (range of cells) in which the table is entered is defined by the rwFirst, rwLast, colFirst, and colLast fields. This area is the interior of the table and does not include the outer row or column (these contain the table formulas and/or input values).

In cases where the input cell is a deleted reference (the cell displays #REF!) the rwInp field is –1. The colInp field is unused in this case.

TEMPLATE: Workbook Is a Template (60h)

This record has no record data field. If the TEMPLATE record is present in the Book stream, it signifies that the workbook is a template. The TEMPLATE record, if present, must immediately follow the BOF record.

TOPMARGIN: Top Margin Measurement (28h)

The TOP MARGIN record specifies the top margin in inches when a sheet is printed. The num field is in 8-byte IEEE floating-point format.

Record Data

Offset	Name	Size	Contents
4	num	8	Top margin

UDDESC: Description String for Chart Autoformat (DFh)

This record stores the description string for a custom chart autoformat. The record is written only in the chart autoformat file (XL5GALRY.XLS in Microsoft Excel for Windows).

Record Data

Offset	Name	Size	Contents
4	cch	1	Length of description string
5	rgch	var	Description string

UNCALCED: Recalculation Status (5Eh)

If the UNCALCED record is present in the Book stream, it indicates that the Calculate message was in the status bar when Microsoft Excel saved the file. This occurs if the sheet changed, the Manual calculation option was on, and the Recalculate before Save option was off (Options dialog box, Calculation tab).

Record Data

Offset	Name	Size	Contents
4	(reserved)	2	Reserved; must be zero

VCENTER: Center Between Vertical Margins (84h)

If the Center on Page Vertically option is on in the Page Setup dialog box, Margins tab, then fVCenter = 1.

Record Data

Offset	Name	Size	Contents
4	fVCenter	2	= 1 if sheet is to be centered between vertical margins when printed

VERTICALPAGEBREAKS: Explicit Column Page Breaks (1Ah)

The VERTICALPAGEBREAKS record contains a list of explicit column page breaks. The cbrk field contains the number of page breaks. rgcol is an array of 2-byte integers that specifies columns. Microsoft Excel sets a page break before each column contained in the list of columns in the rgcol field. The columns must be sorted in ascending order.

Record Data

Offset	Name	Size	Contents
4	cbrk	2	Number of page breaks
6	rgcol	var	Array of columns

WINDOW1: Window Information (3Dh)

The WINDOW1 record contains workbook-level window attributes. The xWn and yWn fields contain the location of the window in units of 1/20 of a point, relative to the upper-left corner of the Microsoft Excel window client area. The dxWn and dyWn fields contain the window size, also in units of 1/20 of a point.

Record Data

Offset	Name	Size	Contents
4	xWn	2	Horizontal position of the window
6	yWn	2	Vertical position of the window
8	dxWn	2	Width of the window
10	dyWn	2	Height of the window
12	grbit	2	Option flags
14	itabCur	2	Index of selected workbook tab (0-based)

Offset	Name	Size	Contents
16	itabFirst	2	Index of first displayed workbook tab (0-based)
18	ctabSel	2	Number of workbook tabs that are selected
20	wTabRatio	2	Ratio of width of the workbook tabs to the width of the horizontal scroll bar; to obtain the ratio, convert to decimal and then divide by 1000.

The grbit field contains the following option flags.

Offset	Bits	Mask	Name	Contents
0	0	01h	fHidden	= 1 if the window is hidden
	1	02h	fIconic	= 1 if the window is currently displayed as an icon
	2	04h	(reserved)	
	3	08h	fDspHScroll	= 1 if horizontal scroll bar is displayed
	4	10h	fDspVScroll	= 1 if vertical scroll bar is displayed
	5	20h	fBotAdornment	= 1 if workbook tabs are displayed
	7-6	C0h	(reserved)	
1	7-0	FFh	(reserved)	

WINDOW2: Sheet Window Information (3Eh)

The WINDOW2 record contains window attributes for a sheet in a workbook.

Record Data

Offset	Name	Size	Contents
4	grbit	2	Option flags
6	rwTop	2	Top row visible in the window
8	colLeft	2	Leftmost column visible in the window
10	rgbHdr	4	Row/column heading and gridline color

The grbit field contains the following option flags.

Offset	Bits	Mask	Name	Contents
0	0	01h	fDspFmla	= 1 if the window should display formulas = 0 if the window should display value
	1	02h	fDspGrid	= 1 if the window should display gridlines

Offset	Bits	Mask	Name	Contents
	2	04h	fDspRwCol	= 1 if the window should display row and column headings
	3	08h	fFrozen	= 1 if the panes in the window should be frozen
	4	10h	fDspZeros	= 1 if the window should display zero values = 0 if the window should suppress display of zero values
	5	20h	fDefaultHdr	= 1 (see following explanation) = 0 use rgbHdr color
	6	40h	fArabic	= 1 for Arabic version of Microsoft Excel
	7	80h	fDspGuts	= 1 if outline symbols are displayed
1	0	01h	fFrozenNoSplit	= 1 if the panes in the window are frozen but there is no split
	1	02h	fSelected	= 1 if the sheet tab is selected
	2	04h	fPaged	= 1 if the sheet is currently being displayed in the workbook window
	7–3	F8h	(reserved)	

fDefaultHdr is 1 if the window's row and column headings and gridlines should be drawn in the window's default foreground color. If this field is 0, then the RGB color in the rgbHdr field is used instead.

WINDOWPROTECT: Windows Are Protected (19h)

The WINDOWPROTECT record stores an option from the Protect Workbook dialog box.

Record Data

Offset	Name	Size	Contents
4	fLockWn	2	= 1 if the workbook windows are protected

WRITEACCESS: Write Access User Name (5Ch)

This record contains the user name, which is the name you type when you install Microsoft Excel. The stName field is always padded with spaces (20h) to make the field 31 characters long; however, only the first cch bytes contain the actual user name data.

Record Data

Offset	Name	Size	Contents
4	cch	1	Length of user name
5	stName	31	User name, padded with spaces (20h)

WRITEPROT: Workbook Is Write-Protected (86h)

This record is 4 bytes long, and it has no record data field. If the WRITEPROT record is present in the Book stream, it signifies that the worksheet has a Write Reservation Password (File menu, Save As command, Options dialog box). For information on the password (wResPass), see "FILESHARING" on page 171.

WSBOOL: Additional Workspace Information (81h)

This record stores information on workspace settings.

Record Data

Offset	Name	Size	Contents
4	grbit	2	Option flags

The grbit field contains the following option flags.

Offset	Bits	Mask	Name	Contents
0	0	01h	fShowAutoBreaks	= 1 if automatic page breaks are visible
	3–1	E0h	unused	
	4	10h	fDialog	= 1 if the sheet is a dialog sheet
	5	20h	fApplyStyles	= 0 if automatic styles are applied to outline
	6	40h	fRwSumsBelow	= 1 if summary rows appear below detail in an outline
	7	80h	fColSumsRight	= 1 if summary columns appear to the right of detail in an outline
1	0	01h	fFitToPage	= 1 if Fit option is on (Page Setup dialog box, Page tab)
	1	02h	(reserved)	
	3–2	06h	fDspGuts	= 1 if outline symbols are displayed
	5–4		(reserved)	

Offset	Bits	Mask	Name	Contents
	6		fAee	= 1 if the Alternate Expression Evaluation option is on (Options dialog box, Calculation tab)
	7		fAfe	= 1 if the Alternate Formula Entry option is on (Options dialog box, Calculation tab)

XCT: CRN Record Count (59h)

For BIFF files that contain CRN records, ccrn is the number of CRN records (type 5Ah) in the file. The CRN records immediately follow the XCT record.

Record Data

Offset	Name	Size	Contents
4	ccrn	2	Count of CRN records that follow

XF: Extended Format (E0h)

The XF record stores formatting properties for cells and styles. The ixfe of a cell record (BLANK, LABEL, NUMBER, RK, and so on) points to a cell XF record, and the ixfe of a STYLE record points to a style XF record. Note that in previous BIFF versions, the record number for the XF record was 43h.

A BIFF file can contain as many XF records as necessary to describe the different cell formats and styles in a workbook. The XF records are written in a table in the workbook stream and the index to the XF record table is a zero-based number called ixfe.

The workbook stream must contain a minimum XF table consisting of 15 style XF records and one cell XF record (ixfe=0 through ixfe=15). The first XF record (ixfe=0) is the XF record for Normal style. The next 14 records (ixfe=1 through ixfe=14) are XF records that correspond to outline styles RowLevel_1, ColLevel_1, RowLevel_2, ColLevel_2, and so on. The last record (ixfe=15) is the default cell XF for the workbook.

Following these XF records are five additional style XF records, not strictly required, that correspond to the Comma, Comma [0], Currency, Currency [0], and Percent styles.

Cell XF Record

Record Data

Offset	Bits	Mask	Name	Contents
4	15–0	FFFFh	ifnt	Index to FONT record
6	15-0	FFFFh	ifmt	Index to FORMAT record
8	0	0001h	fLocked	= 1 if the cell is locked
	1	0002h	fHidden	= 1 if the cell is hidden
	2	0004h	fStyle	= 0 for cell XF = 1 for style XF
	3	0008h	f123Prefix	If the Transition Navigation Keys option is off (Options dialog box, Transition tab), then f123Prefix = 1 indicates that a leading apostrophe (single quotation mark) is being used to coerce the cell's contents to a simple string. If the Transition Navigation Keys option is on, then f123Prefix = 1 indicates that the cell formula begins with one of the four Lotus 1-2-3 alignment prefix characters: ' left " right ^ centered \ fill
	15–4	FFF0h	ixfParent	Index to XF record of parent style. Every cell XF must have a parent style XF, which is usually ixfeNormal = 0.
10	2–0	0007h	alc	Alignment: 0 = general 1 = left 2 = center 3 = right 4 = fill 5 = justify 6 = center across selection
	3	0008h	fWrap	= 1 wrap text in cell

Offset	Bits	Mask	Name	Contents
10	6–4	0070h	alcV	Vertical alignment: 0 = top 1 = center 2 = bottom 3 = justify
	7	0080h	fJustLast	(used only in Far East versions of Microsoft Excel)
	9–8	0300h	ori	Orientation of text in cell: = 0 no rotation = 1 text appears top-to-bottom; letters are upright = 2 text is rotated 90 degrees counterclockwise = 3 text is rotated 90 degrees clockwise
	10	0400h	fAtrNum	= 1 if ifmt is not equal to ifmt of parent style XF
	11	0800h	fAtrFnt	= 1 if ifnt is not equal to ifnt of parent style XF
	12	1000h	fAtrAlc	= 1 if either the alc or the fWrap field is not equal to the corresponding field of parent style XF
	13	2000h	fAtrBdr	= 1 if any border line field (dgTop, and so on) is not equal to the corresponding field of parent style XF
	14	4000h	fAtrPat	= 1 if any pattern field (fls, icvFore, icvBack) is not equal to the corresponding field of parent style XF
	15	8000h	fAtrProt	= 1 if either the fLocked or the fHidden field is not equal to the corresponding field of parent style XF
12	6–0	007Fh	icvFore	Index to color palette for foreground color of fill pattern
	12–7	1F80h	icvBack	Index to color palette for background color of fill pattern
	13	2000h	fSxButton	= 1 if the XF record is attached to a PivotTable button
	15-14	C000h	(reserved)	
14	5–0	003Fh	fls	Fill pattern

Offset	Bits	Mask	Name	Contents
14	8-6	01C0h	dgBottom	Border line style (see following illustration)
	15-9	FE00h	icvBottom	Index to color palette for bottom border color
16	2–0	0007h	dgTop	Border line style (see following illustration)
	5-3	0038h	dgLeft	Border line style (see following illustration)
	8-6	01C0h	dgRight	Border line style (see following illustration)
	15-9	FE00h	icvTop	Index to color palette for top border color
18	6-0	007Fh	icvLeft	Index to color palette for left border color
	13-7	3F80h	icvRight	Index to color palette for right border color
	15–14	C000h	(reserved)	

The border line style fields, dgTop, dgLeft, dgBottom, dgRight, correspond to the options in the Format Cells dialog box, Border tab, as shown in the following illustration.

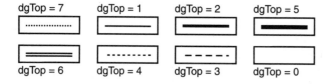

Style XF Record

The style XF record is identical to the cell XF record, except that some of the fields have slightly different meanings.

Record Data

Offset	Bits	Mask	Name	Contents
4	15–0	FFFFh	ifnt	Index to FONT record
6	15-0	FFFFh	ifmt	Index to FORMAT record
8	0	0001h	fLocked	= 1 if the cell is locked
	1	0002h	fHidden	= 1 if the cell is hidden

Offset	Bits	Mask	Name	Contents
8	2	0004h	fStyle	= 0 for cell XF = 1 for style XF
	3	0008h	f123Prefix	This bit is always = 0 for style XF
	15–4	FFF0h	ixfParent	For style XF records, this field equals FFFh (ixfNULL)
10	2–0	0007h	alc	Alignment: 0 = general 1 = left 2 = center 3 = right 4 = fill 5 = justify 6 = center across selection
	3	0008h	fWrap	= 1 wrap text in cell
	6–4	0070h	alcV	Vertical alignment: 0 = top 1 = center 2 = bottom 3 = justify
	7	0080h	fJustLast	(used only in Far East versions of Microsoft Excel)
	9–8	0300h	ori	Orientation of text in cell: = 0 no rotation = 1 text appears top-to-bottom; letters are upright = 2 text is rotated 90 degrees counterclockwise = 3 text is rotated 90 degrees clockwise
	10	0400h	fAtrNum	= 0 if style includes Number (Style dialog box)
	11	0800h	fAtrFnt	= 0 if style includes Font (Style dialog box)
	12	1000h	fAtrAlc	= 0 if style includes Alignment (Style dialog box)
	13	2000h	fAtrBdr	= 0 if style includes Border (Style dialog box)
	14	4000h	fAtrPat	= 0 if style includes Patterns (shading) (Style dialog box)
	15	8000h	fAtrProt	= 0 if style includes Protection (cell protection) (Style dialog box)
12	6–0	007Fh	icvFore	Index to color palette for foreground color of fill pattern

Offset	Bits	Mask	Name	Contents
12	12–7	1F80h	icvBack	Index to color palette for background color of fill pattern
	13	2000h	fSxButton	This bit always = 0 for style XF
	15-14	C000h	(reserved)	
14	5–0	003Fh	fls	Fill pattern
	8-6	01C0h	dgBottom	Border line style (see previous illustration)
	15-9	FE00h	icvBottom	Index to color palette for bottom border color
16	2–0	0007h	dgTop	Border line style (see previous illustration)
	5-3	0038h	dgLeft	Border line style (see previous illustration)
	8-6	01C0h	dgRight	Border line style (see previous illustration)
	15-9	FE00h	icvTop	Index to color palette for top border color
18	6-0	007Fh	icvLeft	Index to color palette for left border color
	13-7	3F80h	icvRight	Index to color palette for right border color
	15–14	C000h	(reserved)	

Finding Cell Records in BIFF Files

Microsoft Excel uses the INDEX and DBCELL records to optimize the lookup of cell records (RK, FORMULA, and so on). You can use these records to optimize your code when reading a BIFF file, or you can simply read the entire workbook stream to find the cell values you want. The unoptimized method may be slower, depending on the size, structure, and complexity of the file.

If your code writes a BIFF file, you must include the INDEX and DBCELL records with correct values in the record fields. If you don't, Microsoft Excel will not be able to optimize lookup, and the program's performance will suffer, especially when the user tries to copy data out of the file that your application has written.

Microsoft Excel stores cell records in blocks that have at most 32 rows. Each row that contains cell records has a corresponding ROW record in the block, and each block contains a DBCELL record at the end of the block.

The following illustration shows how to use the INDEX record to locate the DBCELL records at the end of the record blocks. Notice that the stream position at the start of the first BOF record in the workbook stream is 6F1h. To find the start of each DBCELL record, add this number to each member of the rgibRw array in the INDEX record.

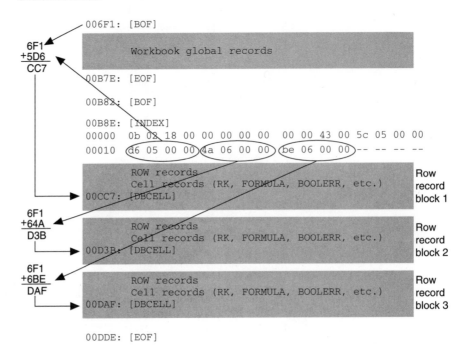

```
006F1: [BOF]
              Workbook global records
00B7E: [EOF]

00B82: [BOF]

00B8E: [INDEX]
00000   0b 08 18 00 00 00 00 00   00 00 43 00 5c 05 00 00
00010   d6 05 00 00 4a 06 00 00 be 06 00 00 -- -- -- --
              ROW records
              Cell records (RK, FORMULA, BOOLERR, etc.)        Row record block 1
00CC7: [DBCELL]

              ROW records
              Cell records (RK, FORMULA, BOOLERR, etc.)        Row record block 2
00D3B: [DBCELL]

              ROW records
              Cell records (RK, FORMULA, BOOLERR, etc.)        Row record block 3
00DAF: [DBCELL]

00DDE: [EOF]
```

```
6F1
+5D6
CC7

6F1
+64A
D3B

6F1
+6BE
DAF
```

After your code has computed the location of the DBCELL records, you can use the dbRtrw field to find the location of the start of the first ROW record for each block. This field is stored as a positive long integer, although the offset is really a "negative" offset to an earlier position in the file. See the following illustration for details.

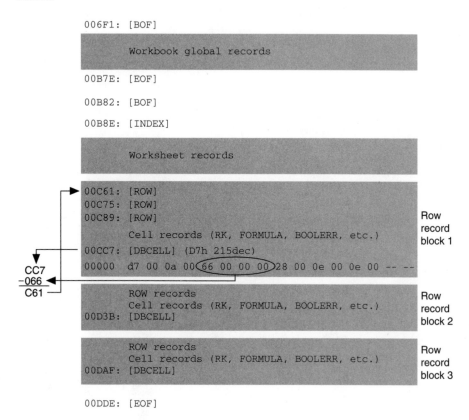

```
006F1: [BOF]

        Workbook global records

00B7E: [EOF]

00B82: [BOF]

00B8E: [INDEX]

        Worksheet records

00C61: [ROW]
00C75: [ROW]                                                    Row
00C89: [ROW]                                                    record
        Cell records (RK, FORMULA, BOOLERR, etc.)               block 1
00CC7: [DBCELL] (D7h 215dec)
00000  d7 00 0a 00 66 00 00 00 28 00 0e 00 0e 00 -- --
CC7
-066    ROW records                                             Row
C61     Cell records (RK, FORMULA, BOOLERR, etc.)               record
00D3B: [DBCELL]                                                 block 2

        ROW records                                             Row
        Cell records (RK, FORMULA, BOOLERR, etc.)               record
00DAF: [DBCELL]                                                 block 3

00DDE: [EOF]
```

Finally, your code can compute the start of each cell record in the block using the members in the rgdb array in the DBCELL record. The offsets in this array use the start of the second ROW record in the block as the initial offset. This is because the code has to read the first ROW record to know what the row number is (and then to make a decision based on the row number), and the stream pointer is at the start of the second ROW record after this. See the following illustration for details.

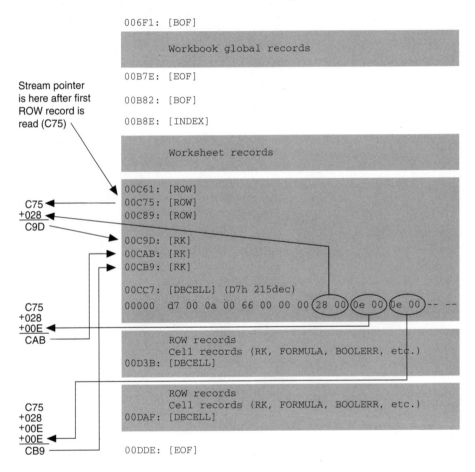

Microsoft Excel Formulas

This section describes how Microsoft Excel stores formulas. Formulas most commonly appear in rgce fields in FORMULA, ARRAY, and NAME records. In this section, *formula* is a synonym for *parsed expression,* which is the internal tokenized representation of a Microsoft Excel formula.

Parsed Expressions and Tokens

Microsoft Excel uses a modified reverse-Polish technique to store parsed expressions. A parsed expression contains a sequence of parse tokens, each of which is either an operand, an operator token, or a control token. Operand tokens push operands onto the stack. Operator tokens perform arithmetic operations upon the operands. Control tokens assist in formula evaluation by describing properties of the formula.

A token consists of two parts: a token type and a token value. A token type is called a *ptg* (Parse ThinG) in Microsoft Excel. A ptg is 1 byte long and has a value from 01h to 7Fh. The ptgs above 7Fh are reserved.

The ptg specifies only what kind of information is contained in a token. The information itself is stored in the token value, which immediately follows the ptg. Some tokens consist only of a ptg, without an accompanying token value. For example, to specify an addition operation, only the token type ptgAdd is required. But to specify an integer operand, both ptgInt and the token value, which is an integer, must be specified.

For example, assume that the formula =5+6 is in cell A1. The parsed expression for this formula consists of three tokens: two integer operand tokens, <token 1> and <token 2>, and an operator token, <token 3>:

<token 1>	<token 2>	<token 3>
ptgInt 0005h	ptgInt 0006h	ptgAdd

Notice that each ptgInt is immediately followed by the integer token value.

If you type this formula into cell A1 and then examine the FORMULA record (using the BiffView utility), you will see the following:

```
00000   06 00 1d 00 00 00 00 00 0f 00 00 00 00 00 00 00
00010   26 40 00 00 00 00 e0 fc 07 00 1e 05 00 1e 06 00
00020   03 -- -- -- -- -- -- -- -- -- -- -- -- -- -- --
```

The first 26 bytes of the hex dump contain the record number, record length, rw, col, ixfe, num, grbit, chn, and cce fields. The remaining 7 bytes contain the two ptgInt (1Eh) tokens, which contain the token values that represent the integers 5 and

6 (0005h and 0006h), and the ptgAdd (03h) token. If the formula were changed to =5*6, then the third token would be ptgMul (05h). For more information about the FORMULA record, see "FORMULA" on page 173.

In many cases, the token value consists of a structure of two or more fields. In these cases, offset-zero is assumed to be the first byte of the token value, that is, the first byte immediately following the token type.

Microsoft Excel ptgs

The following table contains all ptgs that appear in BIFF files. All other ptgs are reserved.

New ptgs for Microsoft Excel version 5.0 and ptgs that changed from version 4.0 to version 5.0 are marked with a CHANGED or NEW note in the right-hand column of the table.

The ptgSheet and ptgEndSheet tokens are no longer used. The external sheet references are contained in the ptgNameX, ptgRef3d, and ptgArea3d tokens.

Name	Ptg	Type
ptgExp	01h	control
ptgTbl	02h	control
ptgAdd	03h	operator
ptgSub	04h	operator
ptgMul	05h	operator
ptgDiv	06h	operator
ptgPower	07h	operator
ptgConcat	08h	operator
ptgLT	09h	operator
ptgLE	0Ah	operator
ptgEQ	0Bh	operator
ptgGE	0Ch	operator
ptgGT	0Dh	operator
ptgNE	0Eh	operator
ptgIsect	0Fh	operator
ptgUnion	10h	operator
ptgRange	11h	operator
ptgUplus	12h	operator
ptgUminus	13h	operator
ptgPercent	14h	operator

Name	Ptg	Type
ptgParen	15h	control
ptgMissArg	16h	operand
ptgStr	17h	operand
ptgAttr	19h	control
ptgSheet	1Ah	(ptg DELETED)
ptgEndSheet	1Bh	(ptg DELETED)
ptgErr	1Ch	operand
ptgBool	1Dh	operand
ptgInt	1Eh	operand
ptgNum	1Fh	operand
ptgArray	20h	operand, reference class
ptgFunc	21h	operator
ptgFuncVar	22h	operator
ptgName	23h	operand, reference class (CHANGED ptg)
ptgRef	24h	operand, reference class
ptgArea	25h	operand, reference class
ptgMemArea	26h	operand, reference class
ptgMemErr	27h	operand, reference class
ptgMemNoMem	28h	control
ptgMemFunc	29h	control
ptgRefErr	2Ah	operand, reference class
ptgAreaErr	2Bh	operand, reference class
ptgRefN	2Ch	operand, reference class (CHANGED ptg)
ptgAreaN	2Dh	operand, reference class (CHANGED ptg)
ptgMemAreaN	2Eh	control
ptgMemNoMemN	2Fh	control
ptgNameX	39h	operand, reference class (NEW ptg)
ptgRef3d	3Ah	operand, reference class (NEW ptg)
ptgArea3d	3Bh	operand, reference class (NEW ptg)
ptgRefErr3d	3Ch	operand, reference class (NEW ptg)
ptgAreaErr3d	3Dh	operand, reference class (NEW ptg)
ptgArrayV	40h	operand, value class
ptgFuncV	41h	operator
ptgFuncVarV	42h	operator
ptgNameV	43h	operand, value class (CHANGED ptg)

Name	Ptg	Type
ptgRefV	44h	operand, value class
ptgAreaV	45h	operand, value class
ptgMemAreaV	46h	operand, value class
ptgMemErrV	47h	operand, value class
ptgMemNoMemV	48h	control
ptgMemFuncV	49h	control
ptgRefErrV	4Ah	operand, value class
ptgAreaErrV	4Bh	operand, value class
ptgRefNV	4Ch	operand, value class (CHANGED ptg)
ptgAreaNV	4Dh	operand, value class (CHANGED ptg)
ptgMemAreaNV	4Eh	control
ptgMemNoMemNV	4Fh	control
ptgFuncCEV	58h	operator
ptgNameXV	59h	operand, value class (NEW ptg)
ptgRef3dV	5Ah	operand, value class (NEW ptg)
ptgArea3dV	5Bh	operand, value class (NEW ptg)
ptgRefErr3dV	5Ch	operand, value class (NEW ptg)
ptgAreaErr3dV	5Dh	operand, value class (NEW ptg)
ptgArrayA	60h	operand, array class
ptgFuncA	61h	operator
ptgFuncVarA	62h	operator
ptgNameA	63h	operand, array class (CHANGED ptg)
ptgRefA	64h	operand, array class
ptgAreaA	65h	operand, array class
ptgMemAreaA	66h	operand, array class
ptgMemErrA	67h	operand, array class
ptgMemNoMemA	68h	control
ptgMemFuncA	69h	control
ptgRefErrA	6Ah	operand, array class
ptgAreaErrA	6Bh	operand, array class
ptgRefNA	6Ch	operand, array class (CHANGED ptg)
ptgAreaNA	6Dh	operand, array class (CHANGED ptg)
ptgMemAreaNA	6Eh	control
ptgMemNoMemNA	6Fh	control
ptgFuncCEA	78h	operator

Name	Ptg	Type
ptgNameXA	79h	operand, array class (NEW ptg)
ptgRef3dA	7Ah	operand, array class (NEW ptg)
ptgArea3dA	7Bh	operand, array class (NEW ptg)
ptgRefErr3dA	7Ch	operand, array class (NEW ptg)
ptgAreaErr3dA	7Dh	operand, array class (NEW ptg)

Expression Evaluation

Calculation of Microsoft Excel formulas is a straightforward process. A last-in-first-out (LIFO) stack, the operand stack, is maintained during calculation. When an operand is encountered, it is pushed onto the stack. When an operator is encountered, it operates on the topmost operand or operands. Operator precedence is irrelevant at evaluation time; operators are handled as soon as they are encountered.

There are three kinds of operators: unary, binary, and function. Unary operators, such as the minus sign that negates a number, operate only on the top operand. Binary operators, such as the addition operator, operate on the top two operands. Function operators, which implement Microsoft Excel functions, operate on a variable number of operands, depending on how many arguments the function accepts.

All operators work by popping the required operands from the stack, performing calculations, and pushing the result back onto the operand stack.

Scanning a Parsed Expression

One fairly common operation on parsed expressions is to scan them, taking appropriate actions at each ptg. You can do this with a loop using a pointer variable that points to the next ptg to scan. However, you must increment this pointer carefully, because different ptgs may have token values of different lengths.

One approach is to maintain an array with one element per ptg. Each element contains the size of the token value. To increment the pointer, add the array element corresponding to the current ptg to the pointer. A possible way to reduce the array size is to limit the array indexes to the range 0–3Fh and then index it using the reference-class ptg (the base ptg) instead of the value- or array-class ptg. This is possible because the token value is the same for all classes of a particular ptg. For more information about operand classes, see "ptg Values for Operand Tokens" on page 267.

There are two tokens, ptgStr and ptgAttr (when bitFAttrChoose is true), that have variable length and are therefore special cases to the preceding description. The first token, ptgStr, is followed by a variable-length string. The token value specifies the length of the string, so the pointer can be incremented by reading the string length (cch) and then adding the string length to the pointer.

The other token is ptgAttr when bitFAttrChoose is true. In this case, the token value contains an optimized CHOOSE function, which contains a variable-length sequence of word offsets into the cases (value1, value2, … arguments) for the CHOOSE function. In this case, you can use the wCases field to calculate the pointer increment.

Unary Operator Tokens

Following are the unary operator tokens for Microsoft Excel. These operators pop the top argument from the operand stack, perform a calculation, and push the result back onto the operand stack.

ptgUplus: Unary Plus (ptg = 12h)

Has no effect on the operand.

ptgUminus: Unary Minus (ptg = 13h)

Negates the operand on the top of the stack.

ptgPercent: Percent Sign (ptg = 14h)

Divides the top operand by 100.

Binary Operator Tokens

There are several binary operator ptgs. All binary operator ptgs pop the top two arguments from the operand stack, perform the associated calculation, and push the result back onto the operand stack.

ptgAdd: Addition (ptg = 03h)

Adds the top two operands.

ptgSub: Subtraction (ptg = 04h)

Subtracts the top operand from the second-to-top operand.

ptgMul: Multiplication (ptg = 05h)

Multiplies the top two operands.

ptgDiv: Division (ptg = 06h)

Divides the top operand by the second-to-top operand.

ptgPower: Exponentiation (ptg = 07h)

Raises the second-to-top operand to the power of the top operand.

ptgConcat: Concatenation (ptg = 08h)

Appends the top operand to the second-to-top operand.

ptgLT: Less Than (ptg = 09h)

Evaluates to TRUE if the second-to-top operand is less than the top operand; evaluates to FALSE otherwise.

ptgLE: Less Than or Equal (ptg = 0Ah)

Evaluates to TRUE if the second-to-top operand is less than or equal to the top operand; evaluates to FALSE otherwise.

ptgEQ: Equal (ptg = 0Bh)

Evaluates to TRUE if the top two operands are equal; evaluates to FALSE otherwise.

ptgGE: Greater Than or Equal (ptg = 0Ch)

Evaluates to TRUE if the second-to-top operand is greater than or equal to the top operand; evaluates to FALSE otherwise.

ptgGT: Greater Than (ptg = 0Dh)

Evaluates to TRUE if the second-to-top operand is greater than the top operand; evaluates to FALSE otherwise.

ptgNE: Not Equal (ptg = 0Eh)

Evaluates to TRUE if the top two operands are not equal; evaluates to FALSE otherwise.

ptgIsect: Intersection (ptg = 0Fh)

Computes the intersection of the top two operands. This is the Microsoft Excel space operator.

ptgUnion: Union (ptg = 10h)

Computes the union of the top two operands. This is the Microsoft Excel comma operator.

ptgRange: Range (ptg = 11h)

Computes the minimal bounding rectangle of the top two operands. This is the Microsoft Excel colon operator.

Operand Tokens: Constant

These operand tokens push a single constant operand onto the operand stack.

ptgMissArg: Missing Argument (Operand, ptg = 16h)

Indicates a missing argument to a Microsoft Excel function. For example, the second (missing) argument to the function DCOUNT(Database,,Criteria) would be stored as a ptgMissArg.

ptgStr: String Constant (Operand, ptg = 17h)

Indicates a string constant ptg followed by a string length field (00 to FFh) and the actual string.

Offset	Name	Size	Contents
0	cch	1	Length of the string
1	rgch	var	The string

ptgStr requires special handling when parsed expressions are scanned. For more information, see "Scanning a Parsed Expression" on page 263.

ptgErr: Error Value (Operand, ptg = 1Ch)

This ptg is followed by the 1-byte error value (err). For a list of error values, see "BOOLERR" on page 152.

Offset	Name	Size	Contents
0	err	1	Error value

ptgBool: Boolean (Operand, ptg = 1Dh)

This ptg is followed by a byte that represents TRUE or FALSE.

Offset	Name	Size	Contents
0	f	1	= 1 for TRUE = 0 for FALSE

ptgInt: Integer (Operand, ptg = 1Eh)

This ptg is followed by a word that contains an unsigned integer.

Offset	Name	Size	Contents
0	w	2	Unsigned integer value

ptgNum: Number (Operand, ptg = 1Fh)

This ptg is followed by an 8-byte IEEE floating-point number.

Offset	Name	Size	Contents
0	num	8	IEEE floating-point number

Operand Tokens

Operand tokens push operand values onto the operand stack. These values fall into one of three classes—reference class, value class, or array class—depending on what type of value the formula expects from the operand. The type of value is determined by the context of the operand when the formula is parsed by Microsoft Excel.

Reference Class

Some operands are required by context to evaluate to references. In this case, the term "reference" is a general term meaning one or more areas on a Microsoft Excel worksheet.

When the Microsoft Excel expression evaluator encounters a reference class operand, it pushes only the reference itself onto the operand stack; it does not dereference it to return the underlying value or values. For example, the function CELL("width",B5) pushes a reference class operand ptgRef (24h) for the second argument. This function returns the column width of cell B5; therefore only the reference to B5 is required, and there is no need to dereference to the value stored in cell B5.

Value Class

This is the most common type of operand. Value class operands push a single dereferenced value onto the operand stack. For example, the formula =A1+1 pushes a value class operand ptgRefV (44h) for the cell reference A1.

Array Class

This operand pushes an array of values onto the operand stack. You can specify the values in an array constant or in a reference to cells. For example, the formula =SUM({1,2,3;4,5,6}) pushes an array class ptgArrayA (60h) to represent the arguments to the function.

ptg Values for Operand Tokens

The three classes of operand tokens are numerically divided as shown in the following table.

Operand class	Ptg values
Reference	20h–3Fh
Value	40h–5Fh
Array	60h–7Fh

The arithmetic difference between ptg classes is 20h. This is the basis for forming the class variants of ptgs. Class variants of ptgs are formed from the reference class ptg, also known as the base ptg. To form the value class ptg from the base ptg, add 20h to the ptg and append V (for Value) to the ptg name. To form the Array class ptg from the base ptg, add 40h to the ptg and append A (for Array) to the ptg name. These rules are summarized in the following table for a sample base ptg, ptgRef.

Class	Name	Ptg
Reference	ptgRef	24h
Value	ptgRefV	44h
Array	ptgRefA	64h

Here is a suggested method for calculating the base ptg from any class variant:

```
if (ptg & 40h)
    {
    /* Value class ptg. Set the 20h bit to
       make it Reference class, then strip
       off the high-order bits. */
    ptgBase = (ptg | 20h) & 3Fh;
    }
else
    {
    /* Reference or Array class ptg. The 20h bit
       is already set, so just have to strip off
       the high-order bits. */
    ptgBase = ptg & 3Fh;
    }
```

A more efficient implementation would define a macro that computes the base ptg:

```
#define PtgBase(ptg) (((ptg & 0x40) ? (ptg | 0x20): ptg) & 0x3F)
```

Operand Tokens: Base

This section describes the operand tokens in their base form (also known as reference class operand tokens).

ptgArray: Array Constant (Operand, ptg = 20h)

Array constant followed by 7 reserved bytes.

The token value for ptgArray consists of the array dimensions and the array values. ptgArray differs from most other operand tokens in that the token value does not follow the token type. Instead, the token value is appended to the saved parsed expression, immediately following the last token. The format of the token value is as follows.

Offset	Name	Size	Contents
0	ccol	1	Number of columns in the array constant
1	crw	2	Number of rows in the array constant
3	rgval	var	The array values

An array with 256 columns is stored with a ccol = 0, because a single byte cannot store the integer 256. This is unambiguous, because a zero-column array constant is meaningless.

The number of values in the array constant is equal to the product of the array dimensions, crw*ccol. Each value is either an 8-byte IEEE floating-point number or a string. The two formats for these values are as follows.

IEEE Floating-Point Number

Offset	Name	Size	Contents
0	grbit	1	= 01h
1	num	8	IEEE floating-point number

String

Offset	Name	Size	Contents
0	grbit	1	= 02h
1	cch	1	Length of the string
2	rgch	var	The string

If a formula contains more than one array constant, then the token values for the array constants are appended to the saved parsed expression in order: first the values for the first array constant, then the values for the second, and so on.

If a formula contains very long array constants, then the FORMULA, ARRAY, or NAME record containing the parsed expression may overflow into CONTINUE records (to accommodate all of the array values). In such cases, an individual array value is never split between records, but record boundaries are established between adjacent array values.

The reference class ptgArray never appears in a Microsoft Excel formula; only the ptgArrayV and ptgArrayA classes are used.

ptgName: Name (Operand, ptg = 23h)

This ptg stores the index to a name. The ilbl field is a one-based index to the table of NAME records in the workbook.

Offset	Name	Size	Contents
0	ilbl	2	Index to the NAME table
2	(reserved)	12	Reserved; must be zero

ptgRef: Cell Reference (Operand, ptg = 24h)

This ptg specifies a reference to a single cell. It is followed by the row and column of the cell. The row of the cell is encoded.

Offset	Name	Size	Contents
0	grbitRw	2	(see following table)
2	col	1	Column of the reference

Only the low-order 14 bits of the grbitRw field store the row number of the reference. The 2 MSBs specify whether the row and column references are relative or absolute. The following table shows the bit structure of the grbitRw field.

Bits	Mask	Name	Contents
15	8000h	fRwRel	= 1 if the row offset is relative = 0 otherwise
14	4000h	fColRel	= 1 if the column offset is relative = 0 otherwise
13–0	3FFFh	rw	The row number or row offset (zero-based)

For example, cell C5 is row number 4, column number 2 (Microsoft Excel stores zero-based cell references). Therefore, the absolute reference $C$5 is stored in a ptgRef as shown in the following file fragment:

```
24 04 00 02
```

In this case, grbitRw = 0004h and col = 02h. Notice that bits 14 and 15 of grbitRw are both 0.

The relative reference C5 is stored in a ptgRef as shown in the following file fragment:

```
24 04 C0 02
```

In this case, where grbitRw = C004h and col = 02h, bits 14 and 15 of grbitRw are both 1.

Mixed references are stored in the same way, with appropriate coding in grbitRw.

ptgArea: Area Reference (Operand, ptg = 25h)

This ptg specifies a reference to a rectangle (range) of cells. ptgArea is followed by 6 bytes that define the first row, last row, first column, and last column of the rectangle. The first row and last row are encoded.

Offset	Name	Size	Contents
0	grbitRwFirst	2	(see following table)
2	grbitRwLast	2	(see following table)
4	colFirst	1	First column of the reference
5	colLast	1	Last column of the reference

Only the low-order 14 bits of the grbitRwFirst and grbitRwLast fields store the row offsets of the reference. The 2 MSBs of each field specify whether the row and column offset are relative or absolute. The following table shows the bit structure of the grbitRwFirst and grbitRwLast fields.

Bits	Mask	Name	Contents
15	8000h	fRwRel	= 1 if the row offset is relative = 0 otherwise
14	4000h	fColRel	= 1 if the column offset is relative = 0 otherwise
13–0	3FFFh	rw	The row number or row offset (zero-based)

ptgMemArea: Constant Reference Subexpression (Operand, ptg = 26h)

This ptg is used to optimize reference expressions. A reference expression consists of operands, usually references to cells or areas, joined by reference operators (intersection, union, and range). Following are three examples of reference expressions.

Reference expression	Evaluates to
(A1,C3,D3:D5)	Two single cells and a 3x1 area
(A1:C3) (B2:D4)	A 2x2 area (the space character is the intersection operator)
(Name C3)	The smallest area that contains both C3 and all the cells referenced in Name (the space character is the intersection operator)

Many reference expressions evaluate to constant references. In the preceding examples, the first two expressions always evaluate to the same reference. The third example does not evaluate to a constant reference because the name's definition may change, which may cause the reference expression to evaluate differently.

When a reference expression evaluates to a constant reference, Microsoft Excel stores the constant reference in the parsed formula through a ptgMemArea token. This saves time during expression evaluation, because the constant part of the expression is pre-evaluated. This part of the expression is known as a reference subexpression.

The token value for ptgMemArea consists of two parts: the length of the reference subexpression, and the value of the reference subexpression. The length is stored immediately following the ptgMemArea, but the value is appended to the saved parsed expression, immediately following the last token.

The format of the length is as follows.

Offset	Name	Size	Contents
0	(reserved)	4	
4	cce	2	Length of the reference subexpression

Immediately following this part of the token value is the reference subexpression itself.

The rest of the token value (that is, the value of the reference subexpression) is appended to the parsed expression in the following format.

Offset	Name	Size	Contents
0	cref	2	Number of rectangles to follow
2	rgref	var	Array of rectangles

Each rgref rectangle is 6 bytes long and contains the following fields.

Offset	Name	Size	Contents
0	rwFirst	2	First row
2	rwLast	2	Last row
4	colFirst	1	First column
5	colLast	1	Last column

If a formula contains more than one ptgMemArea, then the token values are appended to the saved parsed expression in order: first, the values for the first ptgMemArea, then the values for the second ptgMemArea, and so on.

If a formula contains very long reference expressions, the BIFF record containing the parsed expression may be too long to fit in a single record. Microsoft Excel will use CONTINUE records to store long formulas. However, an individual rgref rectangle is never split between records; record boundaries occur between successive rectangles. For more information about the CONTINUE records, see "CONTINUE" on page 155.

ptgMemErr: Erroneous Constant Reference Subexpression (Operand, ptg = 27h)

This ptg is closely related to ptgMemArea. It is used for pre-evaluating reference subexpressions that do not evaluate to references.

For example, consider the formula =SUM(C:C 3:3), which is the sum of the intersection of column C and row 3 (the space between C:C and 3:3 is the intersection operator). The argument to the SUM function is a valid reference subexpression that generates a ptgMemArea for pre-evaluation. However, if you delete column C, then the formula adjusts to =SUM(#REF! 3:3). In this case, the argument to SUM is still a constant reference subexpression, but it does not evaluate to a reference. Therefore a ptgMemErr is used for pre-evaluation.

The token value consists of the error value and length of the reference subexpression. Its format is as follows.

Offset	Name	Size	Contents
0	(reserved)	4	
4	cce	2	Length of the reference subexpression

The reference subexpression will contain a ptgRefErr or ptgAreaErr.

ptgRefErr: Deleted Cell Reference (Operand, ptg = 2Ah)

This ptg specifies a cell reference that was adjusted to #REF! as a result of worksheet editing (such as cut, paste, and delete). The ptgRefErr is followed by 3 unused bytes.

Offset	Name	Size	Contents
0	(reserved)	3	

The original base type of the adjusted ptg is ptgRef or ptgRefN.

ptgAreaErr: Deleted Area Reference (Operand, ptg = 2Bh)

This ptg specifies an area reference that was adjusted to #REF! as a result of worksheet editing (such as cutting, pasting, and deleting). The ptgAreaErr is followed by 6 unused bytes.

Offset	Name	Size	Contents
0	(reserved)	6	

The original base type of the adjusted ptg is ptgArea or ptgAreaN.

ptgRefN: Cell Reference Within a Shared Formula (Operand, ptg = 2Ch)

Similar to its ptgRef counterpart, the ptgRefN specifies a reference to a single cell. It is followed by the row and column of the reference; the row of the cell is encoded as bit fields.

In BIFF5, ptgRefN is used only in shared formulas. In earlier versions, it was used in names.

Offset	Name	Size	Contents
0	grbitRw	2	(see following table)
2	col	1	Column (or column offset) of the reference

Only the low-order 14 bits of the grbitRw field store the row number of the reference. The 2 MSBs specify whether the row and column references are relative or absolute. The following table shows the bit structure of the grbitRw field.

Bits	Mask	Name	Contents
15	8000h	fRwRel	= 1 if the row offset is relative = 0 otherwise
14	4000h	fColRel	= 1 if the column offset is relative = 0 otherwise
13–0	3FFFh	rw	The row number or row offset (zero-based)

The only difference between ptgRefN and ptgRef is in the way relative references are stored. Relative references in shared formulas are stored as offsets, not as row and column numbers (as in ptgRef). For more information, see SHRFMLA on page 230.

ptgAreaN: Area Reference Within a Shared Formula (Operand, ptg = 2Dh)

The ptgAreaN token specifies a reference to a rectangle of cells. Both the first row and last row are stored as bit fields.

In BIFF5, ptgAreaN is used only in shared formulas. In earlier versions, it was used in names.

Offset	Name	Size	Contents
0	grbitRwFirst	2	First row of the absolute reference or relative reference offset bit fields
2	grbitRwLast	2	Last row of the absolute reference or relative reference offset bit fields
4	colFirst	1	First column of the reference or column offset
5	colLast	1	Last column of the reference or column offset

Only the low-order 14 bits of the grbitRwFirst and grbitRwLast fields store the row offsets of the reference. The 2 MSBs of each field specify whether the row and column offset are relative or absolute. The following table shows the bit structure of the grbitRwFirst and grbitRwLast fields.

Bits	Mask	Name	Contents
15	8000h	fRwRel	= 1 if the row offset is relative = 0 otherwise
14	4000h	fColRel	= 1 if the column offset is relative = 0 otherwise
13–0	3FFFh	rw	The row number or row offset (zero-based)

The only difference between ptgAreaN and ptgArea is in the way relative references are stored.

ptgNameX: Name or External Name (Operand, ptg = 39h)

This ptg stores the index to a name. If the name is in the current workbook (ixals is negative), then the ilbl field is a one-based index to the table of NAME records. If the name is in another workbook (an external name), then the ilbl field is a one-based index to the table of EXTERNNAME records.

Offset	Name	Size	Contents
0	ixals	2	Index to EXTERNSHEET records. If ixals is negative (for example, FFFFh), then the name is in the current workbook.
2	(reserved)	8	
10	ilbl	2	Index to the NAME or EXTERNNAME table (one-based)
12	(reserved)	12	

ptgRef3d: 3-D Cell Reference (Operand, ptg = 3Ah)

This ptg stores a 3-D cell reference (for example, Sheet1:Sheet3!$A$1). If the reference is to another workbook (ixals is positive), then itabFirst is not used (it will be 0000h), and itabLast is the ixals for the last sheet in the 3-D reference. If itabFirst or itabLast are equal to FFFFh, then that sheet is a deleted sheet.

Offset	Name	Size	Contents
0	ixals	2	Index to EXTERNSHEET records. If ixals is negative (for example, FFFFh), then the reference is in the current workbook.
2	(reserved)	8	
10	itabFirst	2	Index to first sheet in the 3-D reference (zero-based); see text
12	itabLast	2	Index to last sheet in the 3-D reference (zero-based); see text
14	grbitRw	2	(See following table)
16	col	1	Column of the reference, or column offset

Only the low-order 14 bits of the grbitRw field store the row number of the reference. The 2 MSBs specify whether the row and column references are relative or absolute. The following table shows the bit structure of the grbitRw field.

Bits	Mask	Name	Contents
15	8000h	fRwRel	= 1 if the row offset is relative = 0 otherwise
14	4000h	fColRel	= 1 if the column offset is relative = 0 otherwise
13–0	3FFFh	rw	The row number or row offset (zero-based)

ptgArea3d: 3-D Area Reference (Operand, ptg = 3Bh)

This ptg stores a 3-D area reference (for example, Sheet1:Sheet3!A1:E9).

Offset	Name	Size	Contents
0	ixals	2	Index to EXTERNSHEET records. If ixals is negative (for example, FFFFh), then the reference is on another sheet in the same workbook.
2	(reserved)	8	
10	itabFirst	2	Index to first sheet in the 3-D reference (zero-based)
12	itabLast	2	Index to last sheet in the 3-D reference (zero-based)
14	grbitRwFirst	2	First row in area; see following table
16	grbitRwLast	2	Last row in area; see following table
18	colFirst	1	First column of the reference, or column offset
19	colLast	1	Last column of the reference, or column offset

Only the low-order 14 bits of the grbitRwFirst and grbitRwLast fields store the row offsets of the reference. The 2 MSBs of each field specify whether the row and column offset are relative or absolute. The following table shows the bit structure of the grbitRwFirst and grbitRwLast fields.

Bits	Mask	Name	Contents
15	8000h	fRwRel	= 1 if the row offset is relative = 0 otherwise
14	4000h	fColRel	= 1 if the column offset is relative = 0 otherwise
13–0	3FFFh	rw	The row number or row offset (zero-based)

ptgRefErr3d: Deleted 3-D Cell Reference (Operand, ptg = 3Ch)

This ptg stores a 3-D cell reference that was adjusted to #REF! as a result of worksheet editing (such as cut, paste, and delete). The ptgRefErr3d is identical to ptgRef3d.

ptgAreaErr3d: Deleted 3-D Area Reference (Operand, ptg = 3Dh)

This ptg stores a 3-D area reference that was adjusted to #REF! as a result of worksheet editing (such as cut, paste, and delete). The ptgAreaErr3d is identical to ptgArea3d.

Control Tokens

ptgExp: Array Formula or Shared Formula (ptg = 01h)

This ptg indicates an array formula or a shared formula. When ptgExp occurs in a formula, it is the only token in the formula. This indicates that the cell containing the formula is part of an array or part of a shared formula. The actual formula is found in an ARRAY record.

The token value for ptgExp consists of the row and column of the upper-left corner of the array formula.

Offset	Name	Size	Contents
0	rwFirst	2	Row number of upper-left corner
2	colFirst	2	Column number of upper-left corner

ptgTbl: Data Table (ptg = 02h)

This ptg indicates a data table. When ptgTbl occurs in a formula, it is the only token in the formula. This indicates that the cell containing the formula is an interior cell in a data table; the table description is found in a TABLE record. Rows and columns that contain input values to be substituted in the table do not contain ptgTbl.

The token value for ptgTbl consists of the row and column of the upper-left corner of the table's interior.

Offset	Name	Size	Contents
0	rwFirst	2	Row number of upper-left corner
2	colFirst	2	Column number of upper-left corner

ptgParen: Parenthesis (ptg = 15h)

This ptg is used only when Microsoft Excel unparses a parsed expression (for example, to display it in the formula bar). This ptg is not used to evaluate parsed expressions. It indicates that the previous token in the parsed expression should be in parentheses. If the previous token is an operand, then only that operand is in parentheses. If the previous token is an operator, then the operator and all of its operands are in parentheses.

For example, the formula =1+(2) is stored as:

```
ptgInt   0001h
ptgInt   0002h
ptgParen
ptgAdd
```

In this case, only the integer operand 2 is in parentheses.

The formula =(1+2) is stored as:

```
ptgInt   0001h
ptgInt   0002h
ptgAdd
ptgParen
```

In this example, the parenthesized quantity consists of the ptgAdd operator and both of its operands.

ptgAttr: Special Attribute (ptg = 19h)

This ptg is used for several different purposes. In all cases, the token value consists of a group of flag bits and a data word.

BIFF3 and BIFF4

Offset	Name	Size	Contents
0	grbit	1	Option flags
1	w	2	Data word

BIFF4 when bifFAttrSpace = 1

Offset	Name	Size	Contents
0	grbit	1	Option flags
1	bAttrSpace	1	Spacing attribute
2	bSpace	1	Number of spaces

The grbit field contains the following option flags.

Bits	Mask	Name	Contents
0	01h	bitFAttrSemi	= 1 if the formula contains a volatile function
1	02h	bitFAttrIf	= 1 to implement an optimized IF function
2	04h	bitFAttrChoose	= 1 to implement an optimized CHOOSE function
3	08h	bitFAttrGoto	= 1 to jump to another location within the parsed expression
4	10h	bitFAttrSum	= 1 to implement an optimized SUM function
5	20h	bitFAttrBaxcel	= 1 if the formula is a BASIC-style assignment statement
6	40h	bifFAttrSpace	= 1 if the macro formula contains spaces after the equal sign (BIFF3 and BIFF4 only)
7	80	(Unused)	

ptgAttr requires special handling when parsed expressions are scanned. For more information, see "Scanning a Parsed Expression" on page 263.

bitFAttrSemi Set to 1 if the formula contains a volatile function, that is, a function that is calculated in every recalculation. If ptgAttr is used to indicate a volatile function, then it must be the first token in the parsed expression. If grbit = bitFAttrSemi, then the b (or w) field is don't-care.

bitFAttrIf Indicates an optimized IF function. An IF function contains three parts: a condition, a TRUE subexpression, and a FALSE subexpression. The syntax of an associated Microsoft Excel formula would be IF(condition, TRUE subexpression, FALSE subexpression).

bitFAttrIf immediately follows the condition portion of the parsed expression. The b (or w) field specifies the offset to the FALSE subexpression; the TRUE subexpression is found immediately following the ptgAttr token. At the end of the TRUE subexpression, there is a bitFAttrGoto token that causes a jump to beyond the FALSE subexpression. In this way, Microsoft Excel evaluates only the correct subexpression instead of evaluating both of them and discarding the wrong one.

The FALSE subexpression is optional in Microsoft Excel. If it is missing, then the b (or w) field specifies an offset to beyond the TRUE subexpression.

bitFAttrChoose Indicates an optimized CHOOSE function. The cCases (or wCases) field specifies the number of cases in the CHOOSE function. It is followed by an array of word offsets to those cases. The format of this complex token value is shown in the following table.

Offset	Name	Size	Contents
0	grbit	1	bitFAttrChoose (04h)
1	wCases	2	Number of cases in the CHOOSE function
3	rgw	var	A sequence of word offsets to the CHOOSE cases. The number of words in this field is equal to wCases + 1.

bitFAttrGoto Instructs the expression evaluator to skip part of the parsed expression during evaluation. The b (or w) field specifies the number of bytes (or words) to skip, minus one.

bitFAttrSum Indicates an optimized SUM function (a SUM that has a single argument). For example, the sum of the cells in a 3-D reference, which has the formula =SUM(Sheet1:Sheet3!C11) generates a ptgAttr with bitFAttrSum TRUE. The b (or w) field is don't-care.

bifFAttrSpace Indicates that a formula (macro sheet or worksheet) contains spaces or carriage returns. Microsoft Excel retains spaces and returns in macro sheet and worksheet formulas (in version 3.0 and earlier, spaces and returns would have been eliminated when the formula was parsed). The bAttrSpace field contains an attribute code, and the bSpace field contains the number of spaces or returns. The attribute codes are shown in the following table.

Attribute	Value
bitFSpace	00h
bitFEnter	01h
bitFPreSpace	02h
bitFPreEnter	03h
bitFPostSpace	04h
bitFPostEnter	05h
bitFPreFmlaSpace	06h

The bitFSpace and bitFEnter attributes indicate that bSpace contains the number of spaces or returns before the next ptg in the formula.

The bitFPreSpace, bitFPreEnter, bitFPostSpace, and bitFPostEnter attributes occur with a ptgParen. Because one ptgParen represents two matched parentheses, the ptgAttr must encode the position of the space or return if it occurs before either parenthesis. For example, the ptgs that express the worksheet formula = ("spaces"), which contains four spaces before the opening and closing parenthesis, would appear in a formula record as shown in the following table.

Hex dump	Ptg type	Decodes to
17 06 73 70 61 63 65 73	ptgStr	The string "spaces" (operand)
19 40 02 04	ptgAttr	Four spaces before opening parenthesis.
19 40 04 04	ptgAttr	Four spaces after closing parenthesis.
15	ptgParen	Enclose operand (ptgStr) in parentheses

The bitFPreFmlaSpace attribute provides compatibility with BIFF3, where spaces can occur only after the equal sign (before the formula) in macro formulas. If the spaces in a BIFF5 formula are also legal in a BIFF3 formula, then Microsoft Excel writes a bitFPreFmlaSpace attribute to indicate it.

ptgMemNoMem: Incomplete Constant Reference Subexpression (ptg = 28h)

This ptg is closely related to ptgMemArea. It is used to indicate a constant reference subexpression that could not be pre-evaluated because of low memory conditions.

The token value consists of the length of the reference subexpression.

Offset	Name	Size	Contents
0	(reserved)	4	
4	cce	2	Length of the reference subexpression

ptgMemFunc: Variable Reference Subexpression (ptg = 29h)

This ptg indicates a reference subexpression that does not evaluate to a constant reference. Any reference subexpression that contains one or more of the following items will generate a ptgMemFunc.

Subexpression contains	Example
A function	OFFSET(ACTIVE.CELL(),1,1):$C$2
A name	INDEX(first_cell:$D$2,1,1)
An external reference	SALES.XLS!$A$1:SALES.XLS!$C$3

The token value consists of the length of the reference subexpression.

Offset	Name	Size	Contents
0	cce	2	Length of the reference subexpression

ptgMemAreaN: Reference Subexpression Within a Name (ptg = 2Eh)

This ptg contains a constant reference subexpression within a name definition. Unlike ptgMemArea, ptgMemAreaN is not used to pre-evaluate the reference subexpression.

The token value consists of the length of the reference subexpression.

Offset	Name	Size	Contents
0	cce	2	Length of the reference subexpression

ptgMemNoMemN: Incomplete Reference Subexpression Within a Name (ptg = 2Fh)

This ptg is closely related to ptgMemAreaN. It is used to indicate a constant reference subexpression within a name that could not be evaluated because of low memory conditions.

The token value consists of the length of the reference subexpression.

Offset	Name	Size	Contents
0	cce	2	Length of the reference subexpression

Function Operators

The following paragraphs describe the function operator ptgs. All of these operators pop arguments from the operand stack, compute a function, and push the result back onto the operand stack. The number of operands popped from the stack is equal to the number of arguments passed to the Microsoft Excel function. Some Microsoft Excel functions always require a fixed number of arguments, while others may accept a variable number of arguments. The SUM function, for example, accepts a variable number of arguments.

Although they are operators, function tokens also behave like operands in that they can occur in any of the three ptg classes: reference, value, and array.

ptgFunc: Function, Fixed Number of Arguments (Operator, ptg = 21h)

This ptg indicates a Microsoft Excel function with a fixed number of arguments. The ptgFunc is followed by the index to the function table. For a complete listing of the function table, see the section "Built-in Functions and Command Equivalents" in the file XLCALL.H in the INCLUDE directory of the Windows disk that accompanies this book.

Offset	Name	Size	Contents
0	iftab	2	Index to the function table

ptgFuncVar: Function, Variable Number of Arguments (Operator, ptg = 22h)

This ptg indicates a Microsoft Excel function with a variable number of arguments. The ptgFuncVar is followed by the number of arguments (one byte) and then the index to the function table (two bytes). For a complete listing of the function table, see the section "Built-in Functions and Command Equivalents" in the file XLCALL.H in the INCLUDE directory of the Windows disk that accompanies this book.

Offset	Bits	Mask	Name	Contents
0	6–0	7Fh	cargs	Number of arguments to the function
	7	80h	fPrompt	= 1, function prompts the user (macro functions that end with a question mark)
1	14–0	7FFFh	iftab	Index to the function table
	15	8000h	fCE	Function is a command-equivalent

C H A P T E R   4

Binary Interchange File Format for Charts

The binary interchange file format (BIFF) is the file format in which Microsoft Excel documents are saved on disk. This chapter describes the chart BIFF, which contains data objects created by combining chart BIFF records. The chart BIFF is combined with other sheet BIFF records into a workbook BIFF file. This chapter documents only those records unique to charts; these records have record numbers greater than 1000 hex. Chart BIFF also uses records outside this range; for information on those records, see the chapter "File Format," on page 131.

The chart BIFF does not necessarily contain a complete description of a Microsoft Excel chart but rather a description of how the chart differs from the default chart (the simple column chart). Therefore, many of the records in the chart BIFF modify the default chart description.

Although the information contained in BIFF records varies, every record has the same basic format. For more information about the BIFF record format, see "BIFF Record Information" on page 133.

Chart BIFF Hierarchy

The chart BIFF contains a hierarchical series of records that defines the chart format. Much of the chart data is defined as objects; an object starts with a BEGIN record and ends with a matching END record. For example, a series object definition starts with a SERIES record immediately followed by a BEGIN record. All subsequent records up to the matching END record apply to the specified series.

Objects can be nested within objects; nested BEGIN and END records are used as required to describe objects that are part of other objects. The outer object is called the "parent;" the nested object is called a "child."

The BIFF structure is flexible; it varies depending on the chart type and the elements included in the chart. You can examine the record structure of an existing BIFF file with the BiffView utility, included in the BIFF directory on the Windows sample disk.

Series and Categories

All charts, whether in column, bar, line, pie, area, or scatter format, contain series data, category data, and value data. The following column chart explains the difference between series and categories.

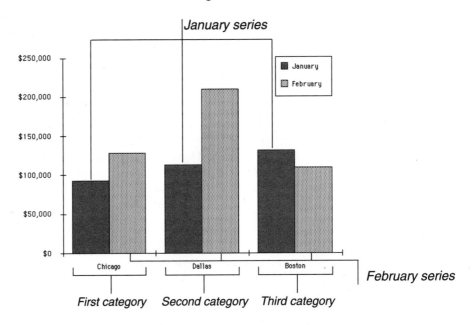

When Microsoft Excel creates a chart from a worksheet, it assigns either the worksheet rows as the series data (and the columns as the category data), or the worksheet columns as the series data (and the rows as categories). If there are fewer rows than columns, then the rows become the series. However, if there are fewer columns than rows, then the columns become the series. If there are an equal number of rows and columns in the range of cells, then the rows become the series.

This algorithm minimizes the number of series on the chart. For example, the following column chart . . .

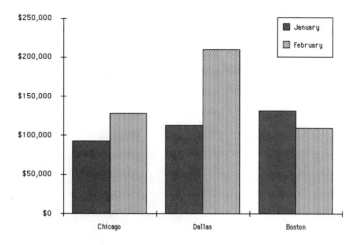

. . . can be created from either of the two following worksheets.

	A	B	C	D
1				
2				
3				
4		January	February	
5	Chicago	$93,000	$128,000	
6	Dallas	$113,000	$210,000	
7	Boston	$132,000	$110,000	
8				

	A	B	C	D	E
1					
2					
3					
4		Chicago	Dallas	Boston	
5	January	$93,000	$113,000	$132,000	
6	February	$128,000	$210,000	$110,000	
7					
8					

In the second worksheet shown here, January and February are the series (because there are fewer rows than columns), and Chicago, Dallas, and Boston are the categories. In these two worksheets, values for each series appear at three locations on the chart.

If you add sales data for March and April, the series are now Chicago, Dallas, and Boston, and the categories are January, February, March, and April. Microsoft Excel automatically exchanges the series and categories to minimize the number of series, as shown in the following chart and worksheet.

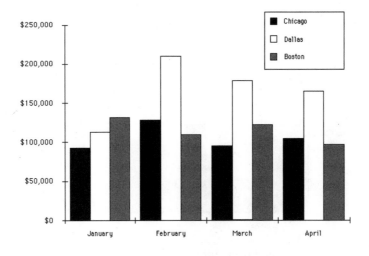

BIFF Records: Alphabetical Order

BIFF Records: Record Number Order

Number	Record	Page
1001	UNITS: Chart Units	321
1002	CHART: Location and Overall Chart Dimensions	299
1003	SERIES: Series Definition	316
1006	DATAFORMAT: Series and Data Point Numbers	301
1007	LINEFORMAT: Style of a Line or Border	306
1009	MARKERFORMAT: Style of a Line Marker	307
100A	AREAFORMAT: Colors and Patterns for an Area	294
100B	PIEFORMAT: Position of the Pie Slice	309
100C	ATTACHEDLABEL: Series Data/Value Labels	295
100D	SERIESTEXT: Legend/Category/Value Text	317
1014	CHARTFORMAT: Parent Record for Chart Group	300
1015	LEGEND: Legend Type and Position	303
1016	SERIESLIST: Specifies the Series in an Overlay Chart	316
1017	BAR: Chart Group is a Bar or Column Chart Group	297
1018	LINE: Chart Group Is a Line Chart Group	305
1019	PIE: Chart Group Is a Pie Chart Group	309
101A	AREA: Chart Group Is an Area Chart Group	294
101B	SCATTER: Chart Group Is a Scatter Chart Group	314
101C	CHARTLINE: Drop/Hi-Lo/Series Lines on a Line Chart	300
101D	AXIS: Axis Type	296
101E	TICK: Tick Marks and Labels Format	320
101F	VALUERANGE: Defines Value Axis Scale	321
1020	CATSERRANGE: Defines a Category or Series Axis	298
1021	AXISLINEFORMAT: Defines a Line That Spans an Axis	296
1022	CHARTFORMATLINK: Not Used	300
1024	DEFAULTTEXT: Default Data Label Text Properties	301
1025	TEXT: Defines Display of Text Fields	319
1026	FONTX: Font Index	302

Record Descriptions

The first two fields in every BIFF record are record number and record length. Because these fields have the same offset and size in every BIFF record, they are not documented in the following descriptions. For more information about the record number and record length fields, see "BIFF Record Information" on page 133.

3D: Chart Group Is a 3-D Chart Group (103Ah)

This record defines a 3-D chart group and also contains generic formatting information.

Record Data

Offset	Name	Size	Contents
4	anRot	2	Rotation angle (0 to 360 degrees)
6	anElev	2	Elevation angle (–90 to +90 degrees)
8	pcDist	2	Distance from eye to chart (0 to 100)
10	pcHeight	2	Height of plot volume relative to width and depth
12	pcDepth	2	Depth of points relative to width
14	pcGap	2	Space between series
16	grbit	2	Option flags

The grbit field contains the following option flags.

Offset	Bits	Mask	Name	Contents
0	0	01h	fPerspective	1 = use perspective transform
0	1	02h	fCluster	1 = 3-D columns are clustered or stacked
0	2	04h	f3DScaling	1 = use auto scaling
0	3	08h	(reserved)	Reserved; must be zero
0	4	10h	(reserved)	Reserved; must be one
0	5	20h	f2DWalls	use 2D walls and gridlines
0	7–2	FAh	(reserved)	Reserved; must be zero
1	7–0	FFh	(reserved)	Reserved; must be zero

AI: Linked Data (1051h)

This record specifies linked series data or text.

Record Data

Offset	Name	Size	Contents
4	id	1	Link index identifier 0 = linking a series title or text 1 = linking series values 2 = linking series categories

Offset	Name	Size	Contents
5	rt	1	Reference type 0 = use default categories 1 = text or value entered directly into the formula bar 2 = linked to worksheet 3 = not used 4 = error reported
6	grbit	2	Flags
8	ifmt	2	Index to number format record
10	cce	2	Size of rgce (in bytes)
12	rgce	var	Parsed formula of link

The grbit field contains the following option flags.

Offset	Bits	Mask	Name	Contents
0	0	01h	fCustomIfmt	TRUE if this object has a custom number format; FALSE if number format is linked to data source
0	1	02h	(reserved)	Reserved; must be zero
0	5-2	3Ch	st	Source type (always zero)
0	7-6	C0h	(reserved)	Reserved; must be zero
1	7-0	FFh	(reserved)	Reserved; must be zero

ALRUNS: Text Formatting (1050h)

This record specifies rich-text formatting (bold, italic, font changes, etc.) within chart titles and data labels.

Record Data

Offset	Name	Size	Contents
4	cRuns	2	Number of rich-text runs
6	rgwRuns	var	Array of cRuns four-byte groups. The first two bytes in each group specifies the first character in the rich-text run. The second two bytes specifies the font index for the text run (see the FONT record for more information about this index).

AREA: Chart Group Is an Area Chart Group (101Ah)

This record defines an area chart group.

Record Data

Offset	Name	Size	Contents
4	grbit	2	format flags

The grbit field contains the following option flags.

Offset	Bits	Mask	Name	Contents
0	0	01h	fStacked	Series in this group are stacked
0	1	02h	f100	Each category is broken down as a percentage
0	7–2	FCh	(reserved)	Reserved; must be zero
1	7–0	FFh	(reserved)	Reserved; must be zero

When fStacked is true, the value indicators (filled areas) are stacked one on top of the next. The f100 bit can be set only when the fStacked bit is set and indicates that each category is broken down into percentages.

AREAFORMAT: Colors and Patterns for an Area (100Ah)

This record describes the patterns and colors used in a filled area.

Record Data

Offset	Name	Size	Contents
4	rgbFore	4	Foreground color: RGB value (high byte = 0)
8	rgbBack	4	Background color: RGB value (high byte = 0)
12	fls	2	Pattern
14	grbit	2	Format flags

The grbit field contains the following option flags.

Offset	Bits	Mask	Name	Contents
0	0	01h	fAuto	Automatic format
0	1	02h	fInvertNeg	Foreground and background are swapped when the data value is negative
0	7–2	FCh	(reserved)	Reserved; must be zero
1	7–0	FFh	(reserved)	Reserved; must be zero

ATTACHEDLABEL: Series Data/Value Labels (100Ch)

The ATTACHEDLABEL record defines the data label type. The ATTACHEDLABEL record applies to the label data identified in the associated DATAFORMAT record.

Record Data

Offset	Name	Size	Contents
4	grbit	2	Value label flags

The grbit field contains the following option flags.

Offset	Bits	Mask	Name	Contents
0	0	01h	fShowValue	1 = show the actual value of the data point
0	1	02h	fShowPercent	1 = show value as a percent of the total. This bit applies only to pie charts
0	2	04h	fShowLabPct	1 = show category label and value as a percentage (pie charts only). Should be 1 if fShowLabel and fShowPerecent are both 1.
0	3	08h	(reserved)	Reserved; must be zero
0	4	10h	fShowLabel	1 = show category label
0	7-5	E0h	(reserved)	Reserved; must be zero
1	7–0	FFh	(reserved)	Reserved; must be zero

AXESUSED: Number of Axes Sets (1046h)

This record specifies the number of axes sets (1 = primary only, 2 = primary and secondary) used on the chart (3-D charts can only have primary axes).

Record Data

Offset	Name	Size	Contents
4	cAxes	2	Number of axes sets

AXIS: Axis Type (101Dh)

This record defines the axis type.

Record Data

Offset	Name	Size	Contents
4	wType	2	Axis type 0 = category axis or x axis on a scatter chart 1 = value axis 2 = series axis
6	(reserved)	16	Reserved; must be zero

AXISLINEFORMAT: Defines a Line That Spans an Axis (1021h)

This record usually follows an AXIS record to define the axis line as it appears on the chart.

Record Data

Offset	Name	Size	Contents
4	id	2	Axis line identifier: 0 = the axis line itself 1 = major grid line along the axis 2 = minor grid line along the axis 3 = walls or floor -- walls if parent axis is type 0 or 2; floor if parent axis is type 1

AXISPARENT: Axis Size and Location (1041h)

This record specifies the location and size of the chart axes, in units of 1/4000 of the chart area.

Record Data

Offset	Name	Size	Contents
4	iax	2	Axis index (0 = main, 1 = secondary)
6	x	4	x coordinate of top left corner
10	y	4	y coordinate of top left corner
14	dx	4	length of x axis
18	dy	4	length of y axis

BAR: Chart Group is a Bar or Column Chart Group (1017h)

This record defines a bar or column chart group.

Record Data

Offset	Name	Size	Contents
4	pcOverlap	2	Space between bars (percent of bar width), default = 0
6	pcGap	2	Space between categories (percent of bar width), default = 50
8	grbit	2	Format flags

The grbit field contains the bar chart display attributes as follows.

Offset	Bits	Mask	Name	Contents
0	0	01h	fTranspose	1 = horizontal bars (bar chart) 0 = vertical bars (column chart)
0	1	02h	fStacked	Stack the displayed values
0	2	04h	f100	Each categpry is displayed as a percentage
0	7–3	FCh	(reserved)	Reserved; must be zero
1	7–0	FFh	(reserved)	Reserved; must be zero

When fStacked is true, the bars or columns within a category are stacked one on top of the next. The f100 bit can be set only when the fStacked bit is set, and indicates that each category is broken down into percentages.

BEGIN: Defines the Beginning of an Object (1033h)

The BEGIN record is a fixed length 4-byte record that indicates the beginning of a block of records that forms a data object. Every BEGIN record must have a corresponding END record. The BEGIN record consists of 10330000h.

CATSERRANGE: Defines a Category or Series Axis (1020h)

This record defines the scaling options for a category or series axis.

Record Data

Offset	Name	Size	Contents
4	catCross	2	Value axis/category crossing point (2-D charts only)
6	catLabel	2	Frequency of labels
8	catMark	2	Frequency of tick marks
10	grbit	2	Format flags

The catCross field defines the point on the category axis where the value axis crosses. A value of 01 indicates that the value axis crosses to the left, or in the center, of the first category (depending on the value of bit 0 of the grbit field); a value of 02 indicates that the value axis crosses to the left or center of the second category, and so on. Bit 2 of the grbit field overrides the value of catCross when set to 1.

The catLabel field defines how often labels appear along the category or series axis. A value of 01 indicates that a category label will appear with each category, a value of 02 means a label appears every other category, and so on.

The catMark field defines how often tick marks appear along the category or series axis. A value of 01 indicates that a tick mark will appear between each category or series; a value of 02 means a label appears between every other category or series, etc.

The grbit field contains the following option flags.

Offset	Bits	Mask	Name	Contents
0	0	01h	fBetween	Value axis crossing 0 = axis crosses mid-category 1 = axis crosses between categories
0	1	02h	fMaxCross	Value axis crosses at the far right category (in a line, bar, column, scatter, or area chart; 2-D charts only)
0	2	04h	fReverse	Display categories in reverse order
0	7–3	F8h	(reserved)	Reserved; must be zero
1	7–0	FFh	(reserved)	Reserved; must be zero

CHART: Location and Overall Chart Dimensions (1002h)

The CHART record marks the start of the chart data substream in the workbook BIFF stream. This record defines the location of the chart on the display and its overall size. The x and y fields define the position of the upper-left corner of the bounding rectangle that encompasses the chart. The position of the chart is referenced to the page.

The dx and dy fields define the overall size (the bounding rectangle) of the chart, including title, pointing arrows, axis labels, etc.

The position and size are specified in points (1/72 inch), using a fixed point format (two bytes integer, two bytes fraction).

Record Data

Offset	Name	Size	Contents
4	x	4	x-position of upper-left corner
8	y	4	y-position of upper-left corner
12	dx	4	x-size
16	dy	4	y-size

CHARTFORMAT: Parent Record for Chart Group (1014h)

This record is the parent record for the chart group format description. Each chart group will have a separate CHARTFORMAT record; followed by a BEGIN record, the chart-group description, and an END record.

Record Data

Offset	Name	Size	Contents
4	(reserved)	16	Reserved; must be zero
20	grbit	2	Format flags
22	icrt	2	Drawing order (0 = bottom of the z-order)

The grbit field contains the following option flags.

Offset	Bits	Mask	Name	Contents
0	0	01h	fVaried	Vary color for each data point
0	7–1	FEh	(reserved)	Reserved; must be zero
1	7–0	FFh	(reserved)	Reserved; must be zero

CHARTFORMATLINK: Not Used (1022h)

This record is written by Microsoft Excel, but it is ignored. Applications writing chart BIFF do not need to write this record, and applications reading chart BIFF can ignore it.

CHARTLINE: Specifies Drop/Hi-Lo/Series Lines on a Line Chart (101Ch)

This record specifies drop lines, hi-lo lines, or series lines on a line chart. If the chart has both drop lines and hi-lo lines, two CHARTLINE records will be present.

Record Data

Offset	Name	Size	Contents
4	id	2	Drop lines/hi-lo lines 0 = drop lines 1 = hi-lo lines 2 = series lines (the lines that connect the columns in a stacked column chart)

DATAFORMAT: Series and Data Point Numbers (1006h)

The DATAFORMAT record contains the zero-based numbers of the data point and series. The subordinate records determine the format of the series or point defined by the DATAFORMAT record.

Record Data

Offset	Name	Size	Contents
4	xi	2	Point number (FFFFh means entire series)
6	yi	2	Series index (file relative)
8	iss	2	Series number (as shown in namebox -- S1, S2, etc.). This can be different from yi if the series order has been changed.
10	grbit	2	format flags

The grbit field contains the following flags.

Offset	Bits	Mask	Name	Contents
0	0	01h	fXL4iss	1 = use Microsoft Excel 4.0 colors for automatic formatting
0	7–1	FEh	(reserved)	Reserved; must be zero
1	7–0	FFh	(reserved)	Reserved; must be zero

DEFAULTTEXT: Default Data Label Text Properties (1024h)

The DEFAULTTEXT record precedes a TEXT record to identify the text defined in the TEXT record as the default properties for certain chart items.

Record Data

Offset	Name	Size	Contents
4	id	2	Object identifier for the text 0 = default text characteristics for "show labels" data labels 1 = default text characteristics for value and percentage data labels 2 = default text characteristics for all text in the chart

DROPBAR: Defines Drop Bars (103Dh)

This record defines drop bars on a line chart. If the chart contains drop bars, the chart BIFF will contain two DROPBAR records. The first DROPBAR record corresponds to the up bar and the second DROPBAR record corresponds to the down bar.

Record Data

Offset	Name	Size	Contents
4	pcGap	2	Drop bar gap width (0 to 100%)

END: Defines the End of an Object (1034h)

This record is a fixed-length 4-byte record that indicates the end of a data object. Every END record has a corresponding BEGIN record. The END record consists of 10340000h.

FONTX: Font Index (1026h)

This record is the child of a TEXT record and defines a text font by indexing the appropriate font in the font table. The font table is built from FONT records.

Record Data

Offset	Name	Size	Contents
4	ifont	2	Index number into the font table

FRAME: Defines Border Shape Around Displayed Text (1032h)

The FRAME record defines the border that is present around a displayed label as a rectangle. A displayed label can include the chart title, the legend (if not a regular rectangle), a category name, or a value amount.

Record Data

Offset	Name	Size	Contents
4	frt	2	0 = regular rectangle/no border 1–3 (reserved) 4 = rectangle with shadow
6	grbit	2	Flags

The frt field defines the format of the frame border, that is, a rectangle or a rectangle with a shadow along two sides. (The format of the rectangle line and the pattern of the background within the rectangle are defined by the subordinate LINEFORMAT and AREAFORMAT records.)

The grbit field contains the following option flags.

Offset	Bits	Mask	Name	Contents
0	0	01h	fAutoSize	Microsoft Excel calculates size
0	1	02h	fAutoPosition	Microsoft Excel calculates position
0	7–2	FCh	(reserved)	Reserved; must be zero
1	7–0	FFh	(reserved)	Reserved; must be zero

The fAutoSize field indicates that the size of the frame is to be calculated by Microsoft Excel. The dx and dy fields in the parent record are ignored.

The fAutoPosition field indicates that the position of the frame is to be calculated by Microsoft Excel. The dx and dy fields in the parent record are ignored.

IFMT: Number-Format Index (104Eh)

This record specifies the number-format index for an axis.

Record Data

Offset	Name	Size	Contents
4	ifmt	2	Number-format index (number of the FORMAT record in the BIFF, begins at zero)

LEGEND: Legend Type and Position (1015h)

The LEGEND record defines the location of the legend on the display and its overall size. The displayed legend contains all series on the chart.

Record Data

Offset	Name	Size	Contents
4	x	4	x-position of upper-left corner
8	y	4	y-position of upper-left corner
12	dx	4	x-size
16	dy	4	y-size

Offset	Name	Size	Contents
20	wType	1	Type 0 = bottom 1 = corner 2 = top 3 = right 4 = left 7 = not docked or inside the plot area
21	wSpacing	1	Spacing 0 = close 1 = medium 2 = open
22	grbit	2	Option flags

The x, y, dx, and dy fields are in units of 1/4000 of the chart area.

The x and y fields define the position of the upper-left corner of the bounding rectangle that encompasses the legend. The position of the legend is referenced to the document window. The dx and dy fields define the overall size (the bounding rectangle) of the legend.

The wType field defines the location of the legend relative to the plot rectangle of the chart. The wSpacing field is always 1 for Microsoft Excel.

The grbit field contains the following option flags.

Offset	Bits	Mask	Name	Contents
0	0	01h	fAutoPosition	Automatic positioning (1 = legend is docked)
0	1	02h	fAutoSeries	Automatic series distribution (TRUE in Microsoft Excel 5.0)
0	2	04h	fAutoPosX	X positioning is automatic
0	3	08h	fAutoPosY	Y positioning is automatic
0	4	10h	fVert	1 = vertical legend (a single column of entries) 0 = horizontal legend (multiple columns of entries) Manual sized legends always have this bit set to zero
0	7–5	E0h	(reserved)	Reserved; must be zero
1	7–0	FFh	(reserved)	Reserved; must be zero

LEGENDXN: Legend Exception (1043h)

This record specifies information about a legend entry which has been changed from the default legend-entry settings.

Record Data

Offset	Name	Size	Contents
4	iss	2	Legend-entry index
6	grbit	2	Flags

The grbit field contains the following option flags.

Offset	Bits	Mask	Name	Contents
0	0	01h	fDeleted	TRUE if the legend entry has been deleted
0	1	02h	fLabel	TRUE if the legend entry has been formatted
0	7-2	FCh	(reserved)	Reserved; must be zero
1	7–0	FFh	(reserved)	Reserved; must be zero

Microsoft Excel uses three legend types. On a chart where the legend lists the series names, the iss field will contain FFFF. On a single-series chart formatted to vary by category (a pie chart or column autoformat number two, for example), the legend lists the categories and the iss field contains the category number. On a surface chart, the legend lists data ranges, and the iss field contains the legend-entry number, starting at zero for the bottom range.

LINE: Chart Group Is a Line Chart Group (1018h)

This record defines a line chart group.

Record Data

Offset	Name	Size	Contents
4	grbit ·	2	format flags

The grbit field contains the following option flags.

Offset	Bits	Mask	Name	Contents
0	0	01h	fStacked	Stack the displayed values
0	1	02h	f100	Each category is broken down as a percentage

Offset	Bits	Mask	Name	Contents
0	7–2	FCh	(reserved)	Reserved; must be zero
1	7–0	FFh	(reserved)	Reserved; must be zero

When fStacked is true, the value indicators within a category are stacked one on top of the next. The f100 bit can be set only when the fStacked bit is set, and indicates that each category is broken down into percentages.

LINEFORMAT: Style of a Line or Border (1007h)

This record defines the appearance of a line, such as an axis line or border.

Record Data

Offset	Name	Size	Contents
4	rgb	4	Color of line; RGB value high byte must be set to zero
8	lns	2	Pattern of line 0 = solid 1 = dash 2 = dot 3 = dash-dot 4 = dash dot-dot 5 = none 6 = dark gray pattern 7 = medium gray pattern 8 = light gray pattern
10	we	2	Weight of line –1 = hairline 0 = narrow (single) 1 = medium (double) 2 = wide (triple)
12	grbit	2	Format flags

The grbit field contains the following option flags.

Offset	Bits	Mask	Name	Contents
0	0	01h	fAuto	Automatic format
0	1	02h	(reserved)	Reserved; must be zero
0	2	04h	fDrawTick	1 = draw tick labels on this axis
0	7–3	F8h	(reserved)	Reserved; must be zero
1	7–0	FFh	(reserved)	Reserved; must be zero

MARKERFORMAT: Style of a Line Marker (1009h)

This record defines the color and shape of the line markers that appear on scatter and line charts.

Record Data

Offset	Name	Size	Contents
4	rgbFore	4	Foreground color: RGB value (high byte = 0)
8	rgbBack	4	Background color: RGB value (high byte = 0)
12	imk	2	Type of marker 0 = no marker 1 = square 2 = diamond 3 = triangle 4 = X 5 = star 6 = Dow-Jones 7 = standard deviation 8 = circle 9 = plus sign
14	grbit	2	Format flags

The rgbBack field describes the color of the marker's background, such as the center of the square, while the rgbFore field describes the color of the border or the marker itself. The imk field defines the type of marker.

The grbit field contains the following option flags.

Offset	Bits	Mask	Name	Contents
0	0	01h	fAuto	Automatic color
0	3-1	0Eh	(reserved)	Reserved; must be zero
0	4	10h	fNotShowInt	1 = "background = none"
0	5	20h	fNotShowBrd	1 = "foreground = none"
0	7-6	C0h	(reserved)	Reserved; must be zero
1	7-0	FFh	(reserved)	Reserved; must be zero

OBJECTLINK: Attaches Text to Chart or to Chart Item (1027h)

This record links a TEXT record to an object on the chart or to the entire chart.

Record Data

Offset	Name	Size	Contents
4	wLinkObj	2	Object text is linked to 1 = entire chart (chart title) 2 = y axis (y axis title) 3 = x axis (x axis title) 4 = data series or data point (data label) 5 not used 6 not used 7 = z axis (z axis title)
6	wLinkVar1	2	Link index 1, series number
8	wLinkVar2	2	Link index 2, data point number

The wLinkObj field specifies which object the text is linked to. The wLinkVar1 and wLinkVar2 fields define the linked object as a specific series number and data point in the series. The wLinkVar1 and wLinkVar2 fields have meaning only if the wLinkObj field equals 4.

PICF: Picture Format (103Ch)

This record defines the format for a picture attached to a data series or point.

Record Data

Offset	Name	Size	Contents
4	ptyp	2	Picture type: = 1, stretched = 2, stacked = 3, stacked and scaled
6	cf	2	Image format: = 2, Windows metafile or Macintosh PICT format = 9, Windows bitmap format
8	grbit	2	Option flags
10	numScale	8	Scaling value for pictures, units/picture (IEEE floating-point number)

The grbit field contains the following option flags.

Offset	Bits	Mask	Name	Contents
0	7–0	FFh	env	Environment from which the file was written: = 1, Microsoft Windows = 2, Apple Macintosh
1	0	01h	fFmtOnly	Formatting only; no picture attached
1	7–1	FEh	(reserved)	Reserved; must be zero

If fFmtOnly is false, then an IMDATA record, which contains the picture itself, follows the PICF record. If fFmtOnly is true, which occurs only if the parent DATAFORMAT record refers to a single data point, then there is no IMDATA record following the PICF record. In this case, the picture specified for the entire series is used, with formatting specified by the PICF record. For more information about the IMDATA record, see "IMDATA" on page 178.

PIE: Chart Group Is a Pie Chart Group (1019h)

This record defines a pie chart group and also specifies the angle of the first slice in the pie.

Record Data

Offset	Name	Size	Contents
4	anStart	2	Angle of the first pie slice expressed in degrees
6	pcDonut	2	0 = true pie chart non-zero = size of center hole in a donut chart (as a percentage)

The angle of the pie slice has a default value of zero and can be any value in the range of 0 to 359 (0000h to 0167h).

PIEFORMAT: Position of the Pie Slice (100Bh)

The distance of an open pie slice from the center of the pie chart is expressed as a percentage of the pie diameter. For example, if the percent = 33 (21h), the pie slice is one-third of the pie diameter away from the pie center.

Record Data

Offset	Name	Size	Contents
4	percent	2	Distance of pie slice from center of pie

PLOTAREA: Frame Belongs to Plot Area (1035h)

This record immediately preceeds a FRAME record. It indicates that the frame record that follows belongs to the plot area.

POS: Position Information (104Fh)

This record defines manual position information for the main-axis plot area, legend, and attached text (data labels, axis labels, and chart title). The record data depends on the record's use, as shown in the following sections.

This record is used very rarely and is usually not required; for most applications, the default size and position settings are sufficient. If your application writes chart BIFF, use the default settings whenever possible. To use the default plot area, set the fManPlotArea bit in the SHTPROPS record. To use a default legend position and size, set the fAutoPosition bit in the LEGEND record, and set the fAutoSize bit in the legend FRAME record. No other settings are required to use the default position for text (data labels, axis labels, and chart title).

Plot Area

The POS record is used only for the main axis. The record describes the plot-area bounding box (the plot-area bounding box includes the plot area, tick marks, and a small border around the tick marks). The fManPlotArea bit in the SHTPROPS record must be 1, or the POS record is ignored.

The top-left position, width, and height fields use units of 1/4000 of the chart area.

Record Data

Offset	Name	Size	Contents
4	mdTopLt	2	Must be 2
6	mdBotRt	2	Must be 2
8	x1	4	x coordinate of bounding box top left corner
12	y1	4	y coordinate of bounding box top left corner
16	x2	4	width of the bounding box
20	y2	4	height of the bounding box

Legend

The POS record describes the legend position and size.

Record Data

Offset	Name	Size	Contents
4	mdTopLt	2	Must be 5
6	mdBotRt	2	1 = use x2 and y2 for legend size 2 = autosize legend (ignore x2, y2). The fAutoSize bit of the legend FRAME record should be 1 if this field is 2.
8	x1	4	x coordinate of legend top left corner, in units of 1/4000 of the chart area
12	y1	4	y coordinate of legend top left corner, in units of 1/4000 of the chart area
16	x2	4	width of the legend, in points (1/72 inch)
20	y2	4	height of the legend, in points

Text (Chart Title)

The POS record sets the chart title position as an offset from the default position, in units of 1/4000 of the chart area.

Record Data

Offset	Name	Size	Contents
4	mdTopLt	2	Must be 2
6	mdTopRt	2	Must be 2
8	x1	4	offset from default horizontal position
12	y1	4	offset from default vertical position
16	x2	4	ignored (you cannot size the chart title)
20	y2	4	ignored

Text (Axis Title)

The POS record sets the axis title position as an offset from the default position.

Record Data

Offset	Name	Size	Contents
4	mdTopLt	2	Must be 2
6	mdTopRt	2	Must be 2

Offset	Name	Size	Contents
8	x1	4	offset perpendicular to the axis, in units of 1/1000 of the plot-area bounding box
12	y1	4	offset parallel to the axis, in units of 1/1000 of the axis length
16	x2	4	ignored (you cannot size the axis title)
20	y2	4	ignored

Text (Data Labels)

The POS record sets the label position as an offset from the default position.

Record Data

Offset	Name	Size	Contents
4	mdTopLt	2	Must be 2
6	mdTopRt	2	Must be 2
8	x1	4	**Pie charts**: offset angle from the default, in radians. **Bar and Column charts**: offset perpendicular to the bar or column, in units of 1/1000 of the plot area **All other chart types**: horizontal offset from the default position, in units of 1/1000 of the plot area
12	y1	4	**Pie charts**: radial offset, in units of 1/1000 of the pie radius. **Bar and Column charts**: offset parallel to the bar or column, in units of 1/1000 of the plot area **All other chart types**: vertical offset from the default position, in units of 1/1000 of the plot area
16	x2	4	ignored (you cannot size the data label)
20	y2	4	ignored

RADAR: Chart Group Is a Radar Chart Group (103Eh)

This record defines a radar chart group.

Record Data

Offset	Name	Size	Contents
4	grbit	2	Option flags

The grbit field contains the following option flags.

Offset	Bits	Mask	Name	Contents
0	0	01h	fRdrAxLab	= 1, chart contains radar axis labels
0	7–1	FEh	(reserved)	Reserved; must be zero
1	7–0	FFh	(reserved)	Reserved; must be zero

RADARAREA: Chart Group Is a Radar Area Chart Group (1040h)

This record defines a radar area chart group.

Record Data

Offset	Name	Size	Contents
4	grbit	2	Option flags

The grbit field contains the following option flags.

Offset	Bits	Mask	Name	Contents
0	0	01h	fRdrAxLab	1 if chart contains radar axis labels
0	7–1	FEh	(reserved)	Reserved; must be zero
1	7–0	FFh	(reserved)	Reserved; must be zero

SBASEREF: PivotTable Reference (1048h)

This record specifies the PivotTable reference used for the chart.

Record Data

Offset	Name	Size	Contents
4	rwFirst	2	First PivotTable row
6	rwLast	2	Last PivotTable row
8	colFirst	2	First PivotTable column
10	colLast	2	Last PivotTable column

SCATTER: Chart Group Is a Scatter Chart Group (101Bh)

This record has no record data field. If the SCATTER record is present in the Chart BIFF, it signifies that the chart group is an XY (scatter) chart group.

SERAUXERRBAR: Series ErrorBar (105Bh)

This record defines series error bars.

Record Data

Offset	Name	Size	Contents
4	sertm	1	Error-bar type: 1 = x-direction plus 2 = x-direction minus 3 = y-direction plus 4 = y-direction minus
5	ebsrc	1	Error-bar value source: 1 = percentage 2 = fixed value 3 = standard deviation 4 = custom 5 = standard error
6	fTeeTop	1	TRUE if the error bars are T-shaped (have a line on the top and bottom)
7	(reserved)	1	Reserved; must be 1
8	numValue	8	IEEE number; specifies the fixed value, percentage, or number of standard deviations for the error bars
16	cnum	2	Number of values or cell references used for custom error bars

SERAUXTREND: Series Trendline (104Bh)

This record defines a series trendline.

Record Data

Offset	Name	Size	Contents
4	regt	1	Regression type: 0 = polynomial 1 = exponential 2 = Logarithmic 3 = Power 4 = moving average (a linear trendline has type 0 with order 1)
5	ordUser	1	Polynomial order or moving average period
6	numIntercept	8	IEEE number; specifies forced intercept (#NA if no intercept is specified)
14	fEquation	1	TRUE if the eqaution is displayed
15	fRSquared	1	TRUE if the R-squared value is displayed
16	numForecast	8	IEEE number; specifies number of periods to forecast forward
24	numBackcast	8	IEEE number; specifies number of periods to forecast backward

SERFMT: Series Format (105Dh)

This record specifies series formatting information.

Record Data

Offset	Name	Size	Contents
0	grbit	2	flags

The grbit field contains the following option flags.

Offset	Bits	Mask	Name	Contents
0	0	01h	fSmoothedLine	TRUE if the line series has a smoothed line
0	7-1	FEh	(reserved)	Reserved; must be zero
1	7-0	FFh	(reserved)	Reserved; must be zero

SERIES: Series Definition (1003h)

This record describes the series of the chart, and contains the type of data and number of data fields that make up the series. Series can contain 4000 points in Microsoft Excel version 5.

The sdtX and sdtY fields define the type of data that is contained in this series. At present, the two types of data used in Microsoft Excel chart series are numeric and text (date and sequence information is not used). The cValx and cValy fields contain the number of cell records in the series.

Record Data

Offset	Name	Size	Contents
4	sdtX	2	Type of data in categories 0 = categories contain date information (not used) 1 = categories contain numeric information 2 = categories contain sequence information (not used) 3 = categories contain text information
8	sdtY	2	Type of data in values 0 = values contain date information (not used) 1 = values contain numeric information 2 = values contain sequence information (not used) 3 = values contain text information
10	cValx	2	Count of categories
12	cValy	2	Count of values

SERIESLIST: Specifies the Series in an Overlay Chart (1016h)

This record is subordinate to the second CHARTFORMAT (overlay) record in a file and defines the series that are displayed as the overlay to the main chart. The first CHARTFORMAT (main chart) record in a file does not require a SERIESLIST record because all series, except those specified for the overlay, are included in the main chart.

Record Data

Offset	Name	Size	Contents
4	cser	2	Count of series (size of rgiser)
6	rgiser	var	List of series numbers (words)

SERIESTEXT: Legend/Category/Value Text (100Dh)

The value of the id field determines the assignment of the text field.

Record Data

Offset	Name	Size	Contents
4	id	2	Text identifier: 0 = series name or text
6	cch	1	Length of text field
7	rgch	var	The series text string

Values greater than zero in the id field do not apply to Microsoft Excel.

SERPARENT: Trendline or ErrorBar Series Index (104Ah)

This record indicates the series index for the series that the trendline or error bar is attached to. The series index is the number of the series in the BIFF (starting with series one).

Record Data

Offset	Name	Size	Contents
4	series	2	Series index for the series that the trendline or error bar is attached to

SERTOCRT: Series Chart-Group Index (1045h)

This record is part of the series specifications and indicates the chart-group index for the series. The chart-group index specifies the number of the chart group (specified by a CHARTFORMAT record) in the BIFF, starting with chart group zero.

Record Data

Offset	Name	Size	Contents
0	chartgroup	2	Chart-group index

SHTPROPS: Sheet Properties (1044h)

This record specifies chart sheet properties.

Record Data

Offset	Name	Size	Contents
4	grbit	2	Property flags
6	mdBlank	1	Empty cells plotted as: 0 = not plotted 1 = zero 2 = interploated

The grbit field contains the following option flags.

Offset	Bits	Mask	Name	Contents
0	0	01h	fManSerAlloc	1 = chart type has been manually formatted (changed from the default)
0	1	02h	fPlotVisOnly	1 = plot visible cells only
0	2	04h	fNotSizeWith	1 = do not size chart with window
0	3	08h	fManPlotArea	0 = use default plot area dimensions 1 = POS record describes plot-area dimensions
0	7-4	F0h	(reserved)	Reserved; must be zero
1	7-0	FFh	(reserved)	Reserved; must be zero

SURFACE: Chart Group Is a Surface Chart Group (103Fh)

This record defines a surface chart group.

Record Data

Offset	Name	Size	Contents
4	grbit	2	Option flags

The grbit field contains the following option flags.

Offset	Bits	Mask	Name	Contents
0	0	01h	fFillSurface	= 1, chart contains color fill for surface
0	7–1	FEh	(reserved)	Reserved; must be zero
1	7–0	FFh	(reserved)	Reserved; must be zero

TEXT: Defines Display of Text Fields (1025h)

This record is used in conjunction with several child records (which further define the text displayed on the chart) to define the alignment, color, position, size, and so on, of text fields that appear on the chart. The fields in this record have meaning according to the TEXT record's parent (CHART, LEGEND, or DEFAULTTEXT).

Record Data

Offset	Name	Size	Contents
4	at	1	Horizontal alignment of the text (1 = left, 2 = center, 3 = bottom, 4 = justify)
5	vat	1	Vertical alignment of the text (1 = top, 2 = center, 3 = bottom, 4 = justify)
6	wBkgMode	2	Display mode of the background 1 = transparent 2 = opaque
8	rgbText	4	Color of the text; RGB value (high byte = 0)
12	x	4	x-position of the text in 1/4000 of chart area
16	y	4	y-position of the text in 1/4000 of chart area
20	dx	4	x-size of the text in 1/4000 of chart area
24	dy	4	y-size of the text in 1/4000 of chart area
28	grbit	2	Display flags

The option flags in the grbit field (like the fields themselves) have meaning according to the TEXT record's parent. The grbit field contains the following option flags.

Offset	Bits	Mask	Name	Contents
0	0	01h	fAutoColor	1 = automatic color 0 = user-selected color
0	1	02h	fShowKey	If text is an attached data label: 1 = draw legend key with data label 0 = no legend key
0	2	04h	fShowValue	1 = text of label is the value of the data point 0 = text is the category label
0	3	08h	fVert	1 = text is not horizontal 0 = text is horizontal
0	4	10h	fAutoText	1 = use automatically generated text string 0 = use user-created text string Must be one for fShowValue to be meaningful.

Offset	Bits	Mask	Name	Contents
0	5	20h	fGenerated	1 = default or unmodified 0 = modified
0	6	40h	fDeleted	1= an Automatic text label has been deleted by the user
0	7	80h	fAutoMode	1 = Background is set to Automatic
1	2–0	07h	rot	0 = no rotation (text appears left-to-right) 1 = text appears top to bottom, letters are upright 2 = text is rotated 90 degrees counterclockwise 3 = text is rotated 90 degrees clockwise
1	3	08h	fShLabPct	1 = show category label and value as a percentage (pie charts only)
1	4	10h	fShowPct	1 = show value as a percent. This bit applies only to pie charts
1	7-5	E0h	(reserved)	Reserved; must be zero

TICK: Tick Marks and Labels Format (101Eh)

This record defines tick mark and tick label formatting.

Record Data

Offset	Name	Size	Contents
4	tktMajor	1	Type of major tick mark 0 = invisible (none) 1 = inside of axis line 2 = outside of axis line 3 = cross axis line
5	tktMinor	1	Type of minor tick mark 0 = invisible (none) 1 = inside of axis line 2 = outside of axis line 3 = cross axis line
6	tlt	1	Tick label position relative to axis line 0 = invisible (none) 1 = low end of plot area 2 = high end of plot area 3 = next to axis
7	wBkgMode	1	Background mode: 1 = transparent 2 = opaque
8	rgb	4	Tick-label text color; RGB value, high byte = 0

Offset	Name	Size	Contents
12	(reserved)	16	Reserved; must be zero
28	grbit	2	Display flags

The grbit field contains the following option flags.

Offset	Bits	Mask	Name	Contents
0	0	01h	fAutoCo	Automatic text color
0	1	02h	fAutoMode	Automatic text background
0	4–2	1Ch	rot	= 0 no rotation (text appears left-to-right) = 1 text appears top to bottom, letters are upright = 2 text is rotated 90 degrees counterclockwise = 3 text is rotated 90 degrees clockwise
0	5	20h	fAutoRot	Automatic rotation
0	7–6	C0h	(reserved)	Reserved; must be zero
1	7–0	FFh	(reserved)	Reserved; must be zero

UNITS: Chart Units (1001h)

Microsoft Excel writes this record, but its value is always zero.

Applications writing BIFF do not need to write this record. If your application writes this record, the wUnits field must be zero.

Record Data

Offset	Name	Size	Contents
4	wUnits	2	Always zero

VALUERANGE: Defines Value Axis Scale (101Fh)

This record defines the value axis.

Record Data

Offset	Name	Size	Contents
4	numMin	8	Minimum value on axis
12	numMax	8	Maximum value on axis
20	numMajor	8	Value of major increment

Offset	Name	Size	Contents
28	numMinor	8	Value of minor increment
36	numCross	8	Value where category axis crosses
44	grbit	2	Format flags

All 8-byte numbers in the preceding table are IEEE floating-point numbers.

The numMin field defines the minimum numeric value that appears along the value axis. This field is all zeros if Auto Minimum is selected on the Scale tab of the Format Axis dialog box. The numMax field defines the maximum value displayed along the value axis and is all zeros if Auto Maximum is selected.

The numMajor field defines the increment (unit) of the major value divisions (gridlines) along the value axis. The numMajor field is all zeros if Auto Major Unit is selected on the Scale tab of the Format Axis dialog box. The numMinor field defines the minor value divisions (gridlines) along the value axis and is all zeros if Auto Minor Unit is selected.

The numCross field defines the value along the value axis at which the category axis crosses. This field is all zeros if Auto Category Axis Crosses At is selected.

The grbit field contains the following option flags.

Offset	Bits	Mask	Name	Contents
0	0	01h	fAutoMin	Automatic minimum selected
0	1	02h	fAutoMax	Automatic maximum selected
0	2	04h	fAutoMajor	Automatic major unit selected
0	3	08h	fAutoMinor	Automatic minor unit selected
0	4	10h	fAutoCross	Automatic category crossing point selected
0	5	20h	fLogScale	Logarithmic scale
0	6	40h	fReverse	Values in reverse order
0	7	80h	fMaxCross	Category axis to cross at maximum value
1	7–0	FFh	(reserved)	Reserved; must be zero

C H A P T E R   5

File Format — Workspace File

This chapter describes the workspace BIFF file, which is the file that Microsoft Excel writes when you choose the Save Workspace command from the File menu. The workspace file stores the position, size, filename, window attributes, and so on, of each workbook window.

The following illustration shows the workspace file for a workspace with two workbook windows. The file contains global BOF, CODEPAGE, and EOF records. There is a set of WNDESK, WINDOW1, and REVERT records for each window, and at the end of the file, an EXTERNSHEET record for each window.

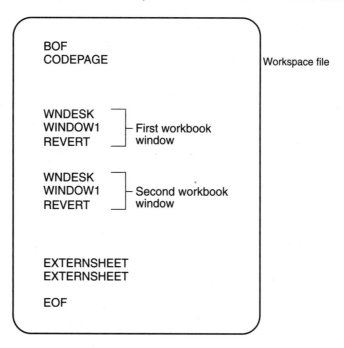

The workspace BIFF file is not an OLE 2 compound file, therefore you must use the DUMPBIFF utility (an MS-DOS program) to examine the file. For general information about BIFF records, see "BIFF Record Information" on page 133.

Record Descriptions

The first two fields in every BIFF record are record number and record length. Because these fields have the same offset and size in every BIFF record, they are not documented in the following descriptions.

BOF: Beginning of File (0809h)

The BOF record marks the beginning of the file.

BOF Record Number Field

Offset	Name	Size	Contents
0	vers	1	ver: = 00 BIFF2 = 02 BIFF3 = 04 BIFF4 = 08 BIFF5
1	bof	1	09h

Record Data

Offset	Name	Size	Contents
4	vers	2	Version number (0500 for BIFF5)
6	dt	2	Substream type: 0005h = Workbook globals 0006h = Visual Basic module 0010h = Worksheet or dialog sheet 0020h = Chart 0040h = Microsoft Excel v4.0 macro sheet 0100h = Workspace file
8	rupBuild	2	Build identifier (internal use only)
10	rupYear	2	Build year (internal use only)

The dt field specifies whether the substream is a module, worksheet, chart, and so on. For the workspace file, dt = 0100h.

The rupBuild and rupYear fields are reserved for internal Microsoft use. If you read a BIFF file, ignore the contents of these bytes. If you write a BIFF file, write 00 00 00 00 to these bytes.

CODEPAGE: Default Code Page (42h)

The CODEPAGE record stores the default code page (character set) that was in use when the workspace was saved.

Record Data

Offset	Name	Size	Contents
4	cv	2	Code page the file is saved in: 01B5h (437 dec.) = IBM PC (Multiplan) 8000h (32768 dec.) = Apple Macintosh 04E4h (1252 dec.) = ANSI (Microsoft Windows)

EOF: End of File (0Ah)

The EOF record marks the end of the file. It has no record data field, and is simply 0A000000h.

EXTERNSHEET: External Reference (17h)

The EXTERNSHEET record specifies an externally referenced workbook in the workspace. You should not change the order of EXTERNSHEET records.

Record Data

Offset	Name	Size	Contents
4	cch	1	Length of filename
5	rgch	var	Filename

The cch field contains the length of the source workbook filename. The rgch field contains the source workbook filename.

Filename Encoding

Whenever possible, filenames are encoded to make BIFF files transportable across file systems. Encoded filenames are identified by the first character of the rgch field. The first character of the rgch field may be any one of the following values.

Name	Value	Meaning
chEmpty	00	Reference to an empty workbook name (see text)
chEncode	01	Filename has been encoded (see following table)
chSelf	02	Self-referential external reference (see text)

chEmpty indicates that the filename is an external reference to an empty workbook name, as in the formula =Sheet1!$A$1.

chSelf indicates that the filename is an external reference where the dependent and source workbooks are the same. An example of this is a workbook SALES.XLS that contains the formula =SALES.XLS!$A$1.

A chEncode at the beginning of rgch indicates that the filename of the source workbook has been encoded to a less system-dependent filename. The following special keys are recognized in the rgch field.

Name	Value	MS-DOS file system	Macintosh file system
chVolume	01	Represents an MS-DOS drive letter. It is followed by the drive letter. For example, the formula ='D:\SALES.XLS'!A1 generates the chVolume key when the dependent workbook is not on the D: drive. UNC filenames, such as \\server\share\myfile.xls generate an @ character after the chVolume key; this replaces the initial double backslash (\\).	Represents a single-character volume name. Because single-character volume names are uncommon on the Macintosh, the chLongVolume key is used to represent volume names that are longer than a single character.
chSameVolume	02	Indicates that the source workbook is on the same drive as the dependent workbook (the drive letter is omitted). For example, the formula ='\SALES.XLS'!A1 generates the chSameVolume key when the dependent workbook is not in the root directory.	Indicates that the source workbook is on the same volume as the dependent workbook (the volume name is omitted).
chDownDir	03	Indicates that the source workbook is in a subdirectory of the current directory. For example, the formula ='XL\SALES.XLS'!A1 generates the chDownDir key. The subdirectory name precedes the chDownDir key, and the filename follows it.	Indicates that the source workbook is in a folder in the current folder. For example, the formula =':XL:Sales1992'!A1 generates the chDownDir key. The folder name precedes the chDownDir key, and the filename follows it.

Name	Value	MS-DOS file system	Macintosh file system
chUpDir	04	Indicates that the source workbook is in the parent directory of the current directory. For example, the formula ='..\SALES.XLS'!A1 generates the chUpDir key.	Indicates that the source workbook is in the parent folder of the current folder. For example, the formula ='::Sales1992'!A1 generates the chUpDir key.
chLongVolume	05	(not used)	The chLongVolume key is followed by the length of the name (1 byte) and then by the volume name string.
chStartupDir	06	Indicates that the source workbook is in the startup directory (the XLSTART subdirectory of the directory that contains EXCEL.EXE).	Indicates that the source workbook is in the Excel Startup Folder (5), which is in the System Folder.
chAltStartupDir	07	Indicates that the source workbook is in the alternate startup directory.	Indicates that the source workbook is in the alternate startup folder.
chLibDir	08	Indicates that the source workbook is in the LIBRARY directory.	Indicates that the source workbook is in the Macro Library folder.

REVERT: Revert Data (DBh)

This record stores internal data for revert-to-saved processing.

Record Data

Offset	Name	Size	Contents
4	rgch	var	Revert array; for internal use only

WINDOW1: Window Information (3Dh)

The WINDOW1 record contains workbook-level window attributes. The xWn and yWn fields contain the location of the window in units of 1/20 of a point, relative to the upper-left corner of the Microsoft Excel window client area. The dxWn and dyWn fields contain the window size, also in units of 1/20 of a point.

Record Data

Offset	Name	Size	Contents
4	xWn	2	Horizontal position of the window
6	yWn	2	Vertical position of the window
8	dxWn	2	Width of the window
10	dyWn	2	Height of the window
12	grbit	2	Option flags
14	itabCur	2	Index of selected workbook tab (0-based)
16	itabFirst	2	Index of first displayed workbook tab (0-based)
18	ctabSel	2	Number of workbook tabs that are selected
20	wTabRatio	2	Ratio of width of the workbook tabs to the width of the horizontal scroll bar; to obtain the ratio, convert to decimal and then divide by 1000.

The grbit field contains the following option flags.

Offset	Bits	Mask	Name	Contents
0	0	01h	fHidden	= 1 if the window is hidden
	1	02h	fIconic	= 1 if the window is currently displayed as an icon
	2	04h	(reserved)	
	3	08h	fDspHScroll	= 1 if horizontal scroll bar is displayed
	4	10h	fDspVScroll	= 1 if vertical scroll bar is displayed
	5	20h	fBotAdornment	= 1 if workbook tabs are displayed
	7-6	C0h	(reserved)	
1	7-0	FFh	(reserved)	

WNDESK: Describes Windows in the Workbook

The WNDESK record describes each window that appears in the workspace.

Offset	Name	Size	Contents
4	ish	2	Document number (zero-based)
6	dt	2	Document type; always = 0005h

C H A P T E R   6

Using DLLs from Visual Basic

Using DLL functions from Visual Basic, Applications Edition, in Microsoft Excel is very similar to using DLL functions from Visual Basic. Chapter 24 of the *Microsoft Visual Basic Programmer's Guide* for version 3.0 of Visual Basic provides detailed guidelines and examples for calling DLL functions from Visual Basic. This chapter provides more specific information about using DLL functions from Visual Basic in Microsoft Excel.

The examples in this chapter were prepared and tested with Microsoft Visual C++ version 1.5, and run on 16-bit Microsoft Windows version 3.1. Visual C++ version 1.5 includes the OLE 2 header files and libraries required to create DLLs using variants, strings, objects, and arrays as described in this chapter (you must include ole2.h and dispatch.h in your code, and link it with ole2disp.lib).

You can use another C compiler and linker if they are capable of creating DLLs. In this case, you must also have the Microsoft OLE 2 Software Developer's Kit (SDK) to create DLLs using variants, strings, objects, or arrays.

In addition to the Help provided with Visual C++ and the OLE 2 SDK, Chapter 6 in Volume 2 of the *OLE 2 Programmer's Reference* provides valuable information about the functions used in the examples in this chapter.

Using the Declare Statement

Before you can call a DLL function from Visual Basic, you must use the Declare statement to identify the function, the name of the DLL where it is located, and its argument types. Once the function is declared in a Visual Basic module, you can call it just as if it were part of your code.

For example, the following C-language function calculates the circumference of a circle given the circle's radius:

```
double FAR PASCAL __export DoubleArg(double dRadius)
{
    return dRadius * 2 * 3.14159;
}
```

In 16-bit windows, DLL functions called from Microsoft Excel must be declared with the FAR PASCAL calling convention; in Windows NT, DLL functions use the __stdcall calling convention; and on the Apple Macintosh, code-resource functions use the pascal calling convention. The examples in this chapter were written to run on 16-bit Microsoft Windows. If you are using Windows NT or the Apple Macintosh, modify the examples accordingly.

This Visual Basic code uses the DoubleArg C function to display a table of circumference values:

```
Declare Function DoubleArg Lib "ADVDLL.DLL" _
    (ByVal radius As Double) As Double

Sub CircumferenceTable()
    Worksheets(1).Activate
    Cells(1, 1) = "Radius"
    Cells(1, 2) = "Circumference"
    For i = 1 To 10
        Cells(i + 1, 1) = i
        Cells(i + 1, 2) = DoubleArg(i)
    Next
    Columns("a:b").AutoFit
End Sub
```

The Declare statement uses the ByVal keyword because the argument is passed by value. Visual Basic coerces the variable *i* to type double even though it is not explicitly declared in the code (with a Dim statement).

The REGISTER Macro Function

In Chapter 1, you used the REGISTER macro function to register a DLL function. The REGISTER function and Declare statement are not related. Using the REGISTER function registers the DLL function only for the macro sheet or the worksheet. You cannot call the function from a Visual Basic module without using the Declare statement, even if you have already used the REGISTER function and called the same DLL function from a macro sheet. You can, however, call the function on a macro sheet by using the ExecuteExcel4Macro method to call the registered DLL function just as you would call any other Microsoft Excel macro function.

Similarly, DLL functions declared as public functions in a Visual Basic module can be called from any Visual Basic module in the workbook, but cannot be called from a macro sheet or worksheet. Public functions are those declared without either the Public or Private keywords (or explicitly declared with the Public keyword). If you declare the DLL function as Private, you can call the function only from the Visual Basic module where it is declared. You must use the REGISTER function before you can call the DLL function from a macro sheet or a worksheet, even if you have already used the Declare statement and called the same DLL function from a Visual Basic module.

To use the same DLL function in Visual Basic, on a macro sheet, and on a worksheet, you must both declare the function in a Visual Basic module *and* use the REGISTER function on the macro sheet and worksheet.

In addition, the REGISTER and UNREGISTER functions allow you to dynamically load and unload DLL functions. This is not possible in Visual Basic. Once a DLL function is loaded by a Visual Basic module (the first time a declared function in the DLL runs), the DLL remains loaded until you close the workbook that contains the Visual Basic module.

You can use the dynamic loading behavior of the REGISTER and UNREGISTER functions by creating a stub macro on a macro sheet. The stub macro should accept appropriate arguments for the DLL function, register the DLL function, call it, unregister it, and return the return value from the DLL function. You can then use the ExecuteExcel4Macro function to call the stub macro from Visual Basic. The stub macro in turn calls the DLL and returns to Visual Basic.

Passing Arguments by Reference

By default, Visual Basic passes arguments by reference, rather than by value. This means that the DLL function can modify the argument. When an argument is passed by reference, you must declare it as a far pointer in the DLL function C-language prototype.

For example, this C-language function modifies its argument by multiplying it by two. The function returns False if the argument is less than zero.

```
BOOL FAR PASCAL __export PointerArg(int FAR *pn)
{
    if (*pn < 0)
        return 0;     // False in Visual Basic

    *pn *= 2;
    return -1;        // True in Visual Basic
}
```

The Visual Basic declaration for this function does not include the ByVal keyword. You may include the ByRef keyword, but it isn't necessary.

```
Declare Function PointerArg Lib "ADVDLL.DLL" _
    (d As Integer) As Boolean

Sub TestPointerArg()
    Dim n As Integer
    n = CInt(InputBox("Number?"))
    r = PointerArg(n)
    MsgBox n & ":" & r
End Sub
```

Using Variants

Passing an argument of Variant data type is very similar to passing any other argument type. In the DLL, you can use the VARIANT data structure to access the data contained in the argument. See Chapter 5 in Volume 2 of the *OLE 2 Programmer's Reference* for descriptions of the VARIANT data type.

The VARIANT type is a C-language structure containing a single member for the variable type, three reserved members, and a large named union that is used to access the variable data depending on the type.

For example, this C-language function determines the data type contained in the VARIANT argument passed by Visual Basic:

```
int FAR PASCAL __export VariantArg(VARIANT vt)
{
    if (vt.vt == VT_DISPATCH)        // variant is an object
        return -1;
    else if (vt.vt == VT_BSTR)       // variant is a string
        return atoi(vt.bstrVal);
    else if (vt.vt == VT_I2)     // variant is an integer
        return vt.iVal;
    else                             // variant is something else
        return -3;
}
```

This Visual Basic code declares and calls the VariantArg function:

```
Declare Function VariantArg Lib "ADVDLL.DLL" _
    (ByVal v As Variant) As Integer

Sub VariantArgTest()
    MsgBox VariantArg(Worksheets(1))      ' -1
    MsgBox VariantArg("25")               ' 25
    MsgBox VariantArg(5)                  ' 5
    MsgBox VariantArg(3.2)                ' -3
End Sub
```

You could use this information to implement a function that accepts either a Range object or a text description of a range. If the argument contains an object, you can use IDispatch to access properties and methods of the object directly. If the argument contains a string, you can use IDispatch to create an object and then access its properties and methods. For more information about using IDispatch, see Chapter 5, "Using the IDispatch Interface."

Visual Basic in Microsoft Excel does not support all the data types supported by the VARIANT structure. The following table shows the allowed data types and their value constants. Microsoft Excel never returns a variant with a data type not shown on this list.

Data Type	Variant Constant
Boolean	VT_BOOL
Currency (scaled integer)	VT_CY
Date	VT_DATE
Double (double-precision floating-point)	VT_R8
Integer	VT_I2
Long (long integer)	VT_I4
Object	VT_DISPATCH
Single (single-precision floating-point)	VT_R4
String	VT_BSTR

Variants and Objects

The VariantArg function shows how you declare and call a DLL function with a Variant passed by value. A Variant passed by reference would be declared in C as a far pointer to a VARIANT structure.

```
void VariantByRef(LPVARIANT *pvar)
```

While it is possible to pass an object as a Variant, it is also possible to specifically declare a function that accepts only an object. An object is passed as a dispatch pointer, either by value:

```
void ObjectByVal(LPDISPATCH pdisp)
```

or by reference:

```
void ObjectByRef(LPDISPATCH FAR *ppdisp)
```

When you pass a variant or object by reference, remember that your DLL code must free any allocated object, string, or array before replacing it. Failure to free allocations results in memory leaks. More information about freeing allocated strings and arrays appears in the following sections, and the ReleaseVariant function example that appears in Chapter 5 shows how this can be done for a variant variable.

Return Values

When your function returns an object, it is declared as returning a dispatch pointer:

```
LPDISPATCH ReturnsObject(void)
```

Returning a Variant is simple:

```
VARIANT ReturnsVariant(void)
```

Using Strings

When Visual Basic passes a string by reference to a C-language DLL, it uses a special OLE 2 data type called a BSTR. OLE Automation allows BSTR strings to be allocated and freed by any component that supports this data type.

In most cases, a BSTR can be treated like a pointer to a null-terminated string. In general, it's best if your C-language code does not directly manipulate the string data. You can dereference the pointer to copy data *from* the BSTR, however.

Instead of directly manipulating BSTR data, OLE Automation provides several functions that should be used to allocate, free, and reallocate BSTR values. These functions are listed in Chapter 6 in Volume 2 of the *OLE 2 Programmer's Reference*.

When you pass a string by reference, your C-language function should declare the argument as a far pointer to a BSTR. The pointer will never be NULL, but if the Visual Basic string is unassigned (that is, created with the Dim statement but not assigned a value), the BSTR pointed to will be NULL. If the string is assigned but empty, the first character will be a null character, and the string length will be zero.

The pointer may also reference a NULL pointer if the original variable was created as a variant but not assigned. Visual Basic would coerce the variant to a string when it called the DLL, but because the variant is empty, it behaves like a declared but unassigned string.

The following code example tests for these conditions:

```
int FAR PASCAL __export SType(BSTR FAR *pbstr)
{
    if (pbstr == NULL)   // pointer is null; will never happen
        return 1;
    if (*pbstr == NULL)  // string (or variant) is allocated by VB
                         // with Dim statement,
                         // but not yet assigned
        return 2;
    if (*pbstr[0] == 0)  // string is allocated
                         // and assigned to empty string ("")
        return 3;
    // string has a value; this value can be accessed at *pbstr
    return 4;
}
```

This Visual Basic code declares and calls the SType function:

```
Declare Function SType Lib "ADVDLL.DLL" _
    (s As String) As Integer

Sub STypeTest()
    Dim s As String
    MsgBox SType(s) 'displays 2
    s = ""
    MsgBox SType(s) 'displays 3
    s = "test"
    MsgBox SType(s) 'displays 4
End Sub
```

Allocating BSTR Values

You should always use OLE functions to operate on BSTR values. If you need to change a BSTR value, first test the BSTR to see if it is already assigned. If it isn't, you may use the SysAllocString or SysAllocStringLen function to assign a value to the BSTR. If the BSTR is already assigned, you must free the current assignment (with the SysFreeString function) before you can use SysAllocString or SysAllocStringLen; or you should use the SysReAllocString or SysReAllocStringLen function to reallocate the string (these functions automatically free the initial assignment).

For example, the following C-language code copies some number of characters from one BSTR into another. Notice that this example tests the second BSTR to see if it is already assigned. If it is, the example uses the SysReAllocStringLen function to free the existing string before replacing it.

```
int FAR PASCAL __export StringArgs(BSTR FAR *pbstrArg1,
    BSTR FAR *pbstrArg2, int cch)
{
    // return error code if requested characters
    // less than zero, or input string is unassigned
    // or has too few characters

    if (cch < 0 || *pbstrArg1 == NULL ||
            (int)SysStringLen(*pbstrArg1) < cch)
        return -1;

    if (*pbstrArg2 == NULL) {    // string is unassigned;
                                 // we can allocate a new one
        if ((*pbstrArg2 = SysAllocStringLen(*pbstrArg1, cch))
                == NULL)
            return -2;
    }
    else {  // argument string is already assigned;
            // we must reallocate
        if (!SysReAllocStringLen(pbstrArg2, *pbstrArg1, cch))
            return -3;
    }

    return 0;
}
```

The calls to the SysAllocStringLen and SysReAllocStringLen functions use the dereferenced BSTR pointer *pbstrArg1 to access the characters in the first argument. This is permitted when you are reading the characters, but you should not write to the dereferenced pointer.

This Visual Basic code declares and calls the StringArgs function:

```
Declare Function StringArgs Lib "ADVDLL.DLL" _
    (inpStr As String, outStr As String, _
    ByVal n As Integer) As Integer

Sub StringArgsTest()
    Dim newStr As String
    x = StringArgs("abracadabra", newStr, 5)
    MsgBox x & ":" & newStr
End Sub
```

Using User-Defined Data Structures

The Type statement in Visual Basic can be used to create user-defined data structures. For example, the following Visual Basic data type and C-language structure are equivalent.

In Visual Basic:

```
Type ARG
    i as Integer
    str as String
End Type
```

In C:

```
typedef struct {
    int i;
    BSTR str;
} ARG;
```

User-defined data types cannot be passed by value; they must be passed by reference. Your C function should declare the argument as a far pointer to the structure. If the structure contains BSTR values (as this example does) the rules discussed above apply to those values; you must test the BSTR before you reassign it (and free it if it is already allocated). You should not manipulate it directly.

For example, this C-language function fills a structure with a string and the length of the string:

```
int FAR PASCAL __export StructArg(ARG FAR *parg, char *szArg)
{
    BSTR bstr;

    if (parg == NULL)
        return -1;

    // allocate a local string first; if this fails,
    // we have not touched the passed-in string

    if ((bstr = SysAllocString(szArg)) == NULL)
        return -1;

    if (parg->bstr != NULL) // string is already assigned
        SysFreeString(parg->bstr);

    parg->i = SysStringLen(bstr);
    parg->bstr = bstr;

    return parg->i;
}
```

Declared and called from Visual Basic:

```
Declare Function StructArg Lib "ADVDLL.DLL" _
    (a As ARG, ByVal s As String) As Integer

Sub StructArgTest()
    Dim x As ARG
    MsgBox StructArg(x, "abracadabra")
    MsgBox x.str & ":" & x.i     'displays string and length
End Sub
```

Using Arrays

OLE 2 provides a special data type for arrays passed from Visual Basic to a DLL. This data type, called a SAFEARRAY, allows both Visual Basic and the DLL to allocate, free, and access array data in a controlled way.

Your DLL should always use OLE Automation functions to allocate and access safe arrays. These functions are described in Chapter 6 in Volume 2 of the *OLE 2 Programmer's Reference*. When OLE Automation passes a safe array to your DLL, you receive a far pointer to a far pointer to the array itself. Like BSTR pointers, a SAFEARRAY pointer may point to a NULL array if the array has been declared but not yet dimensioned:

```
Dim a() as Integer
```

The pointer itself will never be NULL, however.

The following example determines the upper and lower bounds of an array and then loops through the array producing the sum of the elements in the array:

```
int FAR PASCAL __export SumArray(
    FPSAFEARRAY FAR *ppsa, long FAR *plResult)
{
    int iElem;
    long lLb, lUb, l, lResult;

    if (*ppsa == NULL) // array has not been initialized
        return -4;

    if ((*ppsa)->cDims != 1) // check number of dimensions
        return -5;

    // get the upper and lower bounds of the array

    if (FAILED(SafeArrayGetLBound(*ppsa, 1, &lLb)) ||
            FAILED(SafeArrayGetUBound(*ppsa, 1, &lUb)))
        return -1;
```

```
// loop through the array and add the elements

for (l = lLb, lResult = 0; l <= lUb; l++) {
    if (FAILED(SafeArrayGetElement(*ppsa, &l, &iElem)))
        return -2;
    lResult += iElem;
}

*plResult = lResult;
return 0;
}
```

Declared and called from Visual Basic:

```
Declare Function SumArray Lib "ADVDLL.DLL" _
    (a() As Integer, r As Long) As Integer

Sub SumArrayTest()
    Dim n(5) As Integer
    Dim result As Long
    For i = 0 To 5
        n(i) = 2
    Next
    x = SumArray(n, result)
    MsgBox x & ":" & result
End Sub
```

Visual Basic does minimal type checking and enforcement on array element size. Because this function was declared as accepting only an array of integers, it is safe to use an integer element in the call to the SafeArrayGetElement function in the DLL. If the function was declared as accepting an array of any type, however, the Visual Basic code might pass an array of long values; in this case, the C-language function would produce incorrect results. If your DLL function must accept an array of any type, you should use an array of variants and check the variant type in the DLL.

Static Arrays

If you declare and dimension an array:

```
Dim x(5) as String
```

The pointer you receive in your C function points to a static array (the fFeatures element of the SAFEARRAY structure has the FADF_STATIC flag set). You can read and redimension the array, but you cannot modify the pointer, and you cannot copy over the array. If you need to modify the array in the DLL (to create a new one, for example), you must not dimension it in Visual Basic.

Allocating Arrays

Your DLL can create new safe arrays or change the size of existing arrays. When you create a new array, you should use a local variable rather than modify a passed-in array pointer. Once the allocation and any subsequent operations on the array are successful, you can assign the passed-in pointer to the local pointer and return from the function.

The following example accepts an array pointer and creates an array containing 10 integer elements. If the passed-in array has already been initialized, the function redimensions the existing array.

```
int FAR PASCAL __export NewArray(FPSAFEARRAY FAR *ppsa)
{
    SAFEARRAY FAR *psa;
    SAFEARRAYBOUND sa;

    sa.lLbound = 1;
    sa.cElements = 10;

    if (*ppsa == NULL) { //array not yet initialized
        if ((psa = SafeArrayCreate(VT_I2, 1, &sa)) == NULL)
            return -1;
        *ppsa = psa;
    }
    else if (FAILED(SafeArrayRedim(*ppsa, &sa)))
        return -2;

    return 0;
}
```

Declared and called from Visual Basic:

```
Declare Function NewArray Lib "ADVDLL.DLL" _
    (a() As Integer) As Integer

Sub NewArrayTest()
    Dim a(1) As Integer
    MsgBox NewArray(a) & ":" & LBound(a) & ":" & UBound(a)
End Sub
```

Destroying Arrays

Like BSTRs, SAFEARRAYs must be freed before they can be destroyed. When Visual Basic passes an existing array to your DLL, it is passed as a static array that cannot be destroyed. Your DLL can create its own arrays, however. When you no longer need an array, it should be destroyed.

You must be careful when you destroy an existing array. Freeing the array frees only the array memory; if the array contains any pointers (such as BSTR values) these will not be freed. In this case, you must free each BSTR element individually and then free the array. If you do not know what the array contains, you should probably not free or redimension the array.

Using Arrays of Strings

Safe arrays can contain elements of any allowable type, including BSTRs and user-defined data structures. BSTRs inside arrays should be manipulated with the same OLE Automation functions as ordinary BSTRs. Always remember to free any existing BSTR before allocating a new one, or use the reallocation function. Do not directly modify BSTR data.

The following example creates or redimensions an array of strings. Any existing BSTR data in the array is freed before new data is copied into the array.

```
int FAR PASCAL __export StringArray(FPSAFEARRAY FAR *ppsa)
{
    LONG l;
    BSTR bstr;
    SAFEARRAY *psa;
    SAFEARRAYBOUND sa;

    sa.lLbound = 0;
    sa.cElements = 3;

    if ((*ppsa)->cDims != 1) // check array dimensions
        return -1;

    if (*ppsa == NULL) { // array not yet initialized
        if ((psa = SafeArrayCreate(VT_BSTR, 1, &sa)) == NULL)
            return -2;
        *ppsa = psa;
    }
    else if (FAILED(SafeArrayRedim(*ppsa, &sa)))
        return -3;

    // loop through the array; get each element and free
    // any existing string, then allocate the new string
    // and put it in the array

    for (l = sa.lLbound; l < (long)sa.cElements; l++) {
```

```
            if (FAILED(SafeArrayGetElement(*ppsa, &l, &bstr)))
                return -4;
            SysFreeString(bstr);
            if ((bstr = SysAllocString("test string")) == NULL)
                return -5;
            if (FAILED(SafeArrayPutElement(*ppsa, &l, bstr)))
                return -6;
    }

    return 0;
}
```

Declared and called from Visual Basic:

```
Declare Function StringArray Lib "ADVDLL.DLL" _
    (s() As String) As Integer

Sub StringArrayTest()
    Dim s(5) As String
    s(1) = "tt"
    MsgBox StringArray(s) & ":" & s(1)
End Sub
```

Using Arrays of Data Structures

You cannot use the SafeArrayCreate function to create a new array of user-defined structures. Instead, you must use the SafeArrayAllocDescriptor function to create the array descriptor, then use the SafeArrayAllocData function to allocate space for the array data, and finally use the SafeArrayAccessData function to return a pointer to the data. The SafeArrayAccessData function locks the array data; when you are done with the array, you should call the SafeArrayUnaccessData function to unlock it.

You cannot replace an existing array, so if your Visual Basic code passes a dimensioned array you must redimension it. Remember to free any existing BSTR pointers in the array before overwriting them.

The following example creates or redimensions an array of data structures then copies an array of strings into the structures, adding the string length to each structure. Any existing BSTR data in the array is freed before new data is copied into the array.

```
int FAR PASCAL __export StructArray(FPSAFEARRAY FAR *ppsaArg,
    FPSAFEARRAY FAR *ppsaStr)
{
    ARG FAR *parg;
    SAFEARRAY FAR *psa;
    BSTR FAR *pbstr;
    ULONG i, cElements;

    if (*ppsaStr == NULL)
        return -1;

    cElements = (*ppsaStr)->rgsabound[0].cElements;

    if (*ppsaArg == NULL) { // create a new array

        if (FAILED(SafeArrayAllocDescriptor(1, &psa)))
            return -3;

        // set up the SAFEARRAY structure
        // and allocate data space

        psa->fFeatures = 0;
        psa->cbElements = sizeof(ARG);
        psa->rgsabound[0].cElements = cElements;
        psa->rgsabound[0].lLbound = (*ppsaStr)->rgsabound[0].lLbound;

        if (FAILED(SafeArrayAllocData(psa))) {
            SafeArrayDestroyDescriptor(psa);
            return -4;
        }

        // get a pointer to the new data

        if (FAILED(SafeArrayAccessData(psa,
                (void HUGEP* FAR*)&parg))) {
            SafeArrayDestroy(psa);
            return -5;
        }
    }
    else { // redimension the old array
        if (FAILED(SafeArrayRedim(*ppsaArg,
                (*ppsaStr)->rgsabound)))
            return -6;

        // get a pointer to the old data

        if (FAILED(SafeArrayAccessData(*ppsaArg,
                (void HUGEP* FAR*)&parg)))
            return -7;
    }
```

```
    // get a pointer to the string array data

    if (FAILED(SafeArrayAccessData(*ppsaStr,
            (void HUGEP* FAR*)&pbstr)))
        return -8;

    // allocate strings in the structure array and
    // fill them with strings from the string array.
    // free any old BSTRs in the structure

    for (i = 0; i < cElements; i++) {
        SysFreeString(parg[i].bstr);
        parg[i].bstr = SysAllocString(pbstr[i]);
        parg[i].i = SysStringLen(pbstr[i]);
    }

    // release pointers and move the structure
    // array pointer to the new array if we created one

    SafeArrayUnaccessData(*ppsaStr);

    if (*ppsaArg == NULL) {
        SafeArrayUnaccessData(psa);
        *ppsaArg = psa;
    }
    else
        SafeArrayUnaccessData(*ppsaArg);

    return 0;
}
```

Declared and called from Visual Basic:

```
Declare Function StructArray Lib "ADVDLL.DLL" _
    (x() As ARG, s() As String) As Integer

Sub StructArrayTest()
    Dim x() As ARG
    Dim s(1 To 4) As String
    s(1) = "yellow"
    s(2) = "orange"
    s(3) = "blue"
    s(4) = "green"
    n = StructArray(x, s)
    If n = 0 Then
        Worksheets(1).Activate
        Range("a1:c25").Clear
        For i = LBound(x) To UBound(x)
            Cells(i + 1, 1) = i
            Cells(i + 1, 2) = x(i).str
```

```
                Cells(i + 1, 3) = x(i).i
        Next
    Else
        MsgBox "StructArray failed, returned" & n
    End If
End Sub
```

Using the C API and Visual Basic

When you call a DLL function from Visual Basic in Microsoft Excel, the DLL function can use the Microsoft Excel Applications Programming Interface (C API) functions to call back into Microsoft Excel. You cannot use the C API across processes. The DLL using the C API must be called from Visual Basic running in Microsoft Excel (a DLL called from Microsoft Project or Microsoft Visual Basic Professional cannot call the C API). In addition, the C API can only be called after Microsoft Excel has called the DLL. This qualification is met when Visual Basic in Microsoft Excel calls the DLL, and the DLL in turn calls the C API. When the DLL function is called by an external event (such as a DDE command from another application or a Windows timer), the DLL function cannot call the C API.

For more information about using the C API, see Chapter 1, "The Microsoft Excel Applications Programming Interface" and Chapter 2, "Applications Programming Interface Function Reference".

Type Libraries

You can create a type library for your DLL. The type library can contain constant and function declarations and other information about the DLL. Once you have created a type library, you can use the References command on the Tools menu in Microsoft Excel to load the type library. Once loaded, the constant and function declarations are available in Visual Basic without Declare statements.

Visual Basic in Microsoft Excel does not support user-defined data-structure declarations in type libraries. (User-defined data structures are those declared with the Visual Basic "Type" statement or the C/C++ "struct" statement.) To use the structures in your Visual Basic code, you will have to add their declarations to the module.

For more information about creating type libraries, see Chapter 7 in Volume 2 of the *OLE 2 Programmer's Reference*.

C H A P T E R   7

Using the OLE 2 IDispatch Interface

Microsoft Excel exposes its objects as OLE Automation objects. OLE 2 allows another application, called an *OLE Automation Controller,* to access the exposed objects and use their properties and methods with the IDispatch interface. This chapter describes techniques you can use to write an OLE Automation Controller in standard C that can be used to manipulate objects, properties, and methods in Microsoft Excel.

In Chapters 1 and 2, you saw how an application can use the C API interface to call into Microsoft Excel. The C API interface exposes Microsoft Excel macro-language functions and commands. The OLE 2 IDispatch interface allows an application to call Microsoft Excel and manipulate any object, property, or method that can be called from Visual Basic.

This chapter does not discuss techniques for implementing an OLE Server (an application which creates new OLE objects and exposes their properties and methods using an IDispatch interface). Microsoft Excel operates as both an OLE Server (Microsoft Excel creates objects that can be accessed by other applications) and as an OLE Automation Controller (Visual Basic in Microsoft Excel can access objects in other applications which support OLE Automation, and in fact, Visual Basic uses OLE Automation to call Microsoft Excel properties and methods).

The examples in this chapter were built and tested with 16-bit Microsoft Windows version 3.1, using Microsoft Visual C++ version 1.5. Visual C++ version 1.5 includes the OLE 2 header files and libraries required to create OLE Automation Controller applications. If you use another C compiler, you will also need the OLE 2 Software Developer's Kit (SDK).

In addition to the Help provided with Visual C++ and the OLE 2 SDK, Volume 2 of the *OLE 2 Programmer's Reference* provides detailed information about OLE Automation and the IDispatch interface. This chapter focuses mainly on implementation details for using the IDispatch interface with Microsoft Excel. You should use the *OLE 2 Programmer's Reference* together with this chapter to understand the IDispatch interface.

IDispatch Step by Step

Using IDispatch to access exposed OLE Automation objects involves the following steps:

1. Initialize OLE using the OleInitialize function.

2. Create an instance of the object you wish to access using the CoCreateInstance function.

   If the object's application is not yet running, OLE starts it and initializes the object. Note that if OLE starts the application, it may not be visible. With Microsoft Excel, you must set the Visible property for the application to make it visible.

3. Obtain a reference to the object's IDispatch interface using the QueryInterface member function.

   With Microsoft Excel, you can combine steps two and three and obtain the IDispatch reference directly from the CoCreateInstance function.

4. Use the GetIDsOfNames member function to obtain the DISPID values for the desired method or property exposed in the object's IDispatch interface.

5. Use the Invoke member function to access the method or property.

6. Terminate the object by invoking the appropriate method in its IDispatch interface.

7. Uninitialize OLE, using the OleUninitialize function.

Complete information about accessing OLE Automation objects appears in Chapter 3 in Volume 2 of the *OLE 2 Programmer's Reference*.

C++ and C Programming

While the examples in the *OLE 2 Programmer's Reference* were written in C++, the examples in this chapter were written in standard C. The following list describes some of the differences you will encounter.

- Reference data types (such as REFCLSID and REFIID) must be used in standard C with a prepended ampersand (&). In C++, these data types are often used with C++ references, so the ampersand is not required. Because references do not exist in standard C, an explicit address-of operator (the ampersand) is required.

  For example, the CoCreateInstance function uses both a class ID reference (REFCLSID) and an interface ID reference (REFIID) as arguments. In C++, the call to this function can be written as:

  ```
  CoCreateInstance(CLSID_ExcelApp, NULL, CLSCTX_LOCAL_SERVER,
      IID_IDispatch, &pdispExcelpp);
  ```

  In standard C, however, you must use the address-of operator with the first and fourth arguments:

  ```
  CoCreateInstance(&CLSID_ExcelApp, NULL, CLSCTX_LOCAL_SERVER,
      &IID_IDispatch, &pdispExcelApp);
  ```

- In C++, you can call a class member function directly using the member-selection operator (->). In standard C, classes are defined as structures; each structure contains an lpVtbl element which is a pointer to the table of class functions. You must first access the lpVtbl element of the structure and then call the function using a pointer. In addition, the first argument to the function must be the object pointer itself.

  For example, when you are done with an object you have created with the CoCreateInstance function, you should free it with the Release function. In C++, you can call this function directly:

  ```
  pdisp->Release();
  ```

  In standard C, you call the function using the lpVTbl pointer and pass in the dispatch object as the first argument:

  ```
  (*(pdisp->lpVtbl->Release))(pdisp);
  ```

- In C++, you can use the Microsoft Foundation Class library and the ClassWizard in Visual C++ to access OLE methods and properties as member functions of a base class. This simplifies much of the work required to access OLE objects with the IDispatch interface. For more information about using the ClassWizard, see the Visual C++ documentation.

Microsoft Excel Specifics

This section describes some differences between a generic implementation of an OLE Automation Controller and a controller specifically designed to work with Microsoft Excel.

IDispatch and IUnknown

Because Microsoft Excel supports the IDispatch interface, your application does not need to get the IUnknown interface and then query Microsoft Excel for the IDispatch interface. You can use the CoCreateInstance function to directly access the IDispatch interface because you know Microsoft Excel supports IDispatch.

Passed-in Objects

When Visual Basic in Microsoft Excel passes an object reference to your DLL function, the DLL can go directly to step four in the process shown in the preceding section and access the IDispatch interface directly from the object reference. The PropertyPut and PropertyGet examples in the following section show how this is done in a DLL.

Variant Data Types

Visual Basic in Microsoft Excel does not support all the data types supported by the VARIANT structure. The following table shows the allowed data types and their value constants. Microsoft Excel never returns a variant with a data type not shown on this list.

Data Type	Variant Constant
Boolean	VT_BOOL
Currency (scaled integer)	VT_CY
Date	VT_DATE
Double (double-precision floating-point)	VT_R8
Integer	VT_I2
Long (long integer)	VT_I4
Object	VT_DISPATCH
Single (single-precision floating-point)	VT_R4
String	VT_BSTR

Microsoft Excel coerces other data types into one of the supported data types.

Exception Handling

When an error occurs during the execution of the IDispatch Invoke function, Microsoft Excel returns an error code or returns the DISP_E_EXCEPTION error and places information about the error in an EXCEPINFO structure. The error code in the exception info structure will be one of the trappable error values listed in the Visual Basic Help topic "Trappable Errors." When the exception info structure is filled in, your application is responsible for freeing the strings in the structure. A memory leak will result if you do not free the strings before reusing the structure or exiting the application.

The ShowException function discussed later in this chapter is an example of an error-handling function for an OLE Automation Controller. Notice that the Invoke function frees the exception-info strings before it returns.

PropertyPut and PropertyGet

The simplest example of a Microsoft Excel OLE Automation Controller is a DLL function that takes an object as an argument, obtains a DISPID for the object's Value property, and then uses PropertyPut or PropertyGet to set or get the value of the object. This simple example does not need the CoCreateInstance and QueryInterface functions because the function can call the IDispatch interface directly with the object reference.

The CalcCells function is an example of a simple OLE Automation Controller. The function accepts a Range object as its first argument and a variant as its second argument. The function uses the PropertyGet method to obtain the value of the range; if the range contains more than one cell, the value is returned as an array. The function iterates the array, adding the value from each cell to a total (it attempts to coerce any values that are not doubles). Once the total is obtained, the function places the result in the second argument; if the argument specifies another range, the function uses the PropertyPut method to set the range value.

```
SCODE FAR PASCAL __export CalcCells(LPDISPATCH FAR *ppdsSourceRange,
    VARIANTARG FAR *pvtResult)
{
    HRESULT hr;
    EXCEPINFO excep;
    ULONG cElements, i;
    DISPPARAMS dispparams;
    unsigned int uiArgErr, cDims;
    DISPID dispidValue, dispidPut;
    VARIANTARG vSource, vResult, vTemp, FAR *pvdata;

    LPSTR lpszName = "Value";

    hr = (*((*ppdsSourceRange)->lpVtbl->GetIDsOfNames))
            (*ppdsSourceRange, &IID_NULL, (char FAR* FAR*)&lpszName,
            1, LOCALE_SYSTEM_DEFAULT, &dispidValue);
    if (hr != NOERROR)
        goto calc_error;

        // PropertyGet has no arguments

    dispparams.cArgs = 0;
    dispparams.cNamedArgs = 0;

    // Invoke PropertyGet
```

```
        hr = (*((*ppdsSourceRange)->lpVtbl->Invoke))
                (*ppdsSourceRange, dispidValue, &IID_NULL,
                LOCALE_SYSTEM_DEFAULT, DISPATCH_PROPERTYGET,
                &dispparams, &vSource, &excep, &uiArgErr);
        if (hr != NOERROR)
            goto calc_error;

        // initialize the result variant

        VariantInit(&vResult);
        vResult.vt = VT_R8;
        vResult.dblVal = 0.0;

        // If there is more than one cell in the source range,
        // it's a variant containing an array.
        // Access this using the SafeArray functions

        if (vSource.vt & VT_ARRAY) {

            // iterate the dimensions; number of elements is x*y*z
            for (cDims = 0, cElements = 1;
                    cDims < vSource.parray->cDims; cDims++)
                cElements *= vSource.parray->rgsabound[cDims].cElements;

            // get a pointer to the data
            hr = SafeArrayAccessData(vSource.parray, (LPVOID)&pvdata);
            if (hr != NOERROR)
                goto calc_error;

            // iterate the data. try to convert non-double values to double
            for (i = 0; i < cElements; i++) {
                vTemp = pvdata[i];
                if (vTemp.vt != VT_R8) {
                    hr = VariantChangeType(&vTemp,
                        &vTemp, 0, VT_R8);
                    if (hr != NOERROR)
                        goto calc_error;
                }

                // add the data. this is where we could
                // add a more complicated function
                vResult.dblVal += vTemp.dblVal;
            }

            SafeArrayUnaccessData(vSource.parray);
        }
        else {
            // only one cell in the source range.
            // if it's not a double, try to convert it.
            if (vSource.vt != VT_R8) {
```

```
                        hr = VariantChangeType(&vSource, &vSource, 0, VT_R8);
                        if (hr != NOERROR)
                            goto calc_error;
                }
                vResult = vSource;
        }

        // if the result value is an object,
        // get the DISPID for its Value property

        if (pvtResult->vt == VT_DISPATCH) {

                hr = (*(pvtResult->pdispVal->lpVtbl->GetIDsOfNames))
                        (pvtResult->pdispVal, &IID_NULL,
                        (char FAR*FAR*)&lpszName,   1,
                        LOCALE_SYSTEM_DEFAULT, &dispidValue);
                if (hr != NOERROR)
                    goto calc_error;

                dispidPut = DISPID_PROPERTYPUT;

                dispparams.rgdispidNamedArgs = &dispidPut;
                dispparams.rgvarg = &vResult;
                dispparams.cArgs = 1;
                dispparams.cNamedArgs = 1;

                // Invoke PropertyPut

                hr = (*(pvtResult->pdispVal->lpVtbl->Invoke))
                        (pvtResult->pdispVal, dispidValue, &IID_NULL,
                        LOCALE_SYSTEM_DEFAULT, DISPATCH_PROPERTYPUT,
                        &dispparams, NULL, &excep, &uiArgErr);
                if (hr != NOERROR)
                    goto calc_error;
        }
        else {
                // Result is not an object; it's a variable passed by reference.
                // Must free any existing allocation in the variant.
                // The ReleaseVariant function is in dispargs.c

                ReleaseVariant(pvtResult);
                *pvtResult = vResult;
        }

        return 0;

calc_error:
        return GetScode(hr);
}
```

This is a simple example, but it shows the setup for PropertyPut and PropertyGet and how the range value is returned as an array. You could write a more complex data-handling function around this simple example to implement a specialized DLL function. Remember that any variants your DLL function allocates (strings or arrays) must be freed to prevent memory leaks.

The code for this function is included on the samples disk in the SAMPLE\SDISP directory. This directory also includes the make file and module-definition file required to build SDISP.DLL. Once SDISP.DLL is available, you can call this function from Microsoft Excel, as shown in the following example:

```
Declare Function CalcCells Lib "SDISP.DLL" _
    (source As Range, result As Variant) As Integer

Sub Main()
    Worksheets(1).Activate
    Range("A4").Clear
    CalcCells Range("A1:B3"), Range("A4")
End Sub
```

Dispargs.c

Method calls more complex than the PropertyGet and PropertyPut examples shown in the preceding section require extensive setup work. Before you can call the Invoke function, each argument must be placed into the argument array. After the Invoke function call, any variant arguments that were allocated (created BSTR or SAFEARRAY values) must be freed. Creating arrays of BSTR values requires repetitive allocation, testing, and error handling.

The functions provided in dispargs.c on the sample disk (in the SAMPLE\AUTOXL directory) were written to simplify these tasks. The following procedure shows how to use these functions:

1. Use the ClearAllArgs function to clear and reset the argument array.

2. Use the AddArgument*Type* argument-constructor function(s) to set the appropriate argument(s).

3. Use the Invoke function to invoke the method (note that this is the Invoke function in dispargs.c, not the Invoke function provided by OLE 2).

4. Free any arguments not automatically freed by the Invoke function.

5. Free the return value if a return value was requested. Use the ReleaseVariant function to free variant return values and arguments.

The following sections discuss the argument-constructor functions and the Invoke function in more detail.

Argument Information

The argument-constructor functions in dispargs.c place argument information in global arrays.

```
int         g_iArgCount;
int         g_iNamedArgCount;
VARIANTARG  g_aVargs[MAX_DISP_ARGS];
DISPID      g_aDispIds[MAX_DISP_ARGS + 1];
LPSTR       g_alpszArgNames[MAX_DISP_ARGS + 1];
WORD        g_awFlags[MAX_DISP_ARGS];
```

The Vargs array contains the argument values; the lpszArgNames array contains the argument names (unnamed arguments have NULL names); and the wFlags array contains argument flags (such as NOFREEVARIANT). The information in these arrays is used to build the argument list for an IDispatch interface call. The arrays in dispargs.c are statically allocated to reduce complexity; this places a limit on the number of arguments that can be passed. To remove this limit and manage memory more effectively, the code could be modified to allocate memory dynamically.

When the Invoke function is called, it uses the IDispatch::GetIDsOfNames function to convert the names in the lpszArgNames array into DISPID values for the IDispatch::Invoke function. The resulting DISPID values are placed in the DispIds array. The first element of the DispIds array is the DISPID of the method or property, and the first element of the lpszArgNames array is the method or property name.

Utility Functions

Dispargs.c also includes utility functions used to manage variants and argument arrays. The ClearVariant function sets a variant to zero. This function ignores the current contents of the variant. If you are unsure of the current contents of the variant, you should call the ReleaseVariant function before you clear the variant.

```
void ClearVariant(VARIANTARG FAR *pvarg)
{
    pvarg->vt = VT_EMPTY;
    pvarg->wReserved1 = 0;
    pvarg->wReserved2 = 0;
    pvarg->wReserved3 = 0;
    pvarg->lVal = 0;
}
```

The ClearAllArgs function releases any memory in use by the argument array and resets the argument counters. Because these arrays are static, it is important to call the ClearAllArgs function before you begin to set up arguments.

```
void ClearAllArgs()
{
    int i;

    for (i = 0; i < g_iArgCount; i++) {
        if (g_awFlags[i] & DISPARG_NOFREEVARIANT)
            ClearVariant(&g_aVargs[i]);
        else
            ReleaseVariant(&g_aVargs[i]);
    }

    g_iArgCount = 0;
    g_iNamedArgCount = 0;
}
```

The ReleaseVariant function releases any memory allocated for a variant (such as a variant containing a string or array). Use this function any time you set a variant if you are unsure of its current contents. For example, a memory leak will result if you set a variant that currently contains a string without first releasing the string.

This function supports the following data types: integer, Booleans, doubles, objects, strings, and arrays of any of the listed data types.

```
void ReleaseVariant(VARIANTARG FAR *pvarg)
{
    VARTYPE vt;
    VARIANTARG _huge *pvargArray;
    long lLBound, lUBound, l;

    vt = pvarg->vt & 0xfff;      // mask off flags

    // check if an array. If so, free its contents,
    // then the array itself.
    if (V_ISARRAY(pvarg)) {
        // variant arrays are all this routine
        // currently knows about. Since a
        // variant can contain anything (even other arrays),
        // call this function recursively.
        if (vt == VT_VARIANT) {
            SafeArrayGetLBound(pvarg->parray, 1, &lLBound);
            SafeArrayGetUBound(pvarg->parray, 1, &lUBound);

            if (lUBound > lLBound) {
                lUBound -= lLBound;

                SafeArrayAccessData(pvarg->parray, &pvargArray);
```

```
                for (l = 0; l < lUBound; l++) {
                    ReleaseVariant(pvargArray);
                    pvargArray++;
                }

                SafeArrayUnaccessData(pvarg->parray);
            }
        }
        else {
            MessageBox(g_hwndApp,
                "ReleaseVariant: Array contains non-variant type",
                g_szAppTitle, MB_OK | MB_ICONSTOP);
        }

        // Free the array itself.
        SafeArrayDestroy(pvarg->parray);
    }
    else {
        switch (vt) {
            case VT_DISPATCH:
                (*(pvarg->pdispVal->lpVtbl->Release))(pvarg->pdispVal);
                break;

            case VT_BSTR:
                SysFreeString(pvarg->bstrVal);
                break;

            case VT_I2:
            case VT_BOOL:
            case VT_R8:
            case VT_ERROR:        // to avoid erroring
                                  // on an error return from Excel
                // no work for these types
                break;

            default:
                MessageBox(g_hwndApp, "ReleaseVariant: Unknown type",
                    g_szAppTitle, MB_OK | MB_ICONSTOP);
                break;
        }
    }

    ClearVariant(pvarg);
}
```

Argument-Constructor Functions

The argument-constructor functions in dispargs.c are used to set up an argument list before you use the Invoke function. Each argument-constructor function adds a single argument of a specific type to the list of arguments (the global argument arrays). If appropriate, memory may be allocated to represent the argument. This memory will be automatically freed when the ClearAllArgs function is called unless you specify the NOFREEVARIANT flag for the argument. If you specify this flag, it is your responsibility to free the memory allocated for or contained within the argument.

For example, if a method has one Boolean argument and two integer arguments, you would call AddArgumentBool, AddArgumentInt2, AddArgumentInt2. Each AddArgument*Type* function accepts the name of the argument, a flag which tells the function whether the argument should be freed after use, and the value of the argument. Functions are provided for the following data types: integers, Booleans, doubles, objects, strings and arrays of strings. IDispatch is capable of supporting other data types; you can add an argument handler for a data type by writing the appropriate AddArgument*Type* function and adding argument-release code to the ReleaseVariant function.

Arguments may be named. The name string must be a C-style (null-terminated) string, and it is owned by the caller. If the string is dynamically allocated, the caller is responsible for freeing the string.

All named arguments must be set before any positional arguments. The following example shows a Visual Basic call and its equivalent call using the AddArgumentInt2 function (the flags argument is omitted for clarity). Notice that the arguments are added in reverse order (the last argument is added first).

Visual Basic:

```
SomeMethod 5, 2, named1 := 3, named2 := 4
```

Dispargs:

```
AddArgumentInt2("named2", 4);
AddArgumentInt2("named1", 3);
AddArgumentInt2(NULL, 2);
AddArgumentInt2(NULL, 5);
```

If you are using PropertyPut, use a NULL name and add the value to be set as the argument.

All argument-constructor functions use the AddArgumentCommon function to set the name and value of the argument and increment the argument count.

```
void AddArgumentCommon(LPSTR lpszArgName, WORD wFlags, VARTYPE vt)
{
```

```
        ClearVariant(&g_aVargs[g_iArgCount]);

        g_aVargs[g_iArgCount].vt = vt;
        g_awFlags[g_iArgCount] = wFlags;

        if (lpszArgName != NULL) {
            g_alpszArgNames[g_iNamedArgCount + 1] = lpszArgName;
            g_iNamedArgCount++;
        }
}
```

Object Arguments

```
BOOL AddArgumentDispatch(LPSTR lpszArgName, WORD wFlags,
    IDispatch FAR * pdisp)
{
    AddArgumentCommon(lpszArgName, wFlags, VT_DISPATCH);
    g_aVargs[g_iArgCount++].pdispVal = pdisp;
    return TRUE;
}
```

Integer Arguments

```
BOOL AddArgumentInt2(LPSTR lpszArgName, WORD wFlags, int i)
{
    AddArgumentCommon(lpszArgName, wFlags, VT_I2);
    g_aVargs[g_iArgCount++].iVal = i;
    return TRUE;
}
```

Boolean Arguments

```
BOOL AddArgumentBool(LPSTR lpszArgName, WORD wFlags, BOOL b)
{
    AddArgumentCommon(lpszArgName, wFlags, VT_BOOL);
    // Note the variant representation of True as -1
    g_aVargs[g_iArgCount++].bool = b ? -1 : 0;
    return TRUE;
}
```

Double Arguments

```
BOOL AddArgumentDouble(LPSTR lpszArgName, WORD wFlags, double d)
{
    AddArgumentCommon(lpszArgName, wFlags, VT_R8);
    g_aVargs[g_iArgCount++].dblVal = d;
    return TRUE;
}
```

String Arguments

OLE and IDispatch use a BSTR for strings (for more information about BSTR values, see Chapter 6 in Volume 2 of the *OLE 2 Programmer's Reference*. The AddArgumentCString function copies the passed-in C-style string into a BSTR. You must not set the NOFREEVARIANT flag for C-string arguments; the allocated BSTR should be freed by the ReleaseVariant function.

```
BOOL AddArgumentCString(LPSTR lpszArgName, WORD wFlags, LPSTR lpsz)
{
    BSTR b;

    b = SysAllocString(lpsz);
    if (!b)
        return FALSE;
    AddArgumentCommon(lpszArgName, wFlags, VT_BSTR);
    g_aVargs[g_iArgCount++].bstrVal = b;
    return TRUE;
}
```

If you already have a BSTR argument, you should use the AddArgumentBSTR function to avoid making an extra copy of the BSTR. With BSTR arguments, you should set the NOFREEVARIANT flag unless you want the ReleaseVariant function to free the passed-in BSTR (if you plan to use the BSTR after the Invoke function call, you should set this flag).

```
BOOL AddArgumentBSTR(LPSTR lpszArgName, WORD wFlags, BSTR bstr)
{
    AddArgumentCommon(lpszArgName, wFlags, VT_BSTR);
    g_aVargs[g_iArgCount++].bstrVal = bstr;
    return TRUE;
}
```

String-Array Arguments

The following function copies an array of C-style strings into a one-dimensional array of string variants. You should allow the ReleaseVariant function to free the allocated strings; do not set the NOFREEVARIANT flag.

```
BOOL AddArgumentCStringArray(LPSTR lpszArgName, WORD wFlags,
    LPSTR FAR *paszStrings, int iCount)
{
    SAFEARRAY FAR *psa;
    SAFEARRAYBOUND saBound;
    VARIANTARG FAR *pvargBase;
    VARIANTARG FAR *pvarg;
    int i, j;

    saBound.lLbound = 0;
    saBound.cElements = iCount;
```

```
psa = SafeArrayCreate(VT_VARIANT, 1, &saBound);
if (psa == NULL)
    return FALSE;

SafeArrayAccessData(psa, & (VARIANTARG _huge *) pvargBase);

pvarg = pvargBase;
for (i = 0; i < iCount; i++) {
    // copy each string in the list of strings
    ClearVariant(pvarg);
    pvarg->vt = VT_BSTR;
    if ((pvarg->bstrVal = SysAllocString(*paszStrings++)) == NULL) {
        // memory failure:  back out and free strings
        // allocated up to now, and then the array itself.
        pvarg = pvargBase;
        for (j = 0; j < i; i++) {
            SysFreeString(pvarg->bstrVal);
            pvarg++;
        }
        SafeArrayDestroy(psa);
        return FALSE;
    }
    pvarg++;
}

SafeArrayUnaccessData(psa);

// With all memory allocated, setup this argument
AddArgumentCommon(lpszArgName, wFlags, VT_VARIANT | VT_ARRAY);
g_aVargs[g_iArgCount++].parray = psa;
return TRUE;
}
```

The Invoke Function

Once you have set up the argument arrays with the argument-constructor functions, you can use the Invoke function to call a method or to set or get a property.

This function accepts a pointer to the object; the name of the method or property; a pointer to a location for the return value; a flag indicating whether you are calling a method, setting a property, or getting the value of a property; and a flag indicating whether the Invoke function should clear the arguments when it returns.

The Invoke function returns True if the call succeeded and False if an error occurred. A message box will be displayed explaining the error unless the DISP_NOSHOWEXCEPTIONS flag is specified. Errors result from unrecognized method or property names, bad argument names, invalid data types, or run-time exceptions defined by the recipient of the IDispatch call.

After the IDispatch call, the Invoke function calls the ClearAllArgs function to reset the argument list if the DISP_FREEARGS flag is specified. If this flag is not specified, it is up to the caller to call ClearAllArgs.

The return value is placed in the pvargReturn variable, which is allocated by the caller. If no return value is required, this argument should be NULL. It is up to the caller to free the return value (use the ReleaseVariant function).

This function calls IDispatch::GetIDsOfNames every time it is called. This is not very efficient if the same method or property is invoked multiple times, because the DISPID value for a particular method or property will remain the same during the lifetime of an IDispatch object. Modifications could be made to this code to cache DISPID values. If the target application is always the same, you could store the DISPID values at compile time (an application will return the same DISPID values in different sessions). Eliminating the extra cross-process GetIDsOfNames calls can result in a significant time savings.

```
BOOL Invoke(IDispatch FAR *pdisp, LPSTR szMember,
    VARIANTARG FAR * pvargReturn,    WORD wInvokeAction, WORD wFlags)
{
    HRESULT hr;
    DISPPARAMS dispparams;
    unsigned int uiArgErr;
    EXCEPINFO excep;

    // Get the IDs for the member and its arguments.
    // GetIDsOfNames expects the member name as
    // the first name, followed by argument names (if any).
    g_alpszArgNames[0] = szMember;
    hr = (*(pdisp->lpVtbl->GetIDsOfNames))  (pdisp,
            &IID_NULL, g_alpszArgNames, 1 + g_iNamedArgCount,
            LOCALE_SYSTEM_DEFAULT, g_aDispIds);
    if (FAILED(hr)) {
        if (!(wFlags & DISP_NOSHOWEXCEPTIONS))
            ShowException(szMember, hr, NULL, 0);
        return FALSE;
    }
    if (pvargReturn != NULL)
        ClearVariant(pvargReturn);

    // if doing a property put(ref),
    // we need to adjust the first argument to have a
    // named arg of DISPID_PROPERTYPUT.
    if (wInvokeAction & (DISPATCH_PROPERTYPUT |
            DISPATCH_PROPERTYPUTREF)) {
        g_iNamedArgCount = 1;
        g_aDispIds[1] = DISPID_PROPERTYPUT;
        pvargReturn = NULL;
    }
```

```
dispparams.rgdispidNamedArgs = g_aDispIds + 1;
dispparams.rgvarg = g_aVargs;
dispparams.cArgs = g_iArgCount;
dispparams.cNamedArgs = g_iNamedArgCount;

excep.pfnDeferredFillIn = NULL;

hr = (*(pdisp->lpVtbl->Invoke))(pdisp, g_aDispIds[0],
    &IID_NULL, LOCALE_SYSTEM_DEFAULT,    wInvokeAction,
    &dispparams, pvargReturn, &excep, &uiArgErr);

if (wFlags & DISP_FREEARGS)
    ClearAllArgs();

if (FAILED(hr)) {
    // display the exception information if appropriate:
    if (!(wFlags & DISP_NOSHOWEXCEPTIONS))
        ShowException(szMember, hr, &excep, uiArgErr);

    // free exception structure information
    SysFreeString(excep.bstrSource);
    SysFreeString(excep.bstrDescription);
    SysFreeString(excep.bstrHelpFile);

    return FALSE;
}

return TRUE;
}
```

The ShowException Function

If an error occurs as the result of an Invoke function call, the ShowException function attempts to display information about the exception. Note that this function uses a global window handle which must be set before this function can be called.

```
void ShowException(LPSTR szMember, HRESULT hr, EXCEPINFO FAR *pexcep,
    unsigned int uiArgErr)
{
    char szBuf[512];

    switch (GetScode(hr)) {
        case DISP_E_UNKNOWNNAME:
            wsprintf(szBuf, "%s: Unknown name or named argument.",
                szMember);
            break;
```

```
    case DISP_E_BADPARAMCOUNT:
        wsprintf(szBuf, "%s: Incorrect number of arguments.",
            szMember);
        break;

    case DISP_E_EXCEPTION:
        wsprintf(szBuf, "%s: Error %d: ", szMember, pexcep->wCode);
        if (pexcep->bstrDescription != NULL)
            lstrcat(szBuf, pexcep->bstrDescription);
        else
            lstrcat(szBuf, "<<No Description>>");
        break;

    case DISP_E_MEMBERNOTFOUND:
        wsprintf(szBuf, "%s: method or property not found.",
            szMember);
        break;

    case DISP_E_OVERFLOW:
        wsprintf(szBuf, "%s: Overflow coercing argument values.",
            szMember);
        break;

    case DISP_E_NONAMEDARGS:
        wsprintf(szBuf, "%s: Named arguments not supported",
            szMember);
        break;

    case DISP_E_UNKNOWNLCID:
        wsprintf(szBuf, "%s: The locale ID is unknown.", szMember);
        break;

    case DISP_E_PARAMNOTOPTIONAL:
        wsprintf(szBuf, "%s: Missing a required parameter.",
            szMember);
        break;

    case DISP_E_PARAMNOTFOUND:
        wsprintf(szBuf, "%s: Argument not found, argument %d.",
            szMember, uiArgErr);
        break;

    case DISP_E_TYPEMISMATCH:
        wsprintf(szBuf, "%s: Type mismatch, argument %d.",
            szMember, uiArgErr);
        break;

    default:
        wsprintf(szBuf, "%s: Unknown error occured.", szMember);
        break;
```

```
    }

        MessageBox(g_hwndApp, szBuf, g_szAppTitle, MB_OK | MB_ICONSTOP);
}
```

AutoXL: A Detailed Example

AutoXL.exe, included on the sample disk (in the SAMPLE\AUTOXL directory), uses the dispargs functions to implement a more complex OLE Automation Controller. AutoXL uses Microsoft Excel to create a pie chart. It starts Microsoft Excel, adds a new workbook, inserts data into the first worksheet in the workbook, and then uses the ChartWizard method to create a pie chart. The following Visual Basic code shows the equivalent work:

```
Set wb = Application.Workbooks.Add(template := xlWorksheet)
Set ws = wb.Worksheets(1)
ws.Range("A1:D1").Value = Array("North", "South", "East", "West")
ws.Range("A2") = 5.2
ws.Range("B2") = 10
ws.Range("C2") = 8
ws.Range("D2") = 20
set sourceRange = ws.Range("A1:D2")
set crt = wb.Charts.Add
crt.ChartWizard source := sourceRange, gallery := xl3DPie, _
    format := 7, plotBy := xlRows, categoryLabels := 1, _
    seriesLabels := 0, hasLegend := 2, title := "Sales Percentages"
wb.Saved = True
' So that Excel won't ask whether to save this document on close.
```

Wincode.c

The code in wincode.c creates the main window and message queue for AutoXL. This is a fairly typical window-management code module; the interesting portion of this code occurs in the WinMain function. Notice that it increases the size of the message queue and that it initializes and uninitializes OLE.

```
int PASCAL WinMain(HINSTANCE hInst, HINSTANCE hPrevInst,
        LPSTR lpszCmd, int iCmdShow)
{
    MSG msg;
    int iMsg = 96;

    // for OLE, enlarge message queue to be as large as possible
    while (!SetMessageQueue(iMsg) && (iMsg -= 8));

    // various initialization, including OLE
    g_hInstApp = hInst;
```

```
        msg.wParam = FALSE;

        if (!InitApplication(hPrevInst))
            goto ExitApplication;

        if (!InitOLE())
            goto ExitApplication;

        if (!InitInstance(iCmdShow))
            goto ExitApplication;

        // message loop
        while (GetMessage(&msg, NULL, NULL, NULL)) {
            TranslateMessage(&msg);
            DispatchMessage(&msg);
        }

ExitApplication:
        // make sure OLE is cleaned up if init was done
        if (g_fOLEInit)
            OleUninitialize();

        return msg.wParam;
}

BOOL InitOLE()
{
    DWORD dwOleVer;

    dwOleVer = CoBuildVersion();

    // check the OLE library version
    if (rmm != HIWORD(dwOleVer)) {
        MessageBox(NULL, "Incorrect version of OLE libraries.",
            g_szAppTitle, MB_OK | MB_ICONSTOP);
        return FALSE;
    }

    // could also check for minor version, but this application is
    // not sensitive to the minor version of OLE

    // initialize OLE, fail application if we can't get OLE to init.
    if (FAILED(OleInitialize(NULL))) {
        MessageBox(NULL, "Cannot initialize OLE.", g_szAppTitle,
            MB_OK | MB_ICONSTOP);
        return FALSE;
    }
```

```
    // otherwise, init succeeded
    g_fOLEInit = TRUE;

    return TRUE;
}
```

AutoXL.c

The code in autoxl.c actually creates the pie chart using the code in dispargs.c as helper functions to set up the Invoke function calls.

The CLSID for Microsoft Excel is unique and is used by OLE to identify the server to start.

```
DEFINE_OLEGUID(CLSID_ExcelApp, 0x20841, 0, 0);
```

Excel Instance-Management Functions

The StartExcel, ReleaseExcel, IsExcelRunning, and SetExcelVisible functions are used to manage an instance of Microsoft Excel. The StartExcel function uses the CoCreateInstance function to create an instance of Excel. The ReleaseExcel function invokes the Quit method for the Microsoft Excel Application object (this causes Excel to exit), and shuts down the OLE server. The SetExcelVisible function invokes the Visible method for the Application object, making the instance of Microsoft Excel visible.

```
IDispatch FAR* pdispExcelApp = NULL;

BOOL StartExcel()
{
    // if Excel is already running, return with current instance
    if (pdispExcelApp != NULL)
        return TRUE;

    // start a new copy of Excel, grab the IDispatch interface
    if (FAILED(CoCreateInstance(&CLSID_ExcelApp, NULL,
            CLSCTX_LOCAL_SERVER, &IID_IDispatch, &pdispExcelApp))) {
        MessageBox(g_hwndApp,
            "Cannot start an instance of Excel for Automation.",
            g_szAppTitle, MB_OK | MB_ICONSTOP);
        return FALSE;
    }

    return TRUE;
}

BOOL ReleaseExcel()
{
```

```
        if (pdispExcelApp == NULL)
            return TRUE;

        // Tell Excel to quit, since for automation
        // simply releasing the IDispatch object isn't
        // enough to get the server to shut down.

        // Note that this code will hang if Excel tries to
        // display any message boxes. This can occur if a document needs
        // to be saved. The CreateChart() code always clears the
        // dirty bit on the documents it creates, avoiding this problem.

        ClearAllArgs();
        Invoke(pdispExcelApp, "Quit", NULL, DISPATCH_METHOD, 0);

        // Even though Excel has been told to Quit,
        // we still need to release the
        // OLE object to account for all memory.
        (*(pdispExcelApp->lpVtbl->Release))(pdispExcelApp);

        pdispExcelApp = NULL;
        return TRUE;
}

BOOL IsExcelRunning()
{
    return pdispExcelApp != NULL;
}

BOOL SetExcelVisible(BOOL fVisible)
{
    if (!IsExcelRunning())
        return FALSE;

    ClearAllArgs();
    AddArgumentBool(NULL, 0, fVisible);
    return Invoke(pdispExcelApp, "Visible", NULL,
        DISPATCH_PROPERTYPUT, DISP_FREEARGS);
}
```

SetRangeValueDouble Function

The SetRangeValueDouble function uses PropertyPut to set the value of a range given the cell reference as a string. The CreateChart function calls this function several times to set cell values.

```
BOOL SetRangeValueDouble(IDispatch FAR *pdispWs,
    LPSTR lpszRef, double d)
{
```

```
    VARIANTARG vargRng;
    BOOL fResult;

    ClearAllArgs();
    AddArgumentCString(NULL, 0, lpszRef);
    if (!Invoke(pdispWs, "Range", &vargRng,
            DISPATCH_METHOD, DISP_FREEARGS))
        return FALSE;

    AddArgumentDouble(NULL, 0, d);
    fResult = Invoke(vargRng.pdispVal, "Value", NULL,
        DISPATCH_PROPERTYPUT, 0);
    ReleaseVariant(&vargRng);

    return fResult;
}
```

CreateChart Function

The CreateChart function uses the argument-constructor functions and the Invoke function to create a pie chart in Microsoft Excel. The Visual Basic equivalent calls are described in the comments immediately preceding the AddArgument*Type* and Invoke function calls.

```
BOOL CreateChart()
{
    BOOL fResult;
    VARIANTARG varg1, varg2;
    IDispatch FAR *pdispWorkbook = NULL;
    IDispatch FAR *pdispWorksheet = NULL;
    IDispatch FAR *pdispRange = NULL;
    IDispatch FAR *pdispCrt = NULL;
    LPSTR apszNames[4] = { "North", "South", "East", "West" };

    // Set wb = [application].Workbooks.Add(template := xlWorksheet)
    ClearAllArgs();
    if (!Invoke(pdispExcelApp, "Workbooks", &varg1, DISPATCH_METHOD, 0))
        return FALSE;

    ClearAllArgs();
    AddArgumentInt2("Template", 0, xlWorksheet);
    fResult = Invoke(varg1.pdispVal, "Add", &varg2, DISPATCH_METHOD, 0);
    ReleaseVariant(&varg1);
    if (!fResult)
        return FALSE;
    pdispWorkbook = varg2.pdispVal;

    // Set ws = wb.Worksheets(1)
    ClearAllArgs();
    AddArgumentInt2(NULL, 0, 1);
```

```
    if (!Invoke(pdispWorkbook, "Worksheets", &varg2,
            DISPATCH_METHOD, 0))
        goto CreateChartBail;
    pdispWorksheet = varg2.pdispVal;


    // setup the data labels

    // ws.Range("A1:D1").Value = Array("North", "South", "East", "West")
    ClearAllArgs();
    AddArgumentCString(NULL, 0, "A1:D1");
    if (!Invoke(pdispWorksheet, "Range", &varg2, DISPATCH_METHOD,
            DISP_FREEARGS))
        goto CreateChartBail;

    AddArgumentCStringArray(NULL, 0, apszNames, 4);
    fResult = Invoke(varg2.pdispVal, "Value", NULL,
            DISPATCH_PROPERTYPUT, DISP_FREEARGS);
    ReleaseVariant(&varg2);
    if (!fResult)
        goto CreateChartBail;


    // set up the data series values

    // ws.Range("A2") = 5.2
    if (!SetRangeValueDouble(pdispWorksheet, "A2", 5.2))
        goto CreateChartBail;
    // ws.Range("B2") = 10
    if (!SetRangeValueDouble(pdispWorksheet, "B2", 10.0))
        goto CreateChartBail;
    // ws.Range("C2") = 8
    if (!SetRangeValueDouble(pdispWorksheet, "C2", 8.0))
        goto CreateChartBail;
    // ws.Range("D2") = 20
    if (!SetRangeValueDouble(pdispWorksheet, "D2", 20))
        goto CreateChartBail;


    // set sourceRange = ws.Range("A1:D2")
    ClearAllArgs();
    AddArgumentCString(NULL, 0, "A1:D2");
    if (!Invoke(pdispWorksheet, "Range", &varg2,
            DISPATCH_METHOD, DISP_FREEARGS))
        goto CreateChartBail;
    pdispRange = varg2.pdispVal;


    // set crt = wb.Charts.Add
    ClearAllArgs();
    if (!Invoke(pdispWorkbook, "Charts", &varg1,
            DISPATCH_METHOD, 0))
        goto CreateChartBail;
```

```
    ClearAllArgs();
    fResult = Invoke(varg1.pdispVal, "Add", &varg2, DISPATCH_METHOD, 0);
    ReleaseVariant(&varg1);
    if (!fResult)
        goto CreateChartBail;
    pdispCrt = varg2.pdispVal;

    // crt.ChartWizard source := sourceRange, gallery := xl3DPie, _
    // format := 7, plotBy := xlRows, categoryLabels := 1, _
    // seriesLabels := 0, hasLegend := 2, _
    // title := "Sales Percentages"
    ClearAllArgs();
    AddArgumentCString("title", 0, "Sales Percentages");
    AddArgumentInt2("hasLegend", 0, 2);
    AddArgumentInt2("seriesLabels", 0, 0);
    AddArgumentInt2("categoryLabels", 0, 1);
    AddArgumentInt2("plotBy", 0, xlRows);
    AddArgumentInt2("format", 0, 7);
    AddArgumentInt2("gallery", 0, xl3DPie);
    AddArgumentDispatch("source", 0, pdispRange);      // will auto-free
    pdispRange = NULL;
    if (!Invoke(pdispCrt, "ChartWizard", NULL, DISPATCH_METHOD,
            DISP_FREEARGS))
        goto CreateChartBail;

    // wb.Saved = True
    // ' So that Excel won't ask whether to save this document on close.
    ClearAllArgs();
    AddArgumentBool(NULL, 0, TRUE);
    Invoke(pdispWorkbook, "Saved", NULL, DISPATCH_PROPERTYPUT, 0);

    fResult = TRUE;

CreateChartExit:
    if (pdispWorkbook != NULL)
        (*(pdispWorkbook->lpVtbl->Release))(pdispWorkbook);
    if (pdispWorksheet != NULL)
        (*(pdispWorksheet->lpVtbl->Release))(pdispWorksheet);
    if (pdispRange != NULL)
        (*(pdispRange->lpVtbl->Release))(pdispRange);
    if (pdispCrt != NULL)
        (*(pdispCrt->lpVtbl->Release))(pdispCrt);
    return fResult;

CreateChartBail:
    fResult = FALSE;
    goto CreateChartExit;
}
```

A P P E N D I X   A

Dynamic Data Exchange
and XlTable Format

Microsoft Windows provides several methods for transferring data between applications. One way to transfer data is to use Windows dynamic data exchange (DDE). DDE is a message protocol for data exchange between Windows programs. It allows software developers to design applications that share data and thereby provide the user with a more integrated Windows environment.

For complete information about DDE, see the documentation for the Microsoft Windows Software Development Kit (SDK). This appendix describes the DDE formats that Microsoft Excel version 5.0 supports, and provides detailed information about the high-performance XlTable DDE format.

DDE Formats

Microsoft Excel supports several DDE formats. The formats are listed in the following table in the order of precedence defined by Microsoft Excel, from highest precedence (XlTable) to lowest precedence (CF_METAFILEPICT). Clipboard formats that begin with CF_ are formats that are already defined in WINDOWS.H. Clipboard formats without CF_ must be registered before use. For more information about registering formats, see "Registering Clipboard Formats" on page 374.

Clipboard format	Description
XlTable	Microsoft Excel fast table format. For more information, see "Fast Table Format" on page 375.
Biff5	Binary interchange file format (BIFF) for Microsoft Excel version 5.0. For more information about the file format, see Chapter 3, "File Format."
Biff4	Binary interchange file format (BIFF) for Microsoft Excel version 4.0.
Biff3	BIFF for Microsoft Excel version 3.0.
Biff	BIFF for Microsoft Excel version 2.x.

Clipboard format	Description
CF_SYLK	Microsoft symbolic link (SYLK) format. Microsoft Excel for the Apple Macintosh was originally designed to use SYLK format, and this format is now supported by Microsoft Excel on both Windows and Macintosh platforms.
Wk1	Lotus® 1-2-3® Release 2.01 and Release 2.2 format.
Csv	Comma-separated values format, commonly used in BASIC language I/O. It is similar to CF_TEXT format, except that Csv uses commas to separate fields.
CF_TEXT	The simplest form of clipboard data. It is a null-terminated string containing a carriage return and linefeed at the end of each line.
Rich Text Format	A method of encoding formatted text and graphics for easy transfer between applications. Rich Text Format (RTF) is commonly used by document processing programs such as Microsoft Word for Windows and Microsoft Word for the Macintosh.
CF_DIF	An ASCII format used by the VisiCalc™ spreadsheet program. The format is under the control of Lotus Development Corporation.
CF_BITMAP	A Windows version 2 compatible bitmap.
CF_METAFILEPICT	A metafile picture structure. For complete information, see the documentation for the Microsoft Windows Software Development Kit.

Registering Clipboard Formats

Whenever an application uses a private clipboard format such as XlTable, Biff5, Biff4, Biff3, Biff, Wk1, Csv, or Rich Text Format, it must register the format before using it. Microsoft Excel registers these private clipboard formats, and your DDE application must also register any of these formats that you want to use to exchange data.

For example, to register XlTable, use the following Windows API function call:

```
wCBformat = RegisterClipboardFormat((LPSTR)"XlTable");
```

If the function call is successful, the return value is equal to the format value for the XlTable format. This format value (type WORD) is between 0xC000 and 0xFFFF, and is equal to the format value that Windows returned to Microsoft Excel when it registered XlTable. If Windows cannot register XlTable, then the function returns zero.

Fast Table Format

The fast table format, XlTable, is designed to maximize the DDE transfer speed of Microsoft Excel. XlTable consists of a sequence of data blocks that represent a rectangular selection of cells (a table). Each data block has three parts:

```
WORD tdt        /* the table data type */
WORD cb         /* the size (count of bytes) of the data */
BYTE data[cb]   /* the data */
```

The first data block is always of type tdtTable, which specifies the number of rows and the number of columns in the table. The data blocks that follow tdtTable represent all the cells in the table. Microsoft Excel renders the reference of the cells in the table (for example, R1C1:R2C4) as the item part of the DDE message.

The cells are always rendered row-wise. In other words, all the cells in the first row of the table appear first, then all the cells in the second row, and so on. To minimize overhead, adjacent cells of the same type (tdt) are represented together in one data block, even if the cells are in different rows. In other words, one tdtFloat can contain several numbers, one tdtString can contain several strings, one tdtBool can contain several Boolean values, and so on. For examples, see the following sections, "XlTable Example 1," and "XlTable Example 2."

The data block types are described in the following table.

Data block type	Value	Description
tdtTable	0x0010	The size of the table. The data (4 bytes, cb=4) consists of two words. The first word is the number of rows, and the second word is the number of columns.
tdtFloat	0x0001	IEEE-format floating-point number. The size of the number is 8 bytes per cell.
tdtString	0x0002	String in st (byte-counted) format. The first byte contains the length of the string (cch). The string is not null-terminated.
tdtBool	0x0003	Boolean value: 1 = TRUE 0 = FALSE The length of the data is 2 bytes per cell.

tdtError	0x0004	Error value: 0 = #NULL!
		7 = #DIV/0!
		15 = #VALUE!
		23 = #REF!
		29 = #NAME?
		36 = #NUM!
		42 = #N/A
		
		The length of the data is 2 bytes per cell.

Data block type	Value	Description
tdtBlank	0x0005	A count of the number of consecutive undefined (blank) cells. The data (2 bytes, cb=2) contains the number of consecutive blank cells.
tdtInt	0x0006	Unsigned integer. The length of the data is 2 bytes per cell. Microsoft Excel can read a number in this format, but it never writes a number in this format.
tdtSkip	0x0007	Number of cells to skip. A skipped cell is a cell that retains its previous value. In other words, a skipped cell is not changed by a WM_DDE_DATA message. You can use tdtSkip to increase DDE performance if your application changes only one or two cells in the middle of a large table. Microsoft Excel does not support tdtSkip when the new cell data is part of a WM_DDE_POKE message. The length of the data is 2 bytes (cb=2).

XlTable Example 1

The following selection of three cells . . .

	A	B	C	D
1	East	West	North	
2				
3				
4				

. . . produces the following XlTable rendering.

Data (hexadecimal)	Description
10 00 04 00 01 00 03 00	tdtTable, cb=4, rows=1, columns=3
02 00 10 00	tdtString, cb=16
04 45 61 73 74	cch=4, East (tdtString continued)
04 57 65 73 74	cch=4, West (tdtString continued)
05 4e 6f 72 74 68	cch=5, North (tdtString continued)

Notice that the table contains three cells, but the XlTable rendering contains only one tdtString data block.

XlTable Example 2

The XlTable format uses the tdtBlank data block to represent blank cells in a table. A sequence of several blank cells may be represented by a single tdtBlank data block.

For example, the following table . . .

	A	B	C
1	2	3	
2	4	5	
3			
4	6	8	
5			

. . . produces the following XlTable rendering.

Data (hexadecimal)	Description
10 00 04 00 02 00 04 00	tdtTable, cb=4, rows=4, columns=2
06 00 08 00 02 00 03 00 04 00 05 00	tdtInt, cb=8, int[0]=2, int[1]=3, int[2]=4, int[3]=5 (Microsoft Excel can read tdtInt as a client, but it would write tdtFloat if it were a server)
05 00 02 00 02 00	tdtBlank, cb=2, data=2 (2 cells are blank)
06 00 04 00 06 00 08 00	tdtInt, cb=4, int[0]=6, int[1]=8

Biff5, Biff4, Biff3, and Biff Formats

The Biff5, Biff4, Biff3, and Biff clipboard formats contain a variable number of records. The records are identical to the corresponding records in the BIFF file. For more information about the BIFF5 records, see Chapter 3, "File Format." The Biff4, Biff3, and Biff formats are available for backward compatibility with existing applications. The Biff clipboard format corresponds to the BIFF2 file format.

If you implement one of the BIFF clipboard formats, your code should be prepared to receive all BIFF records except the file-specific records such as:

WRITEPROT
FILEPASS
TEMPLATE
WRITEACCESS
FILESHARING
CODEPAGE
PUB
SUB
EDG
INDEX

The minimum BIFF records that your code must provide when it writes to the clipboard are:

BOF
DIMENSIONS
Cell record or records (BLANK, BOOLERR, and so on)
EOF

A P P E N D I X   B

The EXCEL5.INI File

When you install Microsoft Excel version 5.0, the Setup program creates a file named EXCEL5.INI in the same directory as your WIN.INI file. On the Apple Macintosh, Setup creates the Excel Settings (5) file and places it in the System Folder or, if you are running system software version 7.0 or later, in the Preferences Folder in the System Folder. Each time you start Microsoft Excel, it checks the EXCEL5.INI or Excel Settings (5) file for startup settings. For example, you can use this file to specify documents that you want opened automatically, whether you want gridlines to appear in new worksheets, or what font you want as the default font.

With Microsoft Windows NT, Microsoft Excel stores preference settings in the registry instead of using a separate file. For more information, see "Specifying Settings with Microsoft Windows NT" on page 394.

This appendix details the functionality of the EXCEL5.INI file. Similar techniques are used with the Macintosh equivalent, Excel Settings (5). The differences are explained in the discussion "Specifying Settings in Microsoft Excel for the Macintosh" on page 394.

Editing the EXCEL5.INI File

You can use almost any text editor or word processor to edit the EXCEL5.INI file to customize your startup settings if you want to; however, you don't have to edit this file to use Microsoft Excel. When you are finished editing the file, you must save it as a text file. For changes to the EXCEL5.INI file to take effect, you must then restart Microsoft Excel.

Note If you install Microsoft Excel 5.0 on a network, Setup creates an EXCEL5.INI file on the drive and directory where you installed Microsoft Excel, in addition to the EXCEL5.INI file it creates in the directory containing your WIN.INI file. Do not edit this additional EXCEL5.INI file; it is for network purposes only. To change your startup settings, edit only the EXCEL5.INI file that is in the same directory as your WIN.INI file.

WIN.INI and EXCEL5.INI

In previous versions of Microsoft Excel, you could customize some startup settings by editing the [Microsoft Excel] section of the WIN.INI file and customize other settings by editing the EXCEL.INI or EXCEL4.INI files. If you already have a [Microsoft Excel] section in your WIN.INI file, its contents (except OPEN= statements specifying documents you want opened automatically) are used to create the EXCEL5.INI file during installation of Microsoft Excel 5.0. Methods for specifying documents you want opened automatically are described later in this appendix. The contents of existing EXCEL.INI or EXCEL4.INI files are not used to create the new EXCEL5.INI file. You must open and edit your EXCEL5.INI file to include any settings from your EXCEL.INI or EXCEL4.INI files. After installation, Microsoft Excel version 5.0 ignores the [Microsoft Excel] section of the WIN.INI file and the EXCEL.INI or EXCEL4.INI files.

Note The name of the .INI file for Microsoft Excel version 5.0 is different from the name of the .INI file for previous versions (EXCEL5.INI rather than EXCEL.INI or EXCEL4.INI). Therefore, you can specify startup settings for version 5.0 without changing your startup settings for earlier versions of Microsoft Excel.

The [Microsoft Excel] Section

The following is an example of the [Microsoft Excel] section:

```
[Microsoft Excel]
Options3=0
Options5=1667
Pos=159,50,808,621
Maximized=0
StickyPtX=383
StickyPtY=198
MenuKey=47
G1Dft-DemoSpd=3
G1Dft-HelpType=1
AltStartup=c:\work\xl
AutoFormat=3
AutoFormat Options=63
```

```
Basics=1
OPEN=/F C:\EXCEL\LIBRARY\CROSSTAB\CROSSFNC.XLA
OPEN1=C:\EXCEL\LIBRARY\CROSSTAB\CROSSTAB.XLL
OPEN2=/F C:\EXCEL\LIBRARY\REPORTS.XLA
OPEN4=/F C:\EXCEL\LIBRARY\SLIDES\SLIDES.XLT
```

Specifying Documents That You Want Opened Automatically

You can use either of the following methods to specify documents that you want opened each time you start Microsoft Excel.

Note You must use one of the following methods even if you specified the documents in the [Microsoft Excel] section of your WIN.INI file for an earlier version of Microsoft Excel.

The XLSTART Directory

The first method you can use to specify a document that you want opened automatically is to place the document in the XLSTART directory. During installation, the XLSTART directory was automatically created in the directory in which Microsoft Excel was installed.

The OPEN= Statement

The second method you can use to specify a document that you want opened automatically is to add an OPEN= statement to the [Microsoft Excel] section of your EXCEL5.INI file. For example, to open BUDGET92.XLS automatically, add the following statement:

```
OPEN= c:\excel5\budget92.xls
```

where \excel5 is the path to the directory containing the file you want to open.

Option Switches for the OPEN= Statement

You can use the /r and /f option switches, alone or together, to modify the behavior of the OPEN= statement. The /r option switch opens the file as read-only. The /f (fast load) option switch places template documents in the New dialog box (accessed from the File menu). When used to open a macro sheet containing custom functions, the /f option switch places those functions in the Function Wizard dialog box. When you use one of the custom functions in a specified document, the macro sheet containing the function is opened automatically.

For example, to open the file BUDGET.XLS as read-only every time Microsoft Excel is started, use the following statement:

```
OPEN= /r c:\excel5\budget92.xls
```

To enter more than one OPEN= statement, you must number them sequentially. For example, OPEN=, OPEN1=, OPEN2=, and so on. The OPEN statements must appear in ascending numeric order.

If you have a macro sheet named CUSTOM.XLM that contains function macros, the following statement will cause it to open automatically, and the functions it contains will be added to the User Defined function category in the Function Wizard dialog box.

```
OPEN= /f c:\excel5\custom.xlm
```

If you want to be able to use the New command on the File menu to create a new slide show, you can add the Slides template to the list of new document types by including the following statement.

```
OPEN= /f c:\excel5\slides.xlt
```

To use the /f switch with add-in macro sheets (.XLA), you must define the name _DemandLoad (the string "DemandLoad" preceded by two underscores) for the workbook. Microsoft Excel checks to see if the name is defined; the actual definition that you use is not important. You can define _DemandLoad as the Boolean value TRUE, for example.

When an OPEN= statement is used to open an add-in macro sheet on which the name _DemandLoad is defined, custom functions are displayed in the Function Wizard dialog box, but the add-in is not actually loaded until one of its functions is recalculated.

Note The Add-In Manager (the Add-Ins command on the Tools menu) reads and writes OPEN= statements.

Specifying Sets of Random Numbers

If you want Microsoft Excel 5.0 to generate a unique set of random numbers each time you use the RAND function, enter RANDOMIZE=1 in the [Microsoft Excel] section of your EXCEL5.INI file.

Setting the Default Font for Microsoft Excel

To set the default font and font size used for new worksheets, enter

```
FONT=font name,font size
```

in the [Microsoft Excel] section of your EXCEL5.INI file. For example,

```
FONT=MS Sans Serif,10
```

The font name you enter must be the name of the font spelled exactly as it appears in the dialog box when you choose the Font tab of the Cells... command from the Format menu. In Microsoft Excel 5.0, the FONT= statement sets the default font used for the Normal style, for row and column headings, and for text in the Info window.

Setting the Default Display Location for Dialog Boxes

There are two entries you can use in the [Microsoft Excel] section, StickyPtX= and StickyPtY=, that indicate the preferred location where dialog boxes appear on the screen: They are updated every time you exit Microsoft Excel.

StickyPtX and StickyPtY are the x and y coordinates of the current "sticky" point. The sticky point is the point on which dialog boxes are centered when they first appear on the screen. When a user moves a dialog box, a new sticky point is calculated based on the location of the dialog box when it is closed. If a custom dialog box is created, starting-point coordinates specified in the dialog-box definition table override the sticky points as defined in EXCEL5.INI.

Setting the Application Window Size

The Maximized= statement indicates the size of the application window and the size of the workbook window when you start Microsoft Excel. Bit zero controls the size of the application window, and bit one controls the size of the workbook window, as shown in the following table.

Maximized=	Indicates
0	Application window fills the screen, workbook window fills available space below toolbars.
1	Application window fills the screen, workbook window is slightly smaller than available space.
2	Application window size and position are set by the Pos= statement in EXCEL5.INI, workbook window fills available space below toolbars.
3	Application window size and position are set by the Pos= statement in EXCEL5.INI, workbook window is slightly smaller than available space.

When the application window is not maximized, the Pos= statement sets the size and position of the window. The first two coordinates set the distance in points (1 point = 1/72 inch) from the left and top of the screen to the top left corner of the window. The second pair of coordinates sets the size of the window, in points.

Specifying the Transition Menu or Help Key

The MenuKey= statement indicates the ASCII value corresponding to the character used to invoke Microsoft Excel menus or help. The default key is the slash (/) key. For example, if you changed the menu key in the Transition tab of the Tools/Options command to the backslash (\) key, the MenuKey= statement recorded in EXCEL5.INI would be

```
MenuKey=92
```

Specifying Options in Help for Lotus 1-2-3 Users

There are two statements, G1Dft-DemoSpeed= and G1Dft-HelpType=, that correspond to options in the Help for Lotus 1-2-3 Users dialog box. The G1Dft-HelpType= statement indicates whether you want Help for Lotus 1-2-3 Users to display a set of instructions (0) or give a demonstration (1) for the typed-in Lotus 1-2-3 commands.

The G1Dft-DemoSpeed= statement controls the speed of the demonstration when 1 (Demo) is indicated as the G1Dft-HelpType= option. This can be a number from 1 to 5, where 1 is slow and 5 is fast.

Specifying a User Name

With the USER= statement, you can enter a user name for your copy of Microsoft Excel. Then, if you are using a shared document and someone else on the network tries to open it, a message is displayed along with the specified user name.

Specifying Automatic Formatting Options

With the AutoFormat= and AutoFormat Options= lines, you can specify a particular default formatting choice to be used when the AutoFormat tool is clicked. For the AutoFormat= line, type a number to specify the format you want. The formats are numbered 1 through 14 according to the order in which they appear in the list in the AutoFormat dialog box.

The AutoFormat Options= line controls which formatting attributes are applied for the format you specified in the AutoFormat= line. The formatting attributes correspond to the options in the AutoFormat dialog box. The values for the formatting attributes are shown in the following table.

AutoFormat Options=	Indicates
1	Number
2	Font
4	Alignment

AutoFormat Options=	Indicates
8	Border
16	Patterns
32	Width/Height

For example, enter AutoFormat Options=10 to specify that just the font and border properties of a format are applied. The number 10 is the sum of 2 (font) and 8 (border). The default value for AutoFormat Options is 63, the sum of all of the numbers, indicating that all of the formatting properties are applied.

Specifying an Alternate Startup Directory

The AltStartup= statement allows you to specify an alternate directory in which to locate files you want to open each time you start Microsoft Excel. When you start Microsoft Excel, files located in the XLSTART directory are loaded automatically, followed by files located in the alternate startup directory. The General tab of the Tools/Options command lets you modify this statement.

Specifying Whether to Run the Online Tutorial at First Startup

Normally, when you start Microsoft Excel for the first time, the online tutorial "Introducing Microsoft Excel" is run automatically. (This is the same tutorial that is run when you choose the Introducing Microsoft Excel command from the Help menu.) This occurs when the Basics= statement is set to 0. After the first startup, the Basics= statement is set to 1 and the tutorial is no longer run at startup. If you reset this to 0, the tutorial will run the next time Microsoft Excel is started, after which it will again be reset to 1.

Specifying the CBT Location

The CBTLOCATION= statement specifies the full path to the CBT (Computer-Based Training) file.

Specifying the Windows Code Page

The optional statement, WinCodePage= specifies the Windows code page. The default is WinCodePage=1252 (or omitted). This value may be different in foreign Windows versions (for example, 1250 for East European Windows). The WinCodePage= statement is directly copied by the Microsoft Excel Setup program from the [Boot] section in the SYSTEM.INI file. WinCodePage is written into the CODEPAGE record of BIFF files, so that they can be loaded correctly under different environments.

Setting the Most-Recently Used Functions List

The MRUFuncs= statement specifies the functions that appear in the most-recently used list in the Function Wizard. In the EXCEL5.ini file, they appear in the order they were used. In the Function Wizard, they appear in alphabetical order. The complete list of function numbers appears in the XLCALL.H file in the INCLUDE directory on the sample disk. For example, function number 6 is the MIN function (xlfMin in XLCALL.H).

Setting the Number of Sheets in New Workbooks

The DefSheets= statement specifies the number of new worksheets in each new workbook. For example, if DefSheets=1 when you create a new workbook, the new workbook will contain one worksheet. You can set this option from the General tab of the Tools/Options command.

Setting the Default Chart Format

The Default Chart= statement specifies the default chart format. You can set this option from the Chart tab of the Tools/Options command.

Setting DDE Advise Format Retention

If the CFDDELink option is set to 1, Microsoft Excel remembers the last clipboard format used for a successful DDE Advise operation; this is used to reduce the time required for future Advise cycles.

Setting Other EXCEL5.INI Options

You can set the following options with the Options3= line in the EXCEL5.INI file.

Options3=	Indicates
0	Alternate menu key on
2	Alternate navigation keys on
4	Lotus 1-2-3 help on
8	Cell note indicators off
32	Macros are saved in the Personal Macro Workbook
16384	Gridlines in new sheets off

For example, you can enter

```
Options3=8
```

to automatically turn off cell note indicators each time you start Microsoft Excel. To specify more than one of these options, add the numbers for the options you want. For example, Options3=6 turns on both alternate navigation keys (2) and Lotus 1-2-3 Help (4).

The Options= line in the EXCEL5.INI file sets the following options:

Options=	Indicates
1	Show scroll bars
2	Show formula bar
4	Show status bar
16	Use A1-style references
64	DDE is enabled
bits 7 and 8	Apple Macintosh command underlines

The Options5= line in the EXCEL5.INI file sets the following options:

Options=	Indicates
bit 0	Tip Wizard is on
bit 1	Prompt for Summary Info
bit 2	Editing directly in cells is not allowed
bit 3	Status bar is visible in full-screen mode
bit 4	Formula bar is visible in full-screen mode
bit 5	Full-screen mode
bit 6	Most-recently used file list is not displayed
bit 7	Cut, copy, and sort objects with cells
bit 8	Tool tips off
bit 9	Small toolbar buttons
bit 10	Toolbar auto-sensing
bit 11	Do not move to next cell after Enter key is pressed
bit 12	Do not warn before drag-drop copy or paste
bit 13	Use black and white toolbar buttons
bit 14	Ask to update automatic links

The [Spell Checker] Section

Following is an example of the [Spell Checker] section.

```
[Spell Checker]
Speller=Spelling 1033,0
Custom Dict 1=C:\WIN3\MSAPPS\PROOF\CUSTOM.DIC
Ignore Caps=0
Suggest Always=1
```

Statement	Description
Speller=Spelling 1033,0	Cross-references the Speller= section of the WIN.INI file. The number 1033 is a country code and the 0 refers to the dictionary type (see the tables later in this section).
Custom Dict 1=	Specifies the name and location of custom dictionaries you want to use with Microsoft Excel. You can specify additional custom dictionaries by sequentially numbering additional entries, such as Custom Dict 2=, and so on.
Ignore Caps=	Uses a Boolean value (0,1) to indicate the state of the Ignore Caps check box in the Spell Check dialog box.
Suggest Always=	Uses a Boolean value (0,1) to indicate the state of the Suggest check box in the Spell Check dialog box.

Note Although you can specify the full path for each of several custom dictionaries using *Custom Dict n=* statements, all custom dictionaries must be placed in the \MSAPPS\PROOF subdirectory of your WINDOWS directory.

The Speller=Spelling 1033,0 statement includes two arguments, Country Code and Dictionary Type. Country Code specifies the proper spelling tool to use with the corresponding language version of Microsoft Excel. The statement cross-references the WIN.INI file so that you can use different language versions of various software packages on the same computer without conflicts, as long as you have the necessary versions of the speller DLL installed and referenced in WIN.INI. The following table shows the various Country Codes.

Country Code	Language
1030	Danish
1031	German
1033	U.S. English
1034	Spanish
1036	French
1040	Italian
1043	Dutch
1044	Norwegian
1054	Swedish
2057	British English
2070	Portuguese
3081	Australian English

The Dictionary Type argument refers to five possible types of dictionaries that can be used by the speller. Microsoft Excel always uses type 0 (Normal). The following table shows the five Dictionary Types.

Dictionary Type	Description
0	Normal
1	Concise (subset of Normal)
2	Complete (includes Medical and Legal)
3	Medical
4	Legal

Defining Custom Menus and Custom Commands

You can use the [Init Menus] and [Init Commands] sections to define custom menus and commands. These custom menus and commands appear every time you start Microsoft Excel and enable you to load add-in macro sheets or standard macro sheets after you choose the custom command.

Note The Add-In Manager (the Add-Ins command on the Tools menu) reads and writes statements in both the [Init Menus] and [Init Commands] sections.

The [Init Menus] Section

The syntax for the [Init Menus] section is as follows:

```
[Init Menus]
<Keyword>=<menu_bar_num>,<menu_name>,<menu_position>
```

Argument	Description
<keyword>	A unique keyword, such as Custom1, that Microsoft Windows uses to identify menus added by the EXCEL5.INI file.
<menu_bar_num>	The number of the built-in menu bar to which you want to add the menu or command.
<menu_name>	The name of the new menu.
<menu_position>	The position of the new menu on the menu bar. This may be the name of the menu after which you want to place the new menu or a number indicating the menu's position from the left of the menu bar.

The following example shows how EXCEL5.INI specifies a custom menu to be added to the right of the Window menu.

```
[Init Menus]
Custom1=1,Work,Window
```

The [Init Commands] Section

The syntax for the [Init Commands] section is as follows:

```
[Init Commands]
<Keyword>=<menu_bar_num>,<menu_name>,<command_name>,<macro>,
<command_position>,<macro_key>,<status_text>,<help_reference>
```

Argument	Description
<keyword>	A unique keyword, such as Scenario, that Microsoft Windows uses to identify commands added by an INI file.
<menu_bar_num>	The number of the built-in menu bar to which you want to add the command.
<menu_name>	The name of the new menu.
<command_name>	The name of the new command.
<macro>	A reference to a macro on an add-in workbook. Choosing the command opens the add-in and runs the specified macro. This macro should delete the command created by EXCEL5.INI and replace it with a command that runs a macro that performs actions associated with the command.
<command_position>	The position of the command on the menu. This may be the name of the command after which you want to place the new command or a number indicating the command's position on the menu. If omitted, the command appears at the end of the menu.
<macro_key>	The key assigned to the macro, if any.
<status_text>	A message to be displayed in the status bar when the command is selected.
<help_reference>	The filename and topic number for a custom Help topic relating to the command.

The following example shows how EXCEL5.INI specifies two commands to be added to built-in menu bar number 1.

```
[Init Commands]
views=1, Window, &View...,'C:\EXCEL\LIBRARY\VIEWS.XLA'!STUB,-,,
Show or define a named view,EXCELHLP.HLP!1730
solver=1, Formula, Sol&ver...,'C:\EXCEL\LIBRARY\SOLVER\SOLVER.XLA'!STUB
,,,Find solution to worksheet model,EXCELHLP.HLP!1830
```

The [Recent File List] Section

The [Recent File List] section corresponds to the list of the four most recently used files at the bottom of the File menu. This list changes each time the user quits Microsoft Excel. The following is an example of the [Recent File List] section.

```
[Recent File List]
File1=C:\ACCTG\CLOSING.XLW
File2=C:\MONTHLY\JANSALES.WK3
File3=C:\ACCTG\SCRATCH.XLS
File4=C:\EXCEL\AMORT.XLS
```

The [Delete Commands] Section

In the [Delete Commands] section of your EXCEL5.INI file, you can delete built-in Microsoft Excel commands. The syntax of the line to delete commands is:

```
<Keyword>=<menu_bar_num>,<menu_name>,<command_position>
```

The definitions of <keyword>, <menu_bar_num>, <menu_name>, and <command_position> are the same as those given in the preceding [Init Commands] section.

Caution Don't delete the Exit command on the File menu unless you've included another way to quit Microsoft Excel!

Note The Add-In Manager (the Add-Ins command on the Tools menu) reads and writes statements in the [Delete Commands] section.

The [WK? Settings] Section

This section contains statements that control settings for opening and saving Lotus 1-2-3 files. Following is an example of the [WK? Settings] section:

```
[WK? Settings]
WYSIWYG_Save=1
Load_Chart_Wnd=1
AFE=2
Monospace=1
Gridlines=0
```

Statement	Description
WYSIWYG_Save=	Controls whether an FMT or FM3 formatting file is saved along with a Lotus 1-2-3 worksheet.
Load_Chart_Wnd=	Controls whether Lotus 1-2-3 graphs are converted into Microsoft Excel charts.
Monospace=	Controls whether Lotus 1-2-3 files are displayed in Microsoft Excel using a monospaced font (10-point Courier). If Monospace=0, then the Normal style is used.

Statement	Description
Gridlines=	Controls the on-screen display of gridlines when a Lotus 1-2-3 worksheet is opened.
AFE=	Controls whether Transition Formula Entry (AFE) is turned on. A value of 2 is used as the default, indicating that AFE is turned on only if a macro name exists on the Lotus 1-2-3 worksheet. Otherwise, a value of 1 causes AFE to always be turned on, while a value of 0 causes AFE to be never turned on.

The [Line Print] Section

Following is an example of the [Line Print] section.

```
[Line Print]
Options=2
LeftMarg=4
RightMarg=76
TopMarg=2
BotMarg=2
PgLen=66
Setup=
```

This section controls settings used in Lotus 1-2-3 macro line printing. These settings are defined using the various Lotus 1-2-3 Worksheet Global Default Printer (/wgdp) commands and are updated in EXCEL5.INI whenever Microsoft Excel encounters a Lotus 1-2-3 Worksheet Global Default Update (/wgdu) command.

The LeftMarg=, RightMarg=, TopMarg=, and BotMarg= statements control the respective margin settings. The values following LeftMarg= and RightMarg= refer to numbers of characters. While these two values can be from 0 to 1000, a standard page is 80 characters wide. The values following TopMarg= and BotMarg= refer to numbers of lines. While these two values can be from 0 to 240, standard 11-inch paper can accommodate a maximum of 66 lines, as indicated by the sample PgLen= statement.

The Setup= statement is equivalent to the Lotus 1-2-3 Worksheet Global Default Printer Settings (/wgdps) command and specifies the printer setup string.

The Options= statement controls four global settings using an 8-bit binary number entered in decimal format. Each bit is either 0, corresponding to N (no); or 1, corresponding to Y (yes). The following table lists the values used with the Options= statement.

Bit	Lotus 1-2-3 /wgdp command
0	Wait
1	Formatted

Bit	Lotus 1-2-3 /wgdp command
2	AutoLf
3	Port (0 through 7)
4	(Used for port)
5	(Used for port)

The best way to determine the appropriate decimal number to use with the Options= statement is to construct the binary number first and then convert it to a decimal value. The default value is Options=2—or, in binary, 0000 0010—meaning that bit 1 is set to the value 1 (the Formatted option set to Y) while all others are set to zero (N). For example, the Options= entry that is written to EXCEL.INI when bits 0, 1, and 2 are set to 1 (0000 0111) is the decimal value 7, meaning that the Wait, Formatted, and AutoLf options are set to Y.

The three bits (3, 4, and 5) that are devoted to the port indicate the setting used by Lotus 1-2-3 to specify the hardware port to be used for printing. With Microsoft Excel, this is interpreted as a logical port. The default port setting is LPT1:, meaning that bits 3, 4, and 5 are all set to zero. The following table shows the binary bit and port settings.

Binary value (bits 3, 4, and 5)	Port
xx00 0xxx	LPT1:
xx00 1xxx	COM1:
xx01 0xxx	LPT2:
xx01 1xxx	COM2:
xx10 0xxx	LPT1:
xx10 1xxx	LPT2:
xx11 0xxx	LPT3:
xx11 1xxx	LPT4:

Note that in the preceding table, LPT1: and LPT2: are each represented twice. Either combination of bits can be used with equivalent results.

The actual decimal number entered in the Options= statement depends on the combination of all the values in the preceding table. For example, if both the Formatted and AutoLf settings are turned on (bits 1 and 2 set to 1), and COM2: is the specified port (bits 3 and 4 set to 1), the statement *Options=30* is written to the [Line Print] section, which is equivalent to the binary number 0001 1110.

Note To assist you in translations between binary and decimal numbers, you can use the BIN2DEC and DEC2BIN add-in functions that are part of the Analysis ToolPak that is shipped with Microsoft Excel 5.0. To load these functions, open the ADDINFNS.XLA macro sheet, located in the LIBRARY\ANALYSIS subdirectory of the directory where Microsoft Excel is installed. On the Macintosh, this add-in macro sheet is called Analysis Functions and is located in the Macro Library:Analysis Tools folder.

The [Converters] Section

This section contains the description and DLL (code resource) location of external file converters such as the Microsoft Multiplan® converter that is shipped with Microsoft Excel. For more information about file converters, see Appendix D, "File Converter API" which begins on page 413. For information about the [Converters] section, see "Exposing the Converter to Microsoft Excel" on page 416.

Specifying Settings with Microsoft Windows NT

With Microsoft Windows NT, Microsoft Excel stores settings in the registry. Microsoft Excel creates a key called 5.0 under the HKEY_CURRENT_USER key, as shown in the following illustration:

```
HKEY_CURRENT_USER\
    Software\
        Microsoft\
            Excel\
                5.0\
```

Under the 5.0 key, Microsft Excel creates a key for each section in the EXCEL5.INI file. For example, the following key contains all of the settings found in the [Microsoft Excel] section of the EXCEL5.INI file:

```
HKEY_CURRENT_USER\Software\Microsoft\Excel\5.0\Microsoft Excel
```

Under each section key, the individual settings in the EXCEL5.INI file exist as key=value pairs. Integer-value settings have type REG_INT. All others have type REG_SZ.

Specifying Settings in Microsoft Excel for the Macintosh

The Macintosh counterpart to the EXCEL5.INI file is the Excel Settings (5) file. This file resides in the System Folder or, if you are running system software version 7.0, in the Preferences Folder in the System Folder. To make modifications to the

Excel Settings (5) file, you must use the ResEdit utility. ResEdit is available through Macintosh user groups or the Apple Programmers and Developers Association (APDA). The telephone numbers for the APDA are (800) 282-2732 (United States only) and (408) 562-3910.

The syntax of the statements used by the Excel Settings (5) file is the same as described for the EXCEL5.INI file, although the Macintosh file is not a text file. Some of the resources contained in the Excel Settings (5) file are presented in hexadecimal format. The Microsoft Excel Software Development Kit includes a resource template called Settings Template to aid in the modification of the hexadecimal resources in this file.

The Excel Settings (5) file contains the sections GRID, INT, and STR, each of which contains resources that correspond to sections described in the discussion of the EXCEL5.INI file earlier in this appendix.

The STR Section

The resources in the STR section can be modified using the templates included with ResEdit. For example, the following illustration shows the window that appears when you double-click the icon representing the STR section.

ID	Size	Name
766	100	"__ICAdd-in Manager"
971	5	"XLINSTALL"
2976	32	"Open1"
4313	135	"__ICSolver Add-in"
4519	41	"Open"
10166	18	"User Dictionary"
10311	112	"__ICReport Manager"
11036	58	"Spelling"
19920	36	"Open3"
21440	101	"__ICView Manager"
21754	34	"Open2"
26352	41	"Open4"
28685	53	"Open5"
30139	40	"Open7"
30732	49	"Open6"
31385	128	"__ICAnalysis Tools"
31572	35	"Open8"
31834	25	"Main Dictionary"
32086	125	"__ICScenario Manager"

STRs from Excel Settings (4)

The resources listed in the STR section correspond to statements listed in the [Microsoft Excel], [Init Commands], [Delete Commands], [Recent File List], and [Spell Checker] sections of EXCEL5.INI. Resources preceded by "IC" are Init Commands, and resources preceded by "DC" are Delete Commands. Other resources are more easily deciphered, such as "Open1" "File1" and "Spelling," which correspond to Open=, File1= and Spelling= statements.

You can easily edit resources listed in the STR section by double-clicking on them. For example, the following figure shows the window that appears when you double-click on the resource named "__ICSolver Add-in."

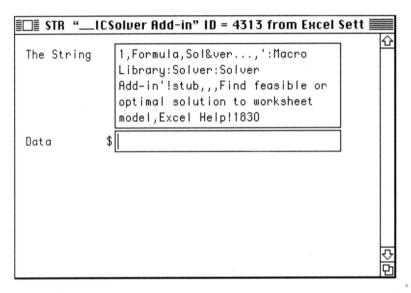

Note that the format of the string is essentially the same as that of the equivalent EXCEL5.INI statement. For more information, see "The [Init Commands] Section" on page 390.

The INT Section

While ResEdit includes a template that allows you to view and edit the contents of the STR section of the Excel Settings (5) file, a similar template is not included with ResEdit to convert the hexadecimal format of the INT section into easily understandable alphanumeric strings. For this reason, the Microsoft Excel Developer's Kit includes a file called Settings Template, which allows you to easily edit the resources listed in the INT section.

Note Your Excel Settings (5) file may not have an INT section, depending on whether you have changed certain settings in your copy of Microsoft Excel.

▶ **To Install the Settings Template**

1. Start ResEdit.

2. In ResEdit, open both the Excel Settings (5) and Settings Template files.

3. Copy the resource called TMPL from the Settings Template file.

4. Paste the TMPL resource into the Excel Settings (5) file.

5. Close the Settings Template file.

6. Save the Excel Settings (5) file.

From now on, whenever you open the Excel Settings (5) file with ResEdit and attempt to modify any of the resources in the INT section, you'll be able to edit using decimal instead of hexadecimal code.

The ALIS Section (System 7.0 Only)

An alias is a resource of the ALIS type that stores information about a particular file. It contains the filename and significant information about the file. An alias is expanded into an actual path by Microsoft Excel calling the Alias Manager. These aliases are stored in the ALIS section of the Excel Settings (5) file.

Microsoft Excel uses the following aliases, each of which is followed in parentheses by the resource ID:

Recently-Used Files (0-3)

These are aliases for the Most Recently Used file list (MRU). When Microsoft Excel saves a file, an alias is created for it.

Excel Installation (128)

This alias is written during Setup and refers to the folder where Microsoft Excel resides. All the entries in the String portion of the Excel Settings (5) file are relative (for example, ":Macro Library:Add-In Manager"), and this alias is used to expand those paths completely. This solves a problem that would otherwise be created by dragging the program icon to the desktop, causing the installable commands to become disabled due to the changed path.

Spelling (511)

This alias is created the first time the Speller is run. Microsoft Excel makes this alias and uses it from then on to locate the Spelling program and its dictionaries.

Excel Help (1967)

This is the alias for the Microsoft Excel Help file. It is created the first time Help is run. It refers to the Help file that is in the Microsoft Excel folder.

Microsoft Help (1968)

This alias is created the first time Help is run. It refers to the Help program that Microsoft Excel installs in the System Folder.

The GRID Section

The GRID section simply acts as a temporary storage space for the Microsoft Excel Setup program and therefore does not require modifications.

APPENDIX C

Displaying Custom Help

With Microsoft Excel, you can display Help to provide users with information about the following custom items:

- Dialog boxes
- Commands
- Menus
- Toolbar buttons
- Alert messages displayed in the course of running a macro

Your Help can include powerful and visually interesting features, such as pop-up windows, graphics, the ability to jump from one topic to another, *hypergraphics* (graphics with one or more hot spots assigned to them), and much more.

To create and compile Help files, you will need the Microsoft Windows Help Compiler version 3.1 or greater. The Help compiler creates Help files for both Windows and Apple Macintosh applications. If you're using Microsoft Excel for the Macintosh, you will first create and compile the source files on a Microsoft Windows-compatible computer and then transfer the compiled files to the Macintosh.

Important Some incompatibilities may arise when using Microsoft Windows Help files with Microsoft Help for the Macintosh. Microsoft Help for the Macintosh supports a subset of the features supported by the Microsoft Windows Help Compiler. Microsoft Corporation does not guarantee Macintosh compatibility of Windows Help files, so you should fully test any compiled Help file before assuming it will work properly on the Macintosh.

The Microsoft Windows Help Compiler (HC31.EXE) creates Help files; it does not display them. To display Help files, you must use one of the two Help *viewers*—Microsoft Windows Help (WINHELP.EXE) or Microsoft Help for the Macintosh, depending on the operating environment in which your Help will be used.

Microsoft Windows Help is included with Microsoft Windows and is usually located in your WINDOWS directory.

Microsoft Help for the Macintosh is included with Microsoft Excel and is usually located in the SYSTEM:EXTENSIONS:MICROSOFT:HELP Folder. You must purchase the Help compiler separately. For information about obtaining the Help compiler, see "Getting More Information about the Microsoft Windows Help Compiler" on page 410.

Note If you plan to use your custom Help system only with Microsoft Excel for the Macintosh, and if your system will not need any advanced features, then you do not need the Help compiler. For more information, see "Working with Help Topics in Plain Text Files" on page 407.

Reviewing How to Create Help Topics

This appendix explains how to display custom Help topics with Microsoft Excel, not how to create and compile Help topics in general. If you need to review basic procedures for creating Help topics, you can examine the example Help files described in the following table. The example files are in the HELP subdirectory of the directory in which you installed the Microsoft Excel Developer's Kit. If you need more detailed information about creating Help topics or obtaining the Help compiler, see "Getting More Information About the Microsoft Windows Help Compiler" on page 410.

Filename	Description
EXAMPLE.HLP	A compiled Help file that explains how to add jumps, graphics, and hypergraphics to your topics and how to use WinHelp macros to add and remove buttons. To display the Help file, see the instructions following this table.
EXAMPLE.DOC	A Microsoft Word for Windows document that contains the source text and *control codes* for the Help topics in EXAMPLE.HLP. Control codes determine how the user can move around the Help system.
EXAMPLE.RTF	The same file as EXAMPLE.DOC, but saved in rich text format (RTF).

Filename	Description
EXAMPLE.HPJ	The Help *project file* used to create EXAMPLE.HLP. The Help project file provides information that the Help compiler needs to build the final Help file.
DLG.SHG	A segmented hypergraphics bitmap file used in EXAMPLE.HLP.
ARROWRT.BMP, DLG.BMP, EXCEL.BMP, and PRESS.BMP	Bitmap files used in several topics in EXAMPLE.HLP.

▶ **To display the example Help file in Microsoft Windows Help**

- In Microsoft Windows File Manager, double-click the filename EXAMPLE.HLP.

▶ **To display the example Help file in Microsoft Help for the Macintosh**

1. In Microsoft Excel, start Help by pressing COMMAND+SHIFT+SLASH or the Help key.
2. From the File menu, choose Open.
3. Specify the path of EXAMPLE.HLP.
4. Double-click EXAMPLE.HLP.

Important Unlike Microsoft Windows Help, Microsoft Help for the Macintosh does not support all of the Help compiler's features. For a list of some of the unsupported features, see "Differences Between Help for Microsoft Windows and the Macintosh" on page 408. You should also check your Help compiler documentation.

Reviewing How to Create a Help System

After you've reviewed how to create Help topics, you're ready to create the Help system for your application in Microsoft Excel. The following list shows the general steps to create a Help system. For specific information about each step, see your Help compiler documentation.

▶ **To create a Help system**

1. After you create the custom commands, dialog boxes, and so on, in Microsoft Excel, gather information for the corresponding custom Help topics.
2. Plan the Help system, deciding which items will need custom Help, what type of Help to provide, how to structure your Help files, and how to structure Help topics within each file.

3. Using your word processing program, write the text for the Help topics in the source files.

4. Enter all required control codes into the source files.

5. Save the source files in rich text format (RTF).

6. Create a project file for the build.

   The *build* is the compiled Help file. Similarly, compiling Help is also called *building* Help in some documentation.

7. Compile the Help file.

8. If you're using Microsoft Excel for the Macintosh, transfer the compiled file from your Microsoft Windows-compatible computer to the Macintosh.

9. Start Microsoft Excel, run your custom application, and try to display custom Help topics.

The next section explains how to display Help topics with Microsoft Excel.

The Help compiler requires certain settings in the Help project file and enough memory and disk space to compile the files you specify. If you want to make sure that everything is set correctly and that the Help compiler is ready to compile Help files, you can compile the example Help files described in the table on page 400.

▶ **To compile the example Help files**

1. Create a temporary directory on your disk.

2. Switch to the temporary directory.

3. Copy all the files listed in the table on page 400, except EXAMPLE.HLP, to the temporary directory.

4. Run the Help compiler using the HC31 command:

   HC31 EXAMPLE.HPJ

   The compiler should create a new file, EXAMPLE.HLP, in the temporary directory. If you have problems, make sure that the directory containing the Help compiler is included in the MS-DOS path. You may also want to try compiling the file when Microsoft Windows is not running (that is, when you're not working in an MS-DOS shell).

Displaying Help Topics with Microsoft Excel

In Microsoft Windows, Help files are displayed using Microsoft Windows Help (WINHELP.EXE), usually located in the WINDOWS directory. On the Macintosh, Help files are displayed using Microsoft Help, usually located in the SYSTEM:EXTENSIONS:MICROSOFT:HELP Folder. Microsoft Windows Help displays only files that have been compiled by the Microsoft Windows Help Compiler. Microsoft Help for the Macintosh displays both compiled files and plain text files.

To display a Help topic in Microsoft Excel, use one of the following:

- The Visual Basic Help method or the HELP macro function
- The Visual Basic MsgBox function or the ALERT macro function
- Help for custom commands and toolbar buttons
- Help for dialog boxes

Displaying Help Topics with the Help method and HELP Macro Function

When you run the Help method in your Visual Basic code, or the HELP macro function in a macro sheet, Microsoft Excel displays the specified Help topic. The Visual Basic Help method has the following syntax:

```
Application.Help "filename", topic_number
```

Here, *filename* is the name of the file containing the topic and can include the full path, and *topic_number* identifies the topic within the Help file. For compiled Help files, *topic_number* is the number you specify in the [MAP] section of the Help project file. For text files, *topic_number* is the number following the initial asterisk (*). The [MAP] section is described on page 406. The initial asterisk is described on page 407.

For example, in Microsoft Excel for Windows, you might use the following Visual Basic code to display Help topic number 103.

```
Application.Help "C:\REPORTS\REPORTS.HLP", 103
```

In Microsoft Excel for the Macintosh, you might use this Visual Basic code to display the same topic.

```
Application.Help "Hard Disk:Reports:Reports Help", 103
```

The HELP macro function has the following syntax:

```
HELP(help_ref)
```

Help_ref is a reference to a topic in a Help file, in the following form:

```
"filename!topic_number"
```

For example, in Microsoft Excel for Windows, you might use the following macro function to display Help topic number 104:

```
=HELP("C:\REPORTS\REPORTS.HLP!104")
```

In Microsoft Excel for the Macintosh, you might use:

```
=HELP("Hard Disk:Reports:Reports Help!104")
```

Displaying Help Topics with the MsgBox Function and ALERT Macro Function

To display Help using the Visual Basic MsgBox function, you must include in its list of arguments a Help file name and topic number. This causes a Help button to be displayed in the message box, and specifies which Help topic will be displayed when the Help button is chosen. For example, in Microsoft Excel for Windows, enter:

```
MsgBox("Delete this item?",vbOKCancel,,"REPORTS.HLP",501)
```

In Microsoft Excel for the Macintosh, enter:

```
MsgBox("Delete this item?",vbOKCancel,,"Reports Help",501)
```

To display Help using the ALERT macro function, enter a Help reference as the third argument. For example, in Microsoft Excel for Windows, enter:

```
=ALERT("Delete this item?",1,"REPORTS.HLP!501")
```

In Microsoft Excel for the Macintosh, enter:

```
=ALERT("Delete this item?",1,"Reports Help!501")
```

Help for Custom Commands and Toolbar Buttons

▶ **To specify a Help topic for a custom command or toolbar button:**

1. From the Tools menu, choose Macro.

2. Select the name of a macro that you have attached to a custom command or toolbar button.

3. Choose the Options button.

4. In the Help File Name box, enter the name of the file that contains the Help topic you wish to display.

5. In the Help Context ID box, enter the topic number of the Help topic you wish to display.

6. Choose the OK button.

7. Choose the Close button.

The topic is displayed by pressing SHIFT+F1 (in Microsoft Excel for Windows) or COMMAND+SHIFT+SLASH or the Help key (in Microsoft Excel for the Macintosh) and then choosing the command from its menu or clicking the tool.

If you are using Microsoft Excel 4.0 macros to create custom commands or toolbar buttons, then you can also specify Help topics within a command table. To specify a Help topic for a command, enter a Help reference in the fifth column of the command table; for a toolbar button, enter the reference in the eighth column. A Help reference has the following syntax:

filename!topic_number

Quotation marks are not necessary because the Help reference is entered as text in a cell.

Help references for custom commands are placed in the fifth column of the definition table.

	E	F	G	H	I
4	**Menu Table**				
5	Name	Command		Status Message	Custom Help
6	mg00r.ProjWorksheetMenu				
7	&Report				
8	&View...	report.xlalmcs14.ViewItemCmd		View a report item	XLREPORT.HLPI400
9	&Edit... (Copy To Disk)	report.xlalmcs15.CopyItemCmd		Copy a report item to the hard drive for editing	XLREPORT.HLPI410
10	&Update...	report.xlalmcs25.UpdateItemCmd		Update a modified report item from a local cop	XLREPORT.HLPI420
11	-				
12	Send &Comments...	report.xlalmcs28.SendMailCmd		Send comments mail to users associated with	XLREPORT.HLPI430
13	-				
14	&Help	report.xlalmcs39.MenuHelpCmd		Display help on the Feature Management Syst	XLREPORT.HLPI200
15	-				
16	C&lean up Local Files	report.xlalmcs38.FlushCacheCmd		Removes previously viewed documents from t	XLREPORT.HLPI450
17	Clo&se Add-in...	report.xlalmcs32.CloseAddinCmd		Close the custom Report add-in	XLREPORT.HLPI460

Help references for custom tools are placed in the eighth column of the definition table.

	E	F	G	H	I	J	K	L
50	UDTs							
51	Tool	Macro	Down	Enabled	Face	Status Message	Balloon Help	Custom Help
52	30	report.xlalmcs50.MultFieldsTool	FALSE	TRUE		Multiplies the sel		XLREPORT.HLPI500

Help for Custom Dialog Boxes

If you are using Visual Basic to create custom dialog boxes, you can use the HelpButton property of buttons in combination with the Help method of the Application object to display Help for dialog boxes.

Each button in a dialog box has a HelpButton property. If the HelpButton property of any button is True, then pressing F1 in Microsoft Excel for Windows (or COMMAND+SLASH in Microsoft Excel for the Macintosh) when the dialog box is displayed causes Microsoft Excel to respond as if you had chosen the button. Microsoft Excel then runs the Visual Basic code attached to the button.

If you want the attached Visual Basic code to display a Help topic, use the Help method of the Application object as described previously. Only one button in a dialog box can have its HelpButton property set to True, so you usually create a button exclusively for displaying Help, with a caption that reads "Help." If no button has its HelpButton property set to True, pressing F1 does nothing.

If you are using Microsoft Excel 4.0 macros to create custom dialog boxes, then you can also specify Help topics within a command table. To display the Help topic for a dialog box, use the custom Help button. Place the Help reference in the first cell of the table.

Help references for dialog boxes are placed in the first cell of the definition table.

	K	L	M	N	O	P	Q
4	UDDs						
5	Item Num	X	Y	Width	Height	Text	Initial Value/Result
6	mg00r.SelectReportDocDialog						
7	XLREPORT.HLP!670			328	98	Select Item Document Type	3
8	14	10	6	200	85	Document Type:	
9	11						1
10	12					&Report Item	
11	12					&TRD	
12	12					Report &Change Log	
13	12					&Test Script	
14	1	224	10	88		OK	
15	2	224	36	88		Cancel	
16	24	224	70	88		Help	

Mapping Context Strings to Topic Numbers in Compiled Help Files

When you create source files for custom Help, you must assign a context string to each Help topic. However, when you specify a help topic to be displayed using any of the methods discussed in this chapter, you must identify the topic using a topic number, not a context string. To map context strings to topic numbers, include a [MAP] section in the Help project file. For more information about the project file, see your Help compiler documentation.

For example, if you have a custom Help file for making reports, with three topics identified by the context strings, Using_Menus, Retrieve_Report_Command, and Open_Any_Command, you might include the following section in the Help project file:

```
[MAP]
Using_Menus 101
Retrieve_Report_Command 102
Open_Any_Command 104
```

To display Help for the Open_Any_Command topic in Microsoft Excel for Windows, you might use the following Visual Basic code.

```
Application.Help "C:\REPORTS\REPORTS.HLP", 104
```

In Microsoft Excel for the Macintosh, you might use this Visual Basic code to display the same topic.

```
Application.Help "Hard Disk:Reports:Reports Help", 104
```

Working with Help Topics in Plain Text Files

This section applies only to Microsoft Excel for the Macintosh.

With text files, you can display simple text information in a Help window, but you cannot include the advanced features that the Help compiler provides. Microsoft Help for the Macintosh automatically switches between compiled Help files and plain text files, so you can use both types of files in your custom Help system.

In a text file, the first line of each Help topic starts with an asterisk and is followed by a space, a topic number, another space, and a short optional comment. The actual Help information begins on subsequent lines. A topic number can be any integer, and the topics don't have to be in consecutive order. You can create your Help topic in a Microsoft Excel worksheet as long as it is saved as text-only.

An asterisk indicates a new topic.

A unique topic number identifies each topic.

You may include an optional comment.

	A
1	* 101 Using the new menus
2	This worksheet automatically replaces
3	Microsoft Excel's menus with menus designed to
4	run our company's reporting system. You can
5	get help on any of the menu commands by
6	pressing Shift+F1 and selecting the command.
7	
8	* 102 Retrieve Report Command
9	The command allows you to open one of the
10	preformatted reports from the Reports
11	directory. This command will only open
12	file in that directory. To open more than one
13	file, use the Open Any command.
14	
15	* 105 Open Any Command

The Help text follows the line that contains the topic number.

You display the Help topics in plain text files in the same way that you display topics in compiled files.

Note When using custom Help, the Next and Previous buttons jump to the next or previous custom Help topics based on their order in the file, not on their topic numbers.

Differences Between Help for Microsoft Windows and the Macintosh

Microsoft Help for the Macintosh does not support all of the features that the Microsoft Windows Help Compiler provides. The following list shows some of the features that are supported by Microsoft Windows Help but not by Microsoft Help for the Macintosh:

- Embedded windows (displayed within the main Help window)
- Secondary windows (displayed next to or on top of the main Help window)
- Customizable menus and buttons in the main Help window
- Support for DLL/XCMD (*hooks* with which a Help file can access the code within a DLL)
- The Windows Help command language
- "Help on top" (the ability to keep the main Help window visible after the user switches back to Microsoft Excel)
- Some API messages (HELP_FORCEFILE, HELP_PARTIALKEY, and so on)

  For more information about API messages, see the description of the WinHelp function in your Help compiler documentation.

Some bitmaps or hypergraphics that are displayed correctly in Windows Help may not be displayed correctly on the Macintosh. To include Macintosh-compatible bitmaps in your compiled Help files, use the Multi-Resolution Bitmap Compiler (MRBC.EXE), which is included with the *Microsoft Windows Help Authoring Guide.* This tool creates bitmap files that can be displayed in multiple resolutions.

▶ **To create Macintosh-compatible bitmaps**

1. Rename the bitmap files so that they have the extension ".MAC"
2. At the MS-DOS prompt, type MRBC /S filename.MAC

   The Multi-Resolution Bitmap Compiler creates a new file with the extension ".MRB." Use this bitmap file the same way you use any .BMP file. For more information, see the *Microsoft Windows Help Authoring Guide.*

If you want to use a resolution other than that of the Macintosh, use an extension beginning with one of the characters listed in the following table.

First character of extension	Resolution
M	Macintosh
8	8514

First character of extension	Resolution
V	VGA (default)
E	EGA
C	CGA

For hypergraphics, the Multi-Resolution Bitmap Compiler (MRBC) converts existing .SHG files into a particular resolution. With Hotspot Editor (SHED.EXE) version 3.5, you can also create the .SHG file in the resolution you want and avoid having to convert it later. The *Microsoft Windows Help Authoring Guide* also includes Hotspot Editor version 3.5. Normally, when the Hotspot Editor saves an existing bitmap in .SHG format, it records the display resolution in the .SHG file based on the resolution of the computer on which it is running (that is, Hotspot Editor ignores the resolution information stored in the original bitmap file).

Hotspot Editor version 3.5 has a switch so you can save the resolution information for a particular monitor. If you use this feature, you do not have to compile hypergraphics with MRBC to make them appear correctly on different displays, including Macintosh displays.

To save resolution information in the hypergraphic, add this line to the SHED.INI file, usually located in your WINDOWS directory:

[Hotspot Editor]

ResBasedOnExt=1

This entry tells Hotspot Editor to save .SHG files with the resolution information of a specific monitor. The monitor type saved depends upon the first letter of the extension of the original bitmap filename, as when using MRBC.

If you compile your bitmaps with MRBC version 1.1, you do not have to author hypergraphics on different machines, and you don't have to use the ResBasedOnExt switch because MRBC will overwrite the resolution information in the graphic.

Other Sample Files and Utilities

In addition to the example Help files, the HELP directory also contains sample files for calling Help from a dynamic link library (DLL) or a stand-alone DLL (XLL) and utilities to make creating and displaying Help topics easier.

Calling Help from a DLL or XLL

- HELPCALL.C contains the C source code for CallHelp, a function that could be used in a DLL or XLL to call Microsoft Windows Help, using the Windows API WinHelp function. CallHelp only displays a Help topic, but you can expand it to use the WinHelp API to more fully control Microsoft Help.

- HELPCALL.DEF and MAKEFILE are files that, along with HELPCALL.C, you will need if you want to compile your own HELPCALL.DLL file. (You will also need the XLCALL.H and XLCALL.LIB files.)

- HELPCALL.DLL is the compiled DLL file.

- HELPCALL.XLM contains a two-line macro that calls the CallHelp function (defined in HELPCALL.C) in the compiled DLL. Use this macro to verify that the DLL works.

Also, from a DLL or XLL, you can use the xlfHelp function from the Microsoft Excel 5.0 API.

Creating Help Topics Automatically

JUMPS.DOC is the source text of a WordBasic macro that automates creating Help topics. The macro displays a dialog box prompting you for the footnote information (context string, search keywords, title, and so on), creates a skeleton topic, and inserts a page break for the next topic. To use the macro, copy the text into your own WinWord macro template.

Getting More Information About the Microsoft Windows Help Compiler

You can obtain the Microsoft Windows Help Compiler and information about how to use it from any of the following sources:

- *The Microsoft Windows Help Authoring Guide,* a CD-ROM product available through the Microsoft Software Developer Network. This comprehensive guide explains how to plan, design, and implement a complete Help system. All the major features of the Microsoft Windows Help Compiler are described in detail, and sample code is provided. The Help compiler is included with the guide. To obtain the *Microsoft Windows Help Authoring Guide,* contact your software vendor or Microsoft Corporation.

- The Microsoft Windows Software Development Kit. The Microsoft Windows SDK includes the Help compiler. The accompanying documentation assumes you know how to author Help using previous versions of the Help compiler. To obtain the Microsoft Windows SDK, contact your software vendor or Microsoft Corporation.

- Microsoft Visual Basic, Professional Edition. This version of Visual Basic includes the Help compiler and documentation explaining how to use it. The documentation is a condensed version of that found in the *Microsoft Windows Help Authoring Guide* but is thorough and should meet the needs of most users.

- Your software vendor may know about other products or publications that include the Help compiler or explain how to use it.

APPENDIX D

File Converter API

Microsoft Excel version 5.0 provides a new file converter application programming interface (API) with which you can write a custom input file converter. For example, the Microsoft Multiplan file converter that ships with Microsoft Excel uses the file converter API.

Although the file converter API is identical across operating environments, a converter is platform-specific, which means that it must be compiled into a 16-bit DLL for Windows, a code resource for the Macintosh, and a 32-bit DLL for Windows NT. For more information about developing DLLs and code resources, see "Creating DLL Files in C" on page 3, and "Creating Code Resource Files in C" on page 4.

This kit includes a sample file converter, UNDUMP.DLL, which converts a text file (.BD5) created by the BiffView utility. The sources and the compiled DLL are in the \SAMPLE\UNDUMP directory on the Windows disk that accompanies this book. The Undump project was prepared and tested with 16-bit Microsoft Windows version 3.1 using Microsoft Visual C++, version 1.5.

File Converter Background

This section describes the file converter user interface, file converter selection algorithm, file converter internals and error handling, and system registry settings that expose the converter to Microsoft Excel.

File Converter User Interface

File converters are seamlessly integrated into the Open dialog box (File menu). To expose the converter to the user, you add a filter option to the List Files of Type box in the Open dialog box. This additional option is created by a string in the EXCEL5.INI file (Excel Settings (5) file on the Macintosh). If you installed the Multiplan converter when you installed Microsoft Excel version 5.0, you can see the Microsoft Multiplan (*.*) filter option in the List Files of Type box in the Open dialog box.

If you did not install the Multiplan converter, you can run the Microsoft Excel setup program to add it. You can also add the option for the UNDUMP.DLL converter to the EXCEL5.INI or Excel Settings (5) file, as described in the following section, "Exposing the Converter to Microsoft Excel," on page 416.

File Converter Selection Algorithm

Microsoft Excel tries to detect the file format automatically when you open a file, as shown in the following pseudo-code:

```
For Each built-in file format except TEXT and CSV
    Test the first n bytes of the file until either a format is
        recognized or until all built-in formats have been tried
        (except TEXT and CSV)

If file format is still not recognized Then
    For each file format in InstallableInputConvertersList
        Tell input converter DLL to sniff the first n bytes of the
            file until either a format is recognized or all of the
            installable input converters have been tried

If file is still not recognized Then
    Assume the file is TEXT format and start the Text Import Wizard
```

You can force Microsoft Excel to try a particular file converter first by selecting the converter's filter option in the List Files of Type box. Microsoft Excel calls the appropriate file converter and then auto-detects only if the file converter does not recognize the file format.

In UNDUMP.C, the IsFormatOk function detects the file format by comparing the passed-in string to the string in the variable szBIFF5.

Inside the File Converter

After your converter has recognized the file format, Microsoft Excel calls the converter's initialization routine to give you an opportunity to do any necessary initialization. The initialization function in UNDUMP.C is called InitLoad.

After initialization, Microsoft Excel repeatedly calls your converter to get BIFF records until the converter returns an EOF record. Your code must provide the BIFF records in the format shown in Chapter 3, "File Format." Your code is also responsible for the actual conversion from the non-native data format to BIFF format.

The converter is called three times for each BIFF record: the first call returns the BIFF record type, the second call returns the number of bytes in the record data, and the third call returns the data. To see examples of these calls in UNDUMP.C, look for the following three functions: `RtNextRecord`, `CbNextRecord`, and `DataNextRecord`.

To help you write a robust converter, Microsoft Excel exposes a callback function that your converter should use for memory management (alloc and free, for example) and for file input/output (read n bytes, get file position, set file position, get file size, for example). For more information, see "Callback Function" on page 422.

You can compile a debug build of UNDUMP.DLL and then use the Visual C++ debugger to watch the entire conversion process. Undump is a very straightforward example of a converter, because there is a one-to-one correspondence between Undump "records" and BIFF records. The records can be processed sequentially, as they are read from the BiffView-created text file.

On the other hand, the Multiplan converter (MPconv) must read the entire Multiplan file before it can convert to BIFF records. Also, in 16-bit Windows, the largest heap block you can allocate is approximately 64K long, therefore MPconv has to break the input Multiplan file into 64K heap blocks before starting the conversion. The Multiplan converter processing can be described by the following pseudo-code:

```
Microsoft Excel calls MPconv to initialize
    For each heap block
        MPconv calls Microsoft Excel to allocate a heap block
            (buffer) for the next part of the file
        MPconv calls Microsoft Excel, instructing it to read part
            of the file into the heap block
    Next heap block
    MPconv does initial file conversion to construct the first
        BIFF record
MPconv returns TRUE

Loop
    Microsoft Excel requests BIFF record
        MPconv returns BIFF record
        MPconv generates next BIFF record
Until conversion is finished (return an EOF record)

MPconv calls Microsoft Excel to free the allocated buffers
Microsoft Excel closes the input file
```

Error Handling

If Microsoft Excel encounters an error during file conversion, it calls your converter before displaying an error to the user. This mechanism gives your code an opportunity to do last-minute cleanup (for example, freeing allocated buffers). Because Microsoft Excel provides the file input/output services, your code does not have to handle file cleanup. In UNDUMP.C, the error handler is the function `AbortLoad` (although there is no error handling in the program, just a short cleanup function).

Your converter can notify Microsoft Excel of a fatal error by returning the special BIFF record type rtNil, which is defined in the header file BIFF.H in the \SAMPLE\UNDUMP directory. This record causes Microsoft Excel to call your error handler and then stop the file load. The rtNil has no record data field.

Exposing the Converter to Microsoft Excel

You must edit the EXCEL5.INI file (the Excel Settings (5) file on the Macintosh, or the System Registry in Windows NT) to expose a converter to Microsoft Excel. When you choose the Open command from the File menu, Excel reads the [Converters] section of EXCEL5.INI (or equivalent) to build a list of installed converters.

Windows   In Microsoft Excel for Windows, the [Converters] section contains the following line when you install the Multiplan converter:

```
conv1=Microsoft Multiplan (*.*) ,C:\XL5\xlconvmp.dll,*.*
```

Each line in the [Converters] section has the following form:

```
<ConverterTag> = <Friendly description>, <DLL filename, including path>,
    <Search filter>
```

Token	Description
<ConverterTag>	A unique tag name in the [Converters] section; ignored by Microsoft Excel
<Friendly description>	The text that appears in the List Files of Type box in the Open dialog box (File menu)
<DLL filename, including path>	The filename and path of the converter DLL. If you omit the path, the DLL must be in the same directory as EXCEL.EXE.
<Search filter>	A file filter string, for example *.XL*

If you provide a setup program with your file converter, it should make the necessary changes to EXCEL5.INI.

Macintosh   On the Macintosh, file extensions (for example, .XLS) are replaced by one or more four-character file types (for example, XCEL). To add file converters to the Excel Preferences (5) file, you must use ResEdit to add a GRID resource. If a GRID resource named Converters does not exist, then create one. Each GRID resource is an array of words that are actually string resource IDs.

Each GRID resource has the following form:

```
<name that appears in drop-down>,"<full path to file converter>",
    <list of 4-letter file types separated by ;>
```

For example,

```
Undump BiffView Files,"HD80:Excel5:undump.res",lttr;XLS5
```

The "full path to file converter" token must contain the full path and filename of the converter code resource, and must be enclosed in quotes as shown. Quotes are optional for the other two tokens.

For more information about editing the Excel Preferences (5) file, see "Specifying Settings in Microsoft Excel for the Macintosh" on page 394

File Converter API Functions

This section describes the EFCP structure, the XlConverter function, and the callback function EfcCallBack.

The EFCP Structure

When Microsoft Excel calls the file converter, it passes a pointer to an EFCP data structure, which is defined in XLCONV.H as follows:

Windows

```
typedef struct _efcParam
    {
    long lcb;
    BYTE FAR *lprgb;
    FARPROC lpfn;
    } EFCP, FAR * LPEFCP;
```

Macintosh

```
typedef struct _efcParam
    {
    long lcb;
    unsigned char *lprgb;
    ProcPtr lpfn;
    } EFCP, * PEFCP;
```

Member	Description
lcb	Count of bytes
lprgb	Pointer to buffer
lpfn	Pointer to Microsoft Excel callback function

For more information about using this structure, see the following descriptions for the converter entry-point function and the callback function.

Converter Entry Point

The file converter should export a single function as its entry point:

Windows (16-bit)
```
short FAR PASCAL __export XlConverter(short iAction, LPEFCP lpefcp)
```

The __export keyword is required in Visual C++.

Macintosh
```
short PASCAL XlConverter(short iAction, LPEFCP lpefcp)
```

Windows NT
```
short __stdcall XlConverter(short iAction, LPEFCP lpefcp)
```

The lpefcp parameter is the pointer to the EFCP structure. The command ID, iAction, is the converter opcode. It has the following values defined in XLCONV.H:

Value	Description
iActionIsFormatOk	Return TRUE if the converter recognizes the file format
iActionInitLoad	Initialize the converter; return TRUE if successful
iActionRtNextRecord	Return the record type of the next BIFF record; the record types are defined in BIFF.H
iActionCbNextRecord	Return the number of bytes in the data field of the next BIFF record
iActionDataNextRecord	Return the data for the next BIFF record; see Chapter 3, "File Format" for record descriptions
iActionAbortLoad	Microsoft Excel has detected a fatal error; clean up now

The following sections describe the opcodes in more detail.

iActionIsFormatOk

Microsoft Excel asks the converter if it recognizes the format of the file that the user is opening.

This is the first opcode sent to the converter. If the converter returns FALSE, then Microsoft Excel does not call the converter again for this file.

Input

Member	Description
lcb	Size of file-recognition string
lprgb	Pointer to buffer containing file-recognition string
lpfn	Unused

Output

None.

Return value

TRUE if the converter recognizes this file format.

FALSE if the converter does not recognize this file format. If FALSE, then Microsoft Excel does not call the converter again.

iActionInitLoad

Microsoft Excel asks the converter to do any pre-conversion initialization. This opcode is sent after the iActionIsFormatOk call has returned TRUE.

Input

Member	Description
lcb	Size of input file
lprgb	Pointer to buffer containing locale ID (LCID) that the converter should assume. For more information about the LCID, see the *OLE 2 Programmer's Reference*.
lpfn	Pointer to callback function

Output

None.

Return value

TRUE if the converter initialized successfully.

FALSE if the converter encountered a fatal error. This return value causes Microsoft Excel to stop the load, so do any internal converter cleanup before returning.

Note This is the only time at which the lpfn member is valid. Converters expecting to return TRUE should save the lpfn value for future use.

---

iActionRtNextRecord

Microsoft Excel asks for the record type of the next BIFF record to be received from the converter. Record types are defined in BIFF.H.

This is one of the three calls (with iActionCbNextRecord and iActionDataNextRecord) in the main conversion loop.

Input

Member	Description
lcb	Unused
lprgb	Unused
lpfn	Unused

Output

None.

Return value

BIFF record type as defined in BIFF.H. The first record type must be rtBOF. Return rtEOF to indicate end of conversion.

iActionCbNextRecord

Microsoft Excel asks the converter for the length of the data in the next BIFF record. The return value is used to allocate buffer storage for the following iActionDataNextRecord call.

This is one of the three calls (with iActionRtNextRecord and iActionDataNextRecord) in the main conversion loop.

Input

Member	Description
lcb	Unused
lprgb	Unused
lpfn	Unused

Output

None.

Return value

Size of the next BIFF record, in bytes. This value must be <=cbBiffMax as defined in BIFF.H; if it is greater, Excel calls iActionAbortLoad.

iActionDataNextRecord

Microsoft Excel asks the converter for the BIFF record data.

This is one of the three calls (with iActionRtNextRecord and iActionCbNextRecord) in the main conversion loop.

Input

Member	Description
lcb	Unused
lprgb	Pointer to buffer for BIFF record data. Size of buffer is cbBiffMax.
lpfn	Unused

Output

Member	Description
lprgb	Pointer to the actual data in the BIFF record; see Chapter 3, "File Format" for BIFF record descriptions. The record data starts at offset 4 in the record descriptions in Chapter 3.

Return value

An integer from 0 to 100 that indicates the percent-complete status of the conversion. Microsoft Excel uses this value to update the load progress indicator in the status bar. The return value should equal 100 when your converter returns rtEOF. See the DataNextRecord function in UNDUMP.C for a example of the percent-complete calculation.

iActionAbortLoad

Microsoft Excel informs the converter that it detected a fatal load error. This is the only chance for the converter to do any necessary cleanup.

Input

Member	Description
lcb	Unused
lprgb	Unused
lpfn	Unused

Output

None.

Return value

Ignored.

Callback Function

Your converter should always use the callback function for memory management and for file input/output. This helps ensure peaceful coexistence with Microsoft Excel. The callback function is declared as:

```
extern short int FAR PASCAL EfcCallBack( short int iefccmd,
                                         BYTE FAR *lpb,
                                         long int lcb)
```

The command ID, iefccmd, is the callback opcode. It has the following values defined in XLCONV.H:

Value	Description
iefccmdCbFromFile	Ask Microsoft Excel to read lcb bytes from the input file stream
iefccmdAllocCb	Ask Microsoft Excel to allocate a buffer
iefccmdFreeCb	Ask Microsoft Excel to free a buffer
iefccmdGetPos	Ask Microsoft Excel to get the current stream position of the file pointer
iefccmdSetPos	Ask Microsoft Excel to set the current stream position of the file pointer

The lpb and lcb parameters take on different meanings, as described in the following sections.

iefccmdCbFromFile

Ask Microsoft Excel to read lcb bytes from the input file stream.

Input

Member	Description
lpb	Pointer to a buffer to hold file data. Remember, the converter is responsible for allocating this buffer.
lcb	Size of file buffer

Output

Member	Description
lpb	Pointer to buffer that contains the file data

Return value

The actual count of bytes written to the file buffer. Microsoft Excel attempts to fill the buffer completely; the actual count will be less than the requested size if an EOF is encountered in the input stream before the buffer is full.

iefccmdAllocCb

Ask Microsoft Excel to allocate a buffer for the converter.

Input

Member	Description
lpb	Pointer to a 32-bit variable (DWORD or long) that stores the address of the allocated buffer
lcb	Requested buffer size

Output

Member	Description
lpb	Pointer to a 32-bit variable (DWORD or long) that stores the address of the allocated buffer

Return value

The actual count of bytes allocated. Returns 0 to indicate an out-of-memory condition and to give your converter an opportunity to request a smaller amount of memory instead.

Note   Under the 16-bit Windows 3.1 and the 16-bit Apple Macintosh operating environments, you can only allocate a 64K buffer (actually slightly less then 64K because of system overhead). On 32-bit Windows NT, you can allocate a buffer up to the available memory limit, or 4 GB, whichever is smaller.

iefccmdFreeCb

Ask Microsoft Excel to free a buffer that was previously allocated using an `iefccmdAllocCb` call.

Input

Member	Description
lpb	Pointer to a 32-bit variable (DWORD or long) that stores the address of the buffer to be freed
lcb	Size of the buffer to be freed

Output

None.

Return value

None. The converter should assume that this call always succeeds.

iefccmdGetPos

Ask Microsoft Excel to get the current (zero-based) offset in the input file stream.

Input

Member	Description
lpb	Pointer to a 32-bit variable (DWORD or long) to store the stream offset
lcb	Unused

Output

Member	Description
lpb	Pointer to a 32-bit variable (DWORD or long) that contains the current input stream offset

Return value

Unused.

iefccmdSetPos

Ask Microsoft Excel to set the current (zero-based) offset in the input file stream.

Input

Member	Description
lpb	Pointer to a 32-bit variable (DWORD or long) that contains the desired offset
lcb	Unused

Output

None; lpb is unchanged.

Return value

Unused.

Using File Converters from the Macro Languages

In Visual Basic, Applications edition, you can use the FileConverters property to return an n x 3 array that contains information about installed converters, where n is equal to the number of installed converters. The other dimension contains the three strings from the entry in the EXCEL5.INI (or equivalent) file.

In the Microsoft Excel version 4.0 macro language, you can use the GET.WORKSPACE(62) macro function to list the installed converters. Array-enter this function in enough cells to store the maximum number of expected converters. Uninstalled converters correspond to the #N/A error value in the cells.

The Open method (Visual Basic) and the OPEN() macro function both contain a Converter argument that can be used to override the converter auto-detect algorithm. The argument is a one-based index to the table of converters (as given by the FileConverters property or by the GET.WORKSPACE(62) macro function).

Index

C

E

M

Y

Z

Books of Choice for Microsoft® Word Users

Microsoft® Word Developer's Kit
Microsoft Corporation

If you want to customize Microsoft Word 6 for Windows to work the way you do, create custom applications, or create macros that streamline routine tasks, the Microsoft Word Developer's Kit is your one-stop solution. You'll find all the technical information and tools you need, including detailed information on using WordBasic, using Workgroup MAPI and ODBC extensions, and using the Word API. The disk includes sample WordBasic macros and dynamic link libraries for putting MAPI and ODBC to work, plus source files and development tools for programming with the Word API.

1024 pages, softcover with one 3.5-inch disk
$39.95 ($53.95 Canada) ISBN 1-55615-630-8

Microsoft® Word 6 for Windows™ Resource Kit
Microsoft Corporation

This is your one-stop guide to installing, customizing, and supporting Word 6 for Windows. It includes information on training new and migrating users, troubleshooting, preventing potential problems, and ensuring that users are taking full advantage of productivity-boosting features. The two accompanying disks include *The Word 6 for Windows Converter*, customizable self-paced training exercises, 250 tips and tricks, and a helpful file to make custom installation easier.

672 pages, softcover with two 3.5-inch disks
$39.95 ($53.95 Canada) ISBN 1-55615-720-7

Word 6 for Windows™ Companion
The Cobb Group with M. David Stone & Alfred Poor and Mark Crane

"This book covers all the bases thoroughly." **PC Magazine**

This is the ultimate reference book, with more than 1000 pages of detailed information on Word 6 for Windows. Written in the clear and easy-to-read style that is the Cobb Group hallmark, this book covers the essentials from the basics to advanced topics. It includes new two-color design with easy lookup features, lots of product tips, and an expanded, fully cross-referenced index.

1072 pages, softcover $29.95 ($39.95 Canada) ISBN 1-55615-575-1

*Microsoft*Press

Information—Direct from the Source

Microsoft® Excel Visual Basic®
for Applications Step by Step
Covers Microsoft Excel version 5 for Windows
Reed Jacobson

Now you can customize Microsoft Excel to work the way you do! Here's the fastest way to learn Visual Basic for Applications, the new macro language in Microsoft Excel. Follow the self-paced lessons with disk-based practice files, and you'll learn to do everything from automating everyday tasks to building a data-extraction utility.
350 pages with one 3.5-inch disk
$29.95 ($39.95 Canada)   ISBN 1-55615-589-1

Microsoft® Excel 5 Visual Basic®
for Applications Reference
Microsoft Corporation

Now programmers have even greater flexibility and power to create custom applications using Microsoft Excel 5's new macro language—Visual Basic for Applications. This complete A–Z reference lists all the objects, properties, methods, functions, and statements, and provides functional descriptions, syntax, and code examples. If you're an Excel power user or a programmer who customizes Microsoft Excel applications, or if you write applications that interact with Microsoft Excel, you need this reference.
736 pages, softcover $24.95 ($33.95 Canada)   ISBN 1-55615-624-3

Microsoft® Excel 5 Worksheet Function Reference
Covers version 5 for Windows™ and the Apple® Macintosh®
Microsoft Corporation

Tap into the number-crunching power of Microsoft Excel by using worksheet functions in your spreadsheets to solve nearly any type of numerical problem—on the job or at home! To use worksheet functions, you don't have to be a genius at mathematics, statistics, or finance. Simply enter the right worksheet function with the required data, and Microsoft Excel does the rest. This reference provides complete information about each of the more than 300 worksheet functions built into Microsoft Excel 5 and is the hard-copy documentation for the Microsoft Excel 5 worksheet function online Help.
336 pages, softcover $12.95 ($16.95 Canada)   ISBN 1-55615-637-5

*Microsoft*Press

IMPORTANT— READ CAREFULLY BEFORE OPENING SOFTWARE PACKET(S). Unless a separate multilingual license booklet is included in your product package, the following License Agreement applies to you. By opening the sealed packet(s) containing the software, you indicate your acceptance of the following Microsoft License Agreement.

Microsoft Excel Developer's Kit
Version 5.0 for Windows and the Apple Macintosh

MICROSOFT LICENSE AGREEMENT
This is a legal agreement between you (either an individual or an entity) and Microsoft Corporation. By opening the sealed software packet(s) you are agreeing to be bound by the terms of this agreement. If you do not agree to the terms of this agreement, promptly return the unopened software packet(s) and the accompanying items (including written materials and binders or other containers) to the place you obtained them for a full refund.

MICROSOFT SOFTWARE LICENSE
1. **GRANT OF LICENSE.** Microsoft grants to you the right to use one copy of the enclosed Microsoft Excel Developer's Kit for use on Microsoft Windows and one copy of the Microsoft Excel Developer's Kit for use on the Apple Macintosh on a single computer (the "SOFTWARE"). The SOFTWARE is in "use" on a computer when it is loaded into temporary memory (i.e.. RAM) or installed into permanent memory (e.g., hard disk, CD-ROM, or other storage device) of that computer. However, installation on a network server for the sole purpose of distribution to one or more other computer(s) shall not constitute "use" for which a separate license is required.

2. **COPYRIGHT.** The SOFTWARE is owned by Microsoft or its suppliers and is protected by United States copyright laws and international treaty provisions. Therefore, you must treat the SOFTWARE like any other copyrighted material (e.g., a book or musical recording) except that you may either (a) make one copy of the SOFTWARE solely for backup or archival purposes, or (b) transfer the SOFTWARE to a single hard disk provided you keep the original solely for backup or archival purposes. You may not copy the written materials accompanying the SOFTWARE.

3. **OTHER RESTRICTIONS.** You may not rent or lease the SOFTWARE, but you may transfer the SOFTWARE and accompanying written materials on a permanent basis provided you retain no copies and the recipient agrees to the terms of this Agreement. You may not reverse engineer, decompile, or disassemble the SOFTWARE. If the SOFTWARE is an update or has been updated, any transfer must include the most recent update and all prior versions.

4. **DUAL MEDIA SOFTWARE.** You may use both disks concurrently but each disk may only be in use on one computer at any time. You may not loan, rent, lease, or transfer the disks to another user except as part of the permanent transfer (as provided above) of all SOFTWARE and written materials.

5. **LICENSE LIMITATIONS.** Microsoft grants you a non-exclusive royalty-free right to use and modify the source code version and to reproduce and distribute the object code version of the SOFTWARE other than the executable files of the SOFTWARE (i.e. those files designated with suffixes .EXE, .HLP, .DLL or .XLL on the Microsoft Windows copy of the SOFTWARE and those files designated as Example, Switchsn or Circum on the Apple Macintosh copy of the Software) (the "LICENSED CODE"), provided that you: (a) distribute the Licensed Code only in conjunction with and as a part of your software application product which is designed to operate in conjunction with Microsoft Excel; (b) do not use Microsoft's name, logo, or trademarks to market your software application product; (c) include Microsoft's copyright notice for the SOFTWARE on your product disk label and/or on the title page of the documentation for your software application product; and (d) agree to indemnify, hold harmless, and defend Microsoft from and against any claims or lawsuits, including attorney's fees, that arise or result from the use or distribution of your software application product.

THE LICENSED CODE IS PROVIDED AS IS WITHOUT WARRANTY OF ANY KIND, EITHER EXPRESS OR IMPLIED, INCLUDING, WITHOUT LIMITATION, THE IMPLIED WARRANTIES OF MERCHANTABILITY OR FITNESS FOR A PARTICULAR PURPOSE AND THE WARRANTY AGAINST INFRINGEMENT.

6. **LIMITED WARRANTY.** Microsoft warrants that (a) the SOFTWARE will perform substantially in accordance with the accompanying written materials for a period of ninety (90) days from the date of receipt, and (b) any hardware accompanying the SOFTWARE will be free from defects in materials and workmanship under normal use and service for a period of one (1) year from the date of receipt. Any implied warranties on the SOFTWARE and hardware are limited to ninety (90) days and one (1) year, respectively. Some states/jurisdictions do not allow limitations on duration of an implied warranty, so the above limitation may not apply to you.

CUSTOMER REMEDIES. Microsoft's and its suppliers' entire liability and your exclusive remedy shall be, at Microsoft's option, either (a) return of the price paid, or (b) repair or replacement of the SOFTWARE or hardware that does not meet Microsoft's Limited Warranty and which is returned to Microsoft with a copy of your receipt. This Limited Warranty is void if failure of the SOFTWARE or hardware has resulted from accident, abuse, or misapplication. Any replacement SOFTWARE or hardware will be warranted for the remainder of the original warranty period or thirty (30) days, whichever is longer. **Outside the United States, these remedies are not available without proof of purchase from an authorized non-U.S. source.**

NO OTHER WARRANTIES. To the maximum extent permitted by law, Microsoft and its suppliers disclaim all other warranties, either express or implied, including, but not limited to implied warranties of merchantability and fitness for a particular purpose, with regard to the SOFTWARE, the accompanying written materials, and any accompanying hardware. This limited warranty gives you specific legal rights. You may have others which vary from state/jurisdiction to state/juridiction.

NO LIABILITY FOR CONSEQUENTIAL DAMAGES. To the maximum extent permitted by law, in no event shall Microsoft or its suppliers be liable for any damages whatsoever (including without limitation, damages for loss of business profits, business interruption, loss of business information, or any other pecuniary loss) arising out of the use of or inability to use this Microsoft product, even if Microsoft has been advised of the possibility of such damages. Because some states/juridictions do not allow the exclusion or limitation of liability for consequential or incidental damages, the above limitation may not apply to you.

U.S. GOVERNMENT RESTRICTED RIGHTS
The SOFTWARE and documentation are provided with RESTRICTED RIGHTS. Use, duplication, or disclosure by the Government is subject to restrictions as set forth in subparagraph (c)(1)(ii) of The Rights in Technical Data and Computer Software clause at DFARS 252.227-7013 or subparagraphs (c)(1) and (2) of the Commercial Computer Software — Restricted Rights 48 CFR 52.227-19, as applicable. Manufacturer is Microsoft Corporation/One Microsoft Way/Redmond, WA 98052-6399.

If you acquired this product in the United States, this Agreement is governed by the laws of the State of Washington.

Should you have any questions concerning this Agreement, or if you desire to contact Microsoft for any reason, please contact your local Microsoft subsidiary or sales office or write: Microsoft Sales and Service/One Microsoft Way/Redmond, WA 98052-6399.

5/94   2276001A.DOC